Practicing Digital Ethnography

Practicing Digital Ethnography offers a comprehensive introduction to the essential methods, concepts, and practices of conducting ethnographic research in digital environments.

Written by 60 global contributors across 12 chapters with accompanying case studies and concept explorations, this book provides both theoretical foundations and practical guidance for digital ethnographic work. It covers research approaches for diverse digital contexts, including social media, virtual spaces, video games, and hybrid physical-technological settings, while addressing the deployment of tools like artificial intelligence, big data, mapping technologies, and multimodal methodologies. This book examines ethical challenges specific to digital research environments while maintaining a commitment to reflexive, co-present research that acknowledges how our interactions with digital technologies transcend boundaries of citizenship, race, gender identity, age, and ability.

Practicing Digital Ethnography is ideal for students and researchers in anthropology, media studies, science and technology studies, and communications who seek to understand contemporary hyper-mediated environments, as well as professionals outside academia who need practical, accessible guidance for conducting rigorous digital research.

Devin Proctor is a cultural anthropologist and Assistant Professor of Anthropology at Elon University, USA.

"This colorful and insightful cornucopia of a book offers enriching and inventive methods and cautions, ones that transcend the specificity of a particular medium, for budding ethnographers for many years to come. For anyone curious about fieldwork online, and these days almost every research has an online component, this book is for you."

    Ilana Gershon, *Professor of Anthropology, Rice University, USA*

"This versatile edited collection provides the basics for beginners, in-depth case studies from an intergenerational slate of authors, and nuanced reflections on concepts like 'virtual' and 'gamer.' It is a fine excursion to ethnography in virtual settings, highly recommended."

    Bonnie Nardi, *Emeritus Professor of the Department of Informatics at the University of California at Irvine, USA*

Practicing Digital Ethnography

Edited by Devin Proctor

Routledge
Taylor & Francis Group
NEW YORK AND LONDON

Designed cover image: Paul Campbell, via Getty Images

First published 2026
by Routledge
605 Third Avenue, New York, NY 10158

and by Routledge
4 Park Square, Milton Park, Abingdon, Oxon, OX14 4RN

Routledge is an imprint of the Taylor & Francis Group, an informa business

© 2026 selection and editorial matter, Devin Proctor; individual chapters, the contributors

The right of Devin Proctor to be identified as the author of the editorial material, and of the authors for their individual chapters, has been asserted in accordance with sections 77 and 78 of the Copyright, Designs and Patents Act 1988.

All rights reserved. No part of this book may be reprinted or reproduced or utilised in any form or by any electronic, mechanical, or other means, now known or hereafter invented, including photocopying and recording, or in any information storage or retrieval system, without permission in writing from the publishers.

For Product Safety Concerns and Information please contact our EU representative GPSR@taylorandfrancis.com. Taylor & Francis Verlag GmbH, Kaufingerstraße 24, 80331 München, Germany.

Trademark notice: Product or corporate names may be trademarks or registered trademarks, and are used only for identification and explanation without intent to infringe.

ISBN: 978-1-032-67264-9 (hbk)
ISBN: 978-1-032-66042-4 (pbk)
ISBN: 978-1-032-67266-3 (ebk)

DOI: 10.4324/9781032672663

Typeset in Sabon
by codeMantra

Contents

List of contributors	*ix*
Foreword	*xvii*
JOHN POSTILL	
Preface and Acknowledgments	*xx*

Introduction   1
DEVIN PROCTOR

0.1   Concept: ethnography   7
       HEATHER A. HORST

0.2   Case study introductory suite: negotiating the on-and-offline   11

       0.2.1   Case study: Zapotec villagers in the digital era   13
               ROBERTO J. GONZÁLEZ

       0.2.2   Case study: selfies, shamans, and social media participation among the Shipibo-Konibo in the Peruvian Amazon   20
               JENNIFER SIERRA

       0.2.3   Case study: digital solidarity and everyday assertion of Dalit identity on WhatsApp in India   26
               RASHMI KUMAR

       0.2.4   Case study: songs of an initiation club in West Africa and its Caribbean Diaspora   33
               IVOR MILLER AND MARGARET M. P. ÒKÔN

1 Digital ethics — 43
MICHELLE CERA

   1.1 Concept: representation — 60
      SERHAT TUTKAL

   1.2 Case study: drug trade on the Polish darknet — 64
      PIOTR SIUDA AND PATRYCJA HEWELT

2 Ethnography about digital media — 71
XINYUAN WANG

   2.1 Concept: affordance — 87
      ANNA COLOM

   2.2 Case study: women Australian Rules footballers' digital self-tracking — 91
      PAUL BOWELL, PAUL SCIFLEET,
      EKATERINA PECHENKINA, AND EMMA SHERRY

3 Ethnography on/in social media — 97
KATRIN TIIDENBERG AND DAVID KNEAS

   3.1 Concept: platform — 114
      CHIARA PERIN

   3.2 Case study: navigating Iranian digital feminist activism through multi-sited mobile ethnography — 118
      MITRA SHAMSI

4 Ethnography in virtual worlds — 125
RACHEL BERRYMAN AND CRYSTAL ABIDIN

   4.1 Concept: virtual — 143
      TOM BOELLSTORFF

   4.2 Case study: work, play, and questioning the binary in EVE Online — 146
      HARISH GOUTAM

5 Linguistic analysis — 153
GRAHAM M. JONES, JISOO HONG, AND MAYA NÁVAR

| | | 5.1 | Concept: meme
İDİL GALIP | 173 |

    5.2 Case study: evaluating emergent Kazakh anti-proverbs using corpus linguistics 177
         ERIK AASLAND AND GULNARA OMARBEKOVA

6 Data analysis 185
ANNA M. GÓRSKA, DARIUSZ JEMIELNIAK, AND NINA KOTULA

    6.1 Concept: data 203
         TONE WALFORD AND HANNAH KNOX

    6.2 Case study: over-the-shoulder observation of Facebook Group admins 208
         ANNA D. GIBSON

7 Spatial analysis 215
GREYSON HARRIS

    7.1 Concept: space 231
         MARK NUNES

    7.2 Case study: implementing GIS in Malmiñañ, Cameroon 235
         VERONICA BAYIHA ÑWA QUILLIEN, JEAN-BAPTISTE QUILLIEN, AND EUGENE BAYIHA BA MAKONN

8 Artificial intelligence 241
MATT ARTZ

    8.1 Concept: algorithm 260
         HEINER HEILAND

    8.2 Case study: using AI for deradicalization 264
         ANDREA RUSSO

9 Multimodal anthropology 273
ISAAC MARRERO-GUILLAMÓN AND ETHIRAJ GABRIEL DATTATREYAN

    9.1 Concept: public 285
         CHRISTOPHER M. KELTY

9.2	Case study: *SAPIENS* magazine as anthropology for the public EMILY SEKINE	289
10	**Video games** LINDSAY GRACE	**295**
10.1	Concept: gamer FLORENCE CHEE	311
10.2	Case study: listening to queer, LGBTQ+, and women Twitch streamers JACK MCLAREN AND LARISA KINGSTON MANN	315
11	**Hybrid installations** ROB EAGLE	**321**
11.1	Concept: hybridity MAXI HEITMAYER	341
11.2	Case study: "In America" COVID memorial art installation on the DC National Mall THE RITUALS IN THE MAKING COLLECTIVE	345

Index   *351*

Contributors

Erik Aasland is Affiliate Assistant Professor of Anthropology at Fuller Theological Seminary in California, USA. He specializes in ethnography, folklore, and digital anthropology. In 2023, he coauthored an edited volume on contemporary Kazakh proverb research. He serves as Past President of the Society for Humanistic Anthropology.

Crystal Abidin is Professor of Internet Studies at Curtin University in Perth, Western Australia. She is the Director of the Influencer Ethnography Research Lab and the Founder of the TikTok Cultures Research Network. Her contributions to this chapter were supported by an ARC DECRA (DE190100789).

Matt Artz is an anthropologist, designer, and technologist specializing in AI product development. He is the founder of Azimuth Labs, an adjunct professor at the University of Pennsylvania, host of the Anthropology in Business and Anthro to UX podcasts, and co-editor of *EmTech Anthropology* and *Anthropology and AI*.

Eugene Bayiha ba Makonn is a retired academic and finance expert affiliated with the Centre Agroecologique Jean Makonn Bayiha. Originally from Cameroon, he has extensive experience in international business, finance, and higher education. His work spans teaching, research, and financial consulting, with a focus on economic development and sustainable financial practices.

Rachel Berryman is a PhD student in the Department of Internet Studies at Curtin University in Perth, Western Australia. Her PhD project examines the evolution, industry, and impact of the social media phenomenon known as "virtual influencers" and is supported by an Australian Government Research Training Program (RTP) Scholarship.

Tom Boellstorff is a Professor in the Departments of Anthropology and Informatics at the University of California, Irvine, USA. Their publications include *Coming of Age in Second Life: An Anthropologist*

Explores the Virtually Human (2008), *Ethnography and Virtual Worlds: A Handbook of Method* (2012), and *Intellivision: How a Videogame System Battled Atari and Almost Bankrupted Barbie®* (2024).

Paul Bowell, an expert in sociology, researches technology's impacts on people and the lived experiences of women athletes. Paul has published in high-ranked, peer-reviewed sport and employment journals and has engaged in various research and consulting projects specializing in sociology, organizational practice, sport sociology, and sport management.

Michelle Cera received her PhD from New York University, USA, where she focused on far-right extremism on social media, gender, and inequality. Her research employed digital ethnography to explore political participation online. She also directed workshops on pedagogy, digital ethnography, and qualitative methods.

Florence Chee is an Associate Professor in the School of Communication, leading the Center for Digital Ethics and Policy (CDEP) and Social & Interactive Media Lab Chicago (SIMLab) at Loyola University Chicago, USA. She is the author of *Digital Game Culture in Korea: The Social at Play* (2023 Bloomsbury).

Anna Colom researches the intersections of data, digital technologies, media, and social change, including the role of online platforms in people's citizenship capabilities. She uses intersectional theory and method to explore power relations. She has led Public Participation Research at the Ada Lovelace Institute and co-led the non-profit The Data Tank.

Ethiraj Gabriel Dattatreyan is Assistant Professor of Anthropology, Core Faculty in the Culture Media Program, and Affiliated Faculty in the Department of Music at New York University, USA. He utilizes collaborative, multimodal, and speculative approaches, researching how media consumption, production, and circulation shape understandings of migration, gender, race, and urban space in diasporic and postcolonial contexts.

Rob Eagle is Research Fellow at the Centre for Cultural Value at the University of Leeds, UK, and Co-Director of the Bradford Digital Arts Lab. With a focus on performance, film, and immersive media, Rob's current research examines community-led and socially engaged approaches in theaters and arts organizations.

İdil Galip is Lecturer of New Media and Digital Culture at the University of Amsterdam, the Netherlands. She holds a PhD in Sociology from the University of Edinburgh, UK. She is the founder of the Meme Studies Research Network.

Anna D. Gibson is a Postdoctoral Associate in Comparative Media Studies/Writing at Massachusetts Institute of Technology, USA. She received her PhD from the Department of Communication at Stanford University.

Roberto J. González is a Professor in the Anthropology Department at San José State University, USA. He is the author of several books, including *Connected: How a Mexican Village Built Its Own Cell Phone Network* (2020) and *Zapotec Science: Farming and Food in the Northern Sierra of Oaxaca* (2001).

Anna M. Górska is an Assistant Professor at Kozminski University, Poland, and Director of the Women and Diversity in Organizations Research Center. She is a member of the Young Academy of the Polish Academy of Sciences. She studies higher education institutions from the perspective of management, communication, and diversity.

Harish Goutam is a doctoral student in the School of Anthropology and Museum Ethnography at the University of Oxford, UK. He previously published a review of Lisa Mitchell's *Hailing the State* in the *Journal of the Anthropological Society*. He researches the notion of trust in the MMORPG, *EVE Online*.

Lindsay Grace is Knight Chair and Director of the MFA in Interactive Media in the School of Communication at the University of Miami, USA. His research focuses on exploring the intersection of play, human behavior, and technology. He has authored and coauthored nearly 100 peer-reviewed works, including three books on games research.

Greyson Harris entered the geospatial profession in 2009. Most recently, he served as Geospatial Coordinator for FEMA, leading GIS operations during major disasters. Prior, he worked at UC Davis, Esri, the Smithsonian Institution, and the US Forest Service. Greyson is a certified GISP and lives in Northern California.

Heiner Heiland is a postdoctoral researcher at the Institute of Sociology at the University of Göttingen, Germany. In his research, he examines labor processes, digitalization, and corporate public spheres and has ethnographically investigated various forms of platform work and algorithmic management.

Maxi Heitmayer is Assistant Professor of Psychology at Rowan University, USA. His research uses video ethnography to study how users interact with their devices in naturally occurring contexts, their routines and behavioral patterns, and how this influences their decision-making processes. He also works on human interactions in digitally augmented and virtual spaces with a focus on social norms and culture.

Patrycja Hewelt (PhD) is employed as an assistant at the Department of New Media in the Institute of Journalism, Media, and Social Communication at Jagiellonian University in Cracow. She holds a PhD in social sciences in the discipline of social communication and media studies. Her research interests focus primarily on the multifaceted analysis of user behaviors, interaction dynamics, and communication strategies used in the context of social media.

Jisoo Hong earned her BS in Computer Science and MS in Technology and Policy from the Massachusetts Institute of Technology, USA, and her JD from UC Berkley Law, USA. Her practice focuses on antitrust and intellectual property litigation.

Heather A. Horst is Professor of Design Anthropology at the Sydney School of Architecture and Design and Planning at the University of Sydney, Australia. A sociocultural anthropologist by training, she researches material culture, mobility, and the mediation of social relations through the study of homes, clothing, and technology.

Dariusz Jemielniak is a Professor at Kozminski University, Poland; Faculty Associate at Berkman-Klein Center for Internet and Society at Harvard University, USA; and Vice President of the Polish Academy of Sciences. His recent books include *Strategizing AI in Business and Education, Collaborative Society, Thick Big Data,* and *Common Knowledge? An Ethnography of Wikipedia.*

Graham M. Jones is Professor of Linguistic Anthropology at the Massachusetts Institute of Technology, USA. Author of *Trade of the Tricks* (2011) and *Magic's Reason* (2017), he studies how people communicate knowledge, negotiating relationships based on what they do—and don't—know.

Christopher M. Kelty is a Professor at the University of California, Los Angeles, USA. He is the author of *Two Bits* (2008) and *The Participant* (2019) as well as articles on freedom, responsibility, participation in science and engineering, and urban ecologies in Los Angeles.

David Kneas is an anthropologist and Associate Professor of Geography at the University of South Carolina, USA. His research examines the cultural processes of resource formation across a variety of settings and materials. He has published in various outlets, including *Geoforum, American Anthropologist, The Journal of Peasant Studies,* and *Environmental History.*

Hannah Knox is Max Gluckman Professor of Social Anthropology at the University of Manchester, UK. She focuses on the anthropology of technology, infrastructure, and climate change. Recent books include *Thinking Like a Climate: Governing a City in Times of Environmental*

Change and Ethnography for a Data Saturated World (co-edited with Dawn Nafus).

Nina Kotula holds a PhD in Management and Quality Sciences. Her work focuses on how sustainability and digital transformation reshape higher education.

Rashmi Kumar is a doctoral candidate at the Department of Humanities and Social Sciences, Indian Institute of Technology Delhi, India. Her research explores intersections of caste, gender, and urbanity. Her doctoral project explores the experiences and negotiations of Dalit communities located in lower-income neighborhoods in urban areas.

Larisa Kingston Mann is an Associate Professor in Media Studies & Production, Klein College, Temple University, USA. Her work examines how marginalized communities' cultural practices resist, negotiate with, and transcend colonial power. She is interested in the technological and legal contexts that allow such cultural spaces to exist and how people redraw them in moments of creativity and communion.

Isaac Marrero-Guillamón is a Serra Hunter Lecturer in Anthropology at the University of Barcelona, Spain. He was previously a Senior Lecturer at Goldsmiths, University of London, UK. He's conducted ethnographic research on spatial conflicts in Barcelona, London, and the Canary Islands, experimenting with visual, multimodal, and collaborative research devices.

Jack McLaren is a Sessional Instructor at the University of Windsor, Canada. He teaches within the Communication, Media, and Film and Interdisciplinary and Critical Studies departments. His research and teaching interests sit at the intersection of game studies, cultural studies, and transgender studies.

Ivor Miller is a Research Affiliate, African Studies Center at Boston University, USA; worked in the Department of History, University of Calabar, Nigeria; National Museum of African Art at the Smithsonian Institution, USA; and was a Fulbright Scholar to Nigeria. His book, *Voice of the Leopard: African Secret Societies and Cuba*, was awarded Honorable Mention by the Association for Africanist Anthropology.

Maya Návar holds a BA in Linguistics and Comparative Literature and an MA in Latin American Studies from Stanford University, USA. She currently works as an urban planner and community engagement specialist in New York City, USA.

Mark Nunes is Professor of Interdisciplinary Studies at Appalachian State University in North Carolina, USA. He is the author of *Cyberspaces of*

Everyday Life, editor of *Error: Glitch, Jam, and Noise in New Media Cultures*, and co-editor of *"You're Muted": Performance, Precarity, and the Logic of Zoom*. His work explores the place of networks, platforms, and digital devices in everyday life.

Margaret M. P. Òkôn—Doctorat de l'Université de la Sorbonne Nouvelle in Linguistics, Paris, France—is a Professor in the Department of Linguistics & Communication Studies at the University of Calabar, Nigeria.

Gulnara Omarbekova is Associate Professor at Nazarbayev University, Kazakhstan. She specializes in comparative linguistics, lingua-cultural studies, and language pedagogy. Over the past 30 years, she has focused on these areas and has published extensively on them from a linguistic perspective.

Ekaterina Pechenkina is a cultural anthropologist and award-winning Lecturer at Swinburne University, Australia. Her research interests include Indigenous education, educational technology, and the sociocultural aspects of technological innovation. Ekaterina's methodological expertise comprises qualitative and quantitative as well as mixed approaches; she is particularly skilled in ethnographic methods of inquiry.

Chiara Perin completed a PhD in Sociology at the University of Milan, Italy. Her thesis examines the construction of masculinity and sexuality in digital environments. She is currently investigating the encounter between social and healthcare services and the LGBTQ+ population under a research grant at the University of Parma.

John Postill is an anthropologist specializing in the study of media, communication, and socio-political change. He has conducted fieldwork in Malaysia, Indonesia, Spain, and (online) in the Anglosphere. Currently, he is a Senior Lecturer in Communication at RMIT University, Melbourne. His publications include *The Anthropology of Digital Practices* (Routledge) and *The Rise of Nerd Politics* (Pluto).

Devin Proctor is a cultural anthropologist and Assistant Professor of Anthropology at Elon University who explores digital culture, identity construction, and new media. His interdisciplinary writing appears in places like *Public Culture, Critique of Anthropology, Communication Theory, Space & Society, SAPIENS, Persona Studies, Media/Culture*, and *Engaging Science and Technology Studies*.

Jean-Baptiste Quillien, Ph.D. is Assistant Professor of Psychology at Northeastern State University, a member of the AI@NSU committee, and Co-Founder and Chief Scientific Officer of Calyssa.ai, a digital platform designed to help individuals explore their inner world through guided journaling, self-reflection, and evidence-based tools supporting emotional well-being and mental health. As Chief Executive Officer of U-Ree-Kah.com, Dr. Quillien leads initiatives that help individuals and organizations thrive in the digital era by integrating large language models (LLMs) and cognitive science to enhance creativity, productivity, and ethical innovation. Trained in learning and cognition, his research and expertise span creativity, scientific reasoning, critical thinking, cognitive flexibility, and human–machine interaction.

Veronica Bayiha ñwa Quillien, Ph.D. is the Co-Founder and Creative Hacker at The Language Attitude Institute. Her research examines the role of the arts in reclaiming and revitalizing cultural, linguistic, and agricultural identities. She investigates how individuals, families, and communities engage in the production and consumption of culture as a practice of self-determination and collective resilience. Her current work documents agricultural land use, land management, and community-based strategies for resilience and climate adaptation.

Rituals in the Making Collective is a National Science Foundation–funded research project based at the Anthropology Department at George Washington University, USA. The project focuses on memorialization, misinformation, and the ongoing consequences of the COVID-19 pandemic. The Rituals in the Making Collective is an attempt to experiment with different modalities of scholarly production that center on non-hierarchy, reciprocity, and mutuality.

Andrea Russo is an Italian sociologist with a PhD in Physics specializing in complex systems. A postdoctoral researcher at the University of Pavia, and previously at Sorbonne University and CNRS, he focuses on computational social science and security, utilizing data mining, natural language processing, and social network analysis to explore sociotechnical dynamics, communication, and information diffusion.

Paul Scifleet is an expert in information systems, researching digital asset management, emerging information technologies, and information governance in business and e-government contexts. Paul approaches his research from the interpretative traditions of digital documentary practice and is a specialist in policy and content analysis and digital ethnographic methods.

Emily Sekine is a writer and an editor at *SAPIENS* magazine, based in the US. She holds a PhD in anthropology from The New School, and her writing explores the relationships between people and nature, especially in the context of the seismic and volcanic landscapes of Japan.

Mitra Shamsi is a postdoctoral research fellow at the Centre for Advanced Internet Studies (CAIS) in Germany. Her research focuses on digital feminist activism in Iran, examining digital feminist discourses constructed both inside the country and within the diaspora. She received her PhD in Media Studies from the University of Tehran, Iran.

Emma Sherry is an expert in sport for development, researching community development through sport, access and equity in sport, and sport for at-risk and marginalized communities. Emma has worked with a range of sports organizations in Australia and globally, including the IOC, Commonwealth Secretariat, VicHealth, Netball Australia, and Tennis Australia.

Jennifer Sierra is a linguistic anthropologist examining the complexities of internet access and social media participation among Shipibo-Konibos in the Peruvian Amazon. Her work merges Indigenous studies, digital media, and linguistics to examine emerging Indigenous human–machine lives. She is currently a Postdoctoral Fellow at the Wolf Humanities Center, University of Pennsylvania.

Piotr Siuda is an Associate Professor at Kazimierz Wielki University in Bydgoszcz, Poland, specializing in internet and game studies. Author of articles in journals such as *JCMC*, *Social Media+Society*, and *Games and Culture*, he is also a member of AoIR and Associate Editor for the *SAGE Journal of Creative Communications*.

Katrin Tiidenberg is Professor of Participatory Culture at the Baltic Film, Media and Arts School of Tallinn University, Estonia. She is the author and editor of multiple books on social media, digital visual cultures, and digital research methods and is currently working on visual digital trust and participatory wellbeing.

Serhat Tutkal is a postdoctoral researcher funded by the Secretariat of Science, Humanities, Technology, and Innovation (Secihti), Mexico. He holds a PhD in Human and Social Sciences from the National University of Colombia (UNAL) with his dissertation on the legitimation and delegitimation of state violence in Colombia.

Tone Walford is an Associate Professor in Anthropology at University College London, UK. Their research explores the politics of data and information infrastructures, with an ethnographic focus on the environmental sciences. They work on topics such as informational violence, data justice, and aesthetics.

Xinyuan Wang received her PhD from the Department of Anthropology at University College London, UK. She is the author of *Social Media in Industrial China* (2016) and *Ageing with Smartphones in Urban China* (2023), as well as co-author of *How the World Changed Social Media* (2016) and *The Global Smartphone* (2021).

Foreword

In 2010, Gabriella Coleman published a wide-ranging survey of digital ethnography in the *Annual Review of Anthropology*. To bring some kind of order to what was already a sprawling mess of a literature, she divided it into three overlapping categories: cultural politics, vernacular cultures, and everyday prosaics. By cultural politics she meant how digital media are increasingly entangled with struggles over social, racial, and ethnic identity, often involving marginalized or migrant groups. In contrast, vernacular cultures referred to people who have become reliant on the internet and other digital technologies, such as geeks, hackers, bloggers, internet activists, and meme makers. Finally, prosaics was about the day-to-day living with digital media in all their multiplicity and polyphony (Bakhtin), from the informal media economies of digital piracy to the rituals of online worship.

Coleman argues that although digital media are now integral to the lives of people around the world, we should be skeptical of claims about the universality of digital experience. Through their situated, in-depth studies, ethnographers are in the business of particularizing people's digital practices, even when linking them to large-scale processes. Casting doubt on totalizing theories like Manuel Castells' "network society," she sensibly concludes that digital technologies are clearly important, but that does not mean they are "the basis of planetary transformations" (2010: 489).

Revisiting this seminal text in 2025 is illuminating. After all, a great deal has happened in the world in the last 15 years, not least the Arab Spring, Syria, Occupy, Obama, Xi, Modi, Erdoğan, Brexit, Yemen, Trump, COVID-19, Biden, Putin, Ukraine, Trump again, Musk, and Gaza—to name a few. The global digital landscape has changed, too, dramatically growing in both size and complexity. For instance, the total amount of data generated worldwide has exploded from just 2 zettabytes in 2010 to an estimated 181 zettabytes in 2025. Some of the keywords today are social media, smartphones, podcasts, platforms, TikTok, Twitter/X, Meta, Amazon, 4G networks, 5G networks, military drones, electric vehicles, blockchain, big data, the cloud, algorithms, content creators, influencers, online gurus, broligarchs, disinformation, online hate speech, and generative AI.

Throughout this 15-year period of geopolitical turbulence and technological innovation, digital ethnography has gone from strength to strength. This versatile methodology has now found institutional homes and cross-border networks in many universities, mostly in the Global North (Postill 2024)—an expansion that is likely to continue in the coming years. One sign of its consolidation is the publication of a series of textbooks (e.g., Boellstorff et al. 2012, Geismar and Knox 2021, Hjorth et al. 2017, Pink et al. 2015), including the present volume, *Practicing Digital Ethnography*. At the same time, there are signs of diversification and potential fragmentation as well, for instance, through research events, groups, and networks focusing on ethnographic approaches to a single platform (e.g., TikTok), type of digital actor (influencers), or trending technology (generative AI).

Despite all these developments, Coleman's text remains relevant. The same spirit that animated her pioneering survey can be found in *Practicing Digital Ethnography*. The same interest in the social identities, online cultures, and daily prosaics of the digital realm. The same awe about the sheer diversity of digital lifeworlds found around the globe. The same experimental, open-ended methodological stance. The same keen attention to what people, including ethnographers, actually do with digital technologies. The same skepticism about grand narratives of technological revolution.

The present collection, which brings together both established and emerging scholars, also leads digital ethnography into new terrain. First, its contributors take the first word in the book's title—"practicing"—and run with it through a panoply of examples drawn from their diverse ethnographic practices. Together, these cases give readers a rich set of methods to try out in their own research—as Devin Proctor says in the Introduction, this volume is a user's manual. Second, the volume captures the latest thinking and best practice on new and emergent digital technologies and how ethnographers may go about studying them in collaboration with their research participants. Third, *Practicing Digital Ethnography* grapples with some of the thornier ethical dilemmas that go with studying people's digital lives at a time of surveillance/platform capitalism, growing authoritarianism, and international conflict. Fourth, by focusing on digital keywords like public, affordances, representation, virtual, and memes, it further develops the field's conceptual lexicon, bringing it to life through carefully chosen empirical materials.

In this book, the reader will find an ethnographic treasure trove, including discussions of selfie sharing in the Peruvian Amazon (Sierra), online caste practices in India (Kumar), meaning-making in a Polish dark net drug marketplace (Siuda and Cheba), digital self-tracking in Australian sport (Bowell et al.), migrant digital habitus in China (Wang), online feminism in Iran (Shamsi), and anti-proverb making in Kazakhstan (Aasland and Omarbakova). Running through all these cases is a shared commitment to digital ethnography as a versatile, pragmatic, shape-shifting endeavor. Collectively, this book's contributors demonstrate that digital ethnography is a craft in perpetual flux—a creative undertaking that resists standardization and rewards original insights into the human condition.

John Postill
Melbourne, June 9, 2025

References

Boellstorff, T., Nardi, B., Pearce, C. and Taylor, T.L. 2012, *Ethnography and virtual worlds*, Princeton, NJ, Princeton University Press.

Coleman, E.G., 2010. Ethnographic approaches to digital media. *Annual Review of Anthropology*, 39(1), pp. 487–505.

Geismar, H. and Knox, H. (eds) 2021, *Digital anthropology*, London, Routledge.

Hjorth, L., Horst, H.A., Galloway, A. and Bell, G. (eds) 2017, *The Routledge companion to digital ethnography*, New York, Routledge.

Pink, S., Horst, H., Postill, J., Hjorth, L., Lewis, T. and Tacchi, J. 2015, *Digital ethnography: principles and practice*, London, Sage.

Postill, J., 2024. Doing digital ethnography: a comparison of two social movement studies. In *Handbook of research methods and applications for social movements* edited by L. Cox, A. Arribas, S. Chattopadhyay and A. Szolucha (eds.) Cheltenham (pp. 144–158). Edward Elgar Publishing.

Preface and Acknowledgments

This book is an edited volume aimed largely at undergraduates and a general audience about the practice of digital ethnography. After becoming frustrated over the past several years trying to find these kinds of method-focused readings in the classes I teach on the subject—academically rigorous but still approachable—I just decided to stop waiting and make the book I wanted. So I did, and this is that book. It's not meant (necessarily) to be read cover to cover but rather to be deployed in whatever way proves useful to you and in whatever order: skip whole chapters, only use the case study or concept sub-chapters, spread them out to supplement a syllabus, what have you. Cut it up; rearrange it. It has grown into a tome larger than envisioned, and I hope its breadth serves as an indication of ever-emergent possibilities in the well-established, yet still constantly evolving, field of digital ethnography practice.

Putting together a project of this size, with 60 total authors, can be (has been) overwhelming, and there are some folks who deserve thanks for their help. For her reading and feedback, many thanks go to Ilana Gershon. For more general advice and guidance in the process, I need to thank Sarah Wagner. I also want to recognize the institutions and listservs that hosted and circulated the call for case studies: the Association of Internet Researchers, the American Anthropological Association, the American Studies Association, the European Association of Social Anthropologists, the Oxford Digital Anthropology Group, the Digital Ethnography Collective, WikiCFP, and Humanities and Social Sciences Online. An earlier version of Tom Boellstorff's concept chapter "Virtual" appears in *American Ethnologist* as "Toward Anthropologies of the Metaverse" and is reprinted with revisions here with the permission of Wiley. I would like to acknowledge the efforts and contributions of the Byzantine and sprawling, color-coded, and multi-tabbed spreadsheet that kept this endeavor on track—a document I often wanted to name but never did, as I thought that might induce sentience. Thanks to my kids for forcing me to stop working on weekends (sometimes) and reminding me that I am old (always). And for all things and forever, for more than it's possible to express, Kat.

Introduction

Digital ethnography

Devin Proctor

You are holding a user's manual. In the tradition of user's manuals, it is based on an assumption that you have heard of "digital ethnography" before opening this book: perhaps in passing, or you have read some studies, maybe even taken a class. And now you are ready to give it a try yourself. In the following pages, you will find best practices, examples, histories, products, fieldwork narratives, opinions, tips, tricks, ethical dilemmas, and (sometimes) their resolutions. This book is for people who intend to *do* digital ethnography. You are holding a user's manual.

What is digital ethnography?

The object of this collection is to assist readers in the practice of digital ethnography, which can mean so many things that capturing it requires a whole volume and multiple perspectives. But in this introduction, let's start small. As a foundational definition of "digital ethnography" to build upon, we follow Crystal Abidin and Gabriele de Seta's concise and inclusive, "ethnographic research on, through, and about digital media" (2020). That requires a little massaging, though, as it was written for an audience already conversant in the principles of ethnographic research. In the "concept" chapter following this introduction, Heather A. Horst will further clarify the parameters of "ethnography," but in the interests of arriving at a preliminary definition, we need to do a little work up front due to the term's expansive tendencies.

As it "broke loose from its moorings" in anthropology and into interdisciplinary popularity, the use of ethnography as a method has "lost much of its meaning," often referring to all manner of qualitative research as long as it involves people (Ingold 2014, 383). So, to tighten the definition up, I refer to Peter Forberg and Kristen Schilt, who view ethnographic pursuits as characterized by "co-presence" (2023, 04), involving "reflexive decisions about the researcher's participation and self-presentation that other forms of qualitative digital research do not require" (2023, 02).[1] The need for "co-presence" is a jargony way to refer to researchers being there "in" the field (present) *with* their interlocutors, participating rather than observing from the outside. And just as importantly, for a study to be deemed "ethnographic," it must include considerations of how the researchers and their objectives are presented in the process of study, ranging from anonymity to full transparency.[2]

So, to put that all together, we begin with: digital ethnography is *reflexive and co-present research on, through, and about digital media*. While sticking close to its anthropological foundations, this definition allows for a measure of flexibility in the ethnographic practices, which is necessary as digital contexts become increasingly both ubiquitous and precarious.

What does this book say about it?

This book is mainly about digital ethnographic method and practice as it unfolds in the present, but along with these narratives it also rests on some foundational understandings of the digital. The first is that technology is not neutral. In both use and design, technologies can either reinforce existing structures of power or resist them. Thus, the authors interrogate how digital spaces, tools, theories, and logics are deployed in inherently political ways. Second, researchers are implicated in their studies and products. The reflexive nature of digital ethnography means we must attend to the "positionality" of the researchers—i.e., how their own identities influence their access, assumptions, and findings.

Another shared understanding—less political, more pragmatic—concerns the nature of digital methods themselves as fundamentally platform-dependent, which means that they are all ephemeral. In other words, the specter haunting digital ethnography is inevitable obsolescence. Platforms do not last. And a book focused on methods situated on/through/about specific platforms and programs must confront this problem (see, e.g., Berryman and Abidin, this volume). Some studies in this book use the phrase "Twitter (now X)" because the fieldwork itself was done when X was still called Twitter. This phrasing will undoubtedly date the writing, but due to the meaningful differences in user culture on Twitter and X, it is a necessary contemporary distinction. And these questions of permanence plague the field: as you hold this book, do people still reference "tweets?" Do YouTubers still "influence" anything? Does Instagram's interface allow the same types of signals to be sent? Does TikTok even exist? This is the contemporary shaky reality of the digital.

So I ask you, reader, to proceed with this in mind: while the platforms are perhaps temporary, the findings don't have to be. Maybe try a mind experiment where you switch nouns to a newer, sexier platform? Danah boyd's (2008) work on online identity construction in Friendster remains essential for its contribution of "networked publics" and examination of creative user resistance to platform strictures, even though no one born in the twenty-first century knows what a "friendster" is. Graham M. Jones and Bambi Schieffelin's (2009) insights on YouTube comment threads as performances of "metalinguistic play" still hold weight, long after the phrase "IDK, my BFF Jill" has exited the zeitgeist. And this is not to mention the theoretical tonnage of work situated in Facebook (including my own) that fails to feel relevant the way it used to because, as I am constantly told, Facebook is for old people now. Because every platform—no matter how exciting, groundbreaking, or culture-driving—will someday be for old people.

So what exactly is in this book?

With the understanding that short thematically grouped pieces will be useful to practitioners, students, and curious readers, the content of this book comes in three different forms—"chapters," "concepts," and "case studies"—revolving around shared topics. After this chapter, for instance, in case you want a deeper dive into the concept of "ethnography," Heather A. Horst's micro-chapter will engage with the term itself. This introductory ethnography theme then presents a set of case studies, all ethnographically approaching the negotiation of traditionally "non-digital" practices as they transition into a contemporary reality of daily digital mediation: Roberto J. González reflects on Zapotec villagers' move into a "second village" online; Jennifer Sierra investigates the shamanic use of selfies among the Shipibo-Konibo in the Peruvian Amazon; Rashmi Kumar discusses Dalit resistance of caste hegemony on WhatsApp in India; and Ivor Miller and Margaret Òkôn trace the diaspora of West African ritual songs on cellphone videos throughout the West Indies.

If you are interested in the ethical dilemmas one might face in the field—questions like what can be considered "public" and how do we treat data gathered in the gray areas on the peripheries of this distinction—Michelle Cera's chapter, "Digital Data Ethics," takes us through best practices using examples from her fieldwork on the conspiracy-minded collective QAnon. One of these practices, "representation," is addressed in Serhat Tutkal's concept chapter, and Piotr Siuda and Patrycja Hewelt relay their experiences with thorny ethical choices in their work in a Polish dark net drug marketplace. Along with the introduction, this "ethics" theme completes the first section of the book.

Section 2 focuses on different "sites" of digital ethnography and how the concept of the "field" has changed. If you are wondering how traditional, on-the-ground ethnographic engagement approaches digital media practices, Xinyuan Wang's chapter, "Ethnography about Digital Media," discusses the difficulties and methodological compromises necessary in studying smartphone use among Chinese migrant workers and the elderly in Shanghai. This use involves the navigation of platform "affordance," tackled by Anna Colom, and then further examined by Paul Bowell, Paul Scifleet, Ekaterina Pechenkina, and Emma Sherry in their study of female Australian footballers' relationships to their digital tracking technologies.

When the sites themselves move "into" the digital, as it were, we face questions like should "lurking" count as an ethnographic method, even when others don't know you are there? Chapter 3, "Ethnography on/in Social Media," takes this on and illustrates step-by-step suggestions and considerations for social media ethnography using lessons from Katrin Tiidenburg's work within multiple online "NSFW" groups in different platforms and from David Kneas's studies of on-and-offline seaglass enthusiasts. Chiara Perin then clarifies the more-slippery-than-it-seems "platform," and Mitra Shamsi investigates multi-platform action among Iranian feminist activists.

If your interests lie in the melding of digital and physical realms, turn to Rachel Berryman and Crystal Abidin. They describe the recent phenomenon of virtual influencers in Chapter 4, "Ethnography of the Virtual," investigating the lucrative partnership between K-pop celebrities and video game content, and proposing a platform/virtual framework through which these relations should be viewed. Tom Boellstorff then wonders if we should be using the term "virtual" reality at all—if what we are really talking about is sensorial immersion—and Harish Goutam takes us into the virtual space politics of "nullsec" in the multiplayer online video game *EVE Online*, questioning the value of an on/offline binary paradigm.

Section 3 illustrates how entanglement with the digital can alter various types of analysis.

Those of you who want to study the ways internet culture changes how we speak, for instance, will want to read Chapter 5, "Linguistic Analysis," wherein Graham M. Jones, Jisoo Hong, and Maya Návar explain the prickly nature of "evidence" within Twitter UFO communities. After this, İdil Galip traces the origin of "memes," and Erik Aasland and Gulnara Omarbekova survey "anti-proverbs" in Kazakh social media. All three pieces interrogate the digital genesis of new ways of communicating.

How does ethnography in/of/through the digital context negotiate the divide between quantitative and qualitative digital data? Chapter 6, "Data Analysis," argues for a combination of both approaches that authors Anna Górska, Dariusz Jemielniak, and Nina Kotula call "Thick Big Data" based on their mixed methods work in anti-feminist Twitter groups. Following this, Tone Walford and Hannah Knox have an informal conversation about what "data" means to them, reflecting on experiences across multiple studies. And Anna Gibson proposes a novel data collection technique drawing from her field work gathering "over-the-shoulder" evidence by sharing Facebook moderators' screens in real time.

This section ends with a chapter that might not be considered entirely "ethnographic" at first glance. Greyson Harris—in Chapter 7, "Spatial Analysis"—argues for spatial analysis as a methodological extension that can achieve the "thick description" of ethnographic engagement if deployed correctly. Harris reveals the human narratives necessary in creating geographic information systems (GISs) projections in his work as a geospatial specialist with the US government's Federal Emergency Management Agency (FEMA). Mark Nunes wonders what "space" actually is in a digital context and how this has changed over time, and based on their work in rural Cameroon, Veronica Bayiha ñwa Quillien, Jean-Baptiste Quillien, and Eugene Bayiha Makonn talk about on-the-ground troubleshooting when GIS technologies prove insufficient.

The book's final section consists of four chapters discussing new avenues of ethnographic work being opened up through digital methodologies. One of the most urgent contemporary questions in this area seems to be, How do we ethically incorporate the use of artificial intelligence into ethnographic work? In Chapter 8, "Artificial Intelligence," Matt Artz describes a very near future wherein we use AI technologies as an integral part of our methods, doing anthropology *of*, *by*, and *with* AI. Heiner Heiland then probes the nature of the "algorithm," and Andrea Russo recounts her project to deradicalize members of an anti-vaccination conspiracy group on Telegram by inserting a GPT bot programmed with deradicalization strategies into the community.

If you are excited about the potential offered by digital spaces and platforms not only in how we conduct research but also how we present and interact with our findings, flip forward to Chapter 9, "Multimodal Anthropology," where Isaac Marrero-Guillamón and Ethiraj Gabriel Dattatreyan argue for a multisensory, performative, and collaborative ethnographic engagement based on invention in the field that creates a multitude of products rather than simply text-based monographs. After that, Christopher Kelty explains the inherent politics of the concept of a "public," and Emily Sekine describes her work as an editor of the anthropology magazine *SAPIENS* as anthropology *for* the public. The three pieces help visualize ethnographic work that stretches past the academy and into the domains of more "mainstream" media platforms.

How, you may ask, does this translate into virtual spaces that have their own rules, ends, and stakes that come from a place of "play?" Chapter 10, "Video Games" explores ethnography in game space, with Lindsay Grace suggesting differentiation between states of "user" and "player" as foci of study, followed by Florence Chee considering what the moniker "gamer" means to people who self-identify as such. Then Jack McLaren and Larisa Kingston Mann examine another side of the gaming industry, discussing gamer performance, audience, marginalization, and intimacy, drawing from their work with queer game streamers on Twitch.

Are you intrigued by what the future of the digital might look like, as it encroaches further into and onto the physical world? Chapter 11, "Hybrid Installations," widens the space of the digital into augmented reality (AR) with Rob Eagle's reflections on his ethnographic AR art piece *THROUGH THE WARDROBE* that had club-goers place themselves into others' identities while (quite literally) trying on their clothes. Maxi Heitmayer then explores what "hybridity" means now and might mean in the future, and the volume ends with a collaborative piece by the Rituals in the Making Collective, describing the creation, exhibition, and archiving of a hybrid GIS, internet-hosted, and on-the-ground COVID memorial situated on the US National Mall.

As you can see, this book contains a substantial number of chapters from a great deal of contributors. It's a lot. But it does not necessarily have to be read in any particular order, as the chapters are designed to act as self-supporting units. It's modular, so skip around. Or read it beginning-to-end, that's up to you! More than anything, this book is meant to inform *your* work, *your* ethnographic engagement. So use it that way. You are holding a user's manual.

Notes

1 Thanks to Anna Colom, who pointed me toward this article in an early draft of her chapter. I had not read it, and it has proven quite helpful.
2 For anthropologists, this is not really a decision, as our disciplinary ethics maintain that we should always be fully transparent about our aims and as open about our identities as is possible in the context. For other fields that engage in ethnographic endeavors (e.g., sociology) this remains a situational decision based largely on institutional review boards, researcher preference, and research aims.

References

Abidin, Crystal, and Gabriele de Seta. 2020. "Private Messages from the Field: Confessions on Digital Ethnography and Its Discomforts." *Journal of Digital Social Research (JDSR)* 2(1): 1–19. https://doi.org/10.33621/jdsr.v2i1.35.

boyd, danah. 2008. "None of This Is Real: Identity and Participation in Friendster." In *Structures of Participation in Digital Culture*, edited by Joe Karaganis, 132–57. New York: Social Science Research Council.

Forberg, Peter, and Kristen Schilt. 2023. "What Is Ethnographic about Digital Ethnography? A Sociological Perspective." *Frontiers in Sociology* 8: 1–15 (June). https://doi.org/10.3389/fsoc.2023.1156776.

Ingold, Tim. 2014. "That's Enough about Ethnography!" *HAU: Journal of Ethnographic Theory* 4 (1): 383–95. https://doi.org/10.14318/hau4.1.021.

Jones, Graham M., and Bambi B. Schieffelin. 2009. "Talking Text and Talking Back: 'My BFF Jill' from Boob Tube to YouTube." *Journal of Computer-Mediated Communication* 14 (4): 1050–79. https://doi.org/10.1111/j.1083-6101.2009.01481.x.

0.1

Concept

Ethnography

Heather A. Horst

Introduction

Ethnography is an approach to understanding the world that prioritizes the experiences and meaning of communities, places, and spaces of sociality. As a practice, ethnography seeks to move away from "armchair analyses" of the world as gleaned by books and secondary sources and into the places and spaces where life is lived through what has been termed "participant observation." The aim of ethnographic approaches, historically, has involved an understanding of what people do and what they say they do over time to understand the norms and values of specific contexts. In this conceptual chapter, I explore the ways in which ethnography has transformed in relation to two core changes: interdisciplinary engagement and the increasing influence of digital media and technology in everyday life. I conclude by reflecting upon the challenges of ethnography as research questions move further from community and place-based studies in spaces such as platforms, algorithms, and distributed practices.

Ethnography across disciplines

Ethnographic research is often practiced in interdisciplinary or transdisciplinary settings; however, ethnography remains a distinctly disciplined endeavor. Among cultural studies, scholars' ethnography is a technique used to move beyond textual analysis of narratives and other forms of popular culture to prioritize the different voices or audiences that respond to and engage with these cultural forms (Pertierra 2018). Sociologists utilize ethnography to understand communities or practices through systematic periods of participant observation supplemented by interviews or other qualitative methods (Small 2013). Finally, in anthropology, ethnography is viewed as an overarching research approach that may involve historical analysis, interviews, participation, mapping, questionnaires, diary studies, and other activities depending upon the theoretical questions underpinning the research.

DOI: 10.4324/9781032672663-2

The diversity of ethnography in practice reflects the various traditions and methodological prisms through which disciplinary formations have been forged. For example, sociologists are often concerned with demonstrating representativeness and generalizability, such as ensuring that the same number of genders, classes, ages, or other categories of difference participate in interviews and observations. This focus upon demonstrating balanced perspectives and approaches is especially prominent in American sociology due to the influence of quantitative sociologists in the field. Historically committed to long-term ethnography over a period of years, seasons, or other temporal markers, anthropology often places less priority upon the number or representativeness of research participants. By contrast, cultural studies scholars conduct more targeted research over a delimited period with less concern overall with sample size, representativeness, or long periods of research. These are just a few of the disciplinary differences that shape what ethnography looks like in practice.

Ethnography as an interdisciplinary intervention

Ethnographic practice continues to change with the growth in digital media and technology around the world. New subfields such as digital anthropology and digital sociology have worked to develop new sites and practices for research (e.g., Horst and Miller 2012; Geismar and Knox 2022; Lupton 2015). In one of the first instances of the use of the term "digital anthropology," Cohen and Salazar (2005) build on the tradition of media anthropology to highlight our broader understanding of digital technology as part of other media and communication worlds (Ginsburg et al. 2002, Pertierra 2018). This trajectory sits alongside the scholarship in material culture studies that focuses upon the relationships between people and things, such as the internet, mobile phones, and social media (Miller and Slater 2000; Horst and Miller 2006; Miller et al. 2016).

From "virtual ethnography," "cyber-ethnography," and "netnography," a second strand of scholarship explored the new spaces, places, and everyday use of digital media and technology. Framed through a digital culture analysis, Bonnie Nardi's (2010) study of *World of Warcraft* or Tom Boellstorff's study of *Second Life* represent some of the first examples of these online, virtual, and internet ethnographies. Through a focus on designers, Gabriella Coleman's (2013, 2014) work on the Debian software community and the anonymous hacktivist network, and Thomas Malaby's (2009) work have both highlighted the constructed nature of online spaces. This work sits alongside sustained conversation with human-computer interaction scholars such as Lucy Suchman (2007) as well as the growing influence of Science and Technology Studies perspectives.

A third vein of research focused upon what is sometimes termed "internet ethnography" (Hine 2015) or digital ethnography (Pink et al. 2016). Ethnography for the internet and digital ethnography explore the practices and meaning of engagement with digital technologies and spaces in the contexts of people's everyday lives. In contrast to netnography and other approaches that prioritize examining online practice using formulaic techniques and ways of mapping online spaces, digital ethnography prioritizes everyday experience and develops methods in relation to the theoretical domain of the work, be that through understanding experiences, social networks, and other forms of connection as these move between online, offline, mobile, and other spaces. Such ethnographic work often brings different techniques, such as re-enactments, diary studies, and others, together with analyses of the images, social media profiles, and other activities.

Conclusion

Ethnography has always been a qualitative methodology used by disciplined scholars to achieve specific ends. Yet, as ethnography moved into studying digital media and technology, it also became a flexible, interdisciplinary, and, at times, transdisciplinary framework for understanding everyday practice. This has been particularly valuable—and a much-needed intervention—for scholars working on collaborative projects with other disciplines. However, as I am often reminded by PhD students working in different disciplines, ethnography is not a silver bullet for all research questions. For example, recent work by Seaver (2018) and others has highlighted how much and how little we can gain rapport with entities such as algorithms or GenAI when the "everydayness" of production and even the experience of such entities in action are difficult to see and, at times, trace. Yet, the condition of such production remains a critical dimension of ethnographic inquiry (Arora 2024; Burrell 2016; Gray and Suri 2019). Work on imagining futures, space or otherwise, presents challenges for capturing the "everyday" or "lived" experience of the future (Salazar and Gorman 2023; Salazar et al. 2017). Ethnographic approaches and questions can guide this research, but they are rarely ethnographic practices that we can triangulate through understanding the differences between what people do and what they say.

Bibliography

Arora, Payal. 2024. *From Pessimism to Promise: Lessons from the Global South on Designing Inclusive Tech*. Cambridge: MIT Press.

Boellstorff, Tom. 2009. *Coming of Age in Second Life*. Princeton, NJ: Princeton University Press.

Burrell, Jenna. 2016. "How the Machine 'Thinks': Understanding Opacity in Machine Learning Algorithms." *Big Data & Society* 3 (1): 1–12.
Cohen, Hart, and Juan Francisco Salazar. 2005. "Introduction: Prospects for a Digital Anthropology." *Media International Australia* 116 (1): 5–9.
Coleman, E. Gabriella. 2013. *Coding Freedom: The Ethics and Aesthetics of Hacking*. Princeton, NJ: Princeton University Press.
Coleman, E. Gabriella. 2014. *Hacker, Hoaxer, Whistleblower, Spy: The Many Faces of Anonymous*. London: Verso Press.
Escobar, Arturo. 1994. "Welcome to Cyberia: Notes for an Anthropology of Cyberculture." *Current Anthropology* 35 (3): 211–31.
Geismar, Haidy, and Hannah Knox, eds. 2022. *Digital Anthropology*. 2nd ed. London: Routledge.
Ginsburg, Faye, Lila Abu-Lughod, and Brian Larkin, eds. 2002. *Media Worlds: Anthropology on New Terrain*. Berkeley: University of California Press.
Gray, Mary L., and Siddharth Suri. 2019. *Ghost Work: How to Stop Silicon Valley from Building a New Global Underclass*. Boston, MA: Houghton Mifflin Harcourt.
Hine, Christine. 2015. *Ethnography for the Internet: Embedded, Embodied and Everyday*. London: Bloomsbury.
Horst, Heather A., and Daniel Miller. 2006. *The Cell Phone: An Anthropology of Communication*. London: Berg.
Horst, Heather A., and Daniel Miller, eds. 2012. *Digital Anthropology*. 1st ed. London: Bloomsbury.
Lupton, Deborah. 2015. *Digital Sociology*. London: Routledge.
Malaby, Thomas. 2009. *Making Virtual Worlds: Linden Lab and Second Life*. Ithaca, NY: Cornell University Press.
Miller, Daniel, and Don Slater. 2000. *The Internet: An Ethnographic Approach*. Oxford: Berg.
Miller, Daniel, Elisabetta Costa, Nell Haynes, Tom McDonald, Razvan Nicolescu, Jolynna Sinanan, Juliano Spyer, Shriram Venkatraman, and Xinyuan Wang. 2016. *How the World Changed Social Media*. London: UCL Press.
Nardi, Bonnie. 2010. *My Life as a Night Elf Priest: An Anthropological Account of World of Warcraft*. Ann Arbor: University of Michigan Press.
Pertierra, Anna Cristina. 2018. *Media Anthropology in a Digital Age*. Oxford: Polity.
Pink, Sarah, Heather Horst, John Postill, Larissa Hjorth, Tania Lewis, and Jo Tacchi. 2016. *Digital Ethnography: Principles and Practice*. London: Sage.
Salazar, Juan Francisco, Sarah Pink, Andrew Irving, and Johannes Sjöberg, eds. 2017. *Anthropologies and Futures: Researching Uncertain and Emerging Worlds*. London and New York: Bloomsbury.
Salazar, Juan Francisco, and Alice Gorman, eds. 2023. *Routledge Handbook of Social Studies of Outer Space*. New York and London: Routledge.
Seaver, Nick. 2018. "What Should an Anthropology of Algorithms Do?" *Cultural Anthropology* 33 (3): 375–85.
Small, Mario L. 2013. "Causal Thinking and Ethnographic Research." *American Journal of Sociology* 119 (3): 597–601.
Suchman, Lucy. 2007. *Human-Machine Reconfigurations*. Cambridge: Cambridge University Press.

0.2

Case study introductory suite

Negotiating the on-and-offline

0.2.1

Case study
Zapotec villagers in the digital era

Roberto J. González

For more than a century, the people of Talea de Castro, a remote Zapotec village in the northern mountains of Oaxaca, Mexico, have sought to strengthen their contacts with the outside world. They eagerly accepted telegraph service in the early 1900s, and, in the 1950s, village leaders successfully petitioned the Mexican government to build a road linking their pueblo to Oaxaca City, the state capital. Over the years, it has provided Talea's inhabitants with an important connection to other regions.

More recently, in the early 1990s, villagers lobbied to have Telmex, Mexico's telephone monopoly, provide several dozen telephones (landlines) to the community. And, in 2013, the pueblo made international headlines by creating its own cellphone network, without support from telecom companies or the Mexican government.[1] Today, the internet and smartphones are a part of daily life in Oaxaca's indigenous communities. Digital technologies are transforming local culture, while helping villagers reinforce and reproduce indigenous identities in a global context.

***

I first visited Talea 30 years ago, as an anthropology student. I lived there for two years, toiling in the fields by day and writing fieldnotes by night. It was a humbling yet rewarding experience that gave me a deep appreciation for the sophisticated ecological knowledge of campesinos (González 2001). I never imagined that one day I would be able to keep in touch with villagers by calling or texting them on cellphones. Yet that's exactly what I do now.

A growing number of Taleans spend parts of their lives online. Many are city dwellers who have migrated far away, but some are also resident Taleans, including campesino farmers. The arrival of internet service and cellphones has brought new possibilities—and challenges.

When the internet arrived in Talea in the late 1990s, a virtual version of the pueblo began to take shape. You might say that two distinct Taleas emerged: a *physical* village located in the cloud forests of northern Oaxaca and a *virtual* village located in the ethereal domain of the World Wide Web. Virtual Talea exists on Facebook pages, YouTube videos, Instagram accounts, WhatsApp posts, and other digital spaces.

The inhabitants of the virtual village are widely dispersed and heterogeneous. They include those born in Talea but who migrated far away; those who have never visited Talea but have an ancestral connection to it; one-time visitors to the pueblo or others who enjoy following events there; and resident Taleans.

* * *

How are villagers using the internet, social media, and digital technologies to connect with each other and with the outside world? It was a challenging question for me to address, because, over the years, I had lost touch with Taleans who had opened their homes—and sometimes their hearts—to me. I guess you might say I let them slip away.

As I began conducting my own version of digital ethnography—something I had never done before—I realized that I would need to create my first Facebook account. At times, it was a disorienting process: I would lose myself for hours, compulsively scrolling through villagers' Facebook pages and posts, reviewing their lists of "friends" for familiar names, or shuttling back and forth between a computer screen, my handwritten field notes from the 1990s, and internet search engines. It was a bizarre experience for someone new to social media.

My preliminary journeys across Facebook's blue-bordered two-dimensional world were clumsy efforts to locate Taleans whom I knew during the 1990s. I began by searching for campesinos whom I knew from working in the fields, but I should have known better—they were unlikely to have the time for social media. So, I decided to try searching for their children. After combing through field notes, I compiled a short list of names of people who, according to my calculations, would now be in their teens or early twenties. Here, I had a bit more success, which is all it took to begin locating others using a crude form of social network analysis. Within days, I had tracked down literally hundreds of people who either had listed Talea as their hometown or I recognized from my fieldwork 20 years earlier.

Most Taleans' Facebook posts contain the kind of material that American social media users have come to expect: status updates, inspirational quotes, baby photos, memes, crude jokes, cute videos, political rants, food photos—and, of course, selfies. It quickly became apparent that Talea's most avid Facebook users are native sons and daughters living and working in the US, in places like Grandview, Washington; Chambersburg, Pennsylvania; Madison,

Wisconsin; and most of all, Greater Los Angeles. Many urbanized Taleans who live in Mexican cities, especially Tijuana, Mexico City, and Oaxaca City, also regularly post status updates and photos to Facebook. Several hundred resident Taleans have Facebook accounts too but typically don't post materials as often as their urban counterparts. They're more likely to respond to posts created by non-resident Taleans living in cities.

Perhaps the most creative (and collective) way that the people of Talea have leveraged social media is by creating a Facebook Group, which at the moment has more than 11,000 members—an extraordinary accomplishment, considering the fact that only 2,400 people live in the actual village.[2] On any given day, group members post an astonishingly wide range of messages, many of which include photos. Here are some examples:

"Anyone driving to Oaxaca City tomorrow? I need a ride," reads a post from a high schooler.
"Fresh poultry for sale—place your order now!" writes a young woman who raises chickens and turkeys.
"Delicious tripe soup today at Comedor Lulu—enjoy our regional cuisine!" announces a restaurant owner.
"Four work oxen available for purchase, call for information," says a message from a campesino farmer.

Many Facebook Group posts are also related to important community events. For example, Taleans have migrant associations in Oaxaca City and Mexico City that periodically sponsor fund-raising bazaars where games, food, and drink are sold to support the village's annual fiestas, which typically cost tens of thousands of dollars.

***

Taleans who frequently use social media often include links to YouTube videos. In fact, several villagers are successful "content creators" who produce and post videos. Tomasa Cruz, a native of Talea who resides in Mexico City, is a remarkably prolific producer who often returns to Talea. Cruz, who is in her late fifties, began posting YouTube videos in 2012.[3] Since then, her videos have been viewed more than two million times. She specializes in high-resolution videos featuring public performances by Talea's band, as well as highlights from fiestas. Although it's difficult to calculate a precise figure, Cruz's work has earned her somewhere between US$3,600 and $5,400— worth several years' salary at Mexico City's official minimum wage.

As it exists on YouTube, the virtual version of Talea can be organized into five themes, mostly associated with the village's annual fiestas— four-day extravaganzas with abundant food, drink, music, and amusement for all. These themes are *danzas* or public outdoor plays; musical performances by the village's brass bands; *calendas* or street parades; firework displays; and basketball tournaments. Another category includes scenes from everyday life such as the preparation of regional foods, agricultural work, and Talea's picturesque surroundings.[4]

Like Facebook, YouTube presents a somewhat distorted version of village life, since many posts portray extraordinary events. As the Mexican poet Octavio Paz once noted, "The fiesta is by nature sacred, literally or figuratively, and above all it is the advent of the unusual ... [It] occurs in an enchanted world: time is transformed to a mythical past or a total present" (Paz 1989 [1950]). From another perspective, YouTube provides a window into a hyper-realistic stage: the viewer is often thrust right into the action. These are almost never staged productions—they are eye-level recordings of culturally significant performances.

A particularly memorable YouTube video, *Linda Taleanita* (literally, "charming Talean girl") *is* a staged production: it's a slick music video featuring 40 young musicians from the municipal band, ranging in age from 8 to 18.[5] They are dressed in clothing that would have been popular in Talea a century ago. Boys sport ivory-colored *calzones* (loose-fitting pants and coarse cotton shirts), black broad-brimmed wool hats, and *huaraches* or sandals. Girls don *huipiles* (embroidered cotton blouses), long pastel-colored skirts, and black *rebozos* (shawls) wrapped around their heads. Dramatic clips of Talea's cobblestone streets, majestic church, and municipal palace are interwoven with close-ups of the protagonist—a beautifully poised teenage girl picking coffee and making tortillas. The song also features a gifted singer, a Talean man known locally as *el Pavarotti* because of his operatic voice.

Linda Taleanita encapsulates how technology can transmit a complex set of symbols, laden with cultural meaning, to different audiences simultaneously. For resident Taleans, particularly for village youth, the video is evidence of vibrant traditions that survive into the twenty-first century—music, clothing, religion, and the countryside. For Talean outmigrants, it is a nostalgic reminder of the pueblo's grandeur and enduring beauty. It's also an alluring invitation—the food, scenery, and music beckon them to return to the village and revisit their heritage.

***

As I was completing my digital ethnographic research on Talea, I briefly became the subject of a Facebook Group post—and a lively exchange afterward. During the summer of 2021, I was interviewed by two researchers affiliated with a non-governmental organization dedicated to preserving Zapotec language and culture. They asked me to discuss my first book, an ethnography about the environmental knowledge of Talea's campesinos, and asked permission to post the interview on YouTube.⁶ I agreed, without giving it much thought.

To my surprise, nearly 2,000 people viewed the hour-long interview within a week! I began receiving emails from Taleans in Los Angeles, Mexico City, and the village itself, who expressed gratitude and appreciation. Apparently, my YouTube appearance had gone (somewhat) viral because of a Facebook Group post written by a man whom I first met in 1994, when he was only nine years old. I couldn't help but smile when I read his post, which included a link to my YouTube interview:

> Good evening everyone! Do you remember a "gringo" in the 1990s, who became a campesino, served as a policeman, participated in the village band, learned to speak Zapotec, and got involved in many, many forms of community life? Do you remember him? Well, you can see Roberto in this video, talking about his book *Zapotec Science*.⁷

Soon afterward, other Facebook Group members posted comments that made me nostalgic for village life. Here are a few:

> "Roberto, we all remember you with much affection."
> "He went to harvest sugar cane and never complained, he learned all about farming work, and he was a very humble person."⁸
> "How he adapted to our way of life here! How can I ever forget the anthropologist Roberto?"

For me, this unexpected experience brought to life the emotional power of social media, how it can provoke feelings of intense nostalgia and trigger long-forgotten memories. It also helped me reestablish relationships that I had left behind years earlier.

* * *

Despite the many benefits of the internet, social media, and cellphones, several questions loom large about the long-term consequences of these technologies: To what extent will the pueblo become dependent on digital tools for social interaction? Will face-to-face communication eventually give way to face-to-screen communication, as in so many other parts of the world? (Figure 0.2.1) Will users experience the kinds of behavioral addiction surrounding these irresistible technologies in the US, Europe, East Asia, and other regions (Cash et al. 2012)? And how do these tools make villages more susceptible to forms of digital surveillance and algorithmic modes of governance that have become normalized in many countries? There are still no clear answers to these questions—only time will tell.

Figure 0.2.1 Teenagers from Talea de Castro using their cellphones. Photo taken by the author.

Several years ago, an influential Talean elder had this to say about new technology: "We've all become comfort lovers … [but] what can be bad about new things is not knowing how to use them properly. I'm not against progress, I'm for it. But I think there must be a balance." Finding that balance in the midst of a digital revolution will likely be among the biggest challenges confronting Talea in the twenty-first century.

Notes

1 https://www.sapiens.org/culture/talea-cellphone-network/.
2 https://www.facebook.com/groups/talea/.
3 This and all other names are pseudonyms.
4 https://www.inah.gob.mx/foto-del-dia/villa-talea-de-castro.
5 https://www.youtube.com/watch?v=4FUvZQqcWKo.
6 https://www.youtube.com/watch?v=qmvNaUwgAZc.
7 For the record, I was never fluent in Zapotec (a complex tonal language), although I did learn several dozen words.
8 Harvesting sugarcane is extraordinarily difficult, and apparently some villagers were impressed when I participated in this work several times.

Bibliography

Cash, Hilarie, Cosette D. Rae, Ann H. Steel, and Alexander Winkler. 2012. "Internet Addiction: A Brief Summary of Research and Practice." *Current Psychiatry Reviews* 8 (4): 292–98. https://doi.org/10.2174/157340012803520513.

González, Roberto. 2001. *Zapotec Science: Farming and Food in the Northern Sierra of Oaxaca*. 1st ed. Austin: University of Texas Press.

González, Roberto. 2021. "Why a Mexican Village's DIY Cellphone Network Matters." *SAPIENS*, March 30. https://www.sapiens.org/culture/talea-cellphone-network/.

Paz, Octavio. (1989 [1950]). *The Labyrinth of Solitude and Other Writings*. New York: Grove Press.

0.2.2

Case study
Selfies, shamans, and social media participation among the Shipibo-Konibo in the Peruvian Amazon

Jennifer Sierra

"Uno no debería estar publicando fotos de la cara de uno en Facebook. Los shamanes te pueden hacer daño, pues!" (One should not be posting photos of one's face [up close] on Facebook. Shamans could [use these photos to] harm you!). Members of the Shipibo-Konibo indigenous group (hereafter referred to as Shipibos) repeatedly brought up this warning through several focus groups that I conducted during my long-term ethnographic fieldwork in the Ucayali region of the Peruvian Amazon. Although I spent many hours observing Shipibos' posts on Facebook, their lack of "selfies" on the platform had not caught my attention. Upon hearing the above warning, I revisited the digital data I had collected and scrolled through Shipibos' Facebook accounts. While I did notice a couple of selfies, they were uncommon among Shipibos. This is one example of the connections that exist between Shipibos' Facebook activity and the broader cultural and socio-political dimensions of their lives.

This case study of Shipibos' engagement with digital media technologies draws on 22 months of ethnographic fieldwork conducted in both the city of Pucallpa and the rural Native Community of Callería, located in the Ucayali province within the Peruvian Amazon. It reflects Shipibos' current reality regarding their experiences with digital media. Indigenous Shipibos reside in more than 150 rural villages—many designated as indigenous territories by the Peruvian government—in the Ucayali River basin, as well as in urban areas like Pucallpa and the Peruvian capital, Lima.

Historically, Shipibos constituted three separate ethnic groups: Shipibo, Konibo, and Xetebo. During the twentieth century, they gradually united through marriage, alliances, and the intervention of Protestant missionaries, forming a single ethnic group (Morin, 1998; Tournon, 2002). Today, Shipibo-Konibo-Xetebos refer to themselves as Shipibos, but some of their members continue to trace their Konibo and Xetebo descendancy and speak distinct Shipibo language varieties. Most Shipibos are bilingual: speaking Shipibo and Spanish (Sánchez et al., 2022).

During my fieldwork between 2018 and 2024, I observed how Shipibos' lives were rapidly digitizing despite the inconsistent and unreliable internet access in their communities, especially in the rural settlements. While Shipibos in the city of Pucallpa have had more reliable internet connections—primarily via cell phone data plans—since 2016, many rural villages still lacked internet connections as of 2024. Yet, by 2022, many daily activities for Shipibos, including schoolwork, healthcare, and banking, increasingly required internet access and the use of digital applications. Similarly, Shipibos' social interactions have increasingly occurred in the digital world, primarily on Facebook. However, for Shipibos, connecting to the internet was not as easy as unlocking phone screens and tapping on apps. At the time of this case study, most Shipibo households did not have Wi-Fi (and still do not as of 2025), and those that did complained about its high cost. The most reliable way to access the internet was offered through phone data plans, which included affordable data to use Facebook, WhatsApp, and sometimes Instagram—all owned by Meta Platforms, Inc.

In the early days of my fieldwork, I repeatedly asked Shipibos, "What do you like to do on the internet?" But few people seemed to understand what I meant. This was especially true in the rural Shipibo settlements like the village of Callería. Eventually, someone sought to clarify my question, asking me, "Do you mean Facebook?" This name substitution of the internet with Facebook was meaningful. It pointed to how the partnerships between telecommunication corporations, nation-states, and tech companies (which in Latin America started forming in the 1990s [Mariscal, 2009]) have impacted Shipibos' experiences on digital media. These alliances have been shown to significantly boost the popularity of certain digital platforms, which has raised questions about who is profiting from this provision of internet access (Peña, 2016; Vincent, 2016).

Meta Platforms, Inc., previously known as The Facebook Company, has, for almost a decade, invested in low-data consumption solutions to provide internet connection to rural and low-income populations. These efforts have resulted in products like Facebook's "Free Basics," which grant users free data access to Facebook and other participating apps. Telecommunications companies in Latin America have partnered with Facebook to support affordable internet connections in regions with limited internet access (García, 2020; Reuters, 2015). Thus, because most Shipibos could only afford limited phone data plans, having free or affordable access to Facebook increased their interest in and use of the platform.

On Facebook, Shipibos produced and circulated news relevant to their community, challenging the long-standing practice of local and national Peruvian news outlets, which rarely cover topics or events affecting Amazonian indigenous communities. So, instead of social media activity being about curating individual personas and sharing personal content,

Shipibo content creation was often community-centered. The expectation was that Shipibos would share what mattered to their community; thus, many Shipibo news accounts were created on Facebook. This content included death announcements for Shipibo members as well as social and political commentary—often through comedic posts or memes.

While much information was shared online, evaluations and concerns about social media content were often done offline. For example, Shipibos articulated their ideas about what was considered (in)appropriate behavior on Facebook through face-to-face conversations rather than on the platform itself. This highlights the media ideologies of Shipibos, that is, their collective ideas and evaluations about media technologies that informed what they did on the platforms (Gershon, 2010). For instance, it was common for Shipibos to discuss other members' posts during in-person social gatherings. In these daily conversations, Shipibos judged other members for posting "too much." However, not every series of frequent posts was considered "too much"; only those posts that contained "too personal" content, such as information about dating and breakups, travel, or leisure activities, were considered improper. These posts were thought to bring "too much attention" to the individual, suggesting that the poster was vain. Conversely, posts covering events happening in the different Shipibo villages—such as anniversary celebrations, local elections, and members' health updates—were rarely criticized, even if made frequently, because such content preferences aligned with Shipibos' broader expectation that Facebook should be a community-centered space.

During a fieldwork trip in 2022, Shipibos warned me that their members should not share up-close photos of their faces on Facebook. Sharing selfies is a popular social media activity worldwide, and elsewhere the practice has been associated with building intimacy and creating an experience of togetherness online (Miguel, 2016). However, for Shipibos, sharing selfies was dangerous, as shamans could use these photos to harm the person in the photo. It is important to make two distinctions here. First, my Shipibo interlocutors did not mean that one should not post pictures that included one's face; instead, one should not post *close-up* photos of one's face (i.e., selfies). Second, the term "shaman" is not originally a Shipibo term. The term was introduced to the Amazon region by foreigners (Gow, 2001). Today, Shipibos commonly use the word to refer to a class of healers or sorcerers, also known as "médicos" (healers) (Brabec de Mori, 2012). Shamans were described to me as knowledgeable spiritual leaders who can heal and assist those in need but who can also be envious and harm people. In my experience, Shipibos use the term "médico" in the context of healing, but, when a person is potentially causing harm, the term "shaman" is used. Shipibos' relationship with shamans/médicos is complicated because of the persistent ambiguity surrounding these individuals' activities and intentions (Brabec de Mori, 2013). Thus, many Shipibos viewed shamans as not entirely trustworthy.

Shipibos' use of recent digital media technologies—which have afforded them an expanded indeterminate audience (Cody & Paz, 2021)—has caused them to grapple with the fact that their presence in such public spaces can expose them to danger. When surveying Shipibos in both Pucallpa and Callería about their general social media practices, most, if not all, stated that they did not befriend anyone on Facebook whom they did not already know in person or through in-person networks. However, this did not mean that everyone who could view and interact with their posts was trustworthy. The indeterminacy of social media audiences has been a feature of digital communication technologies previously studied as "context collapse" (Marwick & boyd, 2011). Not being able to fully control who interacts with one's own public content on social media can create anxiety, and it can influence one's decisions about how and what to post to protect oneself and one's community.

There are many strategies that people on social media—just like in other public settings—can adopt to protect the information they consider private or sensitive (Irvine, 1996; Marwick & boyd, 2014). In the case of Shipibos, only befriending people on Facebook whom they already know in person is one strategy to manage their Facebook audience. However, Facebook users who belong to ambiguous categories, like shamans, can be more difficult to manage. While there are many shamans in Pucallpa and in Shipibo rural communities, most Shipibos know who they are and they are often connected through kinship. In this way, shamans belong to their in-person network and so are often befriended on Facebook. As a result, Shipibos have faced the challenge of developing other strategies to manage less trustworthy people who might gain access to their social media content. The example below illustrates one such threat.

Alba, a Shipibo woman in her early thirties, suspected a shaman was harming her using selfies from her Facebook account. At the time of our conversation in 2022, she had been suffering from stomach pain for months. Because doctors could not determine the source of her discomfort, and her symptoms did not improve, she concluded that her stomach pain was the work of an envious shaman. I was told that shamans could exert their powers (whether healing or harmful) on a person (even without their consent), if they obtained a printed photo of them. That is, even if sourced from Facebook, these photos needed to be printed in order for the shaman to use them. So, if a person wanted to help a relative who was physically remote, they could print a photo of that person and bring it to the shaman for them to "act on" their relative and achieve the requested benefit, like improving that person's health. I heard stories of Shipibo members stealing photos from physical photo albums and bringing them to shamans to request particular outcomes. The material potential of digital photos is relevant for thinking about how content on a digital platform like Facebook can affect people's physical lives such as their health. Similarly, I wondered how Shipibos perceived the way that old and new media work together and why they might think one format has greater power than the other. In this case, while digital photos are insufficient on their own, they remain crucial for sourcing physical images for shamanic use.

Shipibos' ideas about selfies demonstrate how digital media technologies disrupt and enter meaningful cultural and socio-political dimensions of life that extend beyond the platform's bounds. For Shipibos, specific posting practices, such as selfies, can affect one's health and well-being. In the same way, more widespread phenomena such as cyberbullying have far-reaching effects. Various societies may consider different kinds of online content to be risky for many reasons. Ideas about what constitutes a threat, who can pose it, and how it can be carried out are tied to long-standing social values and worldviews (Douglas & Wildavsky, 1982).

I only discovered the connections between selfies and the risk of shamanic practices because I conducted long-term immersive ethnography (Irvine, 2012). I learned the nuanced dos and don'ts of Shipibos' Facebook actions, which are not entirely unique. The use of selfies and their associated risks involving shamans is just one example among many worldwide practices where social media users strategize to shield themselves from offline consequences of their online actions. Shipibos use Facebook with caution, employing tactics that consider long-standing contentious social relationships, such as those with shamans, which have now evolved into relationships that must be managed on social media.

References

Brabec de Mori, Bernd. 2012. "About Magical Singing, Sonic Perspectives, Ambient Multinatures, and the Conscious Experience." INDIANA – *Estudios Antropológicos Sobre América Latina y El Caribe* 29(January): 73–101. https://doi.org/10.18441/ind.v29i0.73-101.

Brabec de Mori, Bernd. 2013. "Shipibo Laughing Songs and the Transformative Faculty: Performing or Becoming the Other." *Ethnomusicology Forum* 22 (3): 343–61. https://doi.org/10.1080/17411912.2013.844528.

Cody, Francis, and Alejandro I. Paz. 2021. "Securitizing Communication: On the Indeterminacy of Participant Roles in Online Journalism." *Journal of Linguistic Anthropology* 31 (3): 340–56. https://doi.org/10.1111/jola.12339.

Douglas, Mary, and Aaron Wildavsky. 1982. *Risk and Culture: An Essay on the Selection of Technological and Environmental Dangers*. Berkeley: University of California Press.

García, Lester. 2020. "Impulsando la conectividad en Latinoamérica." *Meta Noticias*. July 2. https://about.fb.com/ltam/news/2020/07/impulsando-la-conectividad-en-latinoamerica/.

Gershon, Ilana. 2010. "Media Ideologies: An Introduction." *Journal of Linguistic Anthropology* 20 (2): 283–93.

Gow, Peter. 2001. *An Amazonian Myth and Its History*. Oxford: Oxford University Press.

Irvine, Judith T. 1996. "Shadow Conversations: The Indeterminacy of Participant Roles." In *Natural Histories of Discourse*, ed. Michael Silverstein and Greg Urban, 131–59. Chicago: University of Chicago Press.

Irvine, Judith T. 2012. "Keeping Ethnography in the Study of Communication." *Langage et Société* 139: 47–66.

Mariscal, Judith. 2009. "Market Structure and Penetration in the Latin American Mobile Sector." Edited by Amy K. Mahan and William H. Melody. *Info* 11 (2): 24–41. https://doi.org/10.1108/14636690910941867.

Marwick, Alice E., and danah boyd. 2011. "I Tweet Honestly, I Tweet Passionately: Twitter Users, Context Collapse, and the Imagined Audience." *New Media & Society* 13 (1): 114–33. https://doi.org/10.1177/1461444810365313.

Marwick, Alice E., and danah boyd. 2014. "Networked Privacy: How Teenagers Negotiate Context in Social Media." *New Media & Society* 16 (7): 1051–67.

Miguel, Cristina. 2016. "Visual Intimacy on Social Media: From Selfies to the Co-Construction of Intimacies through Shared Pictures." *Social Media + Society* 2 (2): 2056305116641705. https://doi.org/10.1177/2056305116641705.

Morin, Françoise. 1998. "Los shipibo-conibo." *Guía etnográfica de la Alta Amazonía* 3: 275–435.

Peña, Paz. 2016. "Free Basics y las batallas políticas de internet." *El Espectador* (Tecnología). January 21. https://www.elespectador.com/tecnologia/free-basics-y-las-batallas-politicas-de-internet-article-611733/.

Reuters. 2015. "Facebook lanza en Colombia una aplicación de acceso gratuito a Internet." *El Mundo*.

Sánchez, Liliana, José Camacho, Elisabeth Mayer, and Carolina Rodríguez Alzza. 2022. "Gender Agreement in a Language Contact Situation." *Languages* 7: 81. https://doi.org/10.3390/languages7020081

Tournon, Jacques. 2002. *La merma mágica: vida e historia de los shipibo-conibo del Ucayali*. Lima: Centro Amazónico de Antropología y Aplicación Práctica (CAAAP).

Vincent, James. 2016. "Facebook's Free Basics Service Has Been Banned in India." *The Verge*. February 8. https://www.theverge.com/2016/2/8/10913398/free-basics-india-regulator-ruling.

0.2.3

Case study

Digital solidarity and everyday assertion of Dalit identity on WhatsApp in India

Rashmi Kumar

Digital access in India has become a prominent part of people's lives through YouTube, reels, and TikTok. Furthermore, WhatsApp and Facebook have become companions of people from youngsters to middle-aged groups to the elderly generations. In the present, especially since COVID-19, this necessity caused people to buy phones, which later increased social media use that highlighted caste as the harsh reality of Indian societies. Upper-caste netizens reject the significance of caste to deny the need for a reservation policy for the marginalized caste community. The presence and representation of the marginalized caste group in the digital sphere should be explored to assert their existence and caste identity against the dominant norms set up by the upper-caste elites.

For upper-caste netizens, the "unfair" policy of reservation is a curse to the meritorious population in the "general category"[1] in India. The economic crisis among the general caste category becomes more vital for upper-caste netizens to oppose the caste-based reservation policy. Instead of questioning the government about the unemployment crisis, upper-caste netizens blame the oppressed caste groups through insensitive humor and memes, calling people from the reserved category "unworthy" or "freeloaders."

Social media and popular pages on the meme front in India witness several posts and videos around "anti-reservation system" or "anti-Ambedkar" as trendy discourses in the digital sphere.[2] These posts often deny any caste impact in "modern" India, and a handful of affluent Dalit people is enough of a cure for the trauma and hostility induced by caste oppression that has been sustained for centuries. They also carry the claim of apparent castelessness and deny the impact of caste oppression in the institutions. The dominant discourses, channels, and media control the everyday reality of caste narratives and experiences within the digital sphere and pop culture. In contemporary times, caste persists by controlling access to types of occupation and its access to influencing positions and elite circles (A. Deshpande 2011). Upper-caste people nonchalantly display their caste pride while claiming that caste is irrelevant in "modern" India, and lower-caste people adopt casteless surnames like Kumar and Rao to avoid discrimination and indifference.

Caste in urban India is practiced discreetly in everyday life, and the culturalization of caste gets played out through caste pride of upper-caste with hashtags like #rajputspride, #brahminsgenes, and #baniyabrain in digital space as a public sphere. The ostracisation and hostility faced by the marginalized groups in the metaphysical world are also replicated in the virtual world by controlling social media (Guru and Sarukkai 2019; Mukherjee 1999; "Caste and the Digital Sphere—उद्भव" 2022). The dominance of the upper caste in digital space is reinforced by their access to material and social capital. In contrast, the digital divide, unequal social structures in the digital realm, and limited resources make it difficult for Dalits to challenge existing inequalities. The emerging trend of caste-based hate speech on social media highlights the discrimination faced by oppressed castes. Devanshu Saljan (2021) discusses how caste slurs are used to de-legitimize Dalits' presence online, with hateful content mocking their culture, associating them with derogatory references, and attacking Ambedkar and the reservation policy. The intent behind these slurs is to intimidate the Dalit community and instill fear, preventing them from asserting their rights.

Digital engagement of lower-caste communities' assertion of caste identity challenges the idea of castelessness and other hegemonic discourses controlled by the caste elites in the virtual sphere. The WhatsApp group titled *Dhusia Samaj Jodo Manch* (Forum to Connect Dhusia community) was organized by the people from the Dhusia caste community as a *samaj*, "a cultural society of caste" (Natrajan 2011). It is a marginalized caste community among the Dalits acquiring the digital space to assert their caste identity, administering a matrimonial network, seeking solidarity and dignity, and accounting for their history.

To explore the understanding of this caste group through the reflexive understanding and Dalit feminist standpoint as a Dhusia woman, I examined the narratives of the Dhusia caste community offline and online. This digital ethnography examines the WhatsApp group as a case study that explores more significant ideas around identity, caste, matrimony, spirituality, and solidarity. Digital ethnography holds the scope of multiplicity, non-digital-centeredness, openness, reflexivity, and unorthodoxy ("Caste and the Digital Sphere—उद्भव" 2022). The case of a digital ethnography on a marginalized caste group entails the narratives of connecting over social media to assert and administrate Dalit collectivization in Delhi.

Caste encryption and digital solidarity

This excerpt from the WhatsApp group is a message from a Dhusia *Samaj* member from Delhi sharing a message for a gathering for the Ambedkar Jayanti celebration:

> "जन सूचना
> सभी धुसिय परविार के बंधुओं को सुचित किया जाता है, किअगामी दनिाक 14 अप्रैल को स्थान नाना राव परकमे dr भीम राव अंबेडकर जी की जयंती के पर्व को हर्षो ओल्लाश से मनाने के लिए कल रविवार के दनि शाम 5 बजे एक मीटगि आयोजति बुलाई गई हैं …जसिमे हम सब कि उपस्थति अनीवार है।"

(Public notice:
We would like to notify all the Dhusia family members that a meeting has been scheduled for this Sunday at 5 p.m. This is to commemorate Dr. Bhim Rao Ambedkar Ji's birth anniversary on April 14 in Nana Rao Parakme. We are all required to be present at this meeting, which has been arranged)

The Dhusia community has an ambiguous caste status in the eyes of the State and has erased micro-histories. Dhusia people in Delhi are mobilizing the community through cultural events in devotion toward a spiritual guru, "Shiv Narayan Maharaj," in festivals like Shivratri and Basant Panchami. With the increasing accessibility and necessity of smartphones and social media, Dhusia people are increasingly joining groups and pages on WhatsApp and Facebook to make accounts of their activities through pictures, videos, and posts.

The study of such digital groups has the potential to explore how caste ideology has been encrypted in the minds of India and how it is translated through virtual engagements, irrespective of the denial of caste in urban spaces, and its impacts disguised as castelessness by the caste elites in contemporary India (S. Deshpande 2013). In urban India, for caste elites, it is convenient to claim the existence of apparent castelessness, as it is established beyond its visceral form of violence through practicing untouchability or ritualized hierarchies. It furthermore hides the structural oppression of caste and its strongholds in the elite sections and occupations. The caste-based violence that is embedded and naturalized through hostility and ostracization is substantiated through psychological trauma and social exclusion (Guru and Sarukkai 2019; S. Deshpande 2013; A. Deshpande 2011).

Digital solidarity counters the denial of caste through collective consciousness and the assertion of Dalit identity. The digital mobilization to assert their identity, challenging hegemonic discourse on caste in India, serves as a significant vignette that depicts the everyday life of Dalit people and the cultural expression of caste in India through the virtual platform. The group has become a platform for Dhusia people for information about gathering for Ambedkarite events or celebrating Ambedkar Jayanti. Moreover, the group brings out events celebrating guru Shiv Narayan Maharaj called *Bandigi* (devotion). Through offline and online engagement, Dhusia people further connected with other *samaj* and local politicians and social leaders in Delhi. The offline and online Dalit assertion in Delhi constitutes the experience of resilience, resistance, and revolution against the hegemony. The emerging digital engagement of lower-class groups—broadly lower-caste communities—led to caste communities forming pages and WhatsApp groups in an attempt to attain solidarity and dignity.

Matrimonial network through social media

This excerpt is a message from the admin of the WhatsApp group, S.P. Dhusia:

"🙏🙏धुसिया समाज जोड़ो मंच के माध्यम से आपको बताना चाहते हैं कि यह गरुप हमने बिखरे हुए समाज को संगठित कर तथा समाज के परिवारों में जो बच्चे शादी योग्य हो चुकें हैं और वर-वधू तलाशने में जो दिक्कतें आ रही हैं उन परिवारों से हमारा निवेदन है कि अपने बच्चों की एक फोटो और बायोडाटा गरुप में भेजें जिसके द्वारा आप को वर-वधू बोलने में कोई दिक्कत ना आए तथा समाज में ही आपकी रिश्तेदारी बन सके."

(🙏🙏Through *Dhusia Samaj Jodo Manch*, we want to tell you that we have organized this group by organizing the scattered society and helping the families of the society whose children have become eligible for marriage and who are facing difficulties in finding a bride and groom. It is requested that you send a photo and biodata of your children to the group so that you do not face any problem in calling yourself bride and groom and you can become related in the society.)

Through my doctoral project, an anthropological inquiry on the Dhusia community, I connected with the founders of this *pan-India* WhatsApp group. I joined the group as a Dhusia person and native academic spectator to study the everyday exchange of digital text, posts, and pictures in the group. This digital group aims to connect the Dhusia caste community primarily to facilitate matrimonial connections among the community and mobilize to build solidarity and recognition within and outside the Dhusia community. The conversations and messages are centered on sharing general WhatsApp forwards and pictures about morality and religion, as well as notes on the history of the Dhusia caste and collective devotion toward a spiritual guru. For matrimonial purposes, the group members regularly share "Biodata" of the eligible bachelors and bachelorettes that include categories like general information, including qualification, occupation and income, family background, *gotra* (lineage), caste, and information on physical characteristics like height, complexion, weight, and more.

Dhusia Samaj Jodo Manch was founded in September 2020 and has been very active through the networking of Dhusia *Sama*j members in different states. The group was founded by Surya Prakash Dhusia (pseudonym), a retired government servant located initially in another Indian state called Madhya Pradesh, who moved a few years back to Delhi. He approached the members of a collective of the Dhusia community called *Dhusia Mahasabha Dilli Pradesh* (DMDP), also known as *Dhusia* Samaj, and suggested the *Pradhan* (Chief) of the *samaj* to make a *Pan-India* group to collectivize Dhusia. The members of Dhusia *Samaj* also run another WhatsApp group to administrate their activities and send information regarding events and general meetings. S.P. Dhusia approached them and discussed how Dhusia people in Delhi avoid using their surnames; it is very difficult to connect with other Dhusia people, and it is difficult for people to recognize other Dhusia people and to organize for solidarity and matrimonial purposes such as arranged marriage within the community.

Initially, in *Dhusia Samaj Jodo Manch*, the group members actively shared biodata of girls and boys in their mid-20s in different states of India from the Dhusia community. Now I witness biodata of middle-aged people—often widowers, divorced, or single due to miscellaneous reasons—and the group also witnessed around ten successful matrimonial arrangements resulting in marriage. Later, the members also consolidated several biodata into different PDFs, such as "girls' biodata" or "boys' biodata," to facilitate the data for proposal seekers. The engagements of the admins of the WhatsApp group and other major members of the offline Dhusia *Samaj* contribute through archiving the data and networking as well.

During the formal interviews for my fieldwork, S.P. Dhusia actively talked about his family, a wife, a daughter, and three sons who helped him make the group on WhatsApp, setting up icons and names. They also help him with designing and setting up digital pamphlets of information on the Dhusia community and the spiritual guru Shiv Narayan Maharaj. S.P. Dhusia discussed how Dhusia men and women face matrimonial crises within the caste group, as Dhusia women who acquire higher education do not seek to get married to Dhusia men, as they are often not very educated and come from a lower-class status. His wife, Veena, talked about how it is difficult to recognize who is Dhusia or seeking platforms for matrimonial prospects for their children.

They mentioned how the online matrimonial websites are unaffordable, so like other Dhusia people, they often relied on the collective gatherings of Dhusia people in events like Basant Panchami, a festival celebrating the festival of spring, and "*kirtan*" or "*Satsang*" as a spiritual gathering, and Shivratri, a festival celebrating the union of Hindu god *Shiva* and goddess *Parvati*. In these festivals, women often bring their daughters eligible for marriage, and mothers of Dhusia men approach them, other relatives, or "*Bicholia*" who are the intermediates for matrimonial purposes to connect families for approaching and arranging meetings. S.P. Dhusia and Veena Dhusia were "open to love marriage," yet they sought a future for their children through marriage through WhatsApp groups, collectivizing the Pan-Indian group of the Dhusia community.

Conclusion

The caste divides and systematic oppression intensely impact India's digital sphere because the social and material capital pertains to class and caste embodiment experience in contemporary India. During COVID, several upper-caste people justified "untouchability" as a scientific approach, like social distancing. This is a predatory use of the hegemonic discourse of upper-caste people who immediately resort to justifying any casteist or patriarchal practice. This case study presents the narratives of a Dalit caste community in Delhi that negotiates to mobilize and bring solidarity through caste identity in digital space. Digital solidarity counters the denial of caste through collective consciousness and the assertion of Dalit identity. The digital ethnography on the Dhusia caste community brings out the paradox of the invisibility and visibility of caste. It counters the discourse of "castelessness" that denies the significance of caste in everyday social life in Indian societies.

Notes

1 The General category includes those individuals who do not belong to reserved categories like Other Backward Classes, Scheduled Castes, Scheduled Tribes, and Economically Weaker Sections and are therefore not eligible for reservation.
2 See, for example, https://www.facebook.com/photo.php?fbid=1569986139749144&id=119204294827343&set=a.120502598030846.

References

Caste and the Digital Sphere – শুদ্ধস্বর. 14 May 2022. https://shuddhashar.com/caste-and-the-digital-sphere/.
Deshpande, Ashwini. 2011. *The Grammar of Caste: Economic Discrimination in Contemporary India*. Oxford: Oxford University Press.

Deshpande, Satish. 2013. "Caste and Castelessness: Towards a Biography of the 'General Category.'" *Economic and Political Weekly* 48 (15): 32–39.

Guru, Gopal, and Sundar Sarukkai. 2019. *Experience, Caste, and the Everyday Social*. Oxford: Oxford University Press.

Mukherjee, Ramkrishna. 1999. "Caste in Itself, Caste and Class, or Caste in Class." *Economic and Political Weekly* 34 (27): 1759–61.

Natrajan, Balmurli. 2011. *The Culturalization of Caste in India: Identity and Inequality in a Multicultural Age*. London: Routledge.

Sajlan, Devanshu. 2021. "Hate Speech against Dalits on Social Media: Would a Penny Sparrow Be Prosecuted in India for Online Hate Speech?" *CASTE/ A Global Journal on Social Exclusion* 2 (1): 77–96. https://doi.org/10.26812/caste.v2i1.260.

0.2.4

Case study
Songs of an initiation club in West Africa and its Caribbean Diaspora

Ivor Miller and Margaret M. P. Òkôn

Within human memory, the main institution federating the West African settlements and trade networks of the Cross River basin and surrounding uplands has been the Ékpè "leopard" initiation society (Ruel 1969; Northrup 1978; Röschenthaler 2011). Developing within an extremely decentralized, multilingual environment, Ékpè elaborated a symbolic system of gestures, body-masks, and other visual and rhythmic signs which were also substantially transmitted to western Cuba during the Spanish slave labor economy of the eighteenth to nineteenth centuries as Abakuá (Dayrell 1910; Leib & Romano 1984; Miller 2009). Verbal texts of Ékpè/Abakuá performance are expressed in auxiliary linguistic codes that reflect the cult's historical development even while remaining semantically opaque; meanwhile, they are pragmatically meaningful to modern participants in the ritual context.

Cuban scholar Lydia Cabrera (1988) pioneered the study of verbal texts of Cuba's three major African source groups: Yorùbá (Lukumí), Kongo, and Abakuá (1957, 1984, 1988). Our project continues this work in West Africa with the documentation and interpretation of Ékpè song performances through audio and video recordings, which are then transcribed and rendered with tone marks by a professional linguist (Miller & Òkôn 2020). Based in Calabar, Nigeria, since 2004, this project engages current initiates by documenting their ceremonial songs to analyze their literal, poetic, and esoteric meanings. Our goal is to characterize these oral productions both as sources of reconstructed history and as mnemonics of esthetic and practical action. Theoretically, the project uses audiovisual evidence to contribute to awareness of a centuries-old African cultural diaspora, first diffused throughout the Cross River basin and subsequently in the Caribbean.

In Calabar, Ékpè activists embraced this project to promote their heritage and its diaspora and organized in 2007 an association of lodges from various ethnic communities, called Calabar Mgbè.[1] This association sent a delegation to Paris in 2007 to perform with a group of Cuban

Abakuá at a festival sponsored by the Musée Quai Branly. This event was video-recorded, and the performers from Cuba and Nigeria were very observant and curious about the performances of their counterparts. Two results from this exchange were released: an essay by Miller about this cultural summit—the first-ever staged interaction between Èkpè and Abakuá—published in 2015 as "Separated by the Slave Trade: Nigerians and Cubans Reunite through a Shared Cultural Practice." Second, the Cuban participants composed and recorded an album (*Ecobio Enyenison* 2009), including songs and rhythms they learned from the Nigerians, fused with their own and arranged in a jazz context. One of the messages of this recording is that centuries-old ritual rhythms and chants have contributed to the development of jazz performance in the US, continuing the creative work of "Chano" Pozo, who brought Abakuá rhythms and chants into his compositions with Dizzy Gillespie in 1947–1948 in New York City (Miller 2000).

Methodology

The recording of Abakuá texts began in Havana in the early 1900s when RCA Victor recorded songs like "Achui Bongó" (africano), composed by Alberto Villalón and performed by the duo Regino López and Adolfo Colombo with guitar [Victor B-13786, 1913] (Discography of American Historical Recordings 2025). Commencing a long history of recording Abakuá ritual phrases within the context of popular music, the texts are intentionally opaque, untranslated, yet intelligible to Cuban initiates and used by them to document their activities. Cognizant of the extensive Cuban discography, Miller was curious if Èkpè songs in Calabar served a similar purpose. Arriving in 2004, Miller requested singers of Èkpè songs to transcribe their lyrics; he also video-recorded songs performed in ceremonial contexts in both Nigeria and Cameroon. In Calabar, most songs were in the Èfịk language as well as Èkpè linguistic codes, Èfịk being the lingua franca of the entire region in recent generations. To professionally document and analyze the song texts, Miller teamed up with trained linguist Professor Margaret Òkôn, who adjusted the transcriptions, provided literal translations, and also marked the corresponding tones. To our knowledge, this is the first linguistic analysis of Èkpè songs ever published.

But Miller had documented Èkpè songs in several languages while traveling throughout the region. They include Kúọ̀ ("Kwa"), Éjághám, Ọ́rọ́n, Boki, Lokaa, and BàLóndó. Through many frustrated attempts at transcribing and translating the songs in these languages, it became clear that very few contemporary speakers of these languages know how to write their speech, while very few Èkpè specialists understand deeply the meanings of the songs and their contexts, even if they claimed otherwise. Professor Òkôn found that the inability of speakers to write their languages is the bane of most Cross River languages, which have been depressed and suffocated by the English, Èfịk, and Ìbìbìò languages and, thus, are without robust speakers. A good number of them are in grave danger of extinction. Òkôn and Noah (2021) reported that, at present, almost no indigenous Nigerian speaks Èfût (a variant of BàLóndó of Cameroon), which is said to be the original language of the Ékpè society (known as "Mgbè" in Èfût language). Therefore, their research on Èfût required learning from a BàLóndó Cameroonian who has lived in Nigeria for much of his adult life due largely to his maternal lineage in Cross River State. Nonetheless, vestiges of the Èfût language and culture survive in libation rituals and in Ékpè songs, but they continue to be influenced by the languages of the neighboring cultures.

Regarding Èfịk Ékpè songs, progress was made thanks to an Ékpè song specialist raised in a family of traditional musicians in rural Creek Town, an epicenter of Ékpè activity outside the city of Calabar: Chief Eyoma E. Edet masterfully reviewed the entire list of songs and brought clarity to their texts and meanings. Miller, it turns out, had been recording songs from several students of Chief Edet, yet none guided the researcher to their teacher! Nevertheless, Chief Edet's corrections enabled the publication "Ékpè 'Leopard' Association Songs from the Cross River Region" by Miller and Òkôn (International Journal of Languages and Communication, 2020, v7: 86–121). The results of this research indeed found some resonance with Cuban popular song texts, specifically pertaining to both phrases and rhythms expressed in rumba and Abakuá song performances.

Examples

Much of the video documentation from this research has been uploaded to Miller's YouTube channel, where many knowledgeable listeners from West Africa have responded with enthusiasm but with little analysis. The following is a list of some of the video recordings and what they inform us about the Ékpè tradition.

Although Ékpè is by and large a cult for males from "royal" lineages, women who know the culture well may be initiated because they contribute to the performance of song and dance. In Calabar, Miller recorded Madam Ekoyo Bassey, who hailed from a Usaghadet (Isangele) community in Cameroon and was initiated into Ékpè in a Calabar lodge because of her extraordinary singing and dancing skills:

> "Ékpè Songs in Calabar." In Calabar, Madam Ekoyo Bassey, an initiate of Èfé Ékpè Èfût Abua, sings Ékpè songs at the home of Obong Ékpè Mr. E. Ekpenyong Eyo, Mboko-Mboko of Èfé Ékpè Éyò Émà, who accompanied her. Ekpenyong Eyo had participated in the Ékpè and Abakuá performance in Paris, 2007. Ékpè auxiliary codes and Èfịk language. 23:01 minutes in length.[2]

The initiation of women coincides with gender as expressed in Èkpè performance, where the most popular body-mask figures represent the "mother" figure of this cult, with accompanying songs of her role:

> "Èkpè song, rural Calabar." In the Èfịk language, the song says: "Èbònkó is the mother of all Èkpè." Ifako-Ọ́kọ́yọ̀ng, Odukpani Local Government Area (LGA). Ọ́kọ́yọ̀ng is a community in the Calabar region that migrated from Ọ́kọ́yọ̀ng, near Mamfe, Cameroon, in the 1800s. Recorded in February 2012. 2:54 minutes in length.[3]

Research in Calabar also revealed that musicians of "traditional" or "cultural" music had recorded Èkpè songs starting in the decade of the 1970s (seven decades after the first Cuban recordings). In the Cuban colony, if Abakuá was criminalized, musician members could avoid censorship while recording ritual languages in popular music contexts, because only they understood the codes. Meanwhile, in Nigeria, Èkpè practice had been publicly submerged due to British colonial and missionary administrations since the late 1800s; the few Èkpè recordings made after independence in 1960 were achieved, therefore, as acts of resistance to assimilation into British culture and remain as rare examples:

> "Nyamkpe preamble and song by Ekpe Ita of Calabar." Obon Music: Eyet Burstic Kingsley Bassey. Ekpe Ita and His Ima Edi Obio Group. 1979. Anodisc Records. ALPS 1051. Stereo. A subsidiary of Anochie, the Anochie Foundation Ltd, 1–3 Pound Road, PO Box 980, Aba, Nigeria. C. Control Èfịk Cultural Music. Èkpè auxiliary codes and Èfịk language. 06:35 minutes in length.[4]

The following are further examples of video recordings produced through fieldwork in Nigeria:

> "Èkpè songs in Efut Abua community, Calabar South, Cross River State, Nigeria." Recorded in April 2013. The Muri Munene (paramount ruler) of Èfût people of Calabar supported Dr. Miller's quest to record Èkpè songs in Èfût (BàLóndó) language. Because the Èfût language had been largely lost through assimilation into Èfịk culture, the Munene invited a community member from the BàLóndó region of Cameroon who sang BàLóndó songs in with the support of Èfût percussionists and Èkpè members. This event was held in the Efe Èkpè Èfût Abua (Èkpè hall of Èfût Abua). 21:27 minutes in length.[5]

An analysis by a BàLóndó (Òrɔ́kɔ̀) speaker reported that, in fact, none of the Calabar participants understood the language of the BàLóndó singer, so they could not repeat the chorus; therefore, the lead singer began to sing simple phrases that were not Ékpè songs. This example demonstrates a desire for "ethnic nationalism" within a Nigerian context but without results.

> "Mr Ekpenyong Itu Ekpenyong." Ekpenyong Itu Ekpenyong and friends perform Ékpè music in Big Qua, Calabar, Cross River State, Nigeria. Ékpè auxiliary codes and Kúọ̀ ("Kwa") language. Recorded by Alex Jomaron and Ivor Miller, 2010. 06:59 minutes in length.[6]

Miller requested an analysis of these songs from the performers, who were unable to transcribe any song and seemed to have been improvising on the spot. This indicates that Ékpè song performance incorporates spontaneous song production during informal sessions.

The following three songs from Nigerian fieldwork have not received any analysis from the performers so far, even after several requests by the researchers:

> "Etara community Mgbe—Song." Recorded in March 2011. During Miller's first visit to the rural Etara community, Ikom LGA, the Ékpè members assemble inside the Ékpè hall, with titleholders at the high table with an *ùkárá* cloth to their backs. A member performs Nsìbìdì gestures to communicate with the participants as they sing in the Éjághám language. 04:10 minutes in length.[7]
>
> "Big Qua Town Ékpè masks and song." Recorded in Calabar Municipality, December 2005. Kúọ̀ ("Kwa") language. 03:23 minutes in length.[8]
>
> "Ebongo Dibó in Big Qua Town, Nigeria." Recorded inside the Ocham Mgbè (Ékpè hall) of Big Qua Town community, Calabar Municipality, where musicians play while the Ìsìm Ékpè ("leopard tail") dancers and Ekọ̀mọ̀ boys ("drum holders") prepare for the procession. An elder (the Ndidem of the Quas) instructs a young man how to dance with bow and arrow in his hands. Then the chiefs lead the Èbòngó mask procession through the town square. Recorded by Ivor Miller, December 25, 2010, Calabar, Cross River State, Nigeria. 06:06 minutes in length.[9]

The following two songs from Nigerian fieldwork have not yet been incorporated into the study of Miller and Òkôn:

> "Ékpè songs in Owai community." Owai community, Akampka LGA, Cross River State. New Yam Festival, October 2012. The first four minutes were in the dark, thus photographs from Owai are placed there. At 4:28 a local elder begins to sing, with an accompanist. A local

guide Michael Joseph Mbe interprets the songs after they are performed. 14:29 minutes in length.[10]

"Èkpè music, Èbònkó rhythm" Recorded in Calabar, Nigeria June 2019, directed by Dr. Kenneth Bilby. Èkpè music is indigenous to southeastern Nigeria and South West Cameroon, a centuries long practice. Èkpè was the system of community justice of the region and has elaborate initiation rites for neophytes, who are traditionally from royal lineages. 11:52 minutes in length.[11]

This example was recorded in the US, where Cameroonian migrants organized an Èkpè club:

"Èkpè USA music rehearsal" August 2011. A rehearsal of Èkpè songs by Èkpè USA, a group of Èkpè titleholders from Cameroon residing in Maryland, led by Seseku Ojong Orok and including Sesekus Mbe Tazi, Joseph Mbu, and Mr. Mforkem M. Asam-Eyong. Seseku Joe Mbu describes Èkpè songs as proverbs recited with percussion and melodies. He translates the first song. 7:49 minutes in length.[12]

This example was recorded by Mr. Opubo Braide at BraideO!'s Sound Lab., Calabar, Nigeria:

"Calabar Rhythm and Songs—Ebonko." August 2017. These songs were transcribed and translated in the video clip. Èkpè auxiliary codes and Èfịk language. 10:29 minutes in length.[13]

This video demonstrates the use of typical percussion of the Calabar region:

"Èkpè drums presentation—Cross River Nigeria." Recorded 2010, by Alex Jomaron and Ivor Miller. Two professional musicians explain the use of the basic drums and gongs of the Calabar region. 06:03 minutes in length.[14]

Conclusions

Even if many of the songs recorded in languages other than Èfịk were not transcribed, this research method reveals the nature of Èkpè song performance. In fact, not all participants in the music performance understand the texts they are singing. This is relevant to the Cuban tradition, where only leading specialists understand the texts they perform.

It's striking to observe that the phenomenon of partial intelligibility of song texts is not limited to Cuba but is widespread in the Nigerian examples. Presumably, some of the translation difficulties encountered in present-day Nigeria result from a century of cultural imperialism at the hands of successive missionaries, colonialists, and nationalist elites, so it's likely that intelligibility was much greater in Nigeria several generations in the past. To that extent, Nigerian Èkpè is becoming more similar to Cuban Abakuá, as its artistic corpus becomes encapsulated and detached from the context of spoken languages. However, this transatlantic parallelism of textual recession is not observed to nearly the same degree in the other major diasporan tradition with Nigerian and Cuban representatives, namely, Yorùbá Òrìṣà and Lukumí Ocha: semantic opacity is widely observed in Lukumí songs and chants but much less so in the Nigerian counterpart. This contrast of intelligibility has multiple explanations.

Esoterism

Participation in Èkpè/Abakuá is scrupulously graded and restricted to initiates, whereas knowledge of Òrìṣà/Ocha is more dispersed across the general population. In both cases, the operative concept of "secrecy" is a prohibition on the "public" display of information without authority, but the contrast remains that access to initiatory information is more restricted in Èkpè.

Auxiliary coding

Èkpè grew in and adapted to a far more multilingual, ethnically diverse population than was the case for Òrìṣà; thus, Èkpè relies inherently on nonlinguistic representations like the Nsìbìdì figures and symbolic gestures.

Segregated oracy

Throughout the twentieth century, standardization of and mass literacy in local languages were generally blocked in the Èkpè zone by a host of political and economic factors, in contrast to the early success of written Yorùbá.

Notes

1 Calabar Mgbè, https://www.afrocubaweb.com/abakwa/calabarmgbe.htm.
2 Èkpè Songs in Calabar, https://www.youtube.com/watch?v=dbp0sWkDddk.
3 Èkpè song, rural Calabar, https://www.youtube.com/watch?v=cmV4O_o-bHQ.
4 Nyamkpe preamble and song by Èkpè Ita of Calabar, https://www.youtube.com/watch?v=bR0fx9-JDGQ.
5 Èkpè songs in Efut Abua community, Calabar South, Cross River State, Nigeria, https://www.youtube.com/watch?v=XedzMJyB7s8.
6 Mr Ekpenyong Itu Ekpenyong, https://www.youtube.com/watch?v=AQFbHC08Gyg.

7 Etara community Mgbè, "Song," https://www.youtube.com/watch?v=8iXRoMlCy4M.
8 Big Qua Town Èkpè masks and song, https://www.youtube.com/watch?v=CLUSooniklI.
9 Ebongo Dibó in Big Qua Town, Nigeria, https://www.youtube.com/watch?v=XVr3wuy29GM.
10 Èkpè songs in Owai community/ Cantos del Èkpè en la comunidad de Owai, https://www.youtube.com/watch?v=lCHlwe8zaO8.
11 Èkpè music, Èbònkó rhythm, https://www.youtube.com/watch?v=zjxcF5GTPT8.
12 Èkpè USA music rehearsal (2), https://www.youtube.com/watch?v=G_2QNE8KJvc.
13 Calabar Rhythm and Songs – Ebonko https://www.youtube.com/watch?v=eVtobMqTZTU.
14 Èkpè drums presentation—Cross River Nigeria, https://www.youtube.com/watch?v=8g2YpbGQAZQ.

References

Cabrera, Lydia. 1957. *Anagó; vocabulario lucumí (el yoruba que se habla en Cuba)*. Prólogo de Roger Bastide. Habana: Ediciones C.R.

Cabrera, Lydia. 1984. *Vocabulario Congo (El Bantú que se habla en Cuba)*. Miami: Colección del Chicherekú en el Exilio.

Cabrera, Lydia. 1988. *La lengua sagrada de los Ñáñigos*. Miami: Colección del Chicherekú.

Dayrell, Elphinstone. 1910. "Some Nsibidi Signs." *Man* 10 (67): 113–14.

Dizzy Gillespie/Max Roach in Paris. *Afro-Cuban Suite*. BMG Music. CD 0902668213-2.

Discography of American Historical Recordings, s.v. "Victor matrix B-13786. Achui bongo/Adolfo Colombo; Regino López," accessed February 28, 2025, https://adp.library.ucsb.edu/index.php/matrix/detail/200014027/B-13786-Achui_bongo.

Ecobio Enyenison. 2009. *Enyenison Enkama Project*. Produced by Roman Díaz, Angel Guerrero, and Pedro Martínez. New York City: Habana|Harlem™.

Leib, Elliot, and Renee Romano. 1984. "Reign of the Leopard: Ngbe Ritual." *African Arts* 18(1): 48–57, 94–96.

Miller, Ivor. 2000. "A Secret Society Goes Public: The Relationship between Abakuá and Cuban Popular Culture." *African Studies Review* 43(1): 161–188.

Miller, Ivor. 2009. *Voice of the Leopard: African Secret Societies and Cuba*. Jackson: University Press of Mississippi.

Miller, Ivor. 2015. "Separated by the Slave Trade: Nigerians and Cubans Reunite through a Shared Cultural Practice." In *African Indigenous Religious Traditions in Local and Global Contexts: Perspectives on Nigeria. A Festschrift in Honour of Jacob K. Olupona*, edited by David O. Ogungbile, 363–88. Lagos: Malthouse Press Ltd.

Miller, Ivor, and Margaret Òkôn. 2020. "Èkpè 'Leopard' Association Songs from the Cross River Region." *International Journal of Languages and Communication* 7: 86–121.

Northrup, David. 1978. *Trade without Rulers: Pre-Colonial Economic Development in South-Eastern Nigeria*. Oxford: Oxford University Press.

Òkôn, Margaret M., and Paulinus Noah. 2021. "Cultural Dominance and Language Endangerment: The Case of Èfût in Cross River State, Nigeria." *Macrolinguistics* 9 (1) (Serial No. 14): 134–50.

Röschenthaler, Ute M. 2011. *Purchasing Culture: The Dissemination of Associations in the Cross River Region of Cameroon and Nigeria.* Trenton, NJ: African World Press.

Ruel, Malcolm. 1969. *Leopards and Leaders: Constitutional Politics among a Cross River People.* London: Tavistock.

Chapter 1

Digital ethics

Lessons from a digital ethnography of QAnon

Michelle Cera

Introduction

As a developing craft in the social sciences, digital ethnography presents unique ethical dilemmas to researchers. Practitioners of digital ethnography must contend with the many challenges posed by the internet. The misrepresentation of identity, the nebulous delineation between public and private within digital spaces, the dynamic and ephemeral nature of online environments, the complexities of anonymization exacerbated by advanced search engines, and the ease of data extraction without consent, among many other dilemmas, contribute to the challenging ethical landscape.

Ethical quandaries are heightened when vulnerable populations or extremist groups are the object of study. This is exemplified in the examination of QAnon, a group that serves as a particularly instructive focal point to think through digital ethics. QAnon emerged on October 28, 2017, when an anonymous account called "Q" posted a cryptic message about an oncoming "storm" on the social media site 4chan (Rothschild 2021). Since then, QAnon has gained a massive following around the world and has been linked to violent events such as the 2016 "Pizzagate" shooting in Washington, D.C., and the storming of the Capitol on January 6th. The crux of their ideology is the proposition that a satanic cabal of elite actors referred to as the "Deep State" is responsible for all social, economic, and political ills. This narrative posits that Donald Trump is a messianic figure in a cosmic battle between good and evil. They believe he will eventually usher in the "storm" to vanquish the cabal (Garry et al. 2021).

This chapter uses the study of QAnon as a case to develop ethical guidelines for digital ethnographic approaches. First, I briefly outline current theoretical debates within the social sciences around digital ethnography and privacy, consent, anonymity, data extraction and protection, and power dynamics. Next, I discuss best practices for digital ethnographers in the stages of data collection, analysis, and publication with concrete examples from the case of QAnon. This section also suggests practices to avoid. Finally, I reflect on how digital ethnography can be a powerful tool for the development of an informed citizenry as well as for understanding many of society's most pressing issues.

Current debates

Ethical guidelines and practices are key to any study but specifically to the practice of ethnography. The need for ethical considerations in ethnographic research stems from the inherently intimate interactions with people's lives, communities, and social worlds. Ethnographers often immerse themselves in the lives of their participants, gaining privileged access to personal stories, relationships, beliefs, and practices. This close engagement necessitates a heightened sense of responsibility to protect participants from harm. Further, power dynamics between the researcher and participants are inherently imbalanced and part of the intrinsic ethical challenges of ethnography (Becker 1998). These power imbalances and closeness to participants require reflexivity, or in other words continuous reflection on how one's presence, perspectives, and actions shape the communities they study (Hammersley and Atkinson 1995). Clifford Geertz, one of the most notable ethnographers, argues that ethnographic writing is not a neutral act but one of subjective interpretation (Geertz 1973). Accordingly, ethnographers carry a unique responsibility to represent the social worlds they study as accurately and fairly as possible.

The Association of Internet Researchers (AoIR), an academic association focused on internet studies, has developed several reports on internet research ethics, which have become standard for digital ethnographers (see AoIR 2020). The core contribution of the report includes understanding privacy as contextual and shaped by local norms, ensuring informed consent whereby participants fully understand what is being asked of them and how their data will be used, de-identifying data to ensure adequate anonymity (while considering the consequences of stripping data of identifiable information), determining a secure plan for data storage, considering the consequences of searchability with tools like Google, and considering power imbalances inherent between the researcher and researched. While useful, the guidelines are often vague. For example, the AoIR guidelines suggest stricter protection of subjects in digital spaces that are considered private and less strict protection for public interactions. Yet, as Bechmann and Kim (2020) point out, designations of public and private are often unclear. There are no guidelines for what kinds of topics are private, how many people need to be in a group for it to be considered public, and how to understand participant expectations of privacy. How digital ethnographers should designate what is public and private on the internet remains up for debate.

Another tension in the literature on digital ethnography ethics is the balance between privacy and transparency (Bechmann and Kim 2020). Privacy is understood as preserving anonymity, confidentiality, and ensuring informed consent. Transparency typically means researchers being open about their participants and offering access to their data for ethical purposes. Those who prioritize privacy tend to pseudonymize their data and delete identifiable information before storing data. Those who prioritize transparency tend to acquire informed consent to retain identifiable information. For example, a researcher studying a particularly vulnerable community, such as any study involving minors, would likely choose to pseudonymize their data. Conversely, a researcher interested in public policy implications might choose to retain identifiable information as a way to enhance the credibility and impact of the research.

Scholars also debate the degree to which ethnographers should be active participants in the digital spaces they study. Some internet scholars argue that the practice of lurking, or in other words observing digital social worlds and extracting data without informing participants of the researcher presence, can be beneficial to the research process by allowing for more natural interactions (Grincheva 2017; Kozinets 2002; Masullo and Coppola 2020; Reilly and Trevisan 2016). Others argue that lurking does not meet the requirements of ethnography (Taylor et al. 2013; Forberg and Schilt 2023; Varis 2014) and should be avoided because of ethical concerns (Hine 2000; Thompson et al. 2021; Yadlin-Segal et al. 2020).

The ease with which individuals can search and trace content online has led to debates around the practice of paraphrasing. Lane and Lingel (2022) argue that digital methods carry particular ethical burdens, as searchability makes the identification of participants much easier. In response to this concern, many digital researchers choose to paraphrase quotes or otherwise alter data (boyd 2016; Markham 2012). Others maintain that data integrity should take priority and choose not to paraphrase or fabricate to avoid distortion of the data (Cera 2023; Reilly and Trevisan 2016).

All in all, questions remain as to the best ethical practices for digital ethnographers. The relatively new set of methods has yet to be standardized. I offer suggestions for best practices and discuss potential pitfalls below.

Best practices

Digital ethnographers have ethical dilemmas to contend with at all stages of the research process. After a discussion of Institutional Review Board (IRB) protocols, this section uses original research on QAnon to highlight ethical practices at the points of collection, analysis, and publication.

IRB

IRBs play a crucial role in ensuring the ethical conduct of research involving human subjects, including those enmeshed in digital worlds. The IRB is tasked with reviewing research proposals to ensure they meet ethical standards in an effort to protect the rights and welfare of participants. This process involves evaluating the risks and benefits of the proposed study, ensuring informed consent is obtained, and that harm to participants is prevented.

The process of obtaining IRB approval, which most scholars need before conducting research on human subjects, can shape the ethical decisions made in a study. This involves a thorough understanding of the ethical guidelines and historical context that necessitated the establishment of IRBs, such as past harm caused to human subjects in research. Researchers will need to anticipate ethical issues before submitting a proposal to the IRB. They should thoroughly consider the risks and benefits to their research participants, develop data protection measures, and make decisions about how to properly gain informed consent from participants. This is complex in digital worlds where massive amounts of data are readily available, it is easy to obscure identity, and it is difficult to determine whether data is private or public. Further, established understandings of informed consent tend to be grounded in offline research. Researchers face new challenges in the digital realm because they have limited control over the longevity and spread of their data, making it difficult to provide participants with a comprehensive understanding of potential risks associated with their involvement (Matzner and Ochs 2017). Researchers will need to be forthcoming with participants about what they can and cannot control.

To best weigh the risks and potential harm to participants, researchers should be keenly aware of the particular norms, values, and expectations of the group they choose to study. Do participants of the group expect their posts to be read or shared by outsiders? Do participants tend to use real names and photos, or do they remain anonymous with usernames? How will you gain access to participants and their groups? How can claims be made about groups of people without full knowledge of participant identities? Understandings of privacy, consent, and identity vary considerably in digital worlds, and IRB proposals should be informed by this variation.

Power dynamics should also inform proposals to the IRB. As discussed in the previous section, power imbalances are inherent to research on human subjects. Researchers should critically assess their positionality in relation to their participants. This might mean considering how differences in age, socioeconomic status, race, ability, gender, and other variables affect all stages of the research process. It also means thinking through the role of the researcher in upholding or deconstructing structures of power and inequality. For example, I often choose not to reproduce QAnon posts that include hateful rhetoric. I choose not to be an active participant in the spread of stereotypes, while also making it clear that this rhetoric exists and is dangerous.

Collection

Digital ethnographers employ multiple methods in their studies, including participant observation, interviews, content analysis, discourse analysis, ethnographic field notes, and surveys. No matter the method, the first practice should be that of informed consent. Informed consent ensures participants enter into studies freely, voluntarily, with all of the information about what their participation will entail, and with consent (University of Oxford 2021). This practice is complicated by the internet, which stores vast amounts of personal data, allows users to obscure their identities, and makes it difficult to ascertain the possible consequences of the use of one's data in publication. It can be tricky to verify if a participant is 18 years of age or older and where in the world they are logging on from. And, with the increasing ease of searchability because of platforms such as Google, researchers may not be able to inform participants of all of the possible consequences of the use of their data. The affordances of the internet, therefore, raise the standards of informed consent.

The first step I take is ensuring my profile on each platform I use publicly indicates my real identity. On my profile on MeWe, a platform frequented by those affiliated with QAnon. I display my real name, a real photo, and indicate "researcher" as my job, along with my institutional affiliation. This allows all those who interact with me to have a way to ascertain who I am and my purposes in being on the platform. It is a simple way to establish the "inform" aspect of informed consent. It should be noted, however, that there are safety concerns associated with using one's real identity online. Caution should be taken when researching extremist or potentially violent groups, as doxxing and vitriol can be commonplace.

Next, if direct interaction with research subjects is part of the research design, informed consent can be achieved through private messages or posts. Many digital platforms allow users to send messages directly to individual users. Because messages on these platforms are easy to ignore and it is simple to block users from contacting you, sending a direct message can be a useful and ethical method to recruit participants. I typically begin by imparting the same information I have in my profile, as well as a bit about my project. For the QAnon adherents I interacted with over the course of a few years, it looked something like this:

> Hi, my name is Michelle and I am a graduate student at NYU. I am conducting a study on how QAnons use social media platforms. I am

looking for participants for anonymous, voluntary interviews. Let me know if you are interested and I would be happy to answer any questions you might have.

In a few sentences, I disclose my real identity, my purposes for messaging them, and create a space for them to gather more information. The same message can also be posted within social media groups rather than sent directly to individuals, and group members can decide whether or not to respond.

Researchers of extremist groups should be aware that they may receive hateful messages or harassment in response to recruitment messages. In my work with QAnon, I occasionally received sexist and anti-Semitic responses to my posts and messages. For example, an anon on the platform Gab once told me, "Women shouldn't be getting their PhDs" and followed this up with jokes about me "going back to the kitchen." Harassment is made easier by digital platforms because one can be completely anonymous, delete messages at will, and on some platforms might not be censored or reported for hateful rhetoric. On some platforms, such as Reddit, it might be the case that the design and moderation policies support the spread of toxic behaviors and hateful discourse (Massanari 2015). It is important to be aware of the dangers of conducting research online, especially with certain groups and on certain platforms.

Another aspect of data collection in digital research that presents ethical dilemmas pertains to the manner in which distinctions between public and private are delineated. We have a fairly agreed-upon sense of what counts as public offline: parks, cafes, sidewalks, and so on. We know the inside of someone's home is a private space we need to get consent to enter and study. Yet the internet blurs boundaries and space in a way that makes this delineation difficult. If I just need to have an account on a social media platform to view the content within a group, is it public? If there are tens of thousands of people within a group, is it inherently public? If I need to request an administrator to join a social media group, is it private? These decisions shape the way in which we collect data, analyze it, and present it to our audiences.

If we designate a digital space as public, we can and should feel more comfortable gathering, storing, and sharing data. A public space likely involves participants who are aware that the content they post and consume is visible to wide audiences. If we designate a digital space as private, we might not want to collect data in the first place, or, if we do, we need to elicit informed consent from participants. Participants in private spaces likely have expectations that their interactions are visible to a particular set of people. So, how do we decide?

First, it is helpful to understand privacy as a spectrum. There are no digital spaces that are completely public nor completely private. Further, individuals in the same space might have different ideas about the nature of the space. In my work on QAnon, I have found it useful to place a digital space along the spectrum by thinking about barriers to access. Barriers to access include any obstacles or restrictions that limit or control entry or participation in a particular space.

Important barriers to access to consider include membership approval processes, visibility of content, searchability, content sharing controls, membership size, membership fees, and community guidelines. We can use these variables to make a determination of where a group or content might fall on the public versus private spectrum. On the public end of the spectrum, content is visible to all users and can be easily shared; there is no membership approval process, the group is large (over 100 or so members), the group or content is easily searchable within the platform or through search engines, no membership fees are present, and community guidelines are nonexistent or simple. On the private end of the spectrum, content is restricted to certain users, membership approval processes exist, the group is small, the group or posts are not easily searchable, membership fees might exist, and community guidelines are strict and detailed.

"Community guidelines" are sometimes specified in the description of the social media group. For example, a group affiliated with QAnon on MeWe states the following in its description:

> In this group we are promoters of the constitution and freedom. We will organize, educate our members, and build communities to unite our people. We stand strongly against communism, fascism, socialism, and Marxism. We stand against lockdowns and infringements upon our freedom. Please abide by the group guidelines for posts or chatting No obscenity No trolling or doxxing No classless attacks on the opposition No promoting violence or illegal activity.

These guidelines specify the kind of individual they want to have access to their group, how they expect individuals to behave, and what kind of behavior will not be tolerated. Rules and guidelines signal to researchers that the space is not fully public. As researchers, we can take the existence of these rules as a form of boundary policing. They signal that outsiders are not fully welcome.

An important practice when it comes to adjudicating between public and private is to make an effort to understand norms and expectations. Privacy is relative. This means considering barriers to access, but it also could mean direct conversations with individuals about their expectations. I often ask anons how they think about the nature of the groups they are in that I want to include in my research. In other cases, such as on Gab, each group has privacy distinctions visible. The designations on Gab include "public," "visible," and "moderated." Members of the group make these decisions in the creation of the group. In allowing participants to make these designations, my research is shaped by the participants themselves.

Scholars continue to debate the practice of lurking versus active participation. At the heart of these debates lies an inherent power imbalance that favors the researcher. When researchers silently observe online interactions without disclosure, they might gain access to unfiltered and authentic interactions. Yet this approach potentially exploits the vulnerability of unsuspecting participants who are unaware of being studied. This covert observation grants researchers a position of knowledge and control over the data they collect, while denying participants the opportunity to provide informed consent or shape the narrative. In my work on QAnon, I have found active participation to be an important part of ethical digital ethnographic practice. I make an effort to interact in a way others interact. I post my own thoughts and articles, and I directly engage with individuals in comments and direct messages. I make it known that I am a researcher. I immerse myself in a way that helps me understand the digital spaces I inhabit. When researchers lurk, they remove agency from the participants in determining the use of their interactions. Lurking also runs contrary to ethnography itself in that it may provide a limited understanding of a space, prevent the development of relationships that are central to holistic knowledge of a space, and provide very few opportunities to validate observations.

Analysis

Analysis often follows the data collection phase. Ethical analysis of data gathered in a digital ethnography should take into account cultural context, an interrogation of identity, and thinking through the kinds of claims one can make.

Although the internet is in many ways universalizing—in that people all around the world who have internet have access to much of the same content—there are distinct subcultures and contexts. This means that different digital spaces tend to have different norms, languages, mediums (images, text, video, etc.), rules, and shared understandings. For example, platforms typically have taken-for-granted norms of engagement. While Instagram tends to be more for individuals posting photos and videos of friends, family, travel, and other lifestyle themes, on Facebook, you might encounter more news, politics, links to articles, and groups. On X, short-form text is the predominant form of engagement, and shared groups such as those that exist on Facebook do not exist. The onus is on the researcher to develop an understanding of these shared norms so as not to disturb the regular flow of the digital world they are interested in studying.

Digital ethics: lessons from a digital ethnography of QAnon 51

The Q clock is a great example of the importance of context in digital ethnography. The first time I encountered a Q clock, I was completely baffled. I had no idea what the numbers and dates meant, why posts were pulled from other social media sites such as X (then Twitter), and how one could use the clock to ascertain a message. It took me many months to develop an understanding of the purpose of the Q clocks as well as how one could use them to "calculate" or decipher messages. It was as though I was learning a new language. I sent individual messages to members of the groups where I regularly saw Q clocks, asking them to help me decipher the clocks. I found that many anons were happy to help me learn how to "calculate," and I simultaneously learned about the importance of calculation and research to anons while I became proficient in using their common tool (Figure 1.1).

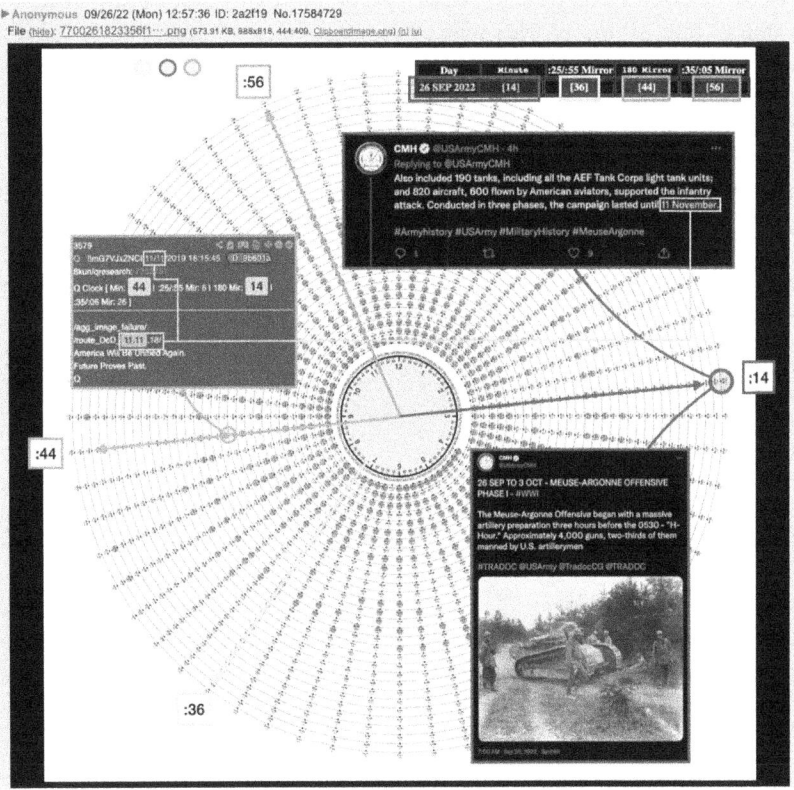

Figure 1.1 Screenshot of a Q Clock, a tool anons use to decipher messages, posted originally on 4chan.

Further, norms surrounding privacy and anonymity vary significantly among QAnon digital spaces. I quickly learned these norms of a QAnon group on the platform Gab by accidentally breaking them in early 2021. I had used my full real name, a real photo of myself as a profile picture, and posted a news article from CNN. In doing so, I had simultaneously broken three norms of engagement. A few angry comments later, I realized that everyone in the group had some sort of emoji as a profile picture, all of them used nicknames such as "Patriot Pat," and CNN was completely off limits. My misunderstanding of the space was disruptive to typical interactions and was quickly noticed. Ethnographers often struggle with affecting or disrupting the social worlds they inhabit, and these challenges remain in online contexts. A proper understanding of platform culture and subgroup culture, including how individuals present themselves, interact with each other, what they post, how they post, and general rules of the space, is helpful in navigating these challenges.

Issues related to identity are also a perennial struggle for ethnographers of online and offline worlds alike. We must contend with the possibility of unequal positions and power dynamics inherent to the relationship between the researcher and the subjects of their study. This is especially true in digital ethnography, where the researcher might have access to a wealth of personal information about their participants. We must also be cognizant of how our own social positions and cultural biases may influence interactions and interpretations. Critical self-reflection is key here. For example, as a progressive person studying a far-right group, I regularly think about how my political views might shape my analysis of their interactions. I am also acutely aware of the possibility that anons lose their jobs if their employers come across their posts. Although I vehemently disagree with anons on their views, I find it important to extend the same ethical considerations to all research participants regardless of my moral objections to their ideologies.

On the contrary, the internet obscures the identities of others in various ways. Internet researchers can never be sure of who is behind the screen. There are a multitude of ways to hide one's identity online or to present false information. Social media is also particularly known for pressuring individuals to present idealized or curated versions of themselves. This raises questions around the extent to which digital identities can be considered "real" for the purposes of ethnographic study. Researchers must grapple with how to ethically represent and analyze these multifaceted digital selves whose identities are hard to verify.

It follows that issues of identity complicate the kinds of claims researchers can make. If we are unsure of who is behind the screen, it becomes more difficult to speak to patterns on the basis of identity as social scientists often do. The researcher's position of power also affects the kinds of claims they can ethically make, especially if the population being studied is vulnerable. Some populations that are particularly vulnerable include minors, the elderly, economically or educationally disadvantaged persons, those with disabilities, people who do not speak the dominant language of the study, and immigrants or refugees. Researchers must also think through the effects of their positionality, as things such as political views, race, gender, nationality, and religion can influence the claims made.

Digital ethnographers might consider asking the following questions to guide their analysis: Do I have an understanding of the norms of the digital space I am studying? Do I have a sense of the regular flow of interactions? How can I immerse myself in a space in the same manner as participants? What are the privacy, anonymity, and security norms of the digital space? How does my identity differ from those of my participants? How can I further verify the identities of participants? How does my position as a researcher and my many identities shape my interpretations and claims?

Publication

Once the data has been gathered and analyzed, digital ethnographers can think about how to present their work. This often will mean presenting their data in a written format such as an article or book. Accordingly, digital ethnographers might think about data fabrication, data security, and sharing drafts with participants for feedback.

Searchability and traceability online, made possible by search engines such as Google, present digital ethnographers with particular ethical quandaries in the process of publishing their research. In other words, digital ethnographers might not want to publish a social media post word-for-word because a reader might be able to search the text and find the person who posted it. Images are similarly susceptible because of reverse image search functions. Accordingly, some researchers choose to paraphrase or "fabricate" their data (see, for example, boyd 2016; Markham 2012; Mukherjee 2017). This typically means maintaining meaning but altering the text such that the original content cannot be traced.

However, data fabrication can itself be considered an unethical practice, especially in the case of QAnon (Cera 2023). First, when researchers reconstruct content produced by someone else, there exists a significant propensity for mischaracterization. It inherently privileges the perspective and interpretation of the researcher while being presented as produced by the participant. For example, I would likely not be able to reproduce the Q clock in such a way that stays true to the original meaning. The figure is far too complex and laden with references to various digital spaces. Second, because the internet has its own cultures and subcultures, researchers may never fully develop the cultural knowledge to meaningfully reproduce data. Figure 1.2 is a portion of a "deep state map" produced by an anon on MeWe. Although I have had a virtual relationship with the person who produced this map for years, I likely will never understand the hundreds of connections this map draws. My reconstruction, or fabrication, of a post like this would inevitably miss the many complexities. Third, and as is the case with QAnon, data fabrication leaves room for reproducing racist, sexist, homophobic, anti-Semitic, or otherwise discriminatory content in the words of the researcher.

Figure 1.2 A portion of a "deep state map" produced by an anon and originally posted on MeWe.

A better practice in place of data fabrication is the use of direct quotes or content (videos, memes, posts, etc.) with informed consent. The researcher can reach out to the original poster to let them know they are interested in using their content directly, where and how their content will be used, and warn of the issues associated with searchability. Participants can then decide for themselves if they are comfortable with their direct posts being distributed beyond the digital space it was originally posted and with the risks associated with search engines. It should be noted that even if the content is de-identified or anonymized, reidentification is possible with the ease of searchability.

In addition to searchability, other aspects of the internet should be discussed candidly with participants. Data security cannot always be guaranteed. Social media users may share personal information or engage in sensitive discussions online, and researchers cannot guarantee that the posts they publish will not be connected to the poster's other interactions, profiles, or groups online. Digital ethnographies also involve collecting large amounts of data, which could be vulnerable to data breaches if the researcher does not ensure secure storage. Researchers should discuss data storage with relevant participants as part of the process of informed consent. In short, digital ethnographies are notably vulnerable to privacy, anonymity, and security issues. Therefore, the onus is on the researcher to be upfront with participants about what they can and cannot control.

Another useful practice that can be considered part of the process of informed consent is sharing drafts of written work with research participants. I regularly share my analyses with relevant participants to ensure I interpreted an interaction or quote accurately. It allows them to see the lens through which I perceive them and their activity and balance it with their own perceptions. I often find that eliciting feedback from participants strengthens my analysis and enriches the data. This collaborative approach helps build trust and ensures the research accurately represents the participants' experiences. Additionally, providing participants with opportunities to review and provide input on the research findings demonstrates respect for their autonomy and agency.

In sum, researchers can think of digital ethnography as a process with roughly three stages. First is data collection, where informed consent, considering the public-private binary, and active engagement are crucial. The second is data analysis, where culture and context, as well as thinking through positionality, help to ensure ethical practice. The third is publication, a stage at which researchers should avoid data fabrication, obtain informed consent for the use of data, be upfront about data security, and consider eliciting feedback from participants. It should be noted that these phases might not occur in chronological order, and it is common practice to move between them at any given point of the study.

Conclusion

Digital ethnography is a relatively new methodology with room for expansion. As our lives become more digital and intertwined with digital spaces, the need for digital ethnography grows. In 2024, the average American spent about eight hours online each day (Statista 2024). Many of our social worlds have online counterparts, and some digital spaces are social worlds of their own. These online environments shape behaviors, ideologies, interactions, and identities in profound ways that cannot be fully understood through traditional in-person ethnography alone. Digital spaces are sites of political contestation, the negotiation of identity, cultural exchange, the dissemination of knowledge, social bonding, economic transactions, and activism. On the contrary, the internet is also full of misinformation, hate speech, fraud, hacking, and other harmful content. By embracing digital ethnography, researchers can gain valuable insights into these important phenomena and, more generally, the increasingly mediated nature of our lives.

Further, the internet has been blamed for many social ills. This includes polarization, mental health issues, election interference, the breakdown of relationships, radicalization and terrorism, declining attention spans, and even genocide in Myanmar (De Guzman 2022; Ferrara et al. 2020; Kubin and von Sikorski 2021; O'Reilly et al. 2018; Primack et al. 2017; Thompson 2011; Thompson 2017). The detailed, immersive, and rich data that comes from digital ethnography is key in addressing the relationships between these social issues and the internet. By closely observing online interactions and content, digital ethnographers can uncover patterns and insights that help explain complex dynamics. This type of in-depth, qualitative research is essential for developing a nuanced understanding of the effect of the internet on society.

Scholarly debates surrounding digital ethnography focus on privacy, transparency, active versus passive engagement, and how to designate digital spaces as public. In addressing these debates and beyond, this chapter offers best practices as well as pitfalls throughout the collection, analysis, and publication phases. It strongly encourages researchers to think through issues of power and inequality relevant to their research. During collection, informed consent, disclosing identity, active engagement, and carefully considering the spectrum from public to private are paramount. During analysis, digital ethnographers should prioritize an understanding of cultural context, an interrogation of their own identities, and use these to shape the kinds of claims that can be made. In the publication phase, where researchers present their work, the direct use of data with informed consent in place of data fabrication is suggested. Candid conversations about data security, in addition to sharing work with participants for feedback, are valuable ways to ensure ethical research.

The advancement of digital ethnography must include serious consideration of ethical dilemmas and solutions. Striking a balance between the investigation of the social issues associated with the internet and the prevention of harm to research subjects is essential. By integrating ethical frameworks such as those proposed in this chapter, digital ethnographers can ensure their work contributes to understanding while upholding the integrity of their research.

References

Association of Internet Researchers. 2020. *Internet Research: Ethical Guidelines 3.0*. https://aoir.org/reports/ethics3.pdf.

Bechmann, Anja, and Jiyoung Ydun Kim. 2020. "Big Data: A Focus on Social Media Research Dilemmas." In *Handbook of Research Ethics and Scientific Integrity*, edited by Robin Iphofen, 427–44. Cham: Springer International Publishing.

Becker, Howard S. 1998. *Tricks of the Trade: How to Think About Your Research While You're Doing it*. Chicago: University of Chicago Press.

boyd, danah. 2016. "Making Sense of Teen Life: Strategies for Capturing Ethnographic Data in a Networked Era." In *Digital Research Confidential: The Secrets of Studying Behavior Online*, edited by E. Hargittai and C. Sandvig, 79–102. Cambridge: MIT Press.

Cera, Michelle. 2023. "Digital Ethnography: Ethics through the Case of QAnon." *Frontiers in Sociology* 8: 1119531.

De Guzman, Chad. 2022. "Report: Facebook Algorithms Promoted Anti-Rohingya Violence." *Time*, September 28. https://time.com/6217730/myanmar-meta-rohingya-facebook/.

Ferrara, Emilio, Herbert Chang, Emily Chen, Goran Muric, and Jaimin Patel. 2020. "Characterizing Social Media Manipulation in the 2020 US Presidential Election." *First Monday*, 1–32. https://firstmonday.org/ojs/index.php/fm/article/view/11431.

Forberg, Peter, and Kristen Schilt. 2023. "What Is Ethnographic About Digital Ethnography? A Sociological Perspective." *Frontiers in Sociology* 8: 1156776.

Garry, Amanda, Samantha Walther, Rukaya Rukaya, and Ayan Mohammed. 2021. "QAnon Conspiracy Theory: Examining Its Evolution and Mechanisms of Radicalization." *Journal for Deradicalization* 26: 152–216.

Geertz, Clifford. 1973. *The Interpretation of Cultures: Selected Essays*. USA: Basic Books.

Grincheva, Natalia. 2017. "Museum Ethnography in the Digital Age." In *Internet Research Ethics for the Social Age*, edited by Michael Zimmer and Katharina Kinder-Kurlanda, 187. New York: Peter Lang Inc., International Academic Publishers.

Hammersley, Martyn. and Atkinson, Paul. 1995. *Ethnography: Principles in Practice* (2nd ed.). London: Routledge.

Hine, Christine. 2000. *Virtual Ethnography*. London: Sage Publications.

Kozinets, Robert V. 2002. "The Field Behind the Screen: Using Netnography for Marketing Research in Online Communities." *Journal of Marketing Research* 39(1): 61–72.

Kubin, Emily, and Christian Von Sikorski. 2021. "The Role of (Social) Media in Political Polarization: A Systematic Review." *Annals of the International Communication Association* 45(3): 188–206.

Lane, Jeffrey, and Jessa Lingel. 2022. "Digital Ethnography for Sociology: Craft, Rigor, and Creativity." *Qualitative Sociology* 45: 319–326.

Markham, Annette. 2012. "Fabrication as Ethical Practice: Qualitative Inquiry in Ambiguous Internet Contexts." *Information, Communication & Society* 15(3): 334–53.

Massanari, Adrienne. 2015. *Participatory Culture, Community, and Play*. New York: Peter Lang Inc.

Masullo, Giuseppe, and Marianna Coppola. 2020. "Socializzazione alla sessualità e Web Society: Una Ricerca Netnografica sulle Donne Lesbiche di Salerno." In *Etnografia e Netnografia: Riflessioni Teoriche, Sfide Metodologiche ed Esperienze di Ricerca*, vol. 1, edited by G. Masullo, F. Addeo, and A. Delli Paoli, 203–17. Napoli: Paolo Loffredo Editore.

Matzner, T., and C. Ochs. 2017. "Sorting Things Out Ethically: Privacy as a Research Issue beyond the Individual." In *Internet Research Ethics for the Social Age: New Challenges, Cases, and Contexts*, edited by M. Zimmer and K. Kinder-Kurlanda, 39–52. New York: Peter Lang.

Mukherjee, Ishani. 2017. "The Social Age of 'It's Not a Private Problem': Case Study of Ethical and Privacy Concerns in a Digital Ethnography of South Asian Blogs Against Intimate Partner Violence." In *Internet Research Ethics for the Social Age: New Challenges, Cases, and Contexts*, edited by Michael Zimmer and Katharina Kinder-Kurlanda, 203–12. New York, NY; Bern: Peter Lang International Academic Publishers.

O'Reilly, Michelle, Nisha Dogra, Natasha Whiteman, Jason Hughes, Seyda Eruyar, and Paul Reilly. 2018. "Is Social Media Bad for Mental Health and Wellbeing? Exploring the Perspectives of Adolescents." *Clinical Child Psychology and Psychiatry* 23(4): 601–13.

Primack, Brian A., Ariel Shensa, Jaime E. Sidani, Erin O. Whaite, Liu yi Lin, Daniel Rosen, Jason B. Colditz, Ana Radovic, and Elizabeth Miller. 2017. "Social Media Use and Perceived Social Isolation Among Young Adults in the US." *American Journal of Preventive Medicine* 53(1): 1–8.

Reilly, Paul, and Filippo Trevisan. 2016. "Researching Protest on Facebook: Developing an Ethical Stance for the Study of Northern Irish Flag Protest Pages." *Information, Communication & Society* 19(3): 419–35.

Rothschild, Mike. 2021. *The Storm Is Upon Us: How QAnon Became a Movement, Cult, and Conspiracy Theory of Everything*. New York: Melville House.

Statista. 2024. "Time Spent with Digital Media in the U.S. 2024." Accessed April 5, 2024. https://www.statista.com/statistics/262340/daily-time-spent-with-digital-media-according-to-us-consumers/.

Taylor, T. L., Tom Boellstorff, Bonnie Nardi, and Celia Pearce. 2013. *Ethnography and Virtual Worlds: A Handbook of Method*. Princeton, NJ: Princeton University Press.

Thompson, Penny. 2017. "Communication Technology Use and Study Skills." *Active Learning in Higher Education* 18(3): 257–70.

Thompson, Robin. 2011. "Radicalization and the Use of Social Media." *Journal of Strategic Security* 4(4): 167–90.

Thompson, Alex, Lindsay Stringfellow, Mairi Maclean, and Amal Nazzal. 2021. "Ethical Considerations and Challenges for Using Digital Ethnography to Research Vulnerable Populations." *Journal of Business Research* 124: 676–683.

University of Oxford. 2021. "Informed Consent." Accessed April 5, 2024. https://researchsupport.admin.ox.ac.uk/governance/ethics/resources/consent#:~:text=Informed%20consent%20is%20one%20of,before%20they%20enter%20the%20research.

Varis, Piia. 2014. "Digital Ethnography." *Tilburg Papers in Culture Studies*, paper 104. https://research.tilburguniversity.edu/en/publications/digital-ethnography-3.

Yadlin-Segal, Aya, Ruth Tsuria, and Wendi Bellar. 2020. "The Ethics of Studying Digital Contexts: Reflections from Three Empirical Case Studies." *Human Behavior and Emerging Technologies* 2(2): 168–78.

Chapter 1.1

Concept: representation
Ethical and methodological challenges in digital ethnography

Serhat Tutkal

Representation

Representation is the process by which we use language (understood as any signifying system) to produce meaning (Hall 1997). This process can occur through various modes, such as written text, still image, music, and even clothing. Modes are our semiotic resources for making meaning (Kress 2010). We communicate through them and represent actors and actions. When we represent actors, we not only represent the others but can also represent ourselves. This is called self-representation, through which we also undertake a process of reflexive self-construction (Fairclough 2001). For example, we can use a haircut or tattoos to convey certain meanings about our identity, which at the same time constructs our identity in the given context. A mustache can be used to indicate following an ideological school of thought in one context or having a nonbinary gender identity in another. The meaning will be transmitted even though we may not be aware of the perceptions, which is why intercultural communication can sometimes lead to great confusion.

The representation conveys two levels of meaning. The first is denotation, which is rather descriptive and responds to the question of "what is being depicted here?" The second level, connotation, is wider and responds to the question of "what ideas are expressed through the representation?" (Barthes 1977). At the descriptive level, we can hear the sound created by the ringing church bells. Most people will be able to hear this sound. However, the second level of meaning can only be understood if we have the tools to decipher the relevant cultural codes, which, in this case, requires a certain level of knowledge about the customs, rituals, and doctrine of the Catholic religion.

When conducting digital ethnography, we see cases of both self-representation and other-representation. These representations occur in a context where we have to rely on cultural codes to achieve an in-depth reading of the representations. Represented social actors and practices will be coded according to cultural structures (Alexander 2003). Through a slow data collection process that helps to foster immersion, we can more successfully interpret the meanings transmitted at the level of connotation.

Actors and practices can be represented in positive or negative ways to legitimize or delegitimize them. These representations may reproduce the status quo, the prevailing power relations, and the resulting domination. However, they may also contest the status quo by questioning it. We must be careful about the legitimation of abuse of power through representations of the other. After all, we will be representing actors and actions through our research. Our research has a social, political, and economic impact (Fals-Borda 2009), and if we fail to critically interpret the representations during our analysis, this may help sustain the prevailing inequalities and violent structures. As researchers, we have a social responsibility since our work does not merely report on a given reality but actually participates in producing new realities (Law 2004). Hiding behind the pretense of scientific objectivity may result in the participation of the prevailing relations of domination through their discursive legitimation and reproduction.

We should keep in mind that meaning is produced and conveyed not only through what is put into words, images, and other modes but also through what is hidden or made invisible (Hansen 2017). While we should study the social, political, and cultural implications of what is depicted, we should also be critical about the implications of what is hidden and the connotation of this invisibilization. Representations of the other in digital spaces can frequently be made in a way that reproduces exclusionary dichotomies such as us-others or friend-enemy. Through stigmatization, dehumanization, or other types of negative presentation of others, their social exclusion and violent victimization can be legitimized. This legitimation can also occur unconsciously. It is important that researchers have a critical perspective regarding the representation of others to avoid the unquestioned reproduction of the meanings conveyed through representation when they publish their research findings.

Digital ethnographies have certain advantages over studies based on data extracted in bulk through application programming interfaces (APIs). The most important is the loss of contextual elements in data obtained through APIs. This is due to resemiotization or how the meaning of any meaning-making social practice changes depending on its context (Iedema 2003). Thus, separating the data from the platform and the context disrupts the link and interactions between different representations and accompanying discourses, which can easily cause misinterpretations. While digital ethnographies are undeniably laborious, the contextualized information resulting from such research leads to a refined interpretation of complex processes of representation, thus allowing for tailor-made proposals to comprehend and resolve social problems.

A specific question regarding representation in digital ethnographies concerns classification: how to classify what we observe in the digital sphere? What are avatars in a massively multiplayer online role-playing game (MMORPG) or profiles on a social media platform? I consider them extensions of our complex identities, produced and reproduced through performative acts. Thus, conducting digital ethnography is not much different from conducting other types of ethnography since it allows us to observe the interactions between actors in a given space, digital or otherwise. Self-representation in digital spaces occurs similarly to self-representation in any other space. The aim is to be perceived by certain audiences as an actor with certain qualities, even though the absence of a physical body leads to a distinct process of self-construction.

Interpreting representations during digital ethnography requires a similar set of abilities as those needed in any ethnographic research. We decode the conveyed meaning with the help of cultural codes. We establish links between what is observed and the context in which the interactions occur, including all cultural, political, social, and economic implications. We also consider the target audience, which shapes the aims of the representation. There are three fundamental questions to which we should respond before our analysis: (1) who is being represented by whom?; (2) what is the target audience?; and (3) what is the aim of the process of representation? Answering all these questions while questioning the possible political implications of the representation will allow for a nuanced reading of the conveyed meanings. Considering that all knowledges are situated, and each researcher speaks from a particular position (Haraway 1988), it would be an unachievable task to avoid our own biases in representing others. In this case, we may follow the posture of critical discourse studies in defining and accepting our biases, thus making them explicit in the research (van Dijk 2001), knowing that all scholarship is biased in some ways, and this does not invalidate our research as long as we do not assume a false pretense of objectivity or strive for unachievable generalizations. In this way, we can make significant contributions to the understanding of complex realities.

References

Alexander, Jeffrey C. 2003. *The Meanings of Social Life: A Cultural Sociology.* New York: Oxford University Press.

Barthes, Roland. 1977. "The Photographic Message." In *Image-Music-Text*, edited by Stephen Heath, 15–31. London: Fontana Press.

Fairclough, Norman. 2001. "Critical Discourse Analysis as a Method in Social Scientific Research." In *Methods of Critical Discourse Analysis*, edited by Ruth Wodak and Michael Meyer, 121–38. London: SAGE.

Fals-Borda, Orlando. 2009. "Cómo Investigar La Realidad Para Transformarla." In *Una Sociología Sentipensante Para América Latina*, edited by Victor Manuel Moncayo, 253–301. Buenos Aires: CLACSO.

Hall, Stuart. 1997. "The Work of Representation." In *Representation: Cultural Representations and Signifying Practices*, edited by Stuart Hall, 13–74. London: SAGE.

Hansen, Lene. 2017. "Reading Comics for the Field of International Relations: Theory, Method and the Bosnian War." *European Journal of International Relations* 23(3): 581–608. https://doi.org/10.1177/1354066116656763.

Haraway, Donna. 1988. "Situated Knowledges: The Science Question in Feminism and the Privilege of Partial Perspective." *Feminist Studies* 14(3): 575–99. https://doi.org/10.2307/3178066.

Iedema, Rick. 2003. "Multimodality, Resemiotization: Extending the Analysis of Discourse as Multi-Semiotic Practice." *Visual Communication* 2(1): 29–57. https://doi.org/10.1177/1470357203002001751.

Kress, Gunther. 2010. *Multimodality: A Social Semiotic Approach to Contemporary Communication*. Oxford: Routledge. https://doi.org/10.4324/9780203970034.

Law, John. 2004. *After Method: Mess in Social Science Research*. Oxford: Routledge.

van Dijk, Teun. 2001. "Multidisciplinary CDA: A Plea for Diversity." In *Methods of Critical Discourse Analysis*, edited by Ruth Wodak and Michael Meyer, 95–120. London: Sage.

Chapter 1.2

Case study: drug trade on the Polish darknet

Releasing control over the research process

Piotr Siuda and Patrycja Hewelt

The presented case study focuses on the digital ethnography of Cebulka, the only Polish-language site used for drug trading on the darknet. Our main argument is that digital ethnographers need to actively gain an understanding of a given community and be involved in its life. However, they should consider incorporating this community into planning and implementing the research at some point, especially when access to the group under study is highly problematic.

This case study is part of a research project financed by the Polish National Science Center titled "Rhizomatic networks, circulation of meanings and contents, and offline contexts of online drug trade," intended to study drug trading online. The project focuses on social media and the darknet, the not-indexed internet accessed by tools like TOR (the Onion Router). This software directs online traffic through multiple relays, significantly decreasing the possibility of tracing the identities and locations of web users.

Cebulka started in 2013, being the heir to the defunct Polish Board & Market. Initially, it functioned without moderation; however, in 2016, PGP keys to encrypt logging and private messages and escrow (money held by a third party, i.e., moderators) for transactions were introduced to bolster users' security and trust, alongside the widely used cryptocurrencies to buy drugs (these sides are called cryptomarkets as using Bitcoin or Monero is the only accepted method of payment) (Barratt and Aldridge 2016; Demant, Munksgaard, and Houborg 2018; Martin et al. 2020; Tsuchiya and Hiramoto 2021). Architecturally, Cebulka is a message board that hosts various threads created by vendors, who may choose to spread their drug offers across several threads or compile them into one. Discussions within these threads can range from evaluating the vendor's credibility through shared experiences to discussing the specifics of the drugs purchased. As of 2024, Cebulka has 59,720 registered users, although determining the actual size of the community is difficult, if not impossible, due to many temporary accounts or the possibility of multiplying them.

The project identified Cebulka not only as transaction-focused but also as playing a vital role in shaping the narratives and discussions prevalent in the online drug subculture (Hunt and Joe-Laidler 2015; Wanke, Piejko-Płonka, and Deutschmann 2022). We are dealing with a stigmatized community, which is also hard to reach (Kaufmann and Tzanetakis 2020) due to the topics discussed and security issues. The difficulty of accessing this community is not so much due to technical problems, such as using TOR and PGP keys to encrypt messages, as these are simple skills to master. This is more an issue of research credibility and establishing trust between researchers and participants, as entering such a community is burdened with mistrust and concealment on both sides (Wright, Klee, and Reid 1998). This has already been well covered in other studies of online drug trafficking sites and other stigmatized or marginalized groups (Kaufmann and Tzanetakis 2020). With this in mind, many researchers consider digital ethnography to provide the best opportunities to establish contact with the studied populations and build the mutual understanding necessary to engage participants.

Barratt and Maddox (2016) emphasize this viewpoint through their examination of the iconic and now-defunct anonymous cryptomarket called Silk Road (Demant, Munksgaard, and Houborg 2018; Barratt, Ferris, and Winstock 2014; Martin 2014), arguing for active engagement. Presenting the stages of their ethnographic research, ethical dilemmas involved, and problems with the volatility of drug trade sites, access, and hate from users, they claim that digital ethnography has a considerable advantage over archival digital traces or Big Data studies. These are usually carried out without overt interaction with the communities under study. Meanwhile, active, participatory research means empowerment for the members of the stigmatized communities. Approaching users means opening channels so they can "keep in touch" with researchers and present their points of view on socially unacceptable activities. Therefore, research becomes more ethical because the balance of power shifts from the research itself to the interaction between researchers and users (Bakardjieva and Feenberg 2001).

The case study presented here supports these views; however, we want to go a step further, arguing that internet-based ethnography should not only actively engage in the community's life but also give that community some control over the research. The idea is to actively shape the entire process by members, especially when this would mean enhancing ethical integrity and facilitating access to otherwise elusive communities.

This two-staged study on Cebulka spanned from February 2023 to February 2024. Initially, the first stage focused on exploring threads and profiles. At the same time, the ethics of the entire study were refined iteratively to be finally defined and approved by the School of Social and

Political Science IRB at the University of Edinburgh[1] and the Faculty of Cultural Studies IRB at the Kazimierz Wielki University in Bydgoszcz, Poland.

When configuring the accounts to browse the site's content, we opted for usernames that do not reveal our real names. This decision was made due to uncertainty about the potential implications of using identifiable handles and with the understanding that we would disclose our identities in the subsequent phase of the study. At first, we followed Gehl's (2014) approach, which is that ethnography in the darknet should be based on pseudonyms because it is not culturally appropriate to do otherwise. Later, we wanted to adopt the dual identity technique indicated by Paechter (2013), aiming to navigate Cebulka as both anonymous users and disclosed researchers, which—as it turned out at the second stage—did not work at all.

Ultimately, the first stage collected 16,842 posts supplemented with 1,299 photos. This rich dataset underwent textual, thematic, and visual analysis. This phase also resulted in the production of internal research team reports totaling 53,171 words, including field data and field notes. From an ethical perspective, this part of the research adopted a "best practices" approach, utilizing several methods outlined in another paper (Harviainen et al. 2021), such as obfuscating all usernames and identifiers like emails or instant messaging numbers found in the posts. The data was carefully curated manually, ensuring that only publicly available information from the sites was released (for ethics, see also Martin and Christin 2016; Haasio, Harviainen, and Savolainen 2020; Harviainen, Haasio, and Hämäläinen 2020).

The second stage assumed interaction with the studied community. Initially, we planned to establish a so-called recruitment thread within one of the forum sections (Barratt and Maddox 2016). We intended to introduce ourselves as researchers and clarify the study's aims to gather the community's perspectives on various topics and recruit participants for interviews. This, however, was intensely discussed within the research team, as there are already many known cases where full disclosure was met with significant hostility from online communities. For example, Barratt and Maddox (2016) reported trolling and unwanted messages of a sexual nature. Similarly, Hout and Bingham (2013) described instances of high suspicion effectively torpedoing the recruitment process, a challenge also echoed in the findings of Van Hout and Bingham (2013).

For these reasons, we first decided to contact Cebulka's admin (also a community manager) to present our current research and ask permission to create a recruitment post and conduct in-depth interviews with users. We demonstrated the interview questions and the information sheet, including the consent forms. The form emphasized that all data obtained will be managed under the strict research ethics mentioned above. In addition to the standard emphasis on anonymity, we gave respondents many opportunities to choose how the interview might look, asking to potentially record while being open to refusal and proposing to utilize encrypted messengers. We informed respondents thoroughly that we were aware that interviews with drug users and darknet community members must be treated with extra care. Information sheets introduced the team members, offered ORCID iDs and email addresses, and assured participants of our adaptable and responsive approach and empathetic and non-judgmental stance.

Contacting the admin defined the shape of the further investigations. Despite our complete transparency, her initial reaction was very suspicious. The admin explained that the community is highly attached to the principles of OPSEC (operational security). If we started a recruitment thread, it would be met with a very adverse reaction, as the thread would be seen as provocative. She also noted that she would probably delete this post and ban our accounts. The forum's history justified this position; over its more than ten years of existence, there had been two attempts to conduct interviews, which, in her view, turned out to be user profiling operations run by law enforcement agencies.

This initial conversation turned into long-term negotiations about the shape of our research. During these talks, all team members had to properly verify themselves by sending control messages to the indicated secure email box using their university emails. Additionally, the admin set a strict framework for interviews, specifying that they could only be conducted using Cebulka's internal system of asynchronous private messages encrypted by PGP keys. This has wholly reformulated all our previous research-based assumptions on how the interviews might look. On the one hand, imposing encryption eliminated many potential ethical difficulties, ensuring safety protocols were implemented. On the other hand, the admin imposed a particular procedure designating only two users of her choosing with whom interviews could occur at a given time. When these interviews concluded, we were obliged to report, and only then were we given the next pair of users to reach out to.

After some time, we started identifying with community members. This happened, for example, when Cheba's account was automatically banned due to browsing the website too quickly, resulting in profound stress. Together, we clarified this with the admin; what is more, she granted our accounts a higher status, allowing us to view more content in a short time. This identification meant that during regular team meetings, we constantly reminded ourselves that giving up some control does not free us from setting clear boundaries regarding our roles and relationships with respondents. The community occasionally reminded us, as exemplified by the admin's messages, that some of our inquiries were flagged as OPSEC violations.

For instance, at one point, the admin suggested that the community was distressed and demanded that the questions about using anonymity tools other than the darknet (e.g., VPN, secure instant messaging) be removed.

Incorporating the community into the study implementation and letting go of complete control of the research process was beneficial for ethical reasons; it bolstered the previously mentioned empowerment of members and allowed us to run the study at all. This does not mean we do not recognize the limitations of the proposed approach. In our case, agreeing to appoint only two interviewees at a given time significantly extended the time needed to gather sufficient interviews. The asynchronous nature of communication and the frequent need to monitor users who did not respond for some time meant that by February 2024, during the four months of the second stage, we had conducted six complete interviews (this research is still ongoing).

Additionally, we realize that exerting substantial influence over the research's procedures and direction by the community may mean less research validity and reliability. For our study, we lost control over who would be selected for interviews. Although the described procedure could be considered a variation of snowball sampling (Parker, Scott, and Geddes 2021), the admin made the decisions arbitrarily. When asked about the selection criteria, she claimed that she was identifying people with extensive knowledge of how the forum functions, first targeting popular and experienced vendors and then regular customers. Assessing the profiles of our respondents, it can be concluded that they were the site's prominent and active users.

For us, agreeing to the rules imposed by the community was necessary. However, we were aware that we could not lose complete control, and one should always be vigilant to ensure that it does not harm research ethics. This was made clear to us when the admin wanted access to the responses of all users interviewed. Naturally, we had to refuse, explaining that sharing was contrary to the ethical guidelines adopted, to which the admin agreed, and that all answers were confidential, encrypted, and stored securely on our hard drives.

Summarizing, this chapter discusses the ethnography of the Polish darknet forum Cebulka, the most significant Polish TOR drug trade space. We claim that digital ethnography should actively engage in the community's life and divest some control over the research to the studied population. Rather than focusing on our research's primary objectives—namely, the meanings attributed to the discussion and trading of drugs—we opted to explain the methodological aspects of our study. We concentrated on the problems and specificity of internet-based ethnography in a particular crime-related environment. As was seen, numerous modifications to standard procedures had to be implemented to gain access to data, especially since some of the posts are hidden, based on the users' status, and the members are highly suspicious and safety-oriented. For us, this particular case study became a new standard for approaching and researching stigmatized and hard-to-reach communities. We also believe this chapter may serve as a guide for other scholars exploring similar sites. Perhaps it could even encourage researchers to use digital ethnography in less controversial settings and evaluate the benefits and drawbacks of their ethical and methodological choices.

Acknowledgment

This research is supported by the Polish National Science Centre (Narodowe Centrum Nauki) grant 2021/43/B/HS6/00710.

Note

1 University of Edinburgh IRB ID: 288628.

References

Bakardjieva, Maria, and Andrew Feenberg. 2001. "Involving the Virtual Subject." *Ethics and Information Technology* 2 (4): 233–40. https://doi.org/10.1023/a:1011454606534.

Barratt, Monica J., and Judith Aldridge. 2016. "Everything You Always Wanted to Know about Drug Cryptomarkets* (*but Were Afraid to Ask)." *The International Journal on Drug Policy* 35: 1–6. https://doi.org/10.1016/j.drugpo.2016.07.005.

Barratt, Monica J., Jason A. Ferris, and Adam R. Winstock. 2014. "Use of Silk Road, the Online Drug Marketplace, in the United Kingdom, Australia and the United States." *Addiction* 109 (5): 774–83. https://doi.org/10.1111/add.12470.

Barratt, Monica J., and Alexia Maddox. 2016. "Active Engagement with Stigmatised Communities through Digital Ethnography." *Qualitative Research* 16 (6): 701–19. https://doi.org/10.1177/1468794116648766.

Demant, Jakob, Rasmus Munksgaard, and Esben Houborg. 2018. "Personal Use, Social Supply or Redistribution? Cryptomarket Demand on Silk Road 2 and Agora." *Trends in Organized Crime* 21 (1): 42–61. https://doi.org/10.1007/s12117-016-9281-4.

Gehl, Robert W. 2014. "Power/Freedom on the Dark Web: A Digital Ethnography of the Dark Web Social Network." *New Media and Society* 18 (7): 1219–35. https://doi.org/10.1177/1461444814554900.

Haasio, Ari, J. Tuomas Harviainen, and Reijo Savolainen. 2020. "Information Needs of Drug Users on a Local Dark Web Marketplace." *Information Processing & Management* 57 (2): 102080. https://doi.org/10.1016/j.ipm.2019.102080.

Harviainen, J. Tuomas, Ari Haasio, and Lasse Hämäläinen. 2020. "Drug Traders on a Local Dark Web Marketplace." In *Proceedings of the 23rd International Conference on Academic Mindtrek*, 20–26. Tampere, Finland: ACM. https://doi.org/10.1145/3377290.3377293.

Harviainen, J. Tuomas, Ari Haasio, Teemu Ruokolainen, Lobna Hassan, Piotr Siuda, and Juho Hamari. 2021. "Information Protection in Dark Web Drug

Markets Research." In *Proceedings of the 54th Hawaii International Conference on System Sciences,* 4673–80. Grand Hyatt Kauai, Hawaii, USA. https://doi.org/10.24251/HICSS.2021.567.

Hout, Marie Claire Van, and Tim Bingham. 2013. "'Surfing the Silk Road': A Study of Users' Experiences." *International Journal of Drug Policy* 24 (6): 524–29. https://doi.org/10.1016/j.drugpo.2013.08.011.

Hunt, Geoffrey, and Karen Joe-Laidler. 2015. "The Culture and Subculture of Illicit Drug Use and Distribution." In *The Handbook of Drugs and Society,* edited by Henry H. Brownstein, 460–81. Chichester: John Wiley & Sons.

Kaufmann, Mareile, and Meropi Tzanetakis. 2020. "Doing Internet Research with Hard-to-Reach Communities: Methodological Reflections on Gaining Meaningful Access." *Qualitative Research* 20 (6): 927–44. https://doi.org/10.1177/1468794120904898.

Martin, James. 2014. "Lost on the Silk Road: Online Drug Distribution and the 'Cryptomarket.'" *Criminology & Criminal Justice* 14 (3): 351–67. https://doi.org/10.1177/1748895813505234.

Martin, James, and Nicolas Christin. 2016. "Ethics in Cryptomarket Research." *International Journal of Drug Policy* 35 (September): 84–91. https://doi.org/10.1016/j.drugpo.2016.05.006.

Martin, James, Rasmus Munksgaard, Ross Coomber, Jakob Demant, and Monica J. Barratt. 2020. "Selling Drugs on Darkweb Cryptomarkets: Differentiated Pathways, Risks and Rewards." *The British Journal of Criminology* 60 (3): 559–78. https://doi.org/10.1093/bjc/azz075.

Paechter, Carrie. 2013. "Researching Sensitive Issues Online: Implications of a Hybrid Insider/Outsider Position in a Retrospective Ethnographic Study." *Qualitative Research* 13 (1): 71–86. https://doi.org/10.1177/1468794112446107.

Parker, Charlie, Sam Scott, and Alistair Geddes. 2021. "Snowball Sampling." In *SAGE Research Methods Foundations,* edited by Paul Atkinson et al. SAGE Publications Ltd. https://methods.sagepub.com/foundations/snowball-sampling.

Tsuchiya, Yoichi, and Naoki Hiramoto. 2021. "Dark Web in the Dark: Investigating When Transactions Take Place on Cryptomarkets." *Forensic Science International: Digital Investigation* 36 (March): 301093. https://doi.org/10.1016/j.fsidi.2020.301093.

Van Hout, Marie Claire, and Tim Bingham. 2013. "'Silk Road,' the Virtual Drug Marketplace: A Single Case Study of User Experiences." *The International Journal on Drug Policy* 24 (5): 385–91. https://doi.org/10.1016/j.drugpo.2013.01.005.

Wanke, Michał, Magdalena Piejko-Płonka, and Marcin Deutschmann. 2022. "Social Worlds and Symbolic Boundaries of Cannabis Users in Poland." *Drugs: Education, Prevention and Policy* 29 (4): 334–44. https://doi.org/10.1080/09687637.2022.2046706.

Wright, Sam, Hilary Klee, and Paul Reid. 1998. "Interviewing Illicit Drug Users: Observations from the Field." *Addiction Research* 6 (6): 517–35. https://doi.org/10.3109/16066359809004369.

Chapter 2

Ethnography about digital media

Xinyuan Wang

As a digital anthropologist, I'm frequently asked about the compatibility of ethnography—a methodology known for being meticulous and long-term—with the breakneck pace of digital media. It is indeed a valid concern: digital technology evolves so rapidly that research findings can feel outdated almost as soon as they're published. The solution lies in recognizing the core focus of digital anthropology. While it involves observing the use of digital technologies, its primary focus is on people. Despite the rapid changes in technology, humanity remains largely constant. The same core emotions and experiences that drove people centuries ago still resonate with us today. Such continuity of humanity is simply evident in the enduring relevance of ancient literature and philosophy, which continue to touch modern readers.

In today's digital age, however, we have a unique opportunity to study human life. The digital realm has the potential to serve as a powerful tool for understanding the essence of humanity, which lies at the core of anthropology's mission as a discipline (Horst & Miller 2012). Digital anthropology pertains to understanding the consequences of digital technology and human lives in the digital age through ethnography (Heather & Miller 2012; Miller 2018). Through digital anthropology, we can gain insights into the complexities of human existence in the context of rapidly evolving technology while drawing on age-old philosophical inquiries that have fascinated us for generations.

Digital ethnography stands apart from online ethnography in its methodology. The latter would confine fieldwork solely to the digital realm. There are cases (e.g., Boellstorff 2008; Nardi 2010) of online ethnography within self-contained and self-reinforcing systems where interactions primarily occur within the confines of the online space, such as the online virtual world *Second Life* and the massively multiplayer online role-playing game *World of Warcraft*. In those cases, the digital domain justifies itself as a comprehensive research field detached from offline realities. Despite existing within an online realm, users and players are inherently rooted in the offline world, and offline circumstances inevitably shape their online actions. The extent to which participants of these online communities can detach themselves from offline influences remains a subject of debate (Gatson 2011; Golub 2010).

For instance, Golub's study (2010) effectively challenged the notion that virtual worlds can be quite separate from the offline world due to their sensory realism and sense of placeness. In Golub's ethnography, highly committed *World of Warcraft* players intentionally reduce the sensory realism of their interfaces to gain practical knowledge about the game world. Furthermore, their commitment to the game leads them to engage in knowledge-making activities outside of it. Therefore, Golub appeals for a more comprehensive account that covers both in-game and out-of-game worlds.

That said, depending on the researcher's objectives, conducting research solely online to comprehend the dynamics of specific online communities and their digital culture is viable. Purely online research is methodologically legitimate. Nonetheless, adapting traditional anthropological approaches to suit the internet's technologically mediated landscape could prove beneficial for ethnographers (Wilson & Peterson 2002; Snodgrass 2014).

The essence of ethnography lies in its dedication to long-term research endeavors. It demands a prolonged participant observation in the field, both online and offline, often spanning beyond a year. It is essential to observe individuals' daily activities over an extended period. People tend not to act naturally if they are conscious of being observed; hence, effective observation truly begins once the researcher blends into the surroundings. In my own experiences, research participants have confessed to me, after knowing me for six months or longer, that the stories they initially shared were not entirely true because they had not fully acquainted themselves with me at the time. Moreover, long-term fieldwork holds significance as it allows the researcher to assimilate into the environment and forge mutual friendships with the people they study.

A substantial portion of digital media usage occurs within private domains, inaccessible to researchers without individuals' willingness to share such materials. For instance, my key research participants would often sit down with me, scrolling through their social media contacts, directly showing me their online conversations, and providing context for each interaction. Similarly, they willingly opened their smartphone photo galleries, explaining the rationale behind selecting certain images for social media posts or specific group shares. Some even entrusted me with their smartphones, allowing me to explore the installed apps and detail their usage patterns and motivations.

As part of the research design, I closely examined smartphone apps with my key research participants in a very specific manner. Rather than discussing smartphone use in abstract or general terms, I asked participants to open their smartphones so I could see every app on every screen, and then we discussed each app one by one. This method was essential because systematically reviewing the apps often prompted participants to recall forgotten apps and their uses. Much like many aspects of daily life, these apps are quickly taken for granted, and memory requires prompting. Pointing to an app icon on the smartphone screen frequently sparked detailed stories or discussions that would not have otherwise arisen.

The smartphone app analysis was conducted during the latter stages of the fieldwork, typically after I had known the research participants for over six months or had met them at least five times. There are several reasons for this approach. First, cultivating trust and friendship takes time. Through frequent interactions in various daily scenarios, such as going to the food market together, picking up grandchildren from kindergarten, and discussing health issues, participants gradually came to trust me and appreciate my presence in their lives. Second, during these daily interactions, participants would often voluntarily show me the content on their smartphones, similar to how friends share information. These normalized daily exposures of their relatively private content mentally and practically paved the way for the final smartphone app analysis, ensuring that no one found it strange or overly intrusive.

Third, my accumulated knowledge of the individuals' lives and social relations contributed to meaningful discussions during the smartphone app analysis. For example, in one of my final meetings with Mr Guo, a retired schoolteacher whom I had known for more than a year, I was able to challenge his self-observations and trigger more in-depth discussions about the "social life" of various apps, thanks to my understanding of him and his family. During the app analysis, I noticed that Mr. Guo did not have a taxi-hailing app, which seemed odd since he had previously complained about arranging a DiDi (a taxi-hailing app) ride for a friend who never repaid him. When I questioned Mr. Guo about not having the DiDi app, he explained that his wife managed all purchasing-related apps, such as taxi-hailing and online shopping apps, via her smartphone. This insight inspired me to compare the smartphone apps of couples. Through this comparison, I discovered patterns of app overlap and differentiation between spouses. For instance, couples in their seventies had become much more interdependent. This interdependency is reflected in a typical pattern of "collective" app use: Since the couples are always together (whether at home or outside), there is no need to have the same app installed on both smartphones (Wang 2023: 134–35).

Without this systematic inspection, I would have been unlikely to gain such a comprehensive understanding of the wide range of tasks now involving smartphones. All these invaluable insights, constituting a significant portion of my ethnographic materials, were made possible by the deep friendships and trust cultivated through long-term, daily interactions, both online and offline. This mutual trust underscores the importance of sustained engagement and rapport-building in ethnographic research.

I usually suggested conducting the final smartphone app analysis in a tone that conveyed my research participants were doing a favor for a friend before I left the field site. By this point, participants were typically comfortable discussing private matters with me, as our interactions over time had built a sense of ease and trust. Before the analysis, I explained the ethical regulations, such as using the data solely for academic research, ensuring data elimination after the project, and guaranteeing anonymity. Introducing formal paperwork and consent forms at the initial stages often intimidates participants before they have established trust with the researcher. People generally harbor suspicions about signing consent forms. My usual practice is to provide oral explanations of my research and ethical considerations during the initial meetings but to postpone the actual signing of formal paperwork until the end of the fieldwork. This approach significantly reduces distrust and suspicion.

Holistic contextualization

While it is common in social science research to begin with specific research hypotheses, digital anthropology diverges from this approach because it recognizes that any hypotheses may introduce bias and limit researchers' perspectives even though it is also true that no anthropologist arrives in the field as a tabula rasa (Clark 2004). "Holistic contextualization," as a methodological approach, is essential during the ethnographic inquiry (Miller et al. 2021). This approach emphasizes that each element under study contributes to the broader context of understanding individuals. From an epistemological standpoint, understanding any one element, such as digital media use, requires making sense of the interconnectedness with other aspects of our lives that are concurrently unfolding and influencing each other. Sometimes, different elements may complement each other, while, at other times, they may appear contradictory. However, this complexity is inherent to humans. Real scholarship involves embracing this complexity rather than attempting to oversimplify it.

Holistic contextualization acknowledges that people are not just defined by one aspect of their lives and certainly not by any specific research instrument. We're not just our families, our jobs, our online personas, our political beliefs, or our digital media use. We're *all* of those things at once. Ethnographers veer away from predetermined hypotheses, embracing uncertainty as they seek to capture the diverse and dialectical aspects of everyday life through careful observation. For example, we cannot predict beforehand why an individual uses social media in a certain way: It could be influenced by personal experiences, community dynamics, occupations, wide social connections, hobbies, and numerous other factors.

Despite research titles focusing on social media or smartphones, both of my long-term fieldwork studies primarily involved traditional offline ethnography. As expected, the online components of the ethnography evolved organically from my offline interactions. As people incorporated digital media into their daily lives and interactions, I actively engaged with them both online and offline. In both cases, my offline participant observation was indispensable, providing an essential understanding of people's daily routines and living conditions. This offline groundwork was pivotal for comprehending their use of digital media in context.

Ethnographic studies on the use of social media and smartphones

My first long-term ethnography explores the phenomenon of rural-to-urban migration in China, described as the largest migration in human history. Over 250 million Chinese have migrated from villages to urban areas in recent years. From 2013 to 2014, I immersed myself in the community of migrants in a small factory town in southeast China, studying their use of social media. While urban populations often dominate social media studies in China, I argue that rural migrants offer a more compelling focus. Despite limited digital access, these young migrants exhibit a radical embrace of social media. They break traditional social constraints, finding expression and connection, notably through social media. Thus, Chinese rural migrants present a unique lens for examining the transformative power of digital platforms.

The rural-to-urban migration signifies a profound rupture, marked by the fragmentation of rural communities and the emergence of a turbulent life characterized by social exclusion. While many young migrants initially viewed migration as a path to a better life, they encountered a harsh reality where their dreams clashed with the challenges of factory work and pervasive social discrimination against rural migrants. Lily, a young factory worker, poignantly expressed this struggle when she lamented, "Life outside the smartphone is unbearable!" Her remark encapsulates a sentiment shared by many, highlighting the online world as a sanctuary for those feeling disconnected from both village and factory life.

During my fieldwork, I witnessed the struggles of young migrants as they grappled with their aspirations and the realities of urban living. I observed how they sought to find their place in the modern China they envisioned, as well as the motivations that drove their rural-to-urban migration. Moreover, I saw how they navigated complex dynamics of friendship, privacy, and diverse aspirations, often finding a more complete expression of modern life in the digital realm. Thus, I argue that a "dual migration" is taking place, one from rural to urban settings, and another from offline to online spaces (Wang 2016). For migrants, real life, or life imbued with meaning, extends beyond physical existence to encompass the online world they have constructed with dignity. Online life isn't separate from reality but an integral part of everyday existence, reflecting and shaping their experiences in profound ways.[1]

My second long-term ethnography was about the use of smartphones among older people in Shanghai, part of a global comparative study on older people's smartphone use, known as the Anthropology of Smartphones and Smart Ageing (ASSA). China has the largest and most rapidly aging population in the world. Chinese individuals in their 70s and 80s have double the life expectancy of their parents' generation. Concurrently, China has leapfrogged most other countries in its rapid digitalization over the past two decades. The state has demonstrated its ambition to become a digital superpower, leading the world in fields such as smartphone ownership, mobile internet penetration, mobile payments, and Big Data surveillance. Smartphones are particularly significant in the Chinese digital landscape as they are the primary devices for accessing the internet, with mobile internet users accounting for over 99% of internet users in China.[2]

Shanghai is at the forefront of both aging and digitalization in China. It has been the "oldest" city in the country for more than three decades and was the first to be categorized as a super-aging society (e.g., Wang 2023: 11). The current eldest generation in Shanghai was born at a time when the average household couldn't afford electric lights, but, today, they can turn lights off via their smartphones, thanks to full 5G coverage in the downtown area since 2020.[3] A unique aspect of this older generation in China is that they are both the first and the last generation to fully embrace the digital possibilities facilitated by smartphones in the later stages of their lives. My fieldwork has documented a wide range of ways in which older people in Shanghai have integrated smartphones into various aspects of their everyday activities, from self-care and maintaining social relationships to redefining their life purpose. The smartphone has transformed people's relationships with the surrounding world, being constantly present and available in almost all daily life scenarios.

My research tackles the intersection between the "two revolutions" experienced by the older generation in Shanghai: the contemporary smartphone-based digital revolution and the earlier communist revolutions (Wang 2023). I find that I can only explain the smartphone revolution if we first appreciate the long-term consequences of these people's experiences during the communist revolutions. The "information revolution" is being experienced by those who were fundamentally shaped by the political revolution early in their lives. There is a prevailing belief that individuals who refuse to adapt to the changes of their time will be "left behind" and become "useless." For instance, Jiuhong, a 69-year-old research participant, started using smartphones after her best friend strongly cautioned her against becoming outdated: "If you don't learn to use the smartphone, you'll be left behind by the times and become completely old and useless (*mei yong*)!"

The tolerance for individuals to remain detached from the era they live is minimal. This attitude aligns with the communist revolutionary discourse of "self-reform," emphasizing that people should not see themselves as unchangeable in an ever-progressing society. Among older people, there is a widely held idea that learning new technology is essential to being valued as a "useful" person. By embracing the advanced productive power latent in digital technology, individuals achieve the self-reform that defines them as "new people" in the digital era. Despite the appalling turmoil, the Cultural Revolution represents a "peak experience" in their lives, imbuing them with meaning and energy. This energy remains evident in the dynamism of older people who have embraced the smartphone in a way that is hard to match among their peers elsewhere in the world.

The widespread adoption of smartphones among older generations symbolizes China's modernity and commitment to national and individual progress. This positions China as a leader in the digital revolution, aligning with its vision for a modern society. The smartphone embodies continuity with the values of the communist revolution, where citizens aim to embody state ideals. On the other hand, the ethnography noted a shift in family dynamics, facilitated by smartphones, moving toward extended kinship connectivity. This transition highlights the device's role in strengthening familial bonds across generations, echoing Confucian principles. I argue that the term "revolution" transcends political rhetoric or media sensationalism when examining how older individuals in China use smartphones. It encapsulates their lived experiences and the real-time transformations they undergo. Understanding this generation necessitates recognizing their lifelong involvement in multiple revolutions, revealing intricate dynamics among individuals, families, and the state, now more discernible through smartphone use. China grapples with a collision of values, where anxiety signifies the nation's pulse. Yet, it's the older generation that epitomizes these profound struggles, embodying a blend of revolution and Confucianism. Comprehending their evolving experiences is pivotal for grasping contemporary China's complexity.

The ethnography further illustrates the pervasive and entrenched influence of the Party-state in ordinary people's lives. It further depicts how people perceive such parent-like forms of structural power. A typical Chinese concept *guan* (discipline and care), viewed as a means of balancing care and surveillance, is considered perfectly justified both in family situations and in relations between the state and individuals. Based on this ethnographic understanding, I further analyze how ordinary Chinese citizens react to ubiquitous surveillance facilitated by advanced digital technology, including the widespread use of AI in facial recognition.

By immersing myself in people's daily lives, both online and offline, I gained a new perspective on people's digital media usage. Such perspective allows my study to challenge some commonly held ideas about the consequences of digital media. For example, the widespread concerns about privacy and the "problem" of digital-mediated relationships being less authentic than face-to-face. My ethnography in China offers contrasting insights. In the West, it has become commonplace to accuse social media of being a threat to privacy. However, what if the very concept and practice of privacy hardly exist in a society? Migrant workers in China often come from village families where there is no provision for individualized space, a situation further compounded in adulthood by shared dormitory living conditions in the factory. Many also adhere to the traditional belief that "anything hidden from others must be something shameful or bad," effectively suggesting that a preference for privacy is inherently negative. Given such factors, the use of social media must be considered from a different perspective. In the real lives of migrant workers, social media has significantly increased their experience of privacy and legitimized their right to it. Migrant workers often face appalling social discrimination offline, prompting them to seek solace and connection online. In the digital sphere, they can freely express personal aspirations and form friendships without fear of judgment or discrimination.

Research on the internet and new media often raises concerns about technology's impact on human interactions. There's a worry that widespread use of digital-mediated communication platforms could lead to a loss of authentic selves and genuine relationships (e.g., Turkle 2011). However, many of my research participants viewed social media as a platform for establishing genuine relationships, liberated from the constraints of offline life. In this Chinese context, relationships mediated by digital technology were perceived as more authentic than offline interactions, which are often influenced by factors like wealth and social status. This challenges the notion of unmediated authenticity, as every aspect of life is shaped by social norms.

In fieldwork, being perceived as a friendly and trustworthy outsider proved to be immensely rewarding. People felt comfortable sharing their thoughts and confiding in me, knowing I wouldn't judge them or divulge their secrets. Interestingly, my position as an outsider appeared to mirror the role of "strangers" in migrant workers' social media interactions. For migrant workers, forming friendships with strangers online has become a significant aspect of their social lives. Unlike offline relationships, which are often influenced by fixed social roles and practical needs, online connections are perceived as more genuine, rooted in emotions rather than obligations.

In our global comparative study on older people's smartphone use (ASSA), we observed a widespread preference for exaggerated social media stickers (such as WeChat in China and LINE in Japan) among participants in China and Japan (Wang & Haapio-Kirk 2021). Initially, the apparent mismatch between a person's genuine emotions and the exaggerated virtual expressions conveyed through these stickers might seem to validate concerns about the authenticity of digitally mediated communication. However, our ethnographies, which extensively engaged with participants' offline daily lives, revealed that this discrepancy actually stems from longstanding social expectations. Individuals are often compelled to engage in highly performative communication that aligns with collective interests or internalized social norms, regardless of their real feelings.

In China, the idea of "wearing" an appropriate facial expression is frequently discussed, with many research participants expressing tiredness from constantly masking their true feelings to meet social expectations in various situations. Online, individuals often delegate the expression of emotions they are expected to convey to WeChat stickers, known as *biaoqing* (facial expressions) in Chinese. This phenomenon is also prevalent in Japan, where the concept of *tatemae* (public facade) plays a significant role in interpersonal communication. For instance, saying sorry is not necessarily reserved for situations where an apology is needed; rather, it serves as a general tool for smoothing social interactions. Research participants note that social media stickers allow them to say sorry with greater ease and efficiency. As one remarks, "Apologizing on LINE is so easy. It's just one sticker, 'sorry!'" Consequently, there is a wide array of exaggerated LINE stickers in Japan designed to express apology, ranging from bowing to crying characters. Our findings in both field sites suggest that social media stickers offer a less emotionally taxing alternative to face-to-face communication for conveying and performing feelings. Instead of undermining the authenticity of communication, these stickers alleviate the "emotion work" (Hochschild 1979, 2012) individuals undertake—the deliberate effort to evoke or suppress emotions to fit a certain situation.

The transformation of human existence by technological mediation is a central theme in the philosophy of technology (Dorrestijn 2016) and the interdisciplinary fields such as Science and Technology Studies and Digital Anthropology. It's crucial to recognize that, from an anthropological perspective, every moment of an individual's life is mediated in some way. Offline interactions are inherently shaped by societal norms, just as our ethnographies suggest that discrepancies between one's real feelings and their facial expression always exist in the predigital age. Interpersonal communication is always mediated by a wider range of social expectations and norms. In this sense, unmediated authenticity does not exist in human society. Digital anthropology must constantly avoid the temptation to simplify or romanticize the predigital world (Miller 2021).

Digital habitus and the "humility" of the digital media

A young child in my Shanghai field site once asked her grandmother, "You told me when you were young, people didn't have laptops and smartphones. So, what did you use for going online?" For this child, digital media are almost as natural as air and water, taken for granted as part of everyday life. For those who remember life before its widespread adoption, digital media seems to still play an overt role as a mediating factor. However, younger generations, born into the digital age, view digital media as an essential aspect of daily life. This ubiquity renders digital media nearly invisible yet incredibly influential in shaping societal norms. This increasingly normative role of digital media in daily life brings us to the theoretical foundation for this chapter, which can be traced back to Pierre Bourdieu's work and his key concept of "habitus" (1977, 1990).

Habitus essentially refers to a set of practices that become habitual and are engaged in without much prior reflection. Bourdieu conceptualizes habitus as shared predispositions to behave in specific ways under particular circumstances. He seeks to explain the processes of social production and reproduction in which individuals may engage without being fully aware of doing so. Through their interactions with objects, individuals internalize societal norms and values, which dictate behaviors such as sitting posture, spatial boundaries, dining etiquette, and displays of respect.

Lau (2004) further emphasizes the practical logic of habitus, focusing on the formation of generalized expectations and behavioral patterns. While the manifestation of habitus varies among individuals, certain regularities can be identified in practice.

The advent of digital media has introduced a new dimension to our understanding of social practices. In today's world, digital media have become a prominent material presence, shaping numerous aspects of daily life and providing the context for forming a new habitus—what I would call "digital habitus." This shift necessitates an exploration of how individuals creatively engage with digital technologies to negotiate social norms and construct their identities within online spaces. The fact that digital integration into daily life is taken for granted, and that our lives are significantly shaped by the use of digital media, brings us to the concept of the "humility of objects."

Based on Bourdieu's habitus theory, Miller (2005) characterizes objects as possessing a form of humility and emphasizes their understated yet profound influence on the formation of self and the dynamics of social situations. Objects establish a context that makes us aware of what is appropriate and inappropriate, thereby shaping not just cultural conventions but also social and ethical connections operating within them (Miller 2010).

In the sense of the humility of objects, digital media operate beyond our conscious recognition of them as inert material entities. The most intimate level of engagement with digital media occurs most powerfully when we are unaware of its influence. This concept of the humility of objects transcends the conventional view of objects as passive artifacts, positing them as active agents in constructing and transforming thought processes. It also emphasizes the importance of studying offline contexts to fully understand digital media's integration into daily life. Ultimately, examining offline realities is essential for comprehending the complexities of digital media usage.

Researcher's positionality and localized Challenges

Engaging in ethnographic research "at home" usually faces challenges as it seems to contrast with anthropology's tradition of studying cultures and people perceived as "others" in distant locations (Carucci & Dominy 2005; Mughal 2015). Hometown ethnography has been noted as granting automatic "insider status," implying a presumed right to knowledge (Wiederhold 2015). It also raises concerns about objectivity, suggesting that an "outsider" may have a more objective position to access the knowledge of others (Heley 2011). Nonetheless, studies conducted by researchers in their familiar environments actively challenge such restrictive characterizations by exploring the complexities of researcher identity and novel opportunities afforded by immersive ethnographies within familiar contexts (Anderson 2021; Stafford 2018). Placing undue emphasis on studying others as a means to achieve objectivity risks prioritizing a superficial approach over a deeper understanding.

Over the past decade, I have conducted two long-term ethnographies in mainland China, my birthplace and home until my early twenties. Maintaining objectivity and cultural awareness entails remaining attuned to social norms often taken for granted by insiders. As a researcher who grew up in China, I possess certain advantages, including fluency in the Chinese language, encompassing not only standard Mandarin but also various dialects. Moreover, my extensive experience of living and working in European countries for almost 15 years provides me with the necessary "cultural distance" to discern differences and reflect on daily activities. I argue that the oversimplified dichotomy between "insider" and "outsider" overlooks the incredible diversity within a society. For instance, my two target populations—the young migrant factory workers in a small factory town and the middle-class retirees in the metropolis—represent distinct segments of mainland China, each markedly different from the world I am familiar with. Consequently, despite our shared Chinese identity, I am considered an outsider to them.

Reyes (2020) further argues for the recognition of each researcher's unique "ethnographic toolkit," which encompasses both visible (e.g., race/ethnicity) and invisible tools (e.g., social capital). This perspective connects ethnography to inquiries into the strategic and varied use of culture, underscoring the importance of understanding local challenges. During actual fieldwork, researchers often encounter localized challenges, as was evident in both of my ethnographies.

In my initial research in the factory town, gaining access to local factories proved to be a significant hurdle. Factory owners commonly held great suspicions that researchers might be undercover journalists, a concern that became apparent on my first day when I was photographing a factory building and promptly confronted by a security guard enforcing their policy against journalists. A Chinese friend suggested that I adopt a typical Chinese approach to gaining access, relying on personal social networks (*guanxi*) rather than official permissions and regulations. According to her observation, the smaller the community, the more indispensable these personal connections become. Following her advice, I navigated through social networks and eventually secured an introduction to a factory owner through a local friend. This connection helped dispel the perception of me as a potential threat. Consequently, I was issued a temporary factory ID card, affording me access to the factory premises without further permissions. Moreover, I was provided with accommodations for my research stay, facilitating my immersion into the factory environment.

Even before setting foot inside the factory, I had learned a valuable lesson about my research site: personal social relationships are foundational in small-sized communities. This understanding shed light on the strategies employed by migrant workers to navigate life in unfamiliar surroundings, where much relied heavily on their personal networks. Leveraging personal networks (*guanxi*) worked well in a small factory town but yielded quite different outcomes sometimes in bustling Shanghai. For that fieldwork, I resided inside a low-rise living compound, pseudonymously called *ForeverGood* in my monograph. As it happened, one of my cross-window neighbors became my first friend. However, as I closely engaged with this household, it led to an assumption among other neighbors that I was favoring this particular group of people. Soon enough, I also realized that she only introduced me to neighbors who shared the same background and spoke negatively about others.

Relying solely on snowballing through personal networks posed the obvious risk of being perceived as biased and reducing my chances of acceptance by other neighbors. I needed to adopt an official role to project an impartial image. Without an official title or endorsement, I was also met with suspicion—a skepticism rooted in historical circumstances.

Situated in the former French Concession of Shanghai, *ForeverGood* was constructed in the late 1940s to house employees of a state-owned institute. During the Cultural Revolution, particularly during the "class struggle" phase, many households were redistributed. Well-off households were compelled to relinquish living space to "working-class" households. This legacy persists, shaping the attitudes of the older residents. For instance, the flat below mine once belonged to a single household before the Revolution. However, during the political upheaval, the head of the household was labeled "a running dog of capitalism," leading to the confiscation of a room for a "working-class" household. This arrangement persisted post-Revolution, resulting in ongoing conflicts between the two households. Such situations are common in many living compounds in the city center, where dwellings intended for one household have been subdivided to accommodate multiple families. Consequently, some older residents live alongside neighbors who once monitored or persecuted them during revolutionary times. While suspicion among neighbors may not always be overt, the threshold for accepting a stranger into different "sectors" of the neighborhood is exceedingly high.

To achieve this official role, I needed to seek the support of the Residents' Committee (*juweihui*), known for its strong Party association. In fieldwork, reciprocity is a guiding principle: If you seek cooperation, you must first offer something of value. Instead of directly requesting permission to conduct research—a move that often raised suspicion and was likely to be turned down—I proposed to offer free English evening classes for neighborhood children every fortnight by myself. This initiative garnered immediate support from the Residents' Committee, and I was introduced to the community as the volunteer English teacher. Given the central role children have assumed in Chinese families, engaging with them often sparks enthusiasm among entire families, spanning multiple generations. As the neighborhood children warmed up to me, so did their parents and grandparents.

The positive reception of the English evening class led to gaining the trust of the Residents' Committee. In turn, they extended an invitation for me to contribute ideas for utilizing an exhibition space within the living compound. This collaboration with the Residents' Committee culminated in curating an exhibition featuring the oral histories and photographs of residents and the neighborhood. This exhibition provided an official pretext for me to visit over 20 households, where residents generously shared their family albums and personal stories. These formal interviews opened doors that would have otherwise remained closed. Consequently, I earned a reputation for reliability, allowing me to cultivate enduring relationships with them as a valued member of the community.

Conclusion

This chapter explores ethnography about digital media from a perspective of digital anthropology, advocating for an approach of "holistic contextualization" to understand today's world, where digital media are ubiquitous. I assert that examining offline contexts is equally important for studying digital media. Digital media have become integral to constructing our habitus, and the fact that people often take their existence for granted highlights their powerful influence on our daily lives.

Drawing on several case studies of digital ethnographies that debunk widely held understandings of digital media use and its consequences, this chapter further emphasizes why a comprehensive understanding of people's lives, both online and offline, is crucial for understanding their use of digital media. The final section of the chapter reflects on my own experiences as a researcher in the ethnographies discussed. The purpose is to highlight the constraints and opportunities that exist simultaneously in any specific ethnographic endeavor.

Typically, readers are presented with polished results of ethnographies without insight into the numerous mistakes that occur during actual fieldwork. However, some of the most valuable lessons can be drawn from these mistakes. Bearing this in mind, I hope that the detailed description of how I presented myself in my fieldwork and how I adjusted specific ethnographic strategies provides an internal view for students and scholars interested in conducting ethnographic research about digital media.

Notes

1 For a video discussing this fieldwork, see https://youtu.be/4XZ0WJrvE_M?si=2oe4S6x8IBtuKMBg.
2 https://techblog.comsoc.org/2020/01/01/china-internet-penetration-reached-61-2-in-1st-half-2019–99-1-access-internet-via-mobile-phones/ (accessed November 1, 2021).
3 http://www.xinhuanet.com/english/2019-07/06/c_138204560.htm (accessed November 1, 2021).

References

Anderson, Esther R. 2021. "Positionality, Privilege, and Possibility: The Ethnographer 'at Home' as an Uncomfortable Insider." *Anthropology and Humanism* 46: 212–25.

Boellstorff, Tom. 2008. *Coming of Age in Second Life: An Anthropologist Explores the Virtually Human.* Princeton, NJ: Princeton University Press.

Bourdieu, Pierre. 1977. *Outline of a Theory of Practice.* Cambridge: Cambridge University Press.

Bourdieu, Pierre. 1990. *The Logic of Practice.* Stanford, CA: Stanford University Press.

Carucci, Laurence M., and Michèle D. Dominy. 2005. "Anthropology in the 'Savage Slot': Reflections on the Epistemology of Knowledge." *Anthropological Forum* 15, no. 3: 223–33.

Clark, David. 2004. "The Field as 'Habitus': Reflections on Inner and Outer Dialogue." *Anthropology Matters* 6, no. 2, 1–10.
Dorrestijn, Steven. 2016. "Theories and Figures of Technical Mediation." In *Design and Anthropology*, 219–30, edited by Wendy Gunn and Jared Donovan. London: Routledge.
Gatson, S. N. 2011. "The Methods, Politics, and Ethics of Representation in Online Ethnography." In *Collecting and Interpreting Qualitative Materials*, 4th ed., 245–75, edited by Norman K. Denzin and Yvonna S. Lincoln. London: Sage.
Golub, Alex. 2010. "Being in the World (of Warcraft): Raiding, Realism, and Knowledge Production in a Massively Multiplayer Online Game." *Anthropological Quarterly* 83, no. 1: 17–45.
Heley, Jesse. 2011. "On the Potential of Being a Village Boy: An Argument for Local Rural Ethnography." *Sociologia Ruralis* 51, no. 3: 219–37.
Hochschild, Arlie R. 1979. "Emotion Work, Feeling Rules, and Social Structure." *American Journal of Sociology* 85, no. 3: 551–75.
Hochschild, Arlie R. 2012. *The Managed Heart: Commercialization of Human Feeling*. Berkeley: University of California Press.
Horst, Heather A., and Daniel Miller, eds. 2012. *Digital Anthropology*. London: Routledge.
Lau, R.K.W. 2004. "Habitus and the Practical Logic of Practice." *Sociology* 38(2): 369–87.
Miller, Daniel. 2010. *Stuff*. Cambridge: Polity.
Miller, Daniel. 2012. "The Anthropology of Social Media." In *Digital Anthropology*, edited by Heather A. Horst and Daniel Miller, 85–100. London: Routledge.
Miller, Daniel. 2018. "Digital Anthropology." In *The Open Encyclopedia of Anthropology*, edited by Felix Stein. https://doi.org/10.29164/18digital. Accessed on 24 September 2025.
Miller, Daniel. 2020. "Individuals and the Aesthetic of Order." In *Anthropology and the Individual*, edited by Daniel Miller, 3–24. London: Routledge.
Miller, Daniel, ed. 2005. *Acknowledging Consumption*. London: Routledge.
Miller, Daniel, Laila Abed Rabho, Paul Awondo, Marleen de Vries, Marianne Duque, Pauline Garvey, and Xinyuan Wang. 2021. *The Global Smartphone: Beyond a Youth Technology*. London: UCL Press.
Mughal, Muhammad. 2015. "Being and Becoming Native: A Methodological Enquiry into Doing Anthropology at Home." *Anthropological Notebooks* 21, no. 1: 121–32.
Nardi, Bonnie. 2010. *My Life as a Night Elf Priest: An Anthropological Account of World of Warcraft*. Ann Arbor: University of Michigan Press.
Reyes, Victoria. 2020. "Ethnographic Toolkit: Strategic Positionality and Researchers' Visible and Invisible Tools in Field Research." *Ethnography* 21, no. 2: 220–40.
Snodgrass, Jeffrey G. 2014. "Ethnography of Online Cultures." In *Handbook of Methods in Cultural Anthropology*, 465–95, edited by H. Russell Bernard and Clarence C. Gravlee. Lanham: Rowman & Littlefield.
Stafford, Charles. 2018. "Moral Judgement Close to Home." *Social Anthropology* 26, no. 1: 117–29.
Turkle, Sherry. 2011. *Alone Together: Why We Expect More from Technology and Less from Each Other*. New York: Basic Books.

Wang, Xinyuan. 2016. *Social Media in Industrial China*. London: UCL Press.
Wang, Xinyuan. 2023. *Ageing with Smartphones in Urban China: From the Cultural to the Digital Revolution in Shanghai*. London: UCL Press.
Wang, Xinyuan, and Laura Haapio-Kirk. 2021. "Emotion Work via Digital Visual Communication: A Comparative Study between China and Japan." *Global Media and China* 6, no. 3: 325–44.
Wiederhold, Anna. 2015. "Conducting Fieldwork at and Away from Home: Shifting Researcher Positionality with Mobile Interviewing Methods." *Qualitative Research* 15(5): 600–15.
Wilson, Samuel M., and Leighton C. Peterson. 2002. "The Anthropology of Online Communities." *Annual Review of Anthropology* 31, no. 1: 449–67.

Chapter 2.1

Concept: affordance

What they are; why they matter in digital ethnography

Anna Colom

As new technologies and tools are developed and adopted by researchers and society more broadly, new opportunities emerge for studying the social world. The scale and pace of digital technological development have raised a multiplicity of research questions across disciplines but also expanded the methodological toolkit for contributing to answering these questions.

Approaches to studying technologies in social sciences have long been criticized for either taking the technological artifact for granted and unexplored or for approaching it from a technological determinist lens (Brevini 2021), "monolithic and homogeneous" (Sein and Harindranath 2004, 17), which fails to appreciate its impacts in both society and the research practice (Joyce et al. 2023). Constructivist approaches in the field of Science and Technology Studies (STS) have challenged the view of technology as either neutral or deterministic and have argued that technologies both construct and are constructed by society (Henwood et al. 2000). However, the most essentialist ends of this view have also been criticized for overlooking the technological artifact itself and the risk that results from under-theorizing technology (Roberts 2017; Walsham and Sahay 2006), when it is "either absent, black-boxed, abstracted from social life, or reduced to surrogate measures" (Orlikowski and Iacono 2001, 130).

Scholars from across disciplines have attempted to find a balance between constructivist approaches that can overlook the technological artifact and essentialist or deterministic approaches to studying technologies. Yet, the "specter of technological determinism" continues to reemerge (Joyce et al. 2023, 146), and therefore it becomes imperative to be reflexive, intentional, and analytical in how we research with, through, and about digital technologies; how we embed them in our research toolkit; and how these choices shape and are shaped by the context in which we work.

Theory of affordances

The theory of affordances has provided a theoretical and empirical basis for a relational approach to studying the technological artifact without overlooking its materiality. It originates from the work of ecological psychologist James Gibson (1977) and was introduced to the study of information and communication technologies by Ian Hutchby (Pozzi et al. 2014; Zammuto et al. 2007).

Hutchby (2001, 2014) argued that different technologies have specific affordances related to their materiality or design that shape how a technology can be interpreted and used. Affordances can be functional or relational. Functional affordances are the range of perceived uses that the materiality of the technology can enable (and also constrain). These characteristics of the artifact "shape the conditions of possibility associated with an action" (2001, 87). They can also be relational, which means that these affordances will vary depending on the context. In addition, scholars have used the additional concept of "affordances in practice" to theorize the resulting uses or processes of social change shaped by the uses of technology once the different subjectivities, power relations, and social settings have been considered (Zheng and Yu 2016). In this sense, it is also important to see affordances through an intersectional lens as affordances in practice will change depending on power relations and the axis of oppression and invisibility in which people are situated (Colom 2022). Affordances are, therefore, action possibilities that stem from the materiality of an artifact but which are dependent both on human agency and on historical and social settings (Zheng and Yu 2016).

Different technologies, then, will add new elements and linkages to the already-complex ensemble of relationality between agency and historical and social settings that characterizes ethnographic research. Theorizing the technology through its affordances can therefore help the digital ethnographer better grasp the complex world of doing ethnographic research across digital and non-digital contexts; across internet-mediated networks, communities, and forms of communication; and across researchers and research participants and the varied contexts and power relations from which these various actors interact.

Affordances in digital ethnography

The concept of digital ethnography has evolved over the years, especially as digital technologies have become more ubiquitous and entangled in our lives: It does not refer to ethnographic research done using digital technologies alone but to ethnographic research that crosses and inhabits online and offline communities and multiple spaces and modes of research and communication. As argued by Postill and Pink, in digital ethnography, the borders of the "field" site become unclear because the researcher follows emerging connections and therefore new "territories and socialities" (Postill and Pink 2012, 124).

The theory of affordances can provide a framework to more systematically study the potential ways in which the uses of digital tools will shape and be shaped by both the research-researched relationship and the ways in which the research methods will contribute to approaching our research questions.

While it might be easier to treat "digital technology" as a tool or object of study separate from the research process and separate from all subjectivities involved in it, this is no longer possible in the current context of "digital confluencies" (Adams and Thompson 2016). The entanglements of our internet-mediated spaces and technologies mean that we need to carefully consider the tools we use and how these are embodied and constructed in and by our research and vice versa. As argued by Zhao and Li, "both the affordances and their disruptions are constitutive components in the formation of the researcher–participant relationship," and this comes with both ethical and methodological implications (2023).

As researchers we make decisions on what tools and digital technologies to use based on the potential of different technologies to help to answer our research questions, to meet methodological and ethical expectations, such as the need for proximity; rapport; reflexivity; re-balancing power relations between researcher and research partners or participants; convenience and practicalities related to time, space, or budget; among many others. Our assumptions on the potential affordances of these tools and spaces will be informed by our own uses, the uses of the research participants or co-researchers, and empirical evidence from existing scholarly work or will be constituted as we use these tools in our own research journeys. These assumed affordances will also be challenged, because, as we have seen, they are only action possibilities but only realize themselves in action, shaped by the various subjectivities and power relations at play, and the different contexts in which the research takes place. This becomes particularly salient by the prolonged and embodied participation and presence in the "field" that characterizes digital ethnography.

References

Adams, Catherine, and Terrie Lynn Thompson. 2016. "Posthuman Confluencies." In *Researching a Posthuman World*, 107–17. London: Palgrave Macmillan UK. https://link.springer.com/book/10.1057/978-1-137-57162-5#toc.

Brevini, Benedetta. 2021. "Creating the Technological Saviour: Discourses on AI in Europe and the Legitimation of Super Capitalism." In *AI for Everyone? Critical Perspectives,* edited by P. Verdeger. Westminster: Westminster University Press. https://www.jstor.org/stable/j.ctv26qjjhj.11.

Colom, Anna. 2022. "WhatsApp Affordances through an Intersectional Lens: Constructing and Rehearsing Citizenship in Western Kenya." In *Freedom and Social Inclusion in a Connected World. ICT4D 2022. IFIP Advances in Information and Communication Technology*, edited by Y. Zheng, P. Abbott, and J. A. Robles-Flores. 566–580. Cham: Springer. https://doi-org.libezproxy.open.ac.uk/10.1007/978-3-031-19429-0_34.

Gibson, J. J. 1977. "The Theory of Affordances." In *Perceiving, Acting, and Knowing: Toward an Ecological Psychology*, edited by R. Shaw and J. Bransford, 67–82. Hillsdale, NJ: Erlbaum.

Henwood, Flis, Sally Wyatt, Nod Miller, and et al. 2000. "Critical Perspectives on Technologies, In/equalities and the Information Society." In *Technology and In/Equality: Questioning the Information Society*, edited by Flis Henwood, Sally Wyatt, Nod Miller, and et al., 1–18. London: Taylor & Francis.

Hutchby, Ian. 2001. "Technologies, Texts and Affordances." *Sociology* 35 (2): 441–56.

Hutchby, Ian. 2014. "Communicative Affordances and Participation Frameworks in Mediated Interaction." *Journal of Pragmatics* 72: 86–89.

Joyce, Simon, Charles Umney, Xanthe Whittaker, and et al. 2023. "New Social Relations of Digital Technology and the Future of Work: Beyond Technological Determinism." *New Technology, Work and Employment* 38 (2): 145–61.

Orlikowski, Wanda J., and Stephen Iacono. 2001. "Desperately Seeking the 'IT' in IT Research: A Call to Theorizing the IT Artifact." *Information Systems Research* 12 (2): 121–34.

Postill, John, and Sarah Pink. 2012. "Social Media Ethnography: The Digital Researcher in a Messy Web." *Media International Australia* 145: 123–34.

Pozzi, Gabriele, Federico Pigni, and Claudio Vitari. 2014. "Affordance Theory in the IS Discipline: A Review and Synthesis of the Literature." *Twentieth Americas Conference on Information Systems*, Savannah, 2014, 13 (August): 1–12.

Roberts, Tony. 2017. "Participatory Technologies: Affordances for Development." In *Information and Communication Technologies for Development. ICT4D 2017. IFIP Advances in Information and Communication Technology*, vol 504, edited by Jyoti Choudrie, M. Sirajul Islam, Fathul Wahid, Julian M. Bass and Johanes Eka Priyatma, 194–205. Cham: Springer.

Sein, Maung K., and G. Harindranath. 2004. "Conceptualizing the ICT Artifact: Toward Understanding the Role of ICT in National Development." *Information Society* 20 (1): 15–24.

Walsham, Geoff, and Sundeep Sahay. 2006. "Research on Information Systems in Developing Countries: Current Landscape and Future Prospects." *Information Technology for Development* 12 (1): 7–24. https://doi.org/10.1002/itdj.20020.

Zammuto, Raymond F., Terri L. Griffith, Ann Majchrzak, and et al. 2007. "Information Technology and the Changing Fabric of Organization." *Organization Science* 18 (5): 749–62.

Zhao, Peng, and Ping Li. 2023. "The Affordances of Videoconferencing Technology for Doing Interviews with Children Online: Methodological Explorations Based on a Critical Ethnography." *Qualitative Inquiry* 29 (10): 1033–44.

Zheng, Yingqin, and Andrea Yu. 2016. "Affordances of Social Media in Collective Action: The Case of Free Lunch for Children in China." *Information Systems Journal* 26 (3): 289–313.

Chapter 2.2

Case study
Women Australian Rules footballers' digital self-tracking

Paul Bowell, Paul Scifleet, Ekaterina Pechenkina, and Emma Sherry

Engagements between athletes and technology are ever-increasing in elite sports (Rapp & Tirabeni 2020). However, these interactions and the subsequent impacts on athletes are not widely understood. This problem drove our digital ethnography, which investigated women Australian Rules footballers' experiences with digital self-tracking: wearable digital sensors that statistically track bodily outputs of differing physical and mundane activities (Bergroth 2019). This case study will highlight our novel and versatile three-tiered digital ethnography, which investigated the relational connections between elite Australian Football League Women's (AFLW) footballers and their digital self-tracking practices.

Case study background

In designing our methodological approach, it was critical to understand how people interact with digital self-tracking devices. These devices include smartwatches, global positioning systems, and heart rate monitors, which track different physical outputs like movement, speed, acceleration, and effort. People can embody digital tracking, changing its meaning and elevating the importance of the activity until it becomes a taken-for-granted part of their lives (Ruckenstein 2014; Fors & Pink 2017). At the core of digital ethnography's principle is the everyday understanding of the relational interactions between people and technology and how this shapes a person's material-sensory-digital lives (Pink 2015; Pink et al. 2016). This embodying potential justified the enlisting of digital ethnography as our methodology to understand AFLW footballers' experiences with digital self-tracking.

Australian Rules—the native football code of Australia—has traditionally been framed socially and culturally as a men's game (Pavlidis et al. 2022; Sanders 2020). Women's participation in Australian Rules football is relatively new, with the elite national women's competition launching in 2017. Socially and culturally, women find their position within the game vexed, as entering these spaces can result in them being treated as outsiders. The team aspect of Australian Rules also offered unique analytical consideration. The individual nature of monitoring oneself has meant that understanding how a community of practice experiences digital self-tracking is under-researched in digital tracking inquiries (Rapp & Tirabeni 2018). Thus, the team aspect of Australian Rules football and the fraughtness of women participating were critical considerations when designing our digital ethnography from an analytical and ethical perspective.

Three-tiered digital ethnography

Our three-tiered digital ethnography featured a data generation approach of interviews, qualitative reflexive surveys, and video re-enactments. Enlisting these three approaches generated in-depth, rich, experiential qualitative data that would not have been possible through a single approach. The thinking behind the three-tiered digital ethnography was that each approach would target different experiences the footballers had with their digital self-tracking. For example, team, personal, and embodied experiences were all captured through the different approaches, while the aim and questioning within each approach remained similar. Still, the distinct features of each data-generating method helped produce differing responses, creating a more well-rounded, comprehensive dataset of the footballers' experiences with digital self-tracking in the tradition of "thick" ethnographic descriptions (Geertz 1973; Kharel 2015).

Our three-tiered digital ethnography began with interviews, designed to capture the team experiences of the footballers—and their teammates—tracking programs. During the interviews, the footballers were asked how they and their teammates used and understood the tracking devices and the data they produced and what challenges, if any, they faced. We also explored individual and team data practices like sharing, reading, discussing, and interpreting. The data generated from the interviews encapsulates the everyday experiences the footballers and their teammates had with digital self-tracking, a critical aim of the study. This included one AFLW footballer's, Leslie, observations of their teammates' tracking behavior:

> I'd probably say everybody wants to know [their data results] because a lot of girls wear [their smartwatch] even during training. They're wearing their watches, and everybody wants to know how many Ks they're doing. I'd say people find it pretty important.

Despite the rich data generated through the interviews, we were acutely aware of the personal nature of tracking different bodily actions, which were likely not all shared in a two-way conversational setting. Hence, the qualitative survey approach accounted for the personal nature of digital self-tracking.

The qualitative reflexive survey offered a platform for the footballers to express the most personal aspects of their digital self-tracking that they might not have addressed in their interview. The survey was framed as a reflexive exercise where the footballers were encouraged to approach the questions as if they were writing in a diary. The footballers embraced the reflexive element of the survey, offering many personal insights into the challenges and concerns they had with digital self-tracking that were not expressed in the other data generation approaches. For example, another AFLW footballer, Hayley, described their experiences of their device not working: "When my watch went flat halfway through a running session, it made me feel upset and frustrated that I didn't have anything to show and look at for what I did." Other personal comments included the footballers speaking of their sadness when their shared data was ranked lower than that of their teammates. Another footballer described their frustration with their data being absent from context, not accounting for life happenings such as hormonal fluctuations or lack of sleep, to explain substandard data outputs.

The reflexive survey also helped to manage an ethical problem of the study. The lead author—who conducted all research activities—needed to consider their positionality as a middle-aged man and how that might impact the footballers' readiness to share their insights. The reflexive survey helped mitigate this issue as the footballers completed the survey away from the researcher's gaze.

The video re-enactments were the third and final approach. Video data collection has been widely used in digital ethnography and offers a unique perspective by capturing hard-to-verbalize embodied aspects of people's interactions with technology (Leder Mackley & Pink 2013; Pink 2014; Richardson & Keogh 2017). With the video re-enactments, the footballers were asked to re-enact a training activity (generally a running or sprinting drill). During the video re-enactment, there was a systematic focus on how the footballer interacted with their device, including reading the data, where and when the data was uploaded, and data curation. This transcended language as there was a focus on touch, sound, haptics, and visual interactions with the device.

By re-enacting the process, embodied understandings were revealed, such as how the tracking device impacted how the footballer felt during the activity. For example, Siobhan stated: "If I'm doing five-minute intervals, I have a guess at when I'm about halfway through and look down, and then I'm normally disappointed to find out I'm only one minute into a five-minute interval." The video re-enactments offered opportunities to capture data that was not possible in the interviews and surveys, creating a more comprehensive qualitative understanding of the players' experiences with digital self-tracking.

To complement the footballers' data, we interviewed their fitness coaches who oversaw the clubs' digital tracking programs. The fitness staff offered understandings that sometimes supported what the players were expressing. At other times, they explained why the footballers found the practice confusing and confounding. For example, the fitness staff highlighted the problematic resource restraints stemming from AFLW footballers being semi-professional athletes and not having access to the club all year round. Cameron, a fitness staff member, went on to explain:

> So, we say to them [the footballers], we'd love to know how you're going [in the off-season]. We can't force you to tell us how you're going, and we can't necessarily keep track of you. We can't send your GPS units all those things, but they have been a self-driven group that have said that we want to be accountable.

As a result, the footballers had limited time at their clubs, and any upskilling around understanding digital self-tracking was left to the players to seek out. They had to be "self-driven." This resulted in a lack of understanding, which led the footballers to notice vagaries and contradictions in how the tracking programs were run. The footballers then passively engaged in the process, which limited their ability to maximize their digital self-tracking. The findings and analysis from our digital ethnography highlighted in this case study can be found in Bowell (forthcoming) and Bowell et al. (2024).

The flexibility of digital ethnography: meeting the challenges of social research

The iterative and reflexive nature of digital ethnography meant that challenges arising throughout the study could be overcome. The study's main challenge was the ever-present nature of the COVID-19 pandemic. At the time of data collection, strict restrictions concerning social distancing were enforced by the Victorian Government (a state government of Australia), the Australian Football League, and Swinburne University of Technology. As a result, all data collection approaches were conducted online through Microsoft Teams or the survey software Qualtrics. We faced some challenges in conducting the research online, such as a lack of human connection or bandwidth. Nevertheless, digital ethnographic studies are well suited to engaging with digital technologies to generate data, which meant this challenge became a strength of the study. Conducting the research online offered flexibility in when and where to hold the research activities, which opened the sample to more participants. For example, one participant conducted their interview and video re-enactment just days after having an operation on their lower leg and being bedridden.

The COVID-19 pandemic also exacerbated the already persistent challenges found among the sample. For instance, the pandemic further highlighted the precarity experienced by AFLW players, which made them hesitant to engage in extracurricular activities. However, practicing reflexivity and being iterative helped us alleviate these challenges. For example, we initially chose focus groups as the interview method, but this was not possible due to the external time pressures the footballers faced. So, we pivoted to didactic interviews, offering convenience to the footballers. Moreover, the external time pressures placed on the AFLW players, as semi-professional athletes, impacted their willingness to participate. Reflexively understanding this during data collection led to the inclusion of the fitness staff members in the sample. As a result, this change significantly improved the dataset, giving greater context to the footballers' experiences. Our case study has demonstrated digital ethnography's iterative and flexible nature, which helped produce in-depth data that offered unique insights.

Conclusion

Our case study of understanding AFLW footballers' digital self-tracking experiences has highlighted digital ethnography in practice. We have demonstrated that digital ethnography allows researchers to consider people's everyday interactions with technology. Digital ethnography also lends itself to creative and innovative data collection methods. The versatility and flexibility of digital ethnography, as demonstrated in this case study, allowed the research design to be crafted and adjusted to suit the focus and participants of the study. Moreover, with the inherent need to be reflexive and iterative throughout digital ethnographic processes, challenges such as sample constraints, ethical issues, and access restrictions to the field could all be overcome.

References

Bergroth, Heli. 2019. "'You Can't Really Control Life': Dis/Assembling Self-Knowledge with Self-Tracking Technologies." *Distinktion: Journal of Social Theory* 20 (2): 190–206. https://doi.org/10.1080/1600910X.2018.1551809.

Bowell, Paul. Forthcoming. "How Do Digitised Sporting Metrics Feel? The Affective Experiences of Women Australian Rules Footballers." In *Routledge Handbook of Digital Technologies in Sport, Exercise and Physical Education*, edited by Victoria Goodyear and Anne Bundon. London: Routledge.

Bowell, Paul, Paul Scifleet, Ekaterina Pechenkina, and Emma Sherry. 2024. "The Carousel of Gendering and Othering: Women Australian Rules Footballers' Affective Experiences of Digital Self-Tracking." *Journal of Sport & Social Issues* 8 (3–4): 107–33. https://doi.org/10.1177/01937235241269960.

Fors, Vaike, and Sarah Pink. 2017. "Pedagogy as Possibility: Health Interventions as Digital Openness." *Social Sciences* 6 (59): 1–12. https://doi.org/10.3390/socsci6020059.

Geertz, Clifford. 1973. "Deep Play: Notes on the Balinese Cockfight." *Daedalus (Cambridge, Mass.)* 134 (4): 56–86. https://doi.org/10.1162/001152605774431563.

Kharel, Dipesh. 2015. "Visual Ethnography, Thick Description and Cultural Representation." *Dhaulagiri Journal of Sociology and Anthropology* 9: 147–60. https://doi.org/10.3126/dsaj.v9i0.14026.

Leder Mackley, Kerstin, and Sarah Pink. 2013. "From Emplaced Knowing to Interdisciplinary Knowledge: Sensory Ethnography in Energy Research." *The Senses and Society* 8 (3): 335–53. https://doi.org/10.2752/174589313X13712175020596.

Pavlidis, Adele, Kim Toffoletti, and Kylie Sanders. 2022. "'Pretty Disgusted Honestly': Exploring Fans' Affective Responses on Facebook to the Modified Rules of Australian Football League Women's." *Journal of Sport and Social Issues* 46 (1): 103–23. https://doi.org/10.1177/0193723520964969.

Pink, Sarah. 2014. "Digital–Visual–Sensory–Design Anthropology: Ethnography, Imagination, and Intervention." *Arts and Humanities in Higher Education* 13 (4): 412–27. https://doi.org/10.1177/1474022214542353.

Pink, Sarah. 2015. "Going Forward Through the World: Thinking Theoretically about First-Person Perspective Digital Ethnography." *Integrative Psychological and Behavioral Science* 49 (2): 239–52. https://doi.org/10.1007/s12124-014-9292-0.

Pink, Sarah, Heather Horst, John Postill, Larissa Hjorth, Tania Lewis, and Jo Tacchi. 2016. *Digital Ethnography: Principles and Practices*. London: Sage Publications.

Rapp, Amon, and Luca Tirabeni. 2018. "Personal Informatics for Sport: Meaning, Body, and Social Relations in Amateur and Elite Athletes." *ACM Transactions on Computer-Human Interaction (TOCHI)* 25 (3): 1–30. https://doi.org/10.1145/3196829.

Rapp, Amon, and Luca Tirabeni. 2020. "Self-Tracking While Doing Sport: Comfort, Motivation, Attention and Lifestyle of Athletes Using Personal Informatics Tools." *International Journal of Human-Computer Studies* 140: 1–14. https://doi.org/10.1016/j.ijhcs.2020.102434.

Richardson, Ingrid, and Brendan Keogh. 2017. "The Ethnography and Phenomenology of Itinerant Interfaces." In *The Routledge Companion to Digital Ethnography*, edited by Larissa Hjorth, Heather Horst, Anne Galloway, and Genevieve Bell, 212–20. London: Routledge.

Ruckenstein, Minna. 2014. "Visualized and Interacted Life: Personal Analytics and Engagements with Data Doubles." *Societies* 4 (1): 68–84. https://doi.org/10.3390/soc4010068.

Sanders, Kylie. 2020. "Sportscapes: Contested Bodies, Gender, and Desire within a Female Australian Rules Football Team." *International Review for the Sociology of Sport* 55 (6): 685–702. https://doi.org/10.1177/1012690219837898.

Chapter 3

Ethnography on/in social media

Fieldwork on platforms

Katrin Tiidenberg and David Kneas

Introduction

How do we understand the ways that people make their lives meaningful in relation to others and in the context of place, practice, and structures of power? What ideas of culture frame these understandings? While speculating on culture and sociality has long philosophical roots, ethnography emerged as a mode of inquiry in the late nineteenth century and is premised upon exploring social life from the vantage point of the people living it. The crux of ethnographic research is embodied situatedness—where researchers position themselves within and among the people they want to study, witnessing, observing, experiencing, and participating (Hammersley and Atkinson 1995). Through a function of time in the field and by engaging in the practices studied, ethnographers produce detailed and nuanced knowledge of the world.

Social media and ethnography present, on the surface, something of a paradox. On the one hand, social media has become a dominant mode of human sociality. Online engagement involves everything that we know structures cultural life: shared symbols, ritualization, languages, values, norms, material artifacts, and meaning-making contexts. It is absolutely where an ethnographer wants to be. On the other hand, if one of the main tools of ethnography is about locating oneself within and in relation to that which we wish to study, then what does this look like on social media? How are key concerns of ethnographic research—time, presence, participant observation, fluency in language or cultural vernaculars, key informants, etc.—enacted online?

There are a number of labels aimed at distinguishing ethnography of social media, or research with a digital fieldwork element, from "conventional" ethnography, e.g., netnography, virtual ethnography, cyberethnography, and digital ethnography. Each term has its own history, proponents, ebbs, and flows of popularity. While the impulse to highlight the digital and the networked makes sense, it is important to recognize how

DOI: 10.4324/9781032672663-14

such qualifications can reinforce a false binary between off and online social phenomena. With the internet becoming more and more domesticated and ubiquitous, with forms of digital and networked relations becoming part of all social practice (Baym 2015), with platform logics infusing economic, political, cultural, and educational structures (van Dijck and Poell 2013), hierarchies between digital and "real" ethnographies make less and less sense. A number of authors (cf Postill and Pink 2012, Boellstorff et al. 2012, Markham 2017) have for years suggested that ethnography is ethnography, despite the field site or the focus of research. It is based on researchers' capacity to immerse themselves within social contexts and to employ tactics best suited to those settings. Looked at this way, the digital, or the socially mediated, is just another context to be accounted for. It is, however, a context that has features and affordances that we need to recognize (Lane and Lingel 2022).

Ethnography is important not only for the types of data it produces but also for the political stakes of that knowledge. Ethnographers can speak from the margins, can access modes of life that would otherwise be sidelined, and explain logics of cultural practices that would otherwise be glossed over as trivial, obscene, marginal, or, in some other form, unworthy. More than just a question of reworking a powerful research tool for online worlds, ethnography on, with, and for social media is a way to understand what today shapes and constrains human agency and relations in a complex world.

This chapter focuses on practical details of ethnographic fieldwork on social media. Our vantage point starts from what happens in specific social media spaces, groups, and communities and how people have incorporated social media into their everyday lives and practices of meaning-making. It is a partial take, as social media ethnography could also focus on the workings of platform companies and industries (Glatt 2023), the logics of platform economies (Bonini and Gandini 2020), or the shared imaginaries regarding algorithms (Seaver 2017). In practice, social media ethnography (as well as other kinds of ethnography) means fieldwork, wherein key moments pertain to (1) delineation of the research field; (2) engagement with people, ideas, and content that necessarily includes participant observation; and (3) turning it all into analyzable material via the practice of fieldnoting. We will share our experiences and suggestions regarding all of these. We do so from a position that reflects our ongoing dialogue about fieldwork. Kat is a social media scholar whose fieldwork has always unfurled online, across a variety of platforms, online communities, and (sub)cultures. David is an anthropologist whose long-term fieldwork was offline—in the mines and fields of Ecuador, but whose research on seaglass now transcends beach and social media. It is through the similarities and differences in our experiences that we are able to share what we hope are useful notes.

The field

What we delineate as "the field" says just as much about who we are as scholars as the questions we ask when we get there. The field implies a boundary, a line that, upon crossing, signals the beginnings and ends of research. Such boundaries are productive. Things that occur within are subject to investigation; things that occur outside can be left alone, a form of demarcation that gives the ethnographer permission to "not notice" (Candea 2007). Twentieth-century anthropology has been underpinned by ideas of entering a community, living there for a year or more, studying and recording everything—what one of David's advisors calls "vacuum ethnography." This means that ethnographies have traditionally been structured by bounded units of space (e.g., a village). While such work was not without important political arguments (Conklin 1957), we now know that it is impossible to study a small community in a place like Puerto Rico, for example, without some contextual framing within histories of sugar, slavery, and capitalism (Mintz 1986). Similarly, it is impossible to discuss a community of neo-pagan witches on Facebook without contextualizing it in the broader processes of platformization and mediatization (Renser and Tiidenberg 2020). The boundaries of the field are not static, and, indeed, they should change through the course of research.

Increasingly, ethnographers agree that "the field" is always constructed, co-constitutive with the research question and thus a direct result of boundary-making by the researcher (Amit 2000, Burrell 2009). At the same time, social life and social relations, both on social media and off, take shape within various borders, boundaries, and other types of circumscriptions. What this means is that fieldwork entails a constant process of negotiation, of reflecting upon what sort of assumptions characterize how we conceptualize the field—or increasingly fields—of our research, and how we identify and work with or across existing fields of social interaction.

Social media fields

Ethnography is about observing, witnessing, and recording practices, utterances, and common-sense understandings of how the world works from situated vantage points (Herzfeld 1997). Social media—by the function of platform companies' business interests, what platforms are built for, and the rules they set for users—profoundly shape those practices, understandings, and situated vantage points. First, social media's business models hinge on engagement—on users spending time on platforms, interacting with each other and content, leaving behind trails of commodifiable data. To entice users into this version of engagement, platforms (in particular, the older generation of generic social media like Facebook, Instagram, and X) have incorporated features that reward self-revelation and invite attention seeking. The persistent siren song of acknowledgment that lures us to post, comment, react, and interact feeds social media sociality but also links in complicated ways to intimacy, trust, and relationship building, which is important both for the kinds of social life ethnographers can observe and also for their relationships with the people they study.

Second, social media platforms make visible, recordable, traceable, searchable, and persistent (boyd 2010) much of what used to be ephemeral about everyday life and interactions—angry diatribes; drunken, post-break-up selfies; fleeting thoughts. This gives researchers unprecedented access to aspects of meaning-making and identity construction. Just by lingering in hashtags or wading through Facebook Groups, researchers are able to access incredibly rich residues of social relations. Such access, however, is tinged with ambiguities regarding whether, what for, when, and for how long these processes should be observed, collected, and preserved for research (Tiidenberg 2018). Things expressed on social media form something of a shadow archive that impacts the present. Expressions and utterances that work one way in particular contexts can become divorced from those contexts in the process of friending, sharing, and reposting and as a result take on new meanings in those new contexts.

Third, interaction on social media is multimodal, with visual and audio elements becoming increasingly central alongside textual communication. This too shapes the social lives and relations that emerge on platforms, as well as how we as ethnographers construe research fields and enact fieldwork. For example, while visuality has been elevated as superior to other modes of communication in terms of generating attention and affective responses (Joffe 2008), visuals are also always polysemous—their meanings are open to interpretation. Whether something is a compliment, an insult, an homage, a parody, or a joke thus deeply depends on context.

Four-fold fieldmaking

If we look at the field as the domain where the social processes we are interested in take place (Burrell 2009, 182), then some notion of it is required to initiate our research and move it forward. However, other articulations of the field may take time to emerge. It's important to be mindful of the relationship fields have to research questions and the research timelines. Here, we describe four kinds of fields we've experienced in social media ethnography.

Platform as a field

Sometimes, the boundaries of a social media field site coincide with those of a platform, existing in computer code and interface design. Typically, only a slice of a platform—like r/GoneWild subreddit (cf van der Nagel and Firth 2015), a Facebook group for new-spiritual healing (Renser and Tiidenberg 2020), or an Instagram account that a group of activists runs to narrate memories of genocide (Davidjants and Tiidenberg 2022)—makes sense as a field site. In a recent study, however, Kat considered the entirety of Libertine Center, a new sexual social media platform intended mostly for non-monogamists, as her research field. This was made possible by the platform's relatively small user base (~50,000), their fairly uniform interests (at least when compared to, for example, the interests of everyone using Instagram or TikTok), and the fact that the developers were generously willing to interact with the researcher, illuminating backend logics and processes. While ethnographic research will inevitably reveal subfields within platforms, a broad platform-based proto-field might be a productive starting point for some studies.

Flow as field

Alternatively, the field can be (or begin as) "stream-based," consisting of people and content that are aggregated in a moment, for example, around a particular hashtag (Markham 2017, Tunçalp and Lê 2014). In this case, the ethnographer may search for keywords pertaining to particular discourse to see if networked publics (boyd 2010, Rambukkana 2015) exist. Typically, a bread-crumb trail toward ethnographically rich and situationally relevant field sites will emerge as the ethnographer follows along, going from keywords to posts, to hashtags, to new posts with more (sub)culturally specific hashtags, to key users or accounts, groups, networks, or threads. This is what Kat did in her study of representations of pregnancy on Instagram, where starting from fairly unimaginative keywords like "pregnant," "pregnancy," and "9 months," she was spun off into alternative linguistic publics (e.g., Russian) and a variety of subcultural subfields (e.g., those related to natural birth, raw food pregnancies, eating disorder pregnancies etc.). Here, algorithmic recommendations become a useful, although inevitably biased, ethnographic tool.

Profile as field

Sometimes the ethnographer does not start from discourse or platform but might know specific individuals who engage in a practice they are interested in. In this case, it makes sense to start from social media accounts, following the hashtags the initial informants use, the accounts that they follow or that follow them, and through that extend to communities, networks, and discursive fields. For example, David's on-beach conversations with seaglass enthusiasts often lead him to platforms like Instagram and

Etsy, connecting not only with these beachcombers themselves but also to accounts, sites, and communities that they reference as networked publics they are part of, or as examples of those they see themselves as distinct from. Moving between material and mediated domains produces serendipitous moments of field convergence, as when, for example, David contacted a beachcomber on Instagram who then realized that they had in fact met on the beach days prior.

Affinity as field

Fields initiate and sustain research questions, but sometimes they can only become apparent through research discovery. This is especially true when the field emerges in relation to a sense of belonging, shared affinity, or language proficiency (actual languages as well as jargon, cf. Markham 2005). Thus, within a subreddit, a hashtag, or a social media group, there might be other, more meaningful field sites, which can only be recognized through sustained (participant) observation. Kat's ethnography of Tumblr sex bloggers started with a half-year immersion in flows of content. Based on this initial observation, she realized that there are indeed a number of tight-knit communities within the broad sphere of NSFW Tumblr, but to recognize their coordinates, she'd need to participate in a particular way, following the tacit rules and norms she'd so far determined (e.g., pseudonymously, but actively; kindly, but with snarky humor; confessionally, but in a curated manner). This slow, participatory process of delineating the field also made evident that, to describe the community with real ethnographic thickness, the invisible had to be included. This meant users who had private (password-protected) blogs or did not post but were actively contributing to and interacting by commenting, submissions, chat, and email. In this case, social dynamics relevant for determining the boundaries of the field only became visible through competence in community vernaculars and insight into how "locals" deal with the affordances of the platform (e.g., which off-platform communication tools do people incorporate in their repertoires when the native messaging system is clunky).

Fieldwork

Certain elements of fieldwork are always present in ethnography. This includes time in the field, a balance of observation and participation, and relationships with key informants. Fieldwork practices tend to be a matter of pragmatic bricolage (Fayard 2017) that reflects both what is germane for the field site and the skills, creativity, and constraints of the specific ethnographer.

While conventions of ethnography often state that a year of sustained fieldwork is necessary, traditions of multi-sited ethnographies (Marcus 1995) and, more recently, patchwork ethnographies (Günel et al. 2020) have introduced some flexibility into what that looks like in practice, e.g., does it presume constant engagement, or can one dip in and out of multiple sites? Time in the field is really about presence, of ensuring that a researcher is around long enough to understand the cultural codes that shape a social practice, to have the wits to witness when there are transgressions of that code, and, ideally, the ability to ask people about both. As we mentioned above, one of the affordances of social media is that digital content (often) remains accessible. This can alter the relationship between ethnography and time. In the same way that archives give historians access to records of activity generated over many years, social media can allow ethnographers to see, over a matter of days, what took weeks, months, or years to accumulate. What the ethnographers witness, however, is not the original situation of interaction. It is vital, therefore, to read that social media content along its archival grain (Stoler 2009), that is, with a sense of contextual and situated meaning.

Observation: lurking and rabbit holes

Unlike in most offline settings, social media ethnographers can see without being seen—an inherently powerful and ethically complicated position that requires reflection (Markham 2017, Tiidenberg 2018). As we discuss below, while participant observation is a critical part of any ethnographic project, observation on its own is a powerful tool. It is also useful to remember that there are different kinds of observation. Michael Agar (2006) writes of abduction, which means letting yourself be carried away based on moments of surprise or particular situational hunches and curiosities. James Spradley (1980) distinguishes between descriptive, focused, and selective observation. In the case of descriptive observation, everything is interesting; the guiding question is: What is going on here? Focused observation is possible when patterns begin to emerge from descriptive observation, and the observer focuses on how the observed phenomena are related. Selective observation is the narrowest of the three; the observer decides which details to focus on based on previous fieldwork and observes them to confirm hunches or answer questions. While these different types of observation are sometimes recommended for different phases of fieldwork, we'd argue that in social media ethnographies, especially in stream-based field sites, it is a good idea to start each episode of fieldwork with some descriptive observation to then move on to focused and selective observation. In the language of social media, it is useful to lurk first, and then to go down some rabbit holes, and then do it all over again.

Table 3.1 Cues to observe on social media

Cues about people's behavior	In "conventional" ethnography	When studying sociality on social media
Social cues	Facial expressions, voice, observable interactions, rituals, language	Visuals (gifs, memes, emoji), acronyms, statuses, check-ins, language
Relationships	Observable interactions, symbols (e.g., wedding ring), legal documents, people's self-reports, language	Profiles, links, likes, friend and follow lists, liked posts, statuses, observable mediated interactions, language
Norms	Conflicts, myths, rules, laws, folklore, language, inferences about social status from the behavior of others	Conflicts, ToS, FAQ, Community Guidelines, default settings, perceptions of affordances, algorithmic lore, lore on shadowbanning and flagging, etc., language
Values and attitudes	Us—them descriptions, myths, folklore, acts of choosing and preference, language, inferences from the behavior of others, gossip	Self-(re)presentation, including visible/ expressed affiliations (fan of, follower, liked by), profile images and frames, badges, subcultural words, and emoji in profiles

Building on Spradley's classic account of the observable characteristics that structure every social situation (e.g., space, actors, objects, goals, feelings), Kat has developed social media-specific recommendations for observing online. In the first column of Table 3.1 are phenomena that ethnographers' typically want to observe, in the second column their expressions in face-to-face situations and, in the third, their expressions on social media. Some of this becomes evident in descriptive observation, or it can be what the ethnographer's attention snags on, inviting a pivot toward focused or selective observation, or perhaps a conversation.

Participation

While observation is an inherent part of how ethnographers navigate networked publics, it is participation that will allow for the most in-depth understanding of social media cultures. By doing what the people we are interested in do—posting selfies, commiserating around diagnoses, seeking lovers, selling artwork—we notice how that feels, what about it propels us into action, what haunts our thoughts when we are off-platform.

These affective responses are individually subjective, of course, and not generalizable but generate better questions, more focused follow-up observations, and more deeply contextualized interpretations. Methodologically, the importance of participant observation stems from the fact that people have a hard time noticing and articulating that which for them is ordinary and obvious, so watching them do it and doing it with them, offers necessary nuance regarding the risks, rewards, and resentments that are part of any practice and culture. For example, when David began photographing seaglass for his own Instagram account, he discovered a assortment of questions he then asked beachcombers about not only photographic techniques but also the value beachcombers place in their own pictures and what they see in others'. Participation also has an ethical parameter. It illuminates potential vulnerabilities and communicates that you take the subjects and social practices of your research seriously.

There are many different modes of participation, which are contingent upon the research question, the field site, and the comfort level and skills of the ethnographer. Peter Ashworth (1995) has argued that participation is a form of conscious social engagement that consists of and depends on empowered membership in a group that shares certain assumptions and concerns. Mirko Tobias Schäfer (2011), while speaking more broadly of participation in the context of digital media, distinguishes between explicit and implicit participation. This invites interrogations of power, both in the sense of the ethnographer's power in relation to their informants and in terms of the potential of one's participation to shape the phenomena one participates in.

While there are field sites where observing without participating is difficult (e.g., studying group dynamics in multiplayer online games), or vice versa, where participating might raise issues, but some form of lurking is possible (e.g., studying the communities of practice of pornographic deepfakes), in most cases, fieldwork is cyclical. There are periods where more observing and less participating make sense—for example, in early stages of fieldwork, as lurking is how all new members learn community norms and platform vernaculars (Baym 2015), and there are moments where more participation is needed to be able to move forward with interpretation.

Getting in, getting on: gatekeepers and key informants

However, to be able to start observing and participating, one needs to access the field site. This can be thought of as a two-stage process—getting in, which is about material and technical access, and getting on, which is about social access (Gobo 2008). Both rely on the ethnographer's interpersonal skills and can be facilitated or hindered by working with gatekeepers and key informants. Gatekeepers are usually individuals who are influential in their group or community through their formal or informal status and position, and whose authorization can create access for the ethnographer (Latchem-Hastings 2019). Beyond having status as a result of one's skill or tenure, gatekeepers in social media communities will often hold platform-specific roles as group administrators or community moderators. Further, it is important to recognize that the platforms themselves function as gatekeepers—their features, settings, and rules significantly shape researcher access but can rarely be negotiated with.

Key informants, who may be, but are not necessarily gatekeepers, are individuals with whom researchers have developed relationships of trust. "Key informants are often socially adept, kind, and alert to the predicaments of the ethnographer. They constitute a special resource and have been a vital part of ethnography since its inception" (Boellstorff et al. 2012, 79). These are the people we can ask more direct and reflexive questions from and can do so on a recurring basis. Relationships to key informants tend to emerge organically, and not every research project will have such a resource. Key informants can also allow for forms of proxied participation. For example, while David does not have an account that is eligible to sell seaglass on a Facebook selling page (according to the rules of longevity established by the group), a key informant allowed him to assist her in the process of assembling glass, photographing it, and posting it online for sale. In witnessing, in real time, who purchased the glass, David was able to ask about social relations between what appeared to be mostly UK sellers and mostly US buyers. He realized that lasting transatlantic friendships were formed via selling and buying, which is a component of seaglass circulation and commodification that would be difficult to appreciate without a key informant and the ability to witness these modes of interaction firsthand.

Fieldnotes

Finally, for any in-depth interpretation and analysis to be possible, fieldwork experiences have to be turned into *data*. This means systematically taking fieldnotes. Fieldnoting helps us capture both the spectacular and the mundane and to move iteratively between research questions, emerging interpretations, the data, and the field. Sarah Tracy (2013) describes the iterative process as a zigzag or spiral, where a researcher enters the field with an interest and a conceptual preference; both of these change with some fieldwork, which then leads to new perspectives on the field, a need for new forms of participation and observation, new rounds of fieldwork, and so on. Further, writing stimulates our brain, and recording observations and reflecting upon them positions us to be more alert to serendipitous moments of discovery. While there are now a number of new technologies for fieldnoting,[1] we emphasize here some key principles for converting observation into data, data into prose, and prose into theory.

First, different fieldnoting styles work for different ethnographers; therefore, we recommend experimenting with a variety to find a system that aligns with your ethnographic sensibilities and routines. However, it is important to keep in mind that what seems most appropriate at the time of observation may in fact be merely the most convenient and may not be very useful at the stage of analysis. The ethnographer's task is to find a way of making field notes that is feasible in the field but affords thickness (Geertz 1973) in later analysis. Even with experimenting, it is sensible to plan when and how you will take notes, as well as what kinds of notes you plan to keep. The simplest way to divide fieldnotes is perhaps into three complementary categories (Spradley 1980, 66–72):

1 *Quick notes* during or immediately following observation (single keywords, phrases, or sentences).
2 *Expanded and condensed notes* after the observation (this is where the quick notes should be further developed so that they are legible, understandable, and meaningful when our memory of the observation fades).
3 *Notes about the notes* (this is the researcher's diary, where initial ideas for analysis develop and insights are gathered piece by piece).

It is important to remember that, when writing notes, including quick notes, language really matters. For example, Spradley (1980, 67–68) describes the *verbatim principle* and the *concrete principle*. Following the first means we write down what someone said without changing the wording. It is not possible to do this for everything said in the field, but a literal recording of some utterance, a peculiar self-expression, or an interesting metaphor, can become useful when we expand our notes and fertile ground as we probe our data for further lines of inquiry. The principle of concreteness is about avoiding preemptive generalization. This means focusing on particular utterances and their moods, for example, writing down things like: "said, repeated, argued, YELLED, repeated angrily," instead of "they discussed strategies" or "people chatted." The concreteness principle is especially important with extended fieldnotes, when we can flesh out and reflect not just the things said but also questions of tone, context, and affect.

These modes of recording our observations apply to any field site. When we observe socially mediated fields, however, we can rely on screenshots to reflect verbatim and concrete observations and do so in ways that allow us to combine quick and extended note-taking. Screenshots alone, however, do not make good fieldnotes. So we recommend contextualizing them or at least making sure we label and tag them. Kat likes to organize her notes in a fairly conventional three-column structure, with the first column containing the time/place of the observation, the second a description of what happened, and the third a reflection. Screenshots, in this case, would go into column 2.

Kat's notes in Table 3.2 illustrate one key idea of fieldwork—that the significance and meaning of ethnographic data stems from the transition between description and reflection. This becomes even more important when expanding notes. Two helpful strategies here are the strategy of *salience hierarchy* and the strategy of *comprehensive description* (Wolfinger 2002). The first essentially means that the ethnographer who sits down to expand the fieldnotes selects the most striking, noteworthy, or interesting episode and writes it out. Often this means focusing on what is atypical or exceptional in relation to personal assumptions or norms, because that is what stands out. The strategy of salience hierarchy is absolutely subjective, but this is not a problem as much as something to reflexively be aware of. Also, why something seemed relevant and noteworthy to you as an ethnographer may deserve noting down in the researcher's diary. The strategy of comprehensive description involves describing what happened in as much detail as possible. Wolfinger (2002) offers a wide range of tactics for this—a narrative faithful to the chronological order of the events: the Who? What? Why? questions, etc. Again, there is no golden rule; each ethnographer must find a way of expanding that suits them and the particular project.

While it is easy to think of fieldnotes as a chronicle of observation, one of the pioneers of interpretive ethnography, H.L. Goodall (2000), argues that notes represent one-third observation and two-thirds interpretation. They do not document as much as they evoke certain images, meanings, and interpretations. He suggests that each ethnographer, in creating their note-taking strategy, should ask themselves what they want their notes to evoke. According to Goodall, fieldnotes can bring forth (1) verbal interactions between people; (2) actions involving both people and things; and (3) inferences and deductions made by the person making the notes about the relationships between the people, things, and actions observed. "In making the fieldnotes, you put down what fascinated and persuaded you; what seemed meaningful, what you interpreted as a pattern" (Goodall 2000, 87). The purpose of the fieldnotes is also "to articulate what was not said, what evoked—casually but perceptibly like smoke between strangers—what was, what could be, and what seemed to be." The fieldnotes are neither direct translations of experience nor a definitive ethnographic text but rather a bridge connecting the two (Goodall 2000, 87). They also include, it should be stressed, notes regarding the researcher's thoughts, actions, and feelings. Such accounts help to ensure self-reflexivity of the ethnographic process and constitute an invaluable resource for the analysis of material collected during fieldwork. As with other types of notes, there are many possible approaches. There are ethnographers who weave self-reflection into their observations. Others prefer

Table 3.2 Excerpt from Kat's fieldnotes in the NSFW Tumblr ethnography

Time	Description	Reflection
24.04.2013, scrolling my "for research" Tumblr feed (e.g., feed comprised of accounts that participate in the study)	There's nothing particularly interesting on my dashboard, typical for a Sunday. I did see that Participant X commented that someone had re-posted her selfie to a *thinspo* blog and hashtagged it *as #thinspo*. She was not at all happy with this Someone asked Participant R about her Fetlife experience and he replied like this: ~ screenshot ~ *Hi,* *I tried it, but it's not for me. Tumblr fulfils most of my sexual needs. It seems to me that if you're more of a soft-core exhibitionist and are interested in real friendships and meaningful interaction (not just having sex with strangers) then Tumblr is much better for that. Plus, I don't like to equate my identity with just my sexuality. I'm a lot of different things - playful, analytical, sensual and a bit naughty - and Tumblr allows me to be multi-faceted and see many facets of other people. Fetlife forces you to define yourself by ticking boxes.* This post currently has 10 hearts and three comments, with people all agreeing with Participant R.	thinspo – interesting, how the wider body positivity ideology of this community doesn't seem to apply to them. **Note to self:** *ask people about that.* R and the people in her comments compare Tumblr and Fetlife, as if they were sites in the same category, as if Tumblr were a place to meet people, or a dating site, rather than a blogging platform. Clearly, these people are using Tumblr as an interactive, social platform, at least here in the NSFW threads focused corner. **Note to self**: *people's definitions of social media? Which platform is for what?* More on multi-faceted identity, **do an analytical memo,** pick out all the references to it, there are so many!

to keep a separate research diary and to collect all the reflexive notes in it. Some have private or shared (with colleagues, with research participants) social media accounts as their researcher diaries.

Concluding discussion

Being reflexive of one's research process and logic is a long-standing tradition in ethnography. It is framed as a universally good thing, if also one that can be amorphous and vague. Tied to the idea of turning one's critical eye back onto oneself, it is a practice that seeks vantage points from which we can see our research and ourselves in new ways. As Marie Buscatto (2018) concisely notes, reflexivity is an attempt to find harmony between two ethnographic drives: involvement and detachment. Reflexivity has taken on greater significance over the past few decades in relation to questions of identity and authorship—a recognition that our subjective selves are the products of inscribed social structures of race, gender, and class that can shape our research in often unintended ways. These have continued, if not increased in salience, in the context of social media ethnography, but, when studying (in) social media, we also need to be reflexive of our perceptions and previous experiences with platforms, their affordances, vernaculars, norms, and governance.

It is easy to assume, even if tacitly, that the lessons learned about "how to Internet," in one social media field will translate to another. They will not. Each field site has to be learned anew; access has to be earned anew. The worst thing we can do is to believe that we have no position, to assume that the research questions we ask and the observations we make are neutral simply because we take them for granted. As ethnographers, we should critically analyze our preferred paradigms, default assumptions, pet peeves, and beloved approaches and account for them when conducting and interpreting fieldwork. This is important for both the rigor and the ethics (which are, of course, linked) of the research (Markham 2007).

While these different registers of reflexivity—reflecting on the research, while also reflecting on the self conducting the research—are vital and co-constitutive, there tends to be less discussion about the actual ways of being reflexive (cf the special issue edited by Abidin and de Seta 2020 as a great example), or advice on how to operationalize reflexivity. Although often framed in terms of a dialogue between the perspective of the informants and the analytical position of the researcher, the primary agent of reflexivity is usually the researcher. This can be lonely and frustrating. Here, we have one final experience to share.

We both did a fellowship at the Institute of Advanced Studies at Durham University at the beginning of 2023. After a discussion of David's study of seaglass and how the beachcombers' practices incorporate social media, Kat joined David on the beach. On this outing, David couldn't help but start chatting with people about what they were doing and where they came from, and while Kat would have been perfectly content petting their dogs, more often than not, she was drawn in as well. After one such conversation, in a discussion about the nuances of fieldwork, we decided to experiment. After the next couple of conversations on the beach, we each made independent audio recordings of those encounters. Later, we made an initial, individual foray into what could be the "seaglass field" on Instagram. Later still, we listened to how each of us encapsulated our beach interactions as well as our notes from Instagram.

While we were part of the very same interactions and started our social media lurking with the same hashtags (#seaglass and a couple of location-specific variations), we were shocked at just how different some of our observations were. In discussing these differences, we realized how our respective training and disciplinary background influenced our understanding of research fields and the questions that animate our fieldwork, while our gender, nationality, accent, and height (!) shaped how people related to us. While sharing drafts and soliciting feedback on research design is common in academia, we tend not to invite others in during fieldwork and rarely share our notes. It is understandable; relationships an ethnographer has to the field and the people within it can feel private, vulnerable even, but such a "buddy system" offers, even as a playful experiment, a lived, actionable practice of reflexivity. It can make us better ethnographers.

Note

1 Digital and communication technologies can be incorporated into fieldnoting, if you are curious, explore Tricia Wang's (2012) live field-noting or note-taking apps such as the Momento App, CaptureNotes, Ethosapp, and Indeemo (many are subscription based).

References

Abidin, Crystal, and Gabriele de Seta. 2020. "Private Messages from the Field: Confessions on Digital Ethnography and Its Discomforts." *Journal of Digital Social Research* 2, no. 1: 1–19. https://doi.org/10.33621/jdsr.v2i1.35.

Agar, Michael. 2006. "An Ethnography by Any Other Name…" *Forum Qualitative Sozialforschung/Forum: Qualitative Social Research* 7, no. 4: Art. 36.

Amit, Vered. 2000. "Introduction: Constructing the Field." In *Constructing the Field: Ethnographic Fieldwork in the Contemporary World*, edited by Vered Amit, 1–18. London: Routledge.

Ashworth, Peter D. 1995. "The Meaning of 'Participation' in Participant Observation." *Qualitative Health Research* 5, no. 3: 366–87. https://doi.org/10.1177/104973239500500307.

Baym, Nancy K. 2015. *Personal Connections in the Digital Age*. 2nd ed. Cambridge: Polity.

Boellstorff, Tom, Bonnie Nardi, Celia Pearce, and T. L. Taylor. 2012. *Ethnography and Virtual Worlds: A Handbook of Method*. Princeton, NJ: Princeton University Press. Kindle edition.

Bonini, Tiziano, and Alessandro Gandini. 2020. "The Field as a Black Box: Ethnographic Research in the Age of Platforms." *Social Media + Society* 6, no. 4: 1–10. https://doi.org/10.1177/2056305120984477.

boyd, danah. 2010. "Social Network Sites as Networked Publics: Affordances, Dynamics, and Implications." In *Networked Self: Identity, Community, and Culture on Social Network Sites*, edited by Zizi Papacharissi, 39–58. New York: Routledge.

Burrell, Jenna. 2009. "The Field Site as a Network: A Strategy for Locating Ethnographic Research." *Field Methods* 21, no. 2: 181–200. https://doi.org/10.1177/1525822X08329699.

Buscatto, Marie. 2018. "Doing Ethnography: Ways and Reasons." In *The Sage Handbook of Qualitative Data Collection*, edited by Uwe Flick, 326–43. London: Sage.

Candea, Matei. 2007. "Arbitrary Locations: In Defence of the Bounded Field-Site." *Journal of the Royal Anthropological Institute* 13, no. 1: 167–84.

Conklin, Harold C. 1957. *Hanunoo Agriculture: A Report on an Integral System of Shifting Cultivation in the Philippines*. Forestry Development Paper 12. Rome: Food and Agriculture Organization of the United Nations.

Davidjants, Jaana, and Katrin Tiidenberg. 2022. "Activist Memory Narration on Social Media: Armenian Genocide on Instagram." *New Media & Society* 24, no. 10: 2191–206.

Fayard, Anne-Laure. 2017. "Bricolage in the Field: Experimenting in Ethnography." In *The Routledge Companion to Qualitative Research in Organization Studies*, edited by Raza Mir and Sanjay Jain, 141–53. New York: Routledge.

Geertz, Clifford. 1973. *The Interpretation of Cultures*. New York: Basic Books.

Glatt, Zoë. 2023. "The Platformised Creative Worker: An Ethnographic Study of Precarity and Inequality in the London Influencer Industry (2017–2022)." PhD diss., London School of Economics and Political Science.

Gobo, Giampetro. 2008. *Doing Ethnography*. Los Angeles, CA: Sage.

Goodall, H. L. 2000. *Writing the New Ethnography*. Walnut Creek, CA: Rowman & Littlefield.

Günel, Gökçe, Saiba Varma, and Chika Watanabe. 2020. "A Manifesto for Patchwork Ethnography." *Member Voices Fieldsights* 9. https://culanth.org/fieldsights/a-manifesto-for-patchwork-ethnography.

Hammersley, Martyn, and Paul Atkinson. 1995. *Ethnography: Principles in Practice*. London: Routledge.

Herzfeld, Michael. 1997. "Anthropology: A Practice of Theory." *International Social Science Journal* 153: 301–18.

Joffe, Hélène. 2008. "The Power of Visual Material: Persuasion, Emotion, and Identification." *Diogenes* 55: 84–93.

Latchem-Hastings, Julie. 2019. "Gatekeepers in Ethnography." In *Sage Research Methods Foundations*, edited by Paul Atkinson et al. London: SAGE Publications. https://doi.org/10.4135/9781526421036835217.

Lane, Jeffrey, and Jessa Lingel. 2022. "Digital Ethnography for Sociology: Craft, Rigor, and Creativity." *Qualitative Sociology* 45: 319–26. https://doi.org/10.1007/s11133-022-09509-3.

Marcus, George E. 1995. "Ethnography In/Of the World System: The Emergence of Multi-Sited Ethnography." *Annual Review of Anthropology* 24: 95–117.

Markham, Annette N. 2005. "The Methods, Politics, and Ethics of Representation in Online Ethnography." In *The Sage Handbook of Qualitative Research*, 3rd ed., edited by Norman Denzin and Yvonna Lincoln, 793–820. Thousand Oaks, CA: Sage.

Markham, Annette N. 2007. "Ethic as Method, Method as Ethic: A Case for Reflexivity." *Journal of Information Ethics* 15, no. 2: 37–54. https://doi.org/10.3172/JIE.15.2.37.

Markham, Annette N. 2017. "Ethnography in the Digital Internet Era." In *The Sage Handbook of Qualitative Research*, edited by Norman K. Denzin and Yvonna S. Lincoln, 650–68. London: SAGE.

Mintz, S. W. 1986. *Sweetness and power*. New York: Penguin Press.

Postill, John, and Sarah Pink. 2012. "Social Media Ethnography: The Digital Researcher in a Messy Web." *Media International Australia, Incorporating Culture and Policy* 145: 123–34

Rambukkana, Nathan, ed. 2015. *Hashtag Publics: The Power and Politics of Discursive Networks*. New York: Peter Lang.

Renser, Berit. and Tiidenberg, Katrin. 2020. "Witches on Facebook: Mediatization of Neo-Paganism." *Social Media + Society* 6(3). https://doi.org/10.1177/2056305120928514 (Original work published 2020)

Schäfer, Mirko Tobias. 2011. *Bastard Culture! How User Participation Transforms Cultural Production*. Amsterdam: Amsterdam University Press.

Seaver, Nick. 2017. "Algorithms as Culture: Some Tactics for the Ethnography of Algorithmic Systems." *Big Data & Society* 4 (2): 1–12. https://doi.org/10.1177/2053951717738104.

Spradley, James. 1980. *Participant Observation*. New York: Holt, Rinehart and Winston.

Stoler, Ann Laura. 2009. *Along the Archival Grain: Epistemic Anxieties and Colonial Common Sense*. Princeton University Press.

Tiidenberg, Katrin. 2018. "Ethics in Digital Research." In *The Sage Handbook of Qualitative Data Collection*, edited by Uwe Flick, 466–79. London: Sage.

Tracy, Sarah J. 2013. *Qualitative Research Methods: Collecting Evidence, Crafting Analysis, Communicating Impact*. Malden, MA: Wiley-Blackwell.

Tunçalp, Deniz, and Patrick L. Lê. 2014. "(Re)Locating Boundaries: A Systematic Review of Online Ethnography." *Journal of Organizational Ethnography* 3, no. 1: 59–79. https://doi.org/10.1108/JOE-11-2012-0048.

Van der Nagel, Emily, and Jordan Frith. 2015. "Anonymity, Pseudonymity, and the Agency of Online Identity: Examining the Social Practices of r/Gonewild." *First Monday* 20, no. 3: 1–10.

Van Dijck, José, and Thomas Poell. 2013. "Understanding Social Media Logic." *Media and Communication* 1, no. 1: 2–14. https://doi.org/10.17645/mac.v1i1.70.

Wang, Tricia. 2012. "Writing Live Fieldnotes, Towards a More Open Ethnography." *Ethnography Matters*. https://ethnographymatters.net/blog/2012/08/02/writing-live-fieldnotes-towards-a-more-open-ethnography/.

Wolfinger, Nicholas H. 2002. "On Writing Fieldnotes: Collection Strategies and Background Expectancies." *Qualitative Research* 2, no. 1: 85–93. https://doi.org/10.1177/1468794102002001640.

Chapter 3.1

Concept: platform

Digiform ethnography: the omnipresent role of platforms in digital ethnography

Chiara Perin

In 2018, authors van Dijck, Poell, and De Waal published the book *The Platform Society*, in which they explain how platforms have become the nerve center of hyper-connected societies, impacting markets, productive and labor relations, social and identity practices, and political investments. This has led to talk about a "platform paradigm" (Burgess 2021) when referring to the prevailing economic-cultural model on the internet (and society at large), on social media, and in media-cultural production. Major players include Google, YouTube, Tencent Video, WeChat (owned by Tencent), iQiyi (controlled by Baidu), X, WhatsApp, Facebook, and Instagram (owned by Facebook), which are in turn populated by other apps such as Twitch, TikTok, and Tumblr (Burgess 2021).

But what do we mean by platforms? The term encompasses a multiplicity of meanings depending on the perspective from which it is approached (Poell et al. 2019). The Oxford English Dictionary identifies 15 different uses of the term (Gillespie 2010), ranging from a more technical approach (software, development, and production) to a more socioeconomic one (Asadullah et al. 2018). The semantic richness, characterizing the term "platform," reflects the complexity of the actors, processes, and material and discursive impacts involved. Poell et al. (2019, 3) provide a definition of "platforms" that attempts to capture this complexity, defining them as sociotechnical digital infrastructures that allow for the structuring of interactions (facilitated by their architecture) between users, who utilize these infrastructures, and "players" who provide interlinked products or services called "complementors." These relationships are structured and organized through systematic collection, selection, and algorithmic processing, as well as monetization of data created by users themselves, often freely and not always regulated, which are then reused to enhance those same services and products and generate profit.

In this regard, the notion of "datafication" (Sadowski 2019, van Dijck 2014, Mayer-Schonberger and Cukier 2013) refers to how digital platforms construct metrics and quantification on data produced by users, provided freely by them through the mere usage of these platforms, in ways that are often elusive or lacking transparency and are not clearly or explicitly communicated to the users themselves. Not only are demographic data or profiling data provided "voluntarily" by users but also behavioral metadata, which are collected through the integration of these platforms across various devices such as smartphones, smartwatches, cars, and household devices. These human interactions—including but not limited to payments, dating, musical and cinematic tastes, movements, health, and sexuality—are then algorithmically processed and either sold to third parties that structure products and services based on the trends and metrics produced by the algorithms themselves or utilized by the platform, which converts these metrics and measurements into semi-automated decisions that push certain content to attract user engagement or advertising revenue.

Helmond (2015) defines "platformization" as the rise of platforms as foundational structures of the economic model of the social web. Economic and governmental processes, as well as the reorganization of cultural practices and imaginaries, are now largely conducted, constructed, and modified through the use of digital platforms (Poell et al. 2019). The processes of platformization are becoming so pervasive in the current socioeconomic system to the point that their logics deeply reshape our society and culture (Burgess 2021, 22). Platforms structure and determine which behaviors and contents can be featured, which cannot, or should be discouraged, thereby significantly impacting our lives, practices, relationships, and identities. This impact is evident through recent techniques, both automated and non-automated, such as deplatforming, shadowbanning, and the recent restriction of content considered political or sensitive. They are deployed by platforms to moderate or restrict content and practices, which are potentially (and discretely) considered risky or contradictory, resulting in the exclusion and alienation of marginalized and stigmatized subjects (Are 2021).

Data are not naturally occurring but are indeed products of platform-driven activities that often perpetuate power inequalities within contemporary capitalism (Sadowski 2020). Given this undeniable prominence, where contemporary everyday cultures are pervaded by digital platforms (Ritter 2021), the literature in social sciences on platforms is increasingly expanding. Particularly, understanding the role and functioning of platforms is crucial for digital ethnographers who seek to comprehend not only the processes structuring social dynamics, identities, interactions, practices, and online communities and how these relationships are mediated by sociotechnical affordances and architectural structures of platforms but also how users engage with these environments, modifying them. And especially how these processes of platformization, as social phenomena, are structured and better understand how they impact society and our daily actions. Ritter (2021) argues that the omnipresence of digital platforms in everyday life challenges the typical categories of ethnography and requires a change in approach. This is because within digital platforms user relations and processes of content production tend to be massive, in real time, networked, and algorithmically structured, and platforms present themselves as very complex, fluid, and fragmented spaces.

We are currently in an era of digital platform-centered capitalism, wherein digital data are shaped, stored, and extracted in ways that facilitate their accumulation, circulation, manipulation, computation, and evaluation to generate capital and monetize human behaviors (Sadowski 2020; Sadowski 2019; Zuboff 2019). The data generation process itself serves as a means of knowledge production, defining who can access data, what qualifies as knowledge and knowledgeable, and how data can be processed (Törnberg and Uitermark 2021). Therefore, it is crucial to acknowledge participants' agency and power over their data while, if feasible, challenging the platform's monopoly on data collection, assessment, and monetization. Conducting ethnography on, through, and about a platform could be a starting point. This is especially relevant because digital ethnography increasingly involves platforms, even when they are not the direct object of study; they constitute structured fields where social processes and interactions are being shaped.

References

Are, Carolina. 2021. "The Shadowban Cycle: An Autoethnography of Pole Dancing, Nudity and Censorship on Instagram." *Feminist Media Studies* 22, no. 8: 2002–19. https://doi.org/10.1080/14680777.2021.1928259.

Asadullah, Ahmad, Isam Faik, and Atreyi Kankanhalli. 2018. "Digital Platforms: A Review and Future Directions." In *Pacific Asia Conference on Information Systems*, Yokohama, Japan.

Burgess, Jean. 2021. "Platform Studies." In *Creator Culture: An Introduction to Global Social Media Entertainment*, edited by Stuart Cunningham and David Craig, 21–38. New York: NYU Press.

Gillespie, Tarleton. 2010. "The Politics of 'Platforms.'" *New Media & Society* 12, no. 3: 347–64. https://doi.org/10.1177/1461444809342738.

Helmond, Anne. 2015. "The Platformization of the Web: Making Web Data Platform Ready." *Social Media + Society* 1, no. 2: 1–11. https://doi.org/10.1177/2056305115603080.

Mayer-Schönberger, Viktor, and Kenneth Cukier. 2013. *Big Data: A Revolution That Will Transform How We Live, Work, and Think*. Boston, MA: Houghton Mifflin Harcourt.

Poell, Thomas, David B. Nieborg, and José Van Dijck. 2019. "Platformisation." *Internet Policy Review* 8, no. 4: 1–13. https://doi.org/10.14763/2019.4.1425.

Ritter, Christian. 2021. "Rethinking Digital Ethnography: A Qualitative Approach to Understanding Interfaces." *Qualitative Research* 22, no. 6: 916–32. https://doi.org/10.1177/14687941211000540.

Sadowski, Jathan. 2019. "When Data Is Capital: Datafication, Accumulation, and Extraction." *Big Data & Society* 6, no. 1: 1–12. https://doi.org/10.1177/2053951718820549.

Sadowski, Jathan. 2020. "The Internet of Landlords: Digital Platforms and New Mechanisms of Rentier Capitalism." *Antipode* 52, no. 2: 562–80. https://doi.org/10.1111/anti.12595.

Törnberg, Petter, and Justus Uitermark. 2021. "For a Heterodox Computational Social Science." *Big Data & Society* 8, no. 2: 1–13. https://doi.org/10.1177/20539517211047725.

Van Dijck, José, Thomas Poell, and Martijn De Waal. 2018. *The Platform Society: Public Values in a Connective World*. Oxford: Oxford University Press.

Van Dijck, José. 2014. "Datafication, Dataism and Dataveillance: Big Data between Scientific Paradigm and Ideology." *Surveillance & Society* 12, no. 2: 197–208. https://doi.org/10.24908/ss.v12i2.4776.

Zuboff, Shoshana. 2019. "Surveillance Capitalism and the Challenge of Collective Action." *New Labor Forum* 28, no. 1: 10–29. https://doi.org/10.1177/1095796018819461.

Chapter 3.2

Case study
Navigating Iranian digital feminist activism through multi-sited mobile ethnography

Mitra Shamsi

In this text, I reflect on my long-term journey conducting digital ethnography to explore *digital feminist activism* in Iran. My project looked at how affordances and mediation opportunities of digital media platforms (Cammaerts 2018, 2012) are being appropriated by Iranian feminist activists and women's rights campaigners to mobilize support and contribute feminist perspectives to ongoing public debates. I also interrogated the production and circulation of *digital feminist discourses*.

Within this narrative, I focus on the methodological challenges encountered while conducting research in a complex, multilayered, and fluid field of study. The subjects of my research included activists' digital practices and interactions, as well as the digital materials they produced and spread across different digital platforms and spaces. To observe and examine events and developments within such a context, I employed a *multi-sited mobile ethnography approach* (Postill and Pink 2012), where the field of study takes shape through the movements of the ethnographer across various spaces, rather than immersing in a single location.

I will unfold the story of my research, from the moment it sparked my interest as a research idea to how it gradually developed and formed along the way, during which I had to deal with methodological confusion and ethical concerns.

Genesis of my research journey

My research traces back to December 2017, when I was captivated by Iranian women employing digital media platforms to raise public awareness about women's issues, address gender-based violence, and resist structural inequalities, particularly within the framework of the popular hybrid and digital campaigns in response to compulsory hijab enforcement.

The Iranian political structure has historically afforded women's movements limited opportunities. The long-standing suppression of women's rights activists intensified after the conservative takeover of the presidency in 2005, which pushed these movements underground, making digital media an alternative spaces for feminist activism. With this context in mind, I began occasionally archiving relevant digital materials on Facebook, and later on Twitter and Instagram, driven by curiosity before developing a clear research focus.

Over the subsequent years, as I became more determined to focus on digital feminist activism, I put more effort into monitoring and archiving events and discussions related to gendered issues from personal and collective public digital media profiles of feminists and women's rights activists. This initial phase of data collection served as a form of descriptive observation (Flick 2018), which introduced me to the research field and enabled me to identify a set of significant active digital spaces. My curiosity evolved into preliminary research questions during this phase, which continued to develop throughout the research process.

Confronting complexities

In February 2019, I began conducting focused observation (Flick 2018) to address the research questions. These questions centered on exploring diverse women's issues and demands communicated through textual and visual content shared on various digital platforms. I also started investigating the media practices and discursive framings employed by feminist activists.

During this data collection stage, I was wandering about multiple sites, including platforms popular in Iran, such as Twitter (X), Instagram, and Telegram Messenger. My observations also involved tracking popular websites and digital campaigns focused on women's causes, as well as digital tools and apps created by activists that addressed women's issues. Media coverage of women's digital and hybrid campaigns also caught my attention, persuading me to follow news media, news websites, and internet TV channels for their report on these campaigns.

These observations provided me with a more comprehensive understanding of developments and complexities in the multidimensional field under study. The subjects I studied were "mobile and multiply situated" (Marcus 1995, 102), encompassing feminist activists' practices, digital materials they produced and circulated across various platforms and spaces, and the mediation of their activism.

Conducting research in this nuanced and intricate field site proved challenging. Women's campaigns were performed in hybrid spaces where online and offline platforms and alternative digital and mainstream media intertwine. These spaces served to mobilize support, attract local and international media, and create counter-narratives through producing and disseminating (self-)mediated textual and visual digital content. Furthermore, feminist activists often travel from one digital media platform to another to reach diverse audiences and utilize the diverse dynamics of each platform.

#MeTooIran, which gained significant momentum in the summer of 2020, exemplifies these dynamics. Starting with Twitter users sharing personal accounts of sexual harassment using viral hashtags such as #rape, it quickly evolved into a collective narrative of sexual abuse cases involving public figures. The campaign led to legal initiatives, collective statements, online petitions, and multimedia productions. These cases garnered extensive media coverage, with domestic outlets often following the lead of international investigative media reports. These reports, which relied on activists' content, sparked further online discussions. The emerging Clubhouse played a significant role in facilitating discussions among feminist activists on topics such as supporting sexual abuse survivors and legal barriers to reporting such cases. Activist efforts expanded to include developing interactive apps for mapping unsafe locations (HarassWatch), launching the "MeTooIran" Instagram profile to collect sexual harassment narratives, and establishing websites to raise awareness. The campaign was rooted in digital storytelling but sustained and propagated through various formats and channels, with narratives migrating across different media spaces.

The field's shifting dynamics were prompted by government disruptions to internet access and the filtering of digital media platforms. Also, activists were constantly posting fluid and ephemeral discussions on women's issues and claims online. They were dynamically entering and exiting the field, with some new activists joining while others closing or restricting their digital spaces temporarily or permanently, possibly due to perceived risks or the significant labor involved.

Facing these intricacies and entanglements led me to conclude that a case study approach involving multiple profiles, pages, and campaigns would not align with my research. The field under study was not a single site location but rather multi-sited, encompassing multiple sites of participation and observation (Marcus 1995; Hine 2007). To effectively capture the fluidity of the field and analyze the developments within this context, I had to opt for a different research approach and practice rather than conventional ethnographic approaches, in which the researcher often immerses in a single location.

Making the ethnographic place

While grappling with the confusion, I came across Jeong's (2020) research on popular feminism in South Korea, which inspired my research direction by introducing me to the concept of mobile ethnography. In this approach, as Postill and Pink (2012) describe, the research field site is shaped within the ethnographer's narratives and movements along paths of ongoing discussions, bringing together diverse things and elements through the research process (Pink 2009). "Objects of ethnography are being reconfigured by focusing on flows and connections rather than specific locations and boundaries" (Hine 2000, 64).

Informed by this approach, I constructed an ethnographic place (Pink 2009) comprising nearly 100 digital entities and spaces such as digital media profiles, channels, websites, and campaigns. I gradually assembled the elements of this "less-structured corpus" (Mayr and Weller 2017, 108), using the mapping techniques proposed by Marcus (1995): following the people (staying with the movement of a particular group of people) and following the things (tracking the circulation of material objects and artifacts); as well as the strategy of following paths, threads, connections, and relationships.

These strategies in my research involved tracking activists and their followers in their everyday interactions and discussions from one place and practice to another. Consequently, I was able to identify new hyperlinked and interlinked debates and spaces where the subject and phenomenon under study were emerging and evolving (Hine 2008). These locations often extended beyond digital platforms, including instances of women's street resistance and activism, public policy debates, offline petitions and campaigns, and media outlets addressing gendered issues and women's claims, which made me traverse online/offline contexts.

Over nearly three years, I explored and observed relevant places and sites, immersing myself in the digital field site of Iranian feminist digital activism. During this period, I followed discussions crucial for understanding the prevailing digital feminist discourses and narratives, applying basic ethnographic research methods, including participant observation of interactions, engaging in informal conversation and small talk with participants, and text and visual analysis of digital materials.

Following Postill and Pink's (2012) recommendations, my research practices throughout the long-term observation included catching up, sharing, exploring, and interacting. As part of my research routines, I monitored updates on digital spaces, tracked the flow of discussions and debates related to women's issues, explored the topics activists were expressing, and archived key texts, when necessary, at least four days a week. Collecting background information, searching, and following hashtags were other regular practices.

As part of my routines, for instance, I followed the popular hashtag campaign, #ReverseCliche (#کلیشه_برعکس), on Farsi Twitter. This satirical initiative, which emerged in September 2017, reverses common female gender stereotypes by applying them to men. The campaign's premise is simple: exposing the absurdity of gender-biased beliefs and behaviors across cultural norms, religion, and laws. A user explained, "#ReverseCliche is about a world where equality doesn't exist, and men are seen as incompetent and unworthy!" I found myself drawn to the playful and often biting content. One tweet criticized the ban on women judges in Iranian criminal courts: "Men are too emotional to be judges!" Interestingly, the campaign incorporated visual and pop culture elements, transforming it into a metaphorical media practice that effectively communicates women's frustrations with normalized gender inequalities. #ReverseCliche gained significant media coverage through its visibility politics.

Throughout my research, I continuously archived relevant data in dedicated research accounts on digital media and organized screenshots in subject-tagged folders on my computer. However, storing samples in my accounts proved unviable due to internet disruptions by the government. During the final analysis, I could not access some samples, even with VPNs, as Instagram was filtered, forcing me to repeat parts of data collection, expending extra time and energy.

During my engagement with the field, I actively participated in the everyday practices and dialogues of participants. This involved leaving comments and reacting to the thread of comments, resharing activists' posts on my research digital accounts, and attending live broadcast events organized by activists. I also signed online petitions and created and published posts regarding women's issues on my profiles, particularly on Instagram.

I conducted systematic observation on digital spaces in the summer of 2022, when my focus was on examining a number of the most popular and visible feminist digital campaigns, profiles, and collectives, each with a considerable number of followers, as instances of feminist digital activism in Iran. This phase involved a process of selective observation (Flick 2018) aimed at identifying and selecting evidence and discussions that I intended to refer to in the final research report to highlight the main aspects of the phenomenon under study.

Ethical considerations

My research corpus included solely public digital content, profiles, collectives, and campaigns, yet recognized that the public availability of user-generated content does not negate users' privacy expectations (Buchanan and Markham 2012). However, the field's fluidity and mobility precluded introducing myself as a researcher and obtaining informed consent from participants.

Acknowledging the problematic nature of invisible presence and engagement in the research field through lurking and covert observation, I implemented several protective measures to mitigate ethical concerns: First, I anonymized participants' information, whether activists or followers, regardless of whether they used real names or pseudonyms, especially for those inside the country. I excluded any sensitive and potentially compromising information that could pose risks to participants. To limit tracking through search engines, I rephrased the content when quoting individual activists from extracted digital texts. I blurred individuals' faces in digital media images to prevent identification. These strategies aimed to safeguard the privacy and safety of participants in sensitive and potentially precarious activist practices.

Final reflections

The field's constantly evolving nature profoundly shaped my research methodology. This fluidity compelled me to track routines, mobility, and socialities rather than focusing on bounded territories and communities, aligning with the concept of mobile ethnography.

My long-term engagement in the field facilitated a thorough investigation into specific aspects of digital feminist activism in Iran that emerged during the project, allowing me to focus adaptively on newly arising areas throughout the research process. I had the chance to explore several important aspects of digital feminist activism in Iran, including the formation of social hierarchies among activists and followers, and the creative use of local languages, particularly in their playful and satirical expressions and practices, which added layers of meaning to the digital narratives.

The multi-sited mobile ethnography approach guided me in my journey through the "messy web" (Postill and Pink 2012) to map digital feminist discourses and identify emerging patterns and themes while capturing the dynamics, interconnectedness, content, and context of feminist digital activism.

References

Buchanan, Elizabeth, and A. Markham. 2012. "Ethical Decision-Making and Internet Research." Recommendations from the AoIR Ethics Working Committee (Version 2.0). *Association of Internet Researchers* (AoIR), 1–19.

Cammaerts, Bart. 2012. "Protest Logics and the Mediation Opportunity Structure." *European Journal of Communication* 27 (2): 117–34.

Cammaerts, Bart. 2018. "The Circuit of Protest: A Conceptual Framework for Studying the Mediation Opportunity Structure." In *Current Perspectives on Communication and Media Research*, edited by Laura Peja, Nico Carpentier, Fausto Colombo, Maria Francesca Murru, Simone Tosoni, Richard Kilborn, Leif Kramp et al., 131–145. Bremen: Edition Lumière.

Flick, Uwe. 2018. *An Introduction to Qualitative Research*. Thousand Oaks, CA: Sage.

Hine, Christine. 2000. *Virtual Ethnography*. London: Sage Publications Ltd.

Hine, Christine. 2007. "Multisited Ethnography as a Middle Range Methodology for Contemporary STS." *Science, Technology, & Human Values* 32 (6): 652–71.

Hine, Christine. 2008. "Virtual Ethnography: Modes, Varieties, Affordances." In *The Sage Handbook of Online Research Methods,* edited by Nigel G. Fielding, Raymond M. Lee and Grant Blank, 257–70. London: SAGE.

Jeong, Euisol. 2020. "Troll Feminism: The Rise of Popular Feminism in South Korea." PhD diss., University of York.

Marcus, George E. 1995. "Ethnography in/of the World System: The Emergence of Multi-Sited." *Annual Review of Anthropology* 24 (1): 95–117.

Mayr, Philipp, and Katrin Weller. 2017. "Think before You Collect: Setting up a Data Collection Approach for Social Media Studies." In *The Sage Handbook of Social Media Research Methods,* edited by Luke Sloan and Anabel Quan-Haase, 107–24. London: SAGE.

Pink, Sarah. 2009. *Doing Sensory Ethnography*. London: Sage.

Postill, John, and Sarah Pink. 2012. "Social Media Ethnography: The Digital Researcher in a Messy Web." *Media International Australia* 145 (1): 123–34.

Chapter 4

Ethnography in virtual worlds

Rachel Berryman and Crystal Abidin

Introduction

In their 2012 book *Virtual Worlds: A Handbook of Method*, digital media scholars Tom Boellstorff, Bonnie Nardi, Celia Pearce, and T.L. Taylor draw on their expertise on *Second Life*, *World of Warcraft*, There.com, and *EverQuest*, respectively, to tease out logistical, institutional, and ethical issues pertaining to virtual worlds research and to offer guidelines and techniques for navigating this emergent terrain. By the early 2010s, scholars had already spent over two decades sinking their teeth into varieties of virtual worlds, including Massively Multiplayer Online Role-Playing Games (MMORPGs) like *World of Warcraft* and *EverQuest*, and 3D societies for communities to hang out, like *Second Life* and There.com. We write this chapter in the mid-2020s, as scholars are grappling with a season of rapid technologization and platformization, in part propelled by a global pandemic that forced our hands into compulsory—even if ad hoc—digitalization across industries worldwide. Specifically, we offer that the discourse around virtual worlds has appeared to take a turn in three instances.

Fantasy socialization vs. pragmatic interactions

First, the early 2010s rhetoric of virtual worlds as a space for fantasy entertainment and socialization has been usurped by the corporate rhetoric of virtual worlds as necessary instruments to overcome physical-world constraints. Specifically, virtual worlds are marketed as tools for lubricating social interactions and fostering productivity and pragmatic interactions amid the forced pivot to mass digitalization in workplaces and educational institutions.

Among the most popular of these corporate virtual worlds is Gather.Town (Gather), promoted as a "virtual HQ" for "distributed" or "remote teams" to "communicate, collaborate, and feel more connected" ("Gather | Virtual HQ for Remote Teams," n.d.). The platform touts its facilitation of both

DOI: 10.4324/9781032672663-17

spontaneous "water cooler chats" and scheduled "productive conversations" ("Gather | Virtual HQ for Remote Teams," n.d.), and frames virtual worlds as a "metaverse" comprising "a virtual layer over the physical world" ("About," n.d.). Higher education institutes have also recommended Gather.Town for its ability to "transform video communication into sociable serendipitous interactions" (Abrego and Xin 2022).

The large-scale consequences of these corporate virtual worlds were anticipated by scholars a decade ago, pointing to the demands of a "presence bleed" (Gregg 2013), where the solicitation of compulsory performances of professionalism online—technologies, platforms, and devices—intrudes into the personal lives of employees in the guise of greater workplace flexibility (Gregg 2011).

Distributive exclusivity vs. discursive inclusivity

Second, the concept of and access to virtual worlds have been mainstreamed by big tech, with corporations/platforms like Meta/Facebook rebranding the discourse as "metaverses." Specifically, Facebook's metaverse describes itself as a "virtual reality space" for socializing and collaborating; the "next evolution in social connection and the successor to the mobile internet"; and a space to "connect," "learn," "shop," "work," and "play" with other metaverse participants ("What is the Metaverse?," n.d.). The mechanics of accessing this metaverse are intertwined with technologies of "virtual reality," "augmented reality," and "smart glasses" ("The Metaverse is the Future of Digital Connection," n.d.), focusing especially on products that are custom-produced and sold without third parties, such as Meta's Quest 3 headset and other compatible accessories ("Meta Quest 3: Mixed Reality VR Headset," n.d.).

Yet, despite the *distributive exclusivity* dominating the mechanics of the metaverse, Meta has labored to produce a *discursive inclusivity* through the branding of its products. In the company's "About" page, Meta claims that the metaverse "isn't just for gamers or developers, it will be for everyone. And our hope is that in the next decade it will reach a billion people" ("What is the Metaverse?," n.d.). It offers the corporate lore that these virtual worlds are "built by everyone ... developed every day by all sorts of imaginative people", and draws on the discourse of co-creation by promoting partnerships with "creators" ("The Metaverse is the Future of Digital Connection," n.d.), and offering "business opportunities" to attract new customers to an augmented reality market that is estimated to be worth USD$82billion by 2025 ("Metaverse for Business: Immersive Experiences for Customers," n.d.). In fact, the company has even outrightly announced that the metaverse is guided by the values of "privacy," "safety," and "inclusivity" for all users ("The Metaverse is the Future of Digital Connection," n.d.).

Spectator sport vs. spectator spot

Third, the flourishing collaborations and collapse of genres across creative industries have seen virtual worlds move from being a *spectator sport* where avatars or gamers perform or compete for a willing audience, to a *spectator spot* where the platform is relegated to a mere hosting site for events, launches, and exclusive access to paywalled perks. This is most evident through the collaborations between virtual worlds and K-pop idol groups, with tech companies leveraging the massive global popularity of specific K-pop groups and artists to launch or reinvigorate interest in virtual world platforms.

This history can be traced back to 2018, when K-pop idols were first invited to perform live at the opening ceremony for the *League of Legends* (LoL) world championship finals (known as "Worlds"), held in Incheon, South Korea. Rapper Bobby of idol group iKON performed the track "RISE" in a mix of Korean and English, alongside artists Mako and The Glitch Mob (League of Legends 2018b). Bobby also featured in the song's official music video produced by Riot Music Team from Riot Games, the company behind the LoL franchise (Shin 2018b). Other Korean artists featured in the opening ceremony included singers Jeon Soyeon and Cho Miyeon from the idol group (G)I-DLE, who performed as part of a LoL-themed girl group called K/DA alongside American singers Madison Beer and Jaira Burns (Shin 2018a). K/DA's performance of their debut single "Pop/Stars" involved an augmented reality element, with the on-stage singers dancing alongside 3D versions of LoL characters to promote the release of new character cosmetics (skins) that could be purchased in-game (League of Legends 2018a; Lee 2018).

Reactions to the 2018 Worlds performances featuring K-pop idols were overwhelmingly warm and welcoming, with myriad fan reactions applauding the collaboration between the LoL virtual world and K-pop industry: "MY TWO WORLDS ARE COLLIDING" (MiggySmallzKPop 2018); "I think BOBBY was a great choice! Not only does his rap work but the dude also plays League (I'm pretty sure). It's great to see an idol fan collab on one of his faves" (MiggySmallzKPop 2018). An enthusiastic response also followed K/DA's debut, with the YouTube video of their performance accumulating over 20 million views in just four days (Crecente 2018). Their single "Pop/Stars" also topped the Billboard and Google Play charts, reaching number two on iTunes, and was soon announced as an addition to the highly anticipated virtual reality (VR) rhythm game *Beat Saber*, scheduled to launch the following month (Crecente 2018).

Following the 2018 Worlds, various music forums registered chatter from both local Korean and international fans strategizing their participation in virtual game worlds like LoL for the opportunity of chancing into their favorite idol-gamer, or for the experience of listening to Riot Games' collaboration songs in-world. Prior research has noted the potential and prowess of K-pop fans for lubricating the establishment of platforms into domestic and foreign markets (Abidin and Lee 2023). Likewise, so successful was the first LoL and K-pop collaboration that in 2020, Riot Games announced that K/DA would release a five-track EP with intentions to reach the Chinese market. Alongside the original four singers and their LoL character counterparts, the EP also featured Chinese singer Lexie Liu (Rowley 2020). Liu provided the voice for a new LoL character called Seraphine, who Riot Games had initially (anonymously) launched on Instagram, Twitter, and Soundcloud, in an effort to crossover with the emerging "virtual influencer" industry, discussed below (Goslin 2020; "Seraphine (@seradotwav)," n.d.).

Amid these evolving discourses and experiences, this chapter reflects on what it means to conduct digital ethnography in virtual worlds as of the mid-2020s. We begin by briefly describing two of the authors' ethnographic projects, which intersected with the shifts in virtual worlds described above. The first project involves "virtual influencers"—fictional, animated characters designed to accumulate audiences on social media—and their evolving performances of "virtuality" in response to COVID-19 lockdowns and metaverse hype between 2020 and 2022. The second project continues the discussion of the remarkable success of K-pop collaborations with virtual worlds, focusing on YG idol girl group BLACKPINK's collaborations with various virtual worlds between 2022 and 2024, and the new genre of virtual worlds enjoyed by both gaming and music fans. Following this, we review how ethnographic approaches have historically been applied to virtual worlds and conclude with recommendations for current and aspiring digital ethnographers, given the ongoing efforts to reimagine the ownership, scope, and appeal of virtual worlds in an era of platformization.

Virtual influencers, metaverse inhabitants

Virtual influencers are fictional characters that are "native to social media, with no singular referent in the offline world" (Berryman, Abidin, and Leaver 2021, 1). Their designation as "influencers" reflects their efforts to accumulate online attention by engaging with the cultures and vernaculars of visual social media platforms like Instagram, Sina Weibo, Xiaohongshu (RedNote), and TikTok. Some virtual influencers are drawn by hand, but most are made using digital animation software, with faces and bodies created with 3D modeling and computer-generated imagery. Virtual influencers can take on a fantastical aspect (appearing as anthropomorphized animals, aliens, and the like), but many of the most popular are highly photorealistic and almost indistinguishable from human influencers.

Virtual influencers entered mainstream view in 2018, following a wave of press coverage about American virtual influencer Miquela Sousa, known then chiefly by her Instagram username "Lil Miquela" (e.g., Bobila 2018). By the early 2020s, the number of virtual influencers on Instagram was estimated to be in the hundreds, with a combined follower count in the multi-millions (Baklanov 2022).

Although virtual influencers are digital entities, they have a strong connection to the actual world. For example, the "look" of virtual influencers is often calibrated to align with regional preferences—particularly along lines of gender, ethnicity, and language—and their content is deliberately styled to resonate with local audiences (Abidin 2023). Much of what virtual influencers post to social media is also grounded in actual locations. Like human influencers, they use visual social media platforms to document moments (both exceptional and mundane) from their lives. In these posts, virtual influencers often appear at cafes and restaurants, galleries and museums, stores, and activations that actually exist. This fusing of virtuality and actuality is a core component of virtual influencers' appeal, serving to visually distinguish their content in online spaces that are hyper-saturated and highly templated. However, a longitudinal analysis of virtual influencers reveals their shifting treatment of virtuality to suit industry trends and to continually reposition themselves as ideal commercial partners.

For instance, in the early days of the COVID-19 pandemic, as people around the world were sheltering in place, several virtual influencers stopped posting new content, perhaps feeling as Hirokuni Genie Miyaji (creator of Japanese virtual influencer Liam Nikuro) that "continuing to post content outdoors would be disrespectful to real people staying at home and doing their part" (Begum 2020). However, for other producers, the newfound value of "virtual" alternatives during the pandemic presented an unmissable opportunity. Establishing new distance from the local contexts that had previously grounded their content, many virtual influencers began drawing attention to their more-than-human capabilities. For example, *Time Out* magazine published an "interview" with Singaporean virtual influencer Rae, where she explained, "Being virtual, I'm not bound by physical or geographical constraints. No stay home notice for this virtual girl. Who needs a passport or vaccine? I can be anywhere I want" (qtd. in Khalid 2021). Press reports suggest that brands were convinced, with one article for *Bloomberg.com* carrying the headline, "Virtual Influencers Make Real Money While Covid Locks Down Human Stars" (Ong 2020).

Another shift occurred amid growing industry hype for the metaverse. Despite an array of definitions, for tech enthusiasts and Silicon Valley entrepreneurs, the dominant vision of the metaverse involved multiple, interoperable platforms that could deliver an immersive and uninterrupted digital experience of all aspects of daily life ("What is the Metaverse?," n.d.). Virtual influencers were a natural fit for this emerging discourse; their digital composition made them prime candidates to serve as the metaverse's first residents (Leaver and Berryman 2022). By this time, virtual influencers had already appeared in other virtual worlds, including multiplayer video games like *Animal Crossing* (e.g., "Imma's Invites Everyone to Visit Her House in Animal Crossing" 2020), as well as social world mobile apps like *Zepeto* (e.g., "Imma in ZEPETO," n.d.) and *Avakin Life* (e.g., Promoview 2022). As interest in the metaverse grew, many virtual influencers integrated the term into their self-branding efforts: Thai virtual influencer Ai Ailynn adopted the label "Metaverse Influencer" (Mei 2021), while others appeared in online marketplaces for virtual goods, such as the NFT (Non-Fungible Token) marketplace OpenSea (e.g., "Esther Olofsson Collectibles," n.d.), and virtual fashion marketplace DressX (e.g., "OHROZY," n.d.). To position themselves as worthy residents of the metaverse, virtual influencers accentuated their distance from actuality, showcasing the effortlessness with which they could access various virtual worlds, and drawing attention to their composition of binary code, pixels, and bytes.

K-pop collaborations with virtual worlds

As evidenced earlier in the chapter, *League of Legends*' collaborations with the K-pop industry to usher in new audiences, consumers, and fans from international markets were met with resounding success. In fact, this formula would go on to be replicated by several virtual gaming worlds, and with many K-pop idol groups and artists in the years to come. This section specifically considers the collaborations of one of the most internationally popular and highest-grossing K-pop idol girl groups of the 2010s and 2020s: BLACKPINK. The idol group features four members of various nationalities, ethnicities, and intercultural backgrounds, spanning the Australian, Korean, New Zealand, and Thai markets.

In July 2022, the virtual world mobile game app *PUBG MOBILE* collaborated with BLACKPINK for the release of a special track, "Ready for Love." Marketed as the "PUBG MOBILE x BLACKPINK SPECIAL TRACK," the song was exclusively debuted in-app at an online event known as "THE VIRTUAL," described as "BLACKPINK'S FIRST IN-GAME CONCERT IN PUBG MOBILE" ("PUBG MOBILE X BLACKPINK," n.d.). *PUBG MOBILE* released an exclusive poster and music video of the four BLACKPINK artists embodied as avatars, with "collaboration outfits and voice packs" offered to users to customize the characters according to styling from hit songs like "Ddu-du Ddu-du," "Kill This Love," and "Lovesick Girls" ("PUBG MOBILE X BLACKPINK," n.d.). The event was highly anticipated by fans worldwide, especially as publicity and preview material were teased on BLACKPINK's official social accounts, and registered over 12.5 million in-game concert views ("PUBG MOBILE X BLACKPINK," n.d.).

Later in October 2022, mobile game app *ZEPETO* followed suit, launching the virtual world "BLACKPINK SQUARE" and enabling fans to play and dance as animated BLACKPINK avatars ("ZEPETO World—BLACKPINK SQUARE," n.d.; LesBleus FFF 2020). The collaboration also featured an exclusive music video "BLACKPINK—'Pink Venom' M/V—ZEPETO version," but this has registered just 119 thousand views at the time of writing (Equinox Entertainment 2022). This discrepancy with *PUBG MOBILE*'s earlier success is likely because publicity and preview material for the collaboration were hosted mostly on the Equinox Entertainment YouTube channel and *ZEPETO*'s official social accounts, which did not adequately appeal to K-pop fans who are more prone to supporting the official accounts of the idol groups. Further, the collaboration did not offer new tracks, which are usually the main draw for fans.

In August 2023, TakeOne Company launched *BLACKPINK THE GAME*, a virtual world game that aims for players to "Become BLACKPINK's producer and manage your own agency, solve puzzles to clear schedules for BLACKPINK" (TakeOne Company, n.d.). The game also provided options for players to customize members in bespoke in-app outfits and complete small quests and games with friends in-world (TakeOne Company). Perhaps learning from the success of the *PUBG MOBILE* collaboration, TakeOne Company also debuted an exclusive music video, "BLACKPINK THE GAME—'THE GIRLS' MV," hosted on BLACKPINK's YouTube channel. The video has registered 108 million views at the time of writing (BLACKPINK 2023).

Following the launch of *PUBG MOBILE*'s special track, *ZEPETO*'s bespoke in-game world, and TakeOne Company's music video, all via avatars in the likeness of BLACKPINK, in December 2023, Meta Quest collaborated with the idol group to promote its Oculus headsets and Meta Quest platform. "BLACKPINK: A VR Encore" was a virtual concert hosted on Meta Quest between December 26, 2023, and January 31, 2024, allowing fans to relive the finale of the Born Pink World Tour at Gocheok Sky Dome in Seoul in a VR format, albeit in a virtual world setting of a desert oasis à la Coachella ("BLACKPINK: A VR Encore," n.d.). This collaboration was a part of Meta Quest's extensive Music Valley Concert Series, which claims to offer "immersive and unparalleled stage views of your favorite music artists without ever having to leave the comfort of your home" ("Music Valley Concert Series," n.d.). The event was sold out ahead of its launch (Vouloumanos 2024).

Taking stock of ethnography in virtual worlds

With these two accounts, we gesture toward the complexities and nuances involved in ethnographic projects involving contemporary virtual worlds. However, scholars have been using ethnographic principles and adapting ethnographic methods to study virtual worlds since the 1990s. The first generation of virtual world ethnographies—published in the late 1990s and early 2000s—coincided with conceptualizations of the internet as a destination (i.e., cyberspace). This vision was compatible with cultural anthropology's tradition of traveling to distant and unfamiliar fields, with scholars recounting their first experiences of "going online" (Markham 1998) and "logging on" (Kendall 2002). Notable studies of early virtual worlds include sociologist Lori Kendall's (2002) analysis of a MUD (Multi-User Dungeon/Domain/Dimension) she calls "BlueSky"; internet studies scholar Annette N. Markham's (1998) study of the online MOO (MUD, Object-Oriented) "Diversity University"; and sociologist T.L. Taylor's (2002) research on the multi-user system known as "The Dreamscape."

Whereas the MUDs and MOOs studied by Kendall (2002) and Markham (1998) were text-based, combining narrative descriptions and user commands (see also Cherny 1999), "The Dreamscape" studied by Taylor (2002) incorporated computer-graphics, and was an early case of a virtual world with visual representations of users and their surroundings, a multimodal experience that would later become the norm for virtual world experiences. These pioneering studies employed ethnography to explore questions of identity and sociality among early internet users and were particularly interested in the affordances of online spaces that encouraged fluidity, creativity, and connection.

The notion of ethnography for virtual worlds was formally expanded by anthropologist Tom Boellstorff (2008) in his study of the popular virtual world *Second Life*. Boellstorff defines virtual worlds as "places of human culture realized by computer programs through the Internet," drawing attention to "three fundamental elements" of virtual worlds as "(1) places, (2) inhabited by persons, and (3) enabled by online technologies" (17).

Drawing from two years of fieldwork in *Second Life*, Boellstorff (2008) sets out to illuminate "the potential of ethnography for studying virtual worlds" (24). His ethnographic approach to studying *Second Life* emphasizes participant observation, taking inspiration from the anthropological canon in which this method is central to unearthing and analyzing tacit "aspects of culture" that are not necessarily "available for conscious reflection" (68). Inspired by his experiences researching gay men in Indonesia, for his study of *Second Life*, Boellstorff "complemented participant observation with interviews, archival research, the analysis of texts, and focus groups" (76). His analysis draws primarily on fieldnotes, but also includes text-based chat logs, in-world screenshots, as well as documents like "websites, blogs, and even full-fledged periodicals (with staff and advertising)" (79). Access to these documents not only afforded commentary useful for contextualizing in-world events but were also resources accessed by *Second Life* residents themselves, contributing to their experience of the virtual world despite technically sitting beyond its boundaries (see also Taylor 1999, 445).

For Boellstorff, the cultures of virtual worlds can and should be studied on their own terms and need not be verified or complemented by fieldwork in the actual world. Other studies of virtual worlds, especially those interested in the relation between "online" and "offline" (e.g., Kendall 2002; Taylor 2002), often incorporate in-person interviews with virtual world users and conduct participant observation at "offline" gatherings and events.

Theorizing digital ethnography in new virtual worlds

In later writing, Boellstorff (2010) identifies three approaches to researching virtual worlds and plots these along an "ethnographic scale" increasingly narrow in focus (129). The first is "virtual/actual interface," examining the interplay between virtual and actual worlds; the second is "virtual/virtual interface," which adopts a comparative approach to analyzing more than one virtual world; and the third is "virtual worlds on their own terms," which focuses on the cultural customs, mores, and traditions experienced within a single virtual world (129–30). We propose that the current configuration of virtual worlds elevates the need to consider a fourth approach, which we might call "virtual/platform interface."

Sitting somewhere between "virtual/actual interface" and "virtual/virtual interface," looking at the interface of virtual and platform involves studying virtual experiences in the context of platformization or "the rise of the platform as the dominant infrastructural and economic model of the social web" (Helmond 2015, 1). The process of platformization has accelerated since the mid-2010s and encompasses how "platforms transform market structures and curate content" as well as how "cultural industries actively organiz[e] production and distribution around platforms" (Nieborg and Poell 2018, 4287). To this end, although there is already a corpus of methodological reflections about ethnography and virtual worlds—including Taylor's (1999) discussion of the "research challenges" of analyzing life in virtual worlds; Boellstorff's (2008) detailed reflection on virtual anthropology and ethics in *Coming of Age in Second Life*; and *Ethnography and Virtual Worlds: A Handbook of Method* (Boellstorff et al. 2012), mentioned in our introduction—with valuable insights to guide aspiring digital ethnographers, we recognize that researching the virtual/platform interface requires heightened attention to several aspects.

Drawing from our own fieldwork experiences, we identify five principles for researchers of contemporary virtual worlds to consider in their ethnographic practice: field agnosticism, user plurality, platform specificity, ethnographer agility, and experience preservation.

Field agnosticism

Recalling the suggestion of anthropologist Sarah Pink and colleagues (2016) that digital ethnographers adopt a "non-digital-centric" approach, we encourage researchers of virtual worlds to remain open to the different environments to which their research questions might lead. By "following" (Postill 2015) their phenomenon of interest, researchers can understand virtual worlds and their cultures within the broader "network" (see Burrell 2009) of environments traversed by users and commercialized by producers. Depending on the research question, this agnosticism may mean incorporating sources such as official websites, promotional materials, and press releases; community forums, user reviews, or social media threads; user-created "mod" (modification) repositories or "CC" (custom content) marketplaces; trade press, developer interviews, software release notes, or investor reports, among others. Embracing this agnosticism may also lead the researcher to conduct fieldwork at industry conventions or fan events, or inform the selection of other methods, like interviews, or app walkthroughs (see Light, Burgess, and Duguay 2018).

User plurality

Despite Silicon Valley's vision of an interoperable infrastructure navigated with a single, persistent online persona, the current landscape of virtual worlds comprises multiple, siloed environments, each running on proprietary systems. Some virtual worlds offer a wider variety of experiences than others, but there is at present no "all-encompassing" architecture for virtual worlds. Users are likely to engage with more than one virtual world, using each for different experiences or communities. Researchers should thus be sensitive to plurality, as users are incarnated as different avatars or take on different personas in different virtual worlds. As the previous section highlighted, questions of identity and embodiment have long been of interest to scholars of virtual worlds. Taylor (1999) points out that "the moment you enter a virtual environment you immediately have *at least* two bodies: a corporeal one and a digital one" (439, original emphasis). This is further complicated by the fact that "some users maintain a consistency within a single avatar or character, [but] many do not"

(Taylor 1999, 439), with "alts"—alternative accounts owned by a single user, which appear as "entirely different avatars with different screen names" (Boellstorff 2008, 80)—being a common practice in virtual worlds. Understanding how and why users design, curate, and present themselves in virtual worlds can help to illuminate perceptions of that virtual world's cultures and norms. Literature about social media self-presentation will no doubt prove useful for these discussions, given that this body of scholarship has already examined how self-presentation is adapted across platforms (e.g., van Dijck 2013) or modulated within the same platform for different audiences (e.g., Darr and Doss 2022) or degrees of disclosure (e.g., Leavitt 2015).

Platform specificity

As with any digital ethnography, researchers studying virtual worlds must be attuned to the unique features, capabilities, or "affordances" (Bucher and Helmond 2018) that shape their field sites. This also has precedence in social media studies: scholars have highlighted the need for "platform-sensitivity" (Bucher and Helmond 2018, 242), called for greater attention to "platform vernaculars" (Gibbs 2018) and "platform specificities" (Kaye et al. 2021), and proposed methods like "visual cross-platform analysis" (W. Pearce et al. 2020) to emphasize the relationship between the design and infrastructure of different online environments to modes of engagement, sociality, and creativity. Additionally, researchers should be attuned to the kinaesthetic and haptic variability of virtual worlds and the impact and experience of the devices, equipment, and hardware required to access them.

Ethnographer agility

The methodological reflections of digital ethnographers remind us that virtual worlds are as unstable and ephemeral as any other online phenomena. A particularly compelling example can be found in social scientist Monica J. Barratt and sociologist Alexia Maddox's (2016) ethnographic research on the dark web: on the first day of fieldwork, the authors discovered that their primary field site—an illicit marketplace called Silk Road—had been seized by the FBI and could no longer be accessed. The researchers were forced to adjust their initial plans and quickly pivoted to following the community from the Silk Road to a series of new online locations (see also Maddox 2020). A similar approach was adopted by game designer and scholar Celia Pearce (2009) in her examination of the afterlives of virtual worlds, and the migration of their users to new online environments and communities. Both studies remind us of the need for agility and adaptation to unforeseen disruptions.

Experience preservation

Finally, under the logic of platformization, virtual worlds have become subject to the same fast-changing priorities, accelerated development, demanding financial expectations, and logics of acquisition as social media platforms. This has important consequences for digital ethnographers studying virtual worlds, as it means they are often researching cultures, phenomena, and technologies that will be inaccessible to future readers. It is thus more important than ever that ethnographers acknowledge the temporal specificity of their research and take seriously ethnography's call to generate "thick descriptions" (Geertz 1973) to document, archive, and preserve the present for researchers in the future.

Conclusion

This chapter has focused on the changing landscape, evolving discourse, and new developments in virtual worlds, especially considering our original research on virtual influencers and K-pop collaborations with virtual worlds. In closing, we offer three reflections on the contemporary trajectory of virtual worlds thus far.

First, despite the initial hype and the extensive corporate branding, several virtual world projects faced significant losses and did not take off. Facebook/Meta's commitment to its metaverse product as the next frontier was widely recognized through its public name change to "Meta" in October 2021, in alignment with the corporate narrative on the "metaverse" (Clayton 2023). However, the company's overt and continued focus on ownership, control, and exclusive dissemination required customers to fully invest in a brand-new platform, and did not offer much (if any) interoperability. In other words, the inertia for buy-in was high. Further, Meta's Reality Labs, which oversees the development of VR and AR, recorded a USD$4.4billion loss in Q3 2024, and accrued more than USD$45billion in losses between 2020 and 2024 (McGuire 2024). These losses are not exclusive to Facebook/Meta; metaverse projects by blue chip companies like Disney and Microsoft were also closed in 2023 (McGuire 2024).

Second, in their quick pivot to the metaverse, many companies and platforms did not offer a holistic virtual world experience, could not fully utilize the features and affordances of virtual worlds, and failed to retain or even attract a user base. For instance, Facebook/Meta launched Horizon Worlds, where users can explore virtual world settings, including "cafes, comedy clubs, night clubs, basketball courts—to hang out and play games," but early waves of users quickly complained that the worlds were often empty and mostly populated by children, and graphics were of poor quality (Clayton 2023). Many reviews of prolific metaverse events also registered disappointment. For instance, a viral review of Meta Quest's "BLACKPINK: A VR Encore" noted that the experience "felt more like watching a live stream on a giant screen than being part of a virtual world," that "the experience wasn't as interactive or immersive," and that users "could've just projected the concert on [their] wall for a similar front-row experience without needing the headset" (Vouloumanos 2024).

Finally, perhaps the most significant milestone that mainstreamed virtual worlds across platforms, genres, and industries was the successful collaborations with already established fields like the K-pop idol market. Loyal fans make for ardent prospective consumers who are happy to support their favorite artists in various collaborations, across platforms, within worlds. BLACKPINK's string of successful virtual game world collaborations drew in new demographics of game consumers, including female, younger, and older fans as players. Following in this trajectory, when Worlds was held in Seoul in 2023, Riot Games engaged Gen Z idol girl group NewJeans to sing its theme (League of Legends 2023), which marked the first time that an entire idol group was featured (Tuting 2023). Hinging on the massive popularity of NewJeans—who, like BLACKPINK, draw on intercultural backgrounds spanning Australian, Korean, and Vietnamese heritage—Riot Games also engaged the group to promote fashion and styling inspired by in-world characters from LoL. But perhaps the most enduring legacy of these successful collaborations is the evolutions that happen at the grassroots level. Alongside the usual fandom vernacular of compiling easter eggs in music videos, curating funny edits and fandom lore, and producing dance covers on YouTube, since 2020, fan-produced 360° VR versions of official K-pop music videos have been growing popular (e.g., BLACKPINK UP n.d.), indicating not only the mainstreaming but also the affective embrace of virtual world platforms, technologies, and creator practices.

References

Abidin, Crystal. 2023. "AI Influencers in Asia: Navigating Cultural Norms and Market Trends." *Digital Business Lab* (blog). November 30. https://digital-business-lab.com/2023/11/ai-influencers-in-asia-navigating-cultural-norms-and-market-trends/.

Abidin, Crystal, and Jin Lee. 2023. "K-Pop TikTok: TikTok's Expansion into South Korea, TikTok Stage, and Platformed Glocalization." *Media International Australia* 188 (1): 86–111. https://doi.org/10.1177/1329878X231186445.

"About." n.d. Gather. Accessed December 10, 2024. https://www.gather.town/about.

Abrego, Josu, and Bonnie Xin. 2022. "Explore Gather.Town and Its Potential as a New Teaching Resource." *UNSW Sydney Education* (blog). February 16. https://www.education.unsw.edu.au/news-events/news/gather.town.

Baklanov, Nick. 2022. "The Top Virtual Instagram Influencers in 2022." *HypeAuditor Blog* (blog). December 21. https://hypeauditor.com/blog/the-top-virtual-instagram-influencers-in-2022/.

Barratt, Monica J, and Alexia Maddox. 2016. "Active Engagement with Stigmatised Communities through Digital Ethnography." *Qualitative Research* 16 (6): 701–19. https://doi.org/10.1177/1468794116648766.

Begum, Haneesa. 2020. "Instagram Influencer, Singer and Model – And Computer Generated: Rise of the Virtual Kings and Queens of Social Media." *South China Morning Post*, July 8, sec. Lifestyle. https://www.scmp.com/lifestyle/arts-culture/article/3091979/instagram-influencer-singer-and-model-and-computer-generated.

Berryman, Rachel, Crystal Abidin, and Tama Leaver. 2021. "A Topography of Virtual Influencers." In *AoIR Selected Papers of Internet Research*. https://doi.org/10.5210/spir.v2021i0.12145.

BLACKPINK, dir. 2023. *Blackpink The Game - 'The Girls' MV*. https://www.youtube.com/watch?v=cSqOY5nktfg.

"BLACKPINK: A VR Encore." n.d. Meta Quest. Accessed January 26, 2025. https://www.oculus.com/experiences/event/993433791717337/.

BLACKPINK UP. n.d. "BLACKPINK 360° VR." YouTube. Accessed January 26, 2025. https://www.youtube.com/playlist?list=PLZ-wvQwY-TR4A0n-eBxQ3_griZeYPmoUl.

Bobila, Maria. 2018. "Can AI-Powered CGI Creations Take Over the Influencer Space?" *Fashionista*, April 20. https://fashionista.com/2018/04/lil-miquela-cgi-influencers-trend.

Boellstorff, Tom. 2008. *Coming of Age in Second Life: An Anthropologist Explores the Virtually Human*. Princeton, NJ: Princeton University Press.

Boellstorff, Tom. 2010. "A Typology of Ethnographic Scales for Virtual Worlds." In *Online Worlds: Convergence of the Real and the Virtual*, edited by William Sims Bainbridge, 123–33. London: Springer London. https://link.springer.com/10.1007/978-1-84882-825-4_10.

Boellstorff, Tom, Bonnie Nardi, Celia Pearce, and T.L. Taylor. 2012. *Ethnography and Virtual Worlds: A Handbook of Method*. Princeton, NJ: Princeton University Press.

Bucher, Taina, and Anne Helmond. 2018. "The Affordances of Social Media Platforms." In *The SAGE Handbook of Social Media*, edited by Jean Burgess, Alice Marwick, and Thomas Poell, 233–53. London: SAGE Publications Ltd. https://doi.org/10.4135/9781473984066.n14.

Burrell, Jenna. 2009. "The Field Site as a Network: A Strategy for Locating Ethnographic Research." *Field Methods* 21 (2): 181–99. https://doi.org/10.1177/1525822X08329699.

Cherny, Lynn. 1999. *Conversation and Community: Chat in a Virtual World*. Center for the Study of Language and Information. https://press.uchicago.edu/ucp/books/book/distributed/C/bo3645191.html.

Clayton, James. 2023. "Metaverse: What Happened to Mark Zuckerberg's Next Big Thing?" *BBC*, September 25. https://www.bbc.com/news/technology-66913551.

Crecente, Brian. 2018. "The Making of 'League of Legends' Augmented Reality 'Pop/Stars.'" *Variety* (blog). December 21. https://variety.com/2018/gaming/features/k-da-pop-stars-beat-saber-1203093283/.

Darr, Christopher R., and Erin F. Doss. 2022. "The Fake One Is the Real One: Finstas, Authenticity, and Context Collapse in Teen Friend Groups." *Journal of Computer-Mediated Communication* 27 (4): 1–10. https://doi.org/10.1093/jcmc/zmac009.

van Dijck, José. 2013. "'You Have One Identity': Performing the Self on Facebook and LinkedIn." *Media, Culture & Society* 35 (2): 199–215. https://doi.org/10.1177/0163443712468605.

Equinox Entertainment, dir. 2022. *BLACKPINK - 'Pink Venom' M/V - ZEPETO Version || Equinox Entertainment*. https://www.youtube.com/watch?v=BYrxZ8V6qHI.

"Esther Olofsson Collectibles." n.d. OpenSea. Accessed January 26, 2025. https://opensea.io/collection/esther-olofsson-collectibles.

"Gather | Virtual HQ for Remote Teams." n.d. Accessed December 10, 2024. https://www.gather.town/.

Geertz, Clifford. 1973. "Thick Description: Toward an Interpretive Theory of Culture." In *The Interpretation of Cultures: Selected Essays*, 310–23. New York: Basic Books, Inc. https://cdn.angkordatabase.asia/libs/docs/clifford-geertz-the-interpretation-of-cultures.pdf.

Gibbs, Graham R. 2018. *Analyzing Qualitative Data*. 2nd ed. London: SAGE Publications Ltd. https://methods.sagepub.com/book/analyzing-qualitative-data-2e.

Goslin, Austen. 2020. "League of Legends Newest Champion, Seraphine, Revealed." *Polygon*, October 13. https://www.polygon.com/2020/10/12/21513037/lol-seraphine-ability-new-champion-kit-league-of-legends-passive-skills-ultimate-skin-kda.

Gregg, Melissa. 2011. *Work's Intimacy*. Cambridge: Polity Press.

Gregg, Melissa. 2013. "Presence Bleed: Performing Professionalism Online." In *Theorizing Cultural Work: Labour, Continuity and Change in the Creative Industries*, edited by Mark Banks, Rosalind Gill, and Stephanie Taylor, 122–34. London and New York: Routledge.

Helmond, Anne. 2015. "The Platformization of the Web: Making Web Data Platform Ready." *Social Media + Society* 1 (2): 2056305115603080. https://doi.org/10.1177/2056305115603080.

"Imma in ZEPETO." n.d. Accessed January 26, 2025. https://web.zepeto.me/share/user/profile/0JEP4P?language=en.

"Imma's Invites Everyone to Visit Her House in Animal Crossing." 2020. *Aww Inc.* (blog). December 3. https://aww.tokyo/news/2020/12/268/.

Kaye, D. Bondy Valdovinos, Jing Zeng, Patrik Wikstrom, Jack Linchuan Qiu, Natalie Ann Hendry, Katrin Tiidenberg, Crystal Abidin, Tim Highfield, Tama Leaver, and Taina Bucher. 2021. "Panel Rationale for "Platform Specificities: The Platform Books Panel"." In *AoIR Selected Papers of Internet Research*. Online Event. https://doi.org/10.5210/spir.v2021i0.12115.

Kendall, Lori. 2002. *Hanging out in the Virtual Pub: Masculinities and Relationships Online*. Berkeley: University of California Press.

Khalid, Cam. 2021. "Meet Rae: Singapore's Virtual Influencer on the Power of Social Media." *Time Out Singapore*, April 16. https://www.timeout.com/singapore/things-to-do/meet-rae-singapores-virtual-influencer-on-the-power-of-social-media.

League of Legends, dir. 2018a. *POP/STARS - Opening Ceremony Presented by Mastercard | Finals | 2018 World Championship*. https://www.youtube.com/watch?v=p9oDlvOV3qs.

League of Legends, dir. 2018b. *RISE - Opening Ceremony Presented by Mastercard | Finals | 2018 World Championship*. https://www.youtube.com/watch?v=177jxGRbPgM.

League of Legends, dir. 2023. *NewJeans (뉴진스) - GODS | Worlds 2023 Finals Opening Ceremony Presented by Mastercard*. https://www.youtube.com/watch?v=uiz7EsMPsuw.

Leaver, Tama, and Rachel Berryman. 2022. "'Virtual Influencers' Are Here, but Should Meta Really Be Setting the Ethical Ground Rules?" *The Conversation* (blog). January 30. https://theconversation.com/virtual-influencers-are-here-but-should-meta-really-be-setting-the-ethical-ground-rules-175524.

Leavitt, Alex. 2015. "'This Is a Throwaway Account': Temporary Technical Identities and Perceptions of Anonymity in a Massive Online Community." In *Proceedings of the 18th ACM Conference on Computer Supported Cooperative Work & Social Computing*, 317–27. CSCW '15. New York: Association for Computing Machinery. https://doi.org/10.1145/2675133.2675175.

Lee, Julia. 2018. "K/DA, Riot Games' Pop Girl Group, Explained." *Polygon* (blog). November 5. https://www.polygon.com/2018/11/5/18064726/league-of-legends-kda-pop-stars-video-akali-ahri-evelynn-kai-sa.

LesBleus FFF. 2020. "200612 BLACKPINK in ZEPETO Area." Reddit Post. *R/BlackPink*. https://www.reddit.com/r/BlackPink/comments/h7g9vz/200612_blackpink_in_zepeto_area/.

Light, Ben, Jean Burgess, and Stefanie Duguay. 2018. "The Walkthrough Method: An Approach to the Study of Apps." *New Media & Society* 20 (3): 881–900. https://doi.org/10.1177/1461444816675438.

Maddox, Alexia. 2020. "Disrupting the Ethnographic Imaginarium: Challenges of Immersion in the Silk Road Cryptomarket Community." *Journal of Digital Social Research* 2 (1): 20–38. https://doi.org/10.33621/jdsr.v2i1.23.

Markham, Annette N. 1998. *Life Online: Researching Real Experience in Virtual Space*. Walnut Creek, CA: Rowman Altamira.

McGuire, Amelia. 2024. "Reality Check: The VR Dream Costing Meta Tens of Billions of Dollars." *Australian Financial Review*, October 31. https://www.afr.com/technology/reality-check-the-vr-dream-costing-meta-tens-of-billions-of-dollars-20241030-p5kmot.

Mei, Tan Tam. 2021. "Thailand's Rise of Virtual Influencers Born out of Covid-19 Curbs That Limit Humans." *The Straits Times*, October 14. https://www.straitstimes.com/asia/se-asia/thailands-rise-of-virtual-influencers-born-out-of-covid-19-curbs-that-limit-humans.

"Meta Quest 3: Mixed Reality VR Headset." n.d. Meta. Accessed December 10, 2024. https://www.meta.com/au/quest/quest-3/.

"Metaverse for Business: Immersive Experiences for Customers." n.d. Meta for Business. Accessed December 10, 2024. https://en-gb.facebook.com/business/metaverse.

MiggySmallzKPop. 2018. "RISE Remix Ft. BOBBY (바비) of iKON | Worlds 2018- League of Legends." Reddit Post. *R/Kpop.* https://www.reddit.com/r/kpop/comments/9r6be5/rise_remix_ft_bobby_바비_of_ikon_worlds_2018_league/.
"Music Valley Concert Series." n.d. Meta Quest. Accessed January 26, 2025. https://www.oculus.com/experiences/event/305157035795903/.
Nieborg, David B., and Thomas Poell. 2018. "The Platformization of Cultural Production: Theorizing the Contingent Cultural Commodity." *New Media & Society* 20 (11): 4275–92. https://doi.org/10.1177/1461444818769694.
"OHROZY." n.d. DRESSX. Accessed January 26, 2025. https://store.dressx.com/collections/vendors?q=ohrozy.
Ong, Thuy. 2020. "Virtual Influencers Make Real Money While Covid Locks Down Human Stars." *Bloomberg.Com*, October 29. https://www.bloomberg.com/news/features/2020-10-29/lil-miquela-lol-s-seraphine-virtual-influencers-make-more-real-money-than-ever.
Pearce, Celia. 2009. *Communities of Play: Emergent Cultures in Multiplayer Games and Virtual Worlds.* Cambridge, MA: MIT Press.
Pearce, Warren, Suay M. Özkula, Amanda K. Greene, Lauren Teeling, Jennifer S. Bansard, Janna Joceli Omena, and Elaine Teixeira Rabello. 2020. "Visual Cross-Platform Analysis: Digital Methods to Research Social Media Images." *Information, Communication & Society* 23 (2): 161–80. https://doi.org/10.1080/1369118X.2018.1486871.
Pink, Sarah, Heather Horst, John Postill, Larissa Hjorth, Tania Lewis, and Jo Tacchi. 2016. *Digital Ethnography: Principles and Practice.* London: SAGE Publications.
Postill, John. 2015. "Six Ways of Doing Digital Ethnography." *Media/Anthropology* (blog). January 16. https://johnpostill.wordpress.com/2015/01/16/13-six-ways-of-researching-new-social-worlds/.
Promoview, Redação. 2022. "Carnaval Do Boticário No Avakin Recebe Satiko." *Promoview - Insights Sobre Brand Experience e Live Marketing* (blog). February 26. https://www.promoview.com.br/tech/o-boticario-evento-carnaval-avakin/.
"PUBG MOBILE X BLACKPINK." n.d. PUBG MOBILE. Accessed January 26, 2025. https://www.pubgmobile.com/images/event/BLACKPINK2022/2/.
Rowley, Glenn. 2020. "Virtual Girl Group K/DA Roar Back With Futuristic Animated Video For 'More': Watch." *Billboard*, October 28. https://www.billboard.com/music/pop/kda-more-video-9474359/.
"Seraphine (@seradotwav)." n.d. Instagram. Accessed January 26, 2025. https://www.instagram.com/seradotwav/.
Shin, Y. 2018a. "iKON and (G)I-DLE Members to Perform at League of Legends' Worlds 2018 Opening Ceremony." Soompi. October 26. https://www.soompi.com/article/1252133wpp/ikon-gi-dle-members-perform-league-legends-worlds-2018-opening-ceremony.
Shin, Y. 2018b. "Watch: iKON's Bobby Features in 'Rise' Remix for League of Legends Worlds 2018 MV." Soompi. October 25. https://www.soompi.com/article/1251519wpp/watch-ikons-bobby-features-rise-remix-league-legends-worlds-2018-mv.
TakeOne Company. n.d. "BLACKPINK THE GAME." Apps on Google Play. Accessed January 26, 2025. https://play.google.com/store/apps/details?id=com.takeonecompany.bptg1&hl=en_AU.

Taylor, T. L. 1999. "Life in Virtual Worlds: Plural Existence, Multimodalities, and Other Online Research Challenges." *American Behavioral Scientist* 43 (3): 436–49. https://doi.org/10.1177/00027649921955362.

Taylor, T. L. 2002. "Living Digitally: Embodiment in Virtual Worlds." In *The Social Life of Avatars: Presence and Interaction in Shared Virtual Environments*, edited by Ralph Schroeder, 40–62. London: Springer-Verlag.

"The Metaverse is the Future of Digital Connection." n.d. Meta. Accessed December 10, 2024. https://about.meta.com/metaverse/.

Tuting, Kristine "Kurisu." 2023. "The Real Reason Why Riot Games Chose NewJeans for the Worlds 2023 Anthem 'Gods.'" ONE Esports. November 15. https://www.oneesports.gg/league-of-legends/newjeans-riot-games-collab/.

Vouloumanos, Victoria. 2024. "I Got a Front-Row Seat to a Sold-Out Blackpink Concert Using Virtual Reality. Here's What the Experience Was Really Like." *BuzzFeed*, January 31. https://www.buzzfeed.com/victoriavouloumanos/blackpink-virtual-reality-concert-meta.

"What is the Metaverse?" n.d. Meta. Accessed December 10, 2024. https://about.meta.com/what-is-the-metaverse/.

"ZEPETO World - BLACKPINK SQUARE." n.d. Accessed January 22, 2025. https://web.zepeto.me/en/detail/com.ygent.blackpinksquare@49932694e958e0d2e7a95bfd9d2a4733.

Chapter 4.1

Concept: virtual

From virtual reality to sensory immersion

Tom Boellstorff

Despite its ups and downs in the hype cycle, "metaverse" is a useful concept. It can serve as a shorthand for the field site of digital ethnography: the diverse places online, intersecting with places offline, where we can engage in participant observation and the other methods ethnographers employ. As we set forth on such research, our starting points matter. How we define and understand online culture has fundamental consequences for how we proceed and the insights we forge. Unfortunately, a range of confusions can interfere with establishing such starting points for research.

One of the most pervasive confusions involves virtual reality (VR). Try it yourself: search for "metaverse" on a popular stock image vendor like Getty Images or iStock. You will primarily find "photos of gawk-mouthed people in VR headsets" (Au 2023, 330). What these people are seeing and experiencing is obscured.

Using virtual reality headgear to stand in for the metaverse reveals a fundamental confusion of interface and place. It is unfortunate that since the 1980s, "virtual reality" has been equated with sensory interface. This most often means movement-tracking headsets with three-dimensional graphics and sound, but it can also mean, for instance, haptic gear allowing one to touch virtual objects. Reality, however, does not inhere in the senses. Persons with visual and auditory impairments have always participated in the metaverse; their practices, selfhoods, and communities are no less real. What makes the metaverse real is social immersion, not sensory immersion (Boellstorff 2015, chap. 4). If I am in the metaverse with a friend, that friendship is real even if I am using a screen and keyboard. If I take a text-based online Italian language class, interacting with my teacher and fellow students using no graphics whatsoever, those interactions are real, and from my learning, I could travel to physical-world Rome and converse with the locals.

In asserting that virtual reality is necessary to the metaverse, some of its promoters are encoding an empirically incorrect and ableist notion of reality as reduced to the senses. Despite beginning with the same word,

DOI: 10.4324/9781032672663-18

virtual reality and *virtual world* are radically distinct: *virtual reality* is about sensory interface, while *virtual world* is about online place. Apple recognized this when announcing its Vision Pro headset in June 2023: the company never used *virtual reality*, opting instead for the phrase *spatial computing*, which was coined by the company Magic Leap. Virtual reality and virtual worlds can overlap, but they are independent. One can use virtual reality gear on a computer disconnected from the internet or, conversely, inhabit virtual worlds with a monitor and mouse. The metaverse is three-dimensional, "3D," and one can use virtual reality "3D" interfaces within it, but these notions of "3D" differ. One can access the metaverse with "2D" interfaces like a monitor, and even "1D" interfaces in the sense that many virtual worlds are composed solely of text. Yet even these text-only virtual worlds are three-dimensional. In such a world, the following text might appear: "You have entered a room with a red chair and yellow chair; Susan is sitting in the yellow chair." In response, you might type, "Sit in the red chair," and you are thus moving in a three-dimensional virtual world space.

I acknowledge that the association of interface with "virtual reality" has become deeply entrenched. Renaming might seem futile, but the attempt is worthwhile even as a provocation. I therefore propose renaming virtual reality "sensory immersion" (SI). At present, this usually means sight and sound, and often body movement and touch (haptics). In the future it could involve smell and taste, or even full-body immersion, as popularized in *The Matrix*. But, as illustrated by another well-known film, *Avatar*, these interfaces could in theory be used to enable users to have another body in the physical world (Boellstorff 2011). SI can exist without the metaverse and vice versa. SI has many fascinating possibilities, but these do not include privileged access to the real. Terming SI "virtual reality" misleadingly implies that the senses are the foundation of human reality. But we are present in places even when we do not sense them in every way. This is the anthropological insight that human reality is made not by individual sensing but by culture—the collective, shared grammars that let us speak and the shared social logics and practices through which human experience arises. Virtual worlds are virtual reality, in and of themselves. Understanding this does not minimize the important impact that SI technologies will have on many people in many corners of the metaverse. Rather, it provides a common language for locating that impact in the cultural contexts that are the metaverse's true reality.

Acknowledgment

Excerpted, with a new introductory paragraph, from Boellstorff (2024), with permission from Wiley.

References

Au, Wagner James. 2023. *Making a Metaverse That Matters: From Snow Crash and Second Life to a Virtual World Worth Fighting For.* Hoboken, NJ: John Wiley.

Boellstorff, Tom. 2011. "Placing the Virtual Body: Avatar, Chora, Cypherg." In *A Companion to the Anthropology of the Body and Embodiment,* edited by Frances E. Mascia-Lees, 504–20. New York: Wiley-Blackwell.

Boellstorff, Tom. 2015. *Coming of Age in Second Life: An Anthropologist Explores the Virtually Human.* 2nd ed. Princeton, NJ: Princeton University Press.

Boellstorff, Tom. 2024. "Toward Anthropologies of the Metaverse." *American Ethnologist* 51: 47–56. https://doi.org/10.1111/amet.13228.

Chapter 4.2

Case study: work, play, and questioning the binary in EVE Online

The virtual state: specters of a polity

Harish Goutam

EVE Online, a massively multiplayer online role-playing game (MMORPG), allows players a great deal of freedom within its simulation of a world set thousands of years in the future, which players traverse via spacecraft. This chapter looks at how ethnographic research blurs the fantastical depiction of EVE with the ordinary lives of its players. In so doing, it leads us to question far more than this dichotomy.

Methodology

Most of this fieldwork was undertaken through a period of extensive participant observation, but I also engaged in some semi-structured interviews with players at a range of both experience and seniority. It should also be mentioned that, within virtual worlds, the emphasis for participant observation is more heavily dependent on participation over observation (see Nardi 2010, 28). In EVE, this was especially true, given the high level of mistrust between players and outside factions in particular.

Situating the field site

Set within the twin galaxies of New Eden and Anoikis, players (also termed pilots) interact with the virtual world primarily through a mixture of charts, user interfaces, and traversal of the space itself via myriad ships. Space is subdivided into three sectors, pertaining largely to its presence of non-player character (NPC) enforcers, otherwise known as CONCORD. These are "lowsec," "highsec," and "nullsec" in New Eden and an additional fourth region, often referred to as "w-space," only accessible by wormholes, comprising all of Anoikis.

Systems within nullsec (as well as lowsec and w-space, nominally) can be controlled by players, who harvest resources to either manufacture into more complex components (up to and including ships themselves) or sell to other players, as part of EVE's robust and complex user-generated economy.

Players throughout EVE organize themselves into distinct groups: corporations (or corps) that may number between ten and a few hundred; alliances, which are collections of corps; and, in nullsec, coalitions that can comprise tens of thousands and attempt to unify a number of alliances as well as at least partially communalize resources and intelligence.

There is much more that could be mentioned in this section regarding EVE, given its vastness, age, and complexity. Suffice it to say, it is a virtual world teeming with social life, which the rest of this piece shall endeavor to explore in fuller detail.

Stumbling into incoherence

Living within EVE was a concept I came to understand relatively shortly after joining the virtual world. Exploring an entire universe rendered through millions of polygons and housed upon a single server, I watched with dismay during one excursion as my ship and its expensive cargo worth tens of millions of InterStellar Kredits (ISK) slowly disintegrated, under fire from a small posse of bandits who had set a "bubble trap" on the exit point of the jump gate I was passing through. The local chat was filled with ASCII art of bees, genitalia, "gg," and other forms of text teasing the destruction of my ship and unsuccessful escape. I had thought taking the jump gate my alliance had constructed might be safer than the NPC-managed stargates; after all, while anyone could use them, the toll for my passage was considerably lower than for those of rival coalitions. But, clearly, watching my cloned body float away as a frozen husk into the black expanse, something had gone awry.

One may be tempted to ask if traversal in EVE can even occasionally lead to the kind of outcome illustrated above, why would a player simply not avoid these areas as best they could? I asked this of a corp mate:

> Phantom
> > The thing is, you can't really live in EVE without ISK. Like, yeah, there's SRP [Ship Replacement Program] and other stuff for newbros but it's kind of shitty if you want to actually make money or have an impact on anything.

> Me
> > But couldn't I just make ISK near the citadel or something?

> Phantom
> > At the beginning, yeah. But you won't get anything from those places cos everyone else is there too. Also you can still get camped if you're not careful.

After joining a Covert Operations Special Interest Group (CovOps SIG), I took Phantom's advice and began to venture further afield in search of ISK to sustain myself within EVE.

Work and play

Parmelo (fleet chat)
> at work, but im on comms now if you get another target (can listen, can't talk:))

Spock (fleet chat)
> I'm missing work for this, lol

Much has been made of the intersection between work and play, and, more pointedly, how MMOs may in themselves constitute work. As I ventured further out from the citadel to harvest minerals and hack data sites for ISK, it occurred to me that I was also encouraged to adopt a regimented, work-like approach.

Mustang (private chat)
> yeah basically eve is just spreadsheets
> long as you keep to timers, you can make a LOT of isk

As I conducted fieldwork in w-space, I found that this style of living in EVE confounded attempts by previous researchers to explain such behavior by reconciling "work-like" activity in a "play-like" environment. These attempts appear more like an internal reconciling on the part of the researcher of what is prima facie an oddity or contradiction; why would someone willingly work while playing?

Archon (external forum)
> relic sites are a good source of income, and pretty easy to start

Howard (external forum)
> You could try huffing gas [...] probably has the lowest start up cost [...]

Bullet (external forum)
> Keep your costs low [...] fly cheap stuff for PvP

Within EVE, financial verbiage was constantly used; ISK generation activities were referred to as streams or sources of income, which players were expected to diversify, items were processed and transported using contracts, with their own courier collateral clauses, and so on. Perhaps the richest industrialist in EVE, Sir SmashAlot, has directly compared his "market PvP" with his past as an equities trader. Moreover, concepts familiar to financial markets were readily leveraged to gain advantages in EVE. Yet despite this outward appearance, for those who lived within the virtual world, this was play. Going beyond, and against, work, play resists compulsion, whereby the player gains from the mere act of playing, which in itself is the reward sought (Black 1991).

Borders in space

As I continued pursuing means of making ISK, I could not ignore the nagging contradiction between my impression of EVE before research and Phantom's words following my ship's destruction; that even at the local citadel, I was still unsafe.

Despite gaming publications and news articles describing nullsec as the "wild west" or "lawless" (Frye 2024; McHugh 2024), the power structures that controlled this area of EVE had seemingly ossified. This coalescing is important to note because rather than a chaotic, dangerous badlands, nullsec more resembled collectivities of insular, federated republics or fiefdoms. Accordingly, at least on first glance, one may traverse EVE within the "borders" of one's alliance or coalition under the assumption of relative safety. As I grew to find out, however, this assumption was misplaced.

During a general fleet, for instance, one (newer) miner complained over voice chat that his ship was destroyed in "alliance space" after leaving his desk for a short time. He was told how to obtain a free replacement for new players but warned against mining "offline" again. This short interaction typified two aspects of EVE I increasingly found. For one, alliance borders were porous and, while providing some semblance of safety, were repeatedly breached, as Phantom alluded to. Second, to mitigate against this, one should not be "offline"; this is despite being very much in the game itself. I came to understand that one may be: offline but in game (or more disparagingly, "botting"); online but only on certain communication platforms (not including EVE); partially online in EVE[1] (that is to say, one would implicitly distinguish between states of readiness, perhaps being "on" but not available); and many more, besides.

In another example, after participating in a large fleet fight that lasted several hours and induced TiDi (time dilation[2]), I asked Mustang why we had left a number of ships stranded in enemy territory following the battle.

Mustang
> Well, we'll probably pick them up later, especially if they're like titans or whatever, but they were offline during extraction so we couldn't wait around.

In this case, offline refers quite literally to logging off EVE and therefore concurs with the more traditional dichotomy between being online and offline. Yet one cannot ignore the other examples cited above and how, undeniably, a multifaceted understanding of these terms was not utilized but arguably critical to adequately play the game.

Thus, differing notions of being offline and online were understood and leveraged by players to attack others, gain material benefit, or ensure safety. All this is ultimately tied to the concept of a coalition or alliance's "borders" in nullsec. After joining a wormhole alliance, my alliance leader put it quite succinctly following our incursion into a nullsec system:

Bullet
> I feel like a barbarian running through the streets of civilization.

Within that pithy phrase, as we laughed at the wreckage of another nullsec exploration frigate, wrought by our ships, there was a great deal of insight. The nullsec blocs were not impenetrable fortresses of defense but in many ways demonstrated a projection of force beyond their actual borders (which often did not extend much beyond the citadel of a system, depending on one's time zone). Put another way, these were rhetorical borders, reified when defended but otherwise ethereal and employed in the creation and reproduction of a very real culture and a community.

Conclusion

The purported divide between the so-called online and offline world (see, e.g., Boellstorff 2008, Nardi 2010) is often expounded and readily accepted in much of the existing research on the subject. That is to say, it is almost a given in much virtual ethnography that one is said to be in a virtual world, so to speak, and that this is in contradistinction to the real (more commonly, actual) world (cf. Deleuze 1997). These dichotomies, being persistent in digital ethnography,[3] are arguably inscriptive, or prescriptive, rather than necessarily emergent categories in and of themselves. Rather than uncritically viewing the virtual as a singular, coherent category, I suggest caution against this practice. Anthropologists can, and do, have totalizing linguistic and authorial power, which may prevent more substantive ethnography on the subject due to a tendency away from more heterogeneous notions of being and place.

By "playing" with the categories of space and place, we may be able to offer insights regarding this heterogeneity or spectral quality in sociality beyond the so-called digital and also demonstrate why interrogating and dismantling an assumed binary (say between "online" and "offline") within this space is so useful for virtual ethnography specifically. As such, the primary part of this chapter attempted to untangle an accidental realization into more practical applications by which we may conduct this destabilization.

Notes

1 Though this employed specific vocabulary, e.g., being "docked."
2 As EVE is played on a single server, when a large number of ships enter a single system, time is slowed or "dilated," so as to prevent inaccurate processing of player actions and provide a level playing field for all players, irrespective of their connection quality.
3 But also ethnographic work in general often conveys culture as dichotomous (see, for instance, Descola 2013).

References

Black, Bob. 1991. "The Abolition of Work." Accessed at: https://inspiracy.com/black/abolition/abolitionofwork.html.

Boellstorff, Tom. 2008. *Coming of Age in Second Life*. Woodstock: Princeton University Press.

Deleuze, Gilles. 1997. *Bergsonism*. New York: Zone Books.

Descola, Philippe. 2013. *Beyond Nature and Culture*. London: University of Chicago Press.

Frye, Brendan. 2024. "New Expansion EVE Online: Equinox Will Empower Players to Seize Control of Nullsec." *CGMagazine*. Accessed at: https://www.cgmagonline.com/news/eve-online-equinox-expansion-nullsec/.

McHugh, Alex. 2024. "Legendary Sci-Fi MMO Gets New Expansion in Lawless Part of Space." *PCGamesN*. Accessed at: https://www.pcgamesn.com/eve-online/nullsec-expansion.

Nardi, Bonnie. 2010. *My Life as a Night Elf Priest: An Anthropological Account of World of Warcraft*. Ann Arbor: University of Michigan Press.

Chapter 5

Linguistic analysis

Lessons from discovering the "Strength of Weak Evidence" among online UFO investigators

Graham M. Jones, Jisoo Hong, and Maya Návar

On November 14, 2004, the Nimitz Carrier Strike Group dispatched four Navy fighter jets to intercept an unidentified flying object (UFO) off the coast of southern California. The combat pilots encountered a perfectly smooth oblong object that looked like a 45-foot Tic-Tac breath mint. For five minutes, it seemed to coyly dance with them, hovering almost still, then veering away suddenly at impossible speeds before disappearing altogether. After poring over onboard video and audio recordings, cross-referencing other tracking systems, and interviewing the crew involved, Naval Intelligence could not explain the UFO. The pilots were left wondering what they had seen.

Almost two decades later, one of them was on CNN recounting her experience. Retired Lieutenant Commander Alex Dietrich described how she eventually found her way to an online network of UFO sleuths linked by the Twitter (now X) hashtag #ufotwitter. "I'm fascinated with their fascination!" she exclaimed. "Whether they are hardcore enthusiasts, or conspiracy theorists, or hardcore debunkers, or … religious fanatics, … at the core, no matter how much they're attacking each other, … they all want answers" (Dietrich 2021). In #ufotwitter, Dietrich had joined a digital subculture that, like so many others, essentially consists of social media users exchanging verbal messages about shared concerns. As digital ethnographers setting out to study that subculture, we needed to understand how its members were using language to constitute and sustain community in the process of debating and debunking UFO evidence. What their language use ultimately revealed to us about online information ecologies has deep implications—both theoretical and methodological—for the anthropology of digital culture.

Introduction

Whether or not digital ethnographers want to focus on language, they cannot avoid it: Digital culture is fundamentally linguistic. Engineers use machine language to build digital infrastructure. Upon that infrastructure, developers use programming languages to build digital platforms. Platform users interact with each other in spoken and written languages to form digital networks, publics, and communities. The most viral digital content usually incorporates visual language.

In its constant evolution, digital language drives trends in digital culture. Digital speech, such as a social media post, can shake world events; subject to intense scrutiny, it often becomes the topic of headline news. Digital communication can democratize language by empowering marginalized voices, increasing channels of participation, nurturing the emergence of new speech communities, and revitalizing endangered languages. It can also be used to weaponize language by providing levers of state surveillance, censorship, and propaganda; fostering corporate control, value extraction, and labor exploitation; and abetting the linguistic dominance of a select few global languages.

Perhaps the biggest methodological problem digital ethnographers face when it comes to language is that there is just so darn much of it. Digital language, except on platforms where it is designed to quickly evanescence, often constitutes "inscriptive speech" (Jones and Schieffelin 2016), self-archiving text that accumulates in chat logs, social media feeds, public comment threads, and online forums. Ethnography traditionally focuses on small-scale datasets collected through the participant observation research of an individual fieldworker. How does one practice interpretive analysis faced with the potential vastness of already accumulated and always still accumulating language available as data?

In this chapter, we propose some responses drawn from our experience carrying out research on the online subculture of #ufotwitter, part of a digital network of UFO investigators who produce extraordinary amounts of inscriptive speech in the process of evaluating putative evidence—photos, videos, audio recordings, eyewitness accounts, etc.—of extraterrestrial contact. Insofar as digital culture is simply culture, traditional approaches from linguistic anthropology are perfectly well suited for many research projects (Johnson and Jones 2021). Although we employed conventional qualitative techniques, we also found the need for quantitative and computational approaches to language that depart from contemporary norms in anthropological ethnography.

Reflecting on this generative methodological fusion, we emphasize lessons we learned related to three closely interconnected themes—*sampling*, *mixed methods*, and *teamwork*—in the hope that they will inspire innovation among other ethnographers of digital language. At a time when sociocultural anthropologists are struggling to reimagine the hard-to-sustain ideal of isolated, long-term, faraway fieldwork (Günel and Watanabe 2024) and ethnographers are struggling to validate qualitative research vis-à-vis the hegemony of quantitative methods (Small and Calarco 2022), we also believe that these reflections can contribute to revitalizing ethnographic methods more broadly.

Sampling is not an issue that most ethnographers consciously consider. In quantitative, "variable-based" studies (Small 2011, 59), researchers *must* select a sample population that serves as a representative subset of some broader demographic to determine how particular factors may or may not affect dependent human behavior within it. In qualitative, "case-based" studies (Small 2011, 59) like all ethnographies, researchers focus on a specific group of people—residents of a village, say, or workers in a lab—to understand, as Erving Goffman (1989, 125) puts it, how they go about "responding to what life does to them." Such sampling is "purposive" (Guest 2015, 234) in that it is driven by an interest in the shared lifeworld of *those particular people* leading lives interconnected within a shared social unit. That unit of interconnection—the village or the lab—is both the sampling frame and the field site.

Although they must obviously have some general ideas about what makes a particular group interesting before embarking on research, ethnographers typically proceed inductively, gradually reaching an understanding of what might be theoretically generalizable about their case by attending to themes emergent in their data (Timmermans and Tavory 2012). Because the sheer and overwhelming amount of verbal data that researchers encounter online can render such an open-ended approach intractable, it is helpful to articulate an explicit theory about why some cases might be more interesting than others (Guest 2015, 222), with the understanding that such a theory will evolve. Our first lesson for digital ethnographers is that *theory-based sampling is an effective strategy for making analytically pertinent decisions about which data to include in or exclude from a study.*

A theoretical sampling strategy has the additional advantage of facilitating *mixed-methods* research that synergistically combines qualitative and quantitative approaches (Small 2011). Common in sociology as well as human behavioral ecology and applied anthropology, it is generally eschewed by sociocultural anthropologists, who view ethnography as their exclusive method. Indeed, they often have a moral aversion to quantification such that preserving the qualitative purity of ethnographic methods becomes nothing short of a ritual imperative. As Paul Radin (1966 [1933], 168) wrote early on, quantification "robs cultural facts of their vitality, of the humanness, of that specific quality which makes them cultural and not biological or physical." This may be, but, for digital ethnographers, dogmatism about the methodological superiority of qualitative research—or, for that matter, the unalloyed "humanness" of "cultural facts"—rests on shaky foundations.

Digital cultures and communities are shaped by the quantitative logics of digital platforms that measure user activity and manipulate user engagement in order to maximize profit. Digital platforms have logics of knowledge production that bear little resemblance to anthropological models, using machine learning algorithms to generate insights into user behavior that can be sold to marketing interest groups seeking to strategically influence that behavior. At the same time, social media platforms provide application programming interfaces (APIs) that allow computational social scientists in fields such as human-computer interaction or communications to download huge datasets for analysis with their own machine learning tools.

Like it or not, digital ethnography on social media platforms already relies on underlying numerical infrastructures with endemic forms of algorithmic power-knowledge and exists alongside quantitative social media research in other fields. This leads to our second lesson: *a mixed-methods approach blending digital ethnography with quantitative analysis and computational social science can leverage metrics* already *baked into digital data to reveal dynamics between micro-level and macro-level patterns.*

Although anthropological ethnography is doggedly individualistic, *teamwork* may be necessary to make this kind of mixed-methods research possible. Unlike technical fields in which co-authorship is becoming increasingly common, anthropologists steadfastly continue to publish alone, as sole collector, analyst, and explicator of their own ethnographic data. This reinforces status hierarchies between senior researchers who have "been to the field" and junior researchers who have not. Reflecting the multifaceted nature of digital language, digital ethnography can benefit from cooperation between researchers from different backgrounds with different, complementary skills and experiences. As our own process of using methods ranging from qualitative digital ethnography to quantitative sociolinguistics and computational natural language processing (NLP) makes clear, such teamwork takes time.

Part of good teamwork is good communication. During our collaboration, we had regular team meetings at least once a week, reviewing the prior week's tasks and setting objectives for the following week. We frequently communicated on the Slack app and built a shared project bibliography with Zotero. In a shared Google folder, we individually authored research memos, short, informal documents summarizing data and proposing interpretations that we could circulate among ourselves and discuss in comment threads. Occasional presentations to colleagues provided opportunities to synthesize findings and receive additional input. Most importantly, we always seemed to be learning from each other and were often amazed by each other's abilities. Thus, our third lesson is that *the kind of interdisciplinary approach that works best for apprehending the multidimensional complexity of digital language may necessitate teamwork, through which teammates can gain insight both* into *and* through *each other's theories, methods, epistemologies, and tools.*

Case study: #ufotwitter and the "Strength of Weak Evidence"

To illustrate how we learned these lessons, we describe the mixed-methods research project that Graham, Jisoo, and Maya conducted together during the Summer and Fall of 2021, which culminated in Jisoo's thesis the following spring (Hong 2022). The project focused on the way UFO investigators use the Twitter hashtag #ufotwitter to engage in what they sometimes call open-source intelligence (OSINT), circulating and collaboratively analyzing purported evidence of extraterrestrial contact. We each came to this project with a unique set of skills, and, as we learned from each other, the focus of the project evolved. Some approaches we tried did not work as hoped; others produced results so astonishing that we had to rethink everything.

We present this research as a sequence of steps, with a particular emphasis on four pivotal findings that punctuated cycles of trial and error. As we progressed, we mixed methods through a kind of iterative bricolage. Sometimes, qualitative observation raised questions that demanded quantitative and/or computational analysis. Sometimes it was the other way around. The interplay between methods was fluid and organic, driven by our evolving questions, not by a preconceived design. The narrative of our research does not trace a linear arc but rather a tightening gyre, as ongoing methodological experimentation converged on ethnographic insight and theoretical discovery. As we sharpened our empirical focus and refined our research question, we developed a theory that we dubbed "The Strength of Weak Evidence" to explain our paradoxical findings.

Theoretical background: epistemic stance

Our project had roots in an earlier, collaborative, mixed-methods study that Graham, a professor of linguistic anthropology, carried out alongside computer scientists during the 2020 COVID lockdown. Led by doctoral student Crystal Lee, that study examined how COVID skeptics in the US repurposed public health data to create visualizations that cast doubt on the scientific consensus about the pandemic (Lee et al. 2022). Using machine learning to track the circulation of competing data visualizations on Twitter, it mapped online social networks associated with orthodox and heterodox interpretations of the same data.

One of the limitations of that study was the inability to account for what linguistic anthropologists call *stance*: the expression of an assessment, evaluation, or judgment toward a shared referent, through which people establish relationships of value alignment (Du Bois 2007). So, although the study could determine whether individuals were in networks associated with mainstream science or heterodox COVID denialism, it had no way of determining (other than manual inspection) the stance of any given social media post toward the data visualization it shared. This was a significant problem because data cannot speak for itself. People on different sides of the ideological spectrum could share the same graph showing falling infection rates, say, in support of diametrically opposed arguments: *either* that public health measures were highly effective *or* that they were utterly useless. To truly understand how people communicate with and through scientific evidence would require a computational approach to analyzing verbal expressions of stance at scale.

The research question: how does stancetaking shape belief?

This is the issue Graham was pondering when he met Jisoo in Spring 2021. Then a master's student in Technology and Public Policy, Jisoo had previous experience as a computer scientist conducting machine learning research in the tech industry. She was wondering how qualitative methods might help better hold the tech companies accountable for some of the perverse effects of their business model, such as the rampant spread of mis- and disinformation on social media platforms. The two of us very quickly agreed on the broad outlines of a shared research question: do the stances social media users take in posts or comments lead to shifts in individual/ collective opinion over time?

Jisoo began by conducting a comprehensive literature review on stance, spanning research in linguistic anthropology, sociolinguistics, and computer science. She found that researchers in NLP had taken on this topic but with limited success. Although linguistic anthropologists approach stancetaking as a dialogical process that emerges through interaction (Du Bois 2007), research in NLP has, of necessity, focused on identifying discrete verbal markers of agreement and disagreement that can be studied at the level of the individual social media post (Kiesling et al. 2018). We hoped to find a way of better integrating the linguistic anthropological perspective on stancetaking as a relational feature of emergent interactional processes with computational methods that had, until then, treated stance as an intrinsic feature of an isolated message or text.

Developing a sampling strategy

Drawing on linguistic anthropological approaches to the relationship between authority and evidence (Kuipers 2013), we wanted to develop a generalizable framework for understanding how language mediates the perceived reliability of information and admissibility of evidence in scientific conversations among lay social media users. Jisoo began by inspecting the dataset that had been collected for the COVID visualization project. Using a variety of computational approaches, she quickly identified a problem: opinion about the pandemic was so diametrically polarized along ideological lines that there seemed to be very little indication of social media users seriously deliberating about evidence in a way that might shift anyone's beliefs.

This posed a sampling problem. If we wanted to study opinion change, we needed a flourishing public sphere—an empirical test-case with (1) extensive online debate about a scientific issue; (2) no central authority to adjudicate truth claims or differentiate between orthodox and heterodox viewpoints; (3) a high degree of disagreement about what constitutes "good" data or "reliable" evidence; and (4) relatively little political polarization of the sort that radicalized disagreements about COVID. After considering a number of possibilities, an auspicious news article (Lewis-Kraus 2021) suggested that we might find these conditions among UFO investigators and skeptics—"ufologists."

It just so happened that the Pentagon was about to release its first-ever unclassified report on UFOs. Around the world, ufologists awaited the report with keen anticipation. The US government's long and complicated history of dissimulation contributed to a culture of mutual mistrust between ufologists and institutional authorities (Eghigian 2017). Amid conspiracy theories about the state's malicious suppression of information (Lepselter 2016), mainstream scientists relegated UFOs to the tabooed category of the "paranormal" phenomena. For some, UFOs began to take on religious undertones (Pasulka 2019). Nevertheless, a growing consensus among public figures and scientific authorities (Agrama 2021) contributed to a feeling that the impending release of classified information portended a legitimization of UFO research and, with it, a new horizon of epistemological possibility (Espírito Santo and Vergara 2020).

Anticipating animated reactions from both UFO enthusiasts and skeptics alike, we decided to focus on the ufology discourse online. We set about understanding how the credibility of putative evidence of UFOs is accepted or rejected in online interactions: Does the way people talk about evidence enhance or diminish its credibility?

Given past precedents, we decided to focus on the micro-blogging platform Twitter. Using the academic research search endpoint of the

Twitter v2 API, we constructed a corpus of more than 3 million tweets using the "ufo" keyword. Unfortunately, the results were riddled with irrelevant content due to the occurrence of our keyword in unrelated discourse about musical groups, movies, games, etc. Through manual inspection, we learned that people most active in ufology often tweeted with the hashtag #ufotwitter to organize themselves into a single, self-selecting speech community. Using this hashtag, a local marker of participation and community membership, as a query term—hence, sampling frame—yielded a corpus of 240,000 tweets between July 1, 2019, and July 16, 2021. With each tweet, we also obtained metadata on the modality of the evidence (image, video, narrative account), engagement metrics (likes, retweets, replies, mentions), and public user information (number of followers, verified status).

Finding 1: competing views, shared networks

Around this time, Maya, an undergraduate double-majoring in linguistics and comparative literature, joined us as a research assistant. Maya's first role was conducting a "hashtag ethnography" (Bonilla and Rosa 2015) to learn about the culture of #ufotwitter. She found a documentary about #ufotwitter on the ufology YouTube channel Engaging the Phenomenon (2020), in which one participant described it as "a [worldwide] think tank." Another called it "a vehicle for participation in the topic of [UFOs], and instead of creating barriers to entry into this topic it removes them." One described a collaborative division of labor:

> Some #ufotwitter participants are breaking stories, putting together new information. And then right behind them you have other participants of #ufotwitter that take those stories and leads and follow up and put together more data and information, and we have a pool of information going on through this activity.

This isn't to say that #ufotwitter was without its factions or conflicts. As one ufologist put it, "a basic interest in discussing the ufo subject is the single-minded basis for #ufotwitter and from that point, clearly defined camps and tribes have staked out their positions" (Jamieson 2020). Two factions emerged as particularly salient in members' accounts: enthusiasts interested in the scientific legitimization of UFO research and skeptics committed to debunking paranormal claims. According to one member, "all the infighting and all the arguing" resulting from clashes between them "really adds an insane amount of ultra-skepticism, which in the long run just causes more division than in the first place" (Engaging the Phenomenon 2020).

We reasoned that because these "camps" or "tribes" were so salient in users' experience of #ufotwitter, a social network analysis would easily surface them. Not so. Jisoo experimented with machine learning algorithms such as the Louvain method (Blondel et al. 2008) to try and cluster the tweets by user interactions within the corpus (retweets, replies, mentions, and quotes), as well as topic models such as Latent Dirichlet allocation that operated on the text itself (to cluster tweets based on content alone). Neither computational approach surfaced clearly differentiated community networks in the #ufotwitter corpus, suggesting that, whatever epistemological schisms there may have been, users were engaged in sustained dialogue with people in competing camps. Although this seemed like a disappointment at the time, subsequent analysis would later reveal it to be an important finding.

Finding 2: nuanced evidential language

Although participants in #ufotwitter described their community as factious, a computational analysis of patterns of interaction between participants did not reveal the kind of intense factionalization previously detected around controversial topics such as COVID. Instead of focusing on interactions between accounts, then, we shifted our attention to the trajectories of conversational threads: if we couldn't use network analysis to identify processes of factionalization, could we use linguistic and interactional analysis to model the processes of consensus and conflict around individual pieces of evidence like photos and videos of UFOs?

As we turned our attention from the social organization of #ufotwitter to the social life of language within this communicative ecology, we quickly found that it is virtually impossible to reliably assign an epistemic stance to many of the tweets reporting evidence or engaging with reports of evidence. In many cases, individual tweets assumed multiple stances or expressed attitudes that were irresolvably ambiguous. Although everyone contributing to #ufotwitter seemed to be engaged with the activity of OSINT, their attitudes toward individual instances of evidence and toward the UFO phenomenon in general were complex, sometimes contradictory, and always difficult to parse. Stance was just too nebulous. To produce a scalable analysis, we needed something concrete. Something like a set of words.

Speakers of every language are concerned with the provenance of information: in the absence of our own firsthand observations, how do we know we can trust evidence reported to us by others (San Roque 2019)? One of the ways speakers of English signal their stance toward the quality of information is by using epistemic adverbs: some, such as "certainly," boost conviction; others, such as "possibly," hedge conviction; others still, such as "allegedly," indicate hearsay. Using an exhaustive list of epistemic adverbs derived from Wierzbicka (2006) and others, we found 1,600 examples of epistemic adverbs in about half as many tweets within the #ufotwitter corpus. Parsing these examples with the Large Language Model (LLM) BERT, Jisoo found the algorithm mapped the 768-dimensional semantic embeddings of epistemic adverbs into distinct clusters highly consistent with taxonomies in the linguistics scholarship we had consulted, confirming the relevance of that literature (Figure 5.1).

Drawing on her training in formal linguistics, Maya performed syntactic analysis to determine which sentential feature the adverbs in our corpus modified. Her tree diagrams of ufology tweets demonstrated that evidential adverbs are highly mobile within a sentence, affording users many choices when it comes to placement possibilities (Conrad and Biber 2000). Curious about what the placement of epistemic adverbs might reveal about a speaker's epistemic stance, we drew on Goffman's (1981) model of reported speech to delineate six syntactically possible objects of epistemic modulation in an evidential report: the UFO *phenomenon* itself; the *principal* who creates the possibility of witnessing; the actual witness who becomes the *author* of the evidence; the *animator* who reports the evidence; the verbal or visual *representation* of that evidence; and the *audience* to whom the animator presents that representation. When adverbs seemed to modulate the entire report, as when they occurred in initial or terminal positions, we designated them as *umbrella* modifiers.

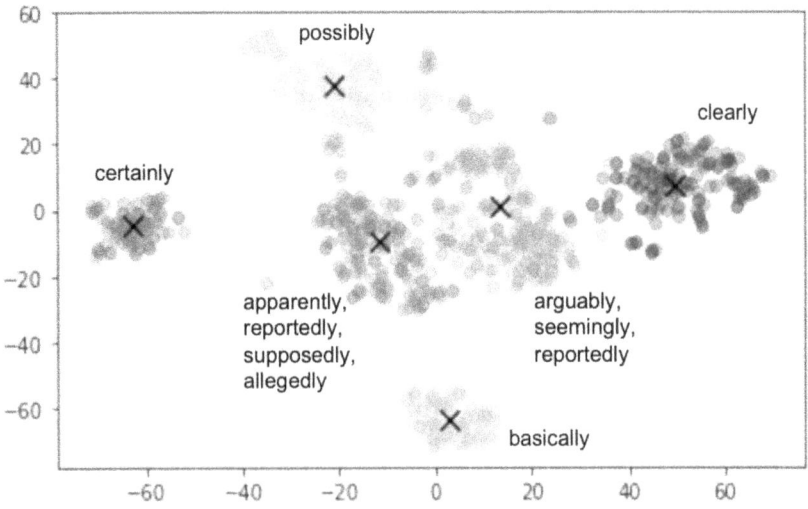

Figure 5.1 Epistemic adverbs grouped according to shared meanings as detected by a machine learning algorithm.

We will describe how we implemented this model in some detail, because the process may be illustrative for anyone conducting team-based, mixed-methods research. We knew that we needed to load the corpus of adverbial tweets onto a platform that would allow us to collaboratively annotate it so that we could work together in real time and cross-check each other's work. Because some tweets had multiple adverbs, we wanted to be able to annotate the data not just at the level of the message but at the level of the individual word. Finally, we wanted a platform that could allow us to quickly explore statistical patterns in the annotated data. After some experimentation with large and expensive qualitative data analysis software (QDAS) packages, we found a convenient and inexpensive collaborative tool in Notion, a shared workspace app with a spreadsheet feature that Jisoo quickly customized.

To calibrate our annotation of the adverbs, we began with two rounds of co-annotation. Jisoo and Maya independently coded small subsets of tweets (40 in the first round, 10 in the second round) and then consulted with Graham to resolve disagreements, further refining the annotation framework. After reaching intercoder reliability with a Krippendorff's alpha of 0.882, Jisoo and Maya annotated the remainder of the tweets on a single-coder basis. Ultimately, we found that evidential adverbs modulate the *phenomenon* and *representation* elements most frequently. This is perhaps to be expected, as conversation on #ufotwitter often revolves around making sense of what blurry pixels in a photograph might signify. Still, a nontrivial number of tweets focus attention on other actors involved in producing or circulating evidence, including the original witness (*author*) and the subsequent reporter (*animator*). This distribution suggests that the language used on #ufotwitter to encode stance reflects a highly nuanced awareness, emergent on the syntactic level, of the multifaceted nature of evidence (Figure 5.2).

Finding 3: the hearsay effect

Out of curiosity, we decided to inspect the subset of #ufotwitter tweets in the evidential adverb corpus from another perspective: user engagement. Statistical analysis revealed a surprising pattern: tweets with certain adverbs received a level of downstream engagement—measured by replies, likes, retweets, and quotes—that was far higher than the baseline average for the overall corpus. While tweets using adverbs such as "certainly," "clearly," or "presumably" engender rates of participation similar to the rest of the corpus, we saw a striking level of deviation for tweets with "allegedly," "arguably," "seemingly," and "supposedly." In particular, tweets with "allegedly" receive, on average, 10.2 times more retweets and 8.5 times more replies than the corpus average.

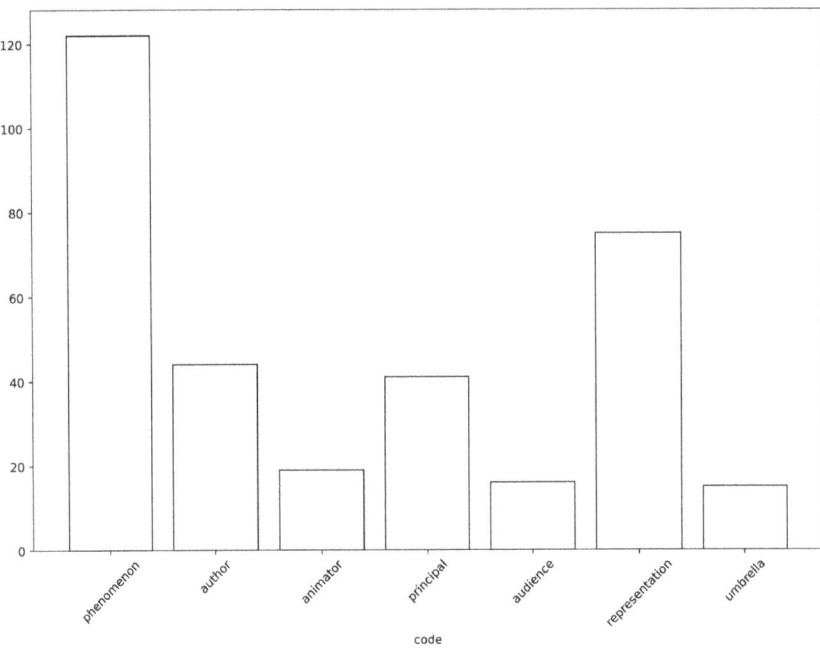

Figure 5.2 Aspect of evidence modified by epistemic adverb.

From a linguistic perspective, this result associated with "allegedly" (and "supposedly") is particularly interesting, as they are part of a small but semantically and pragmatically coherent subset of epistemic adverbs associated with hearsay (Celle 2009; Wierzbicka 2006). These adverbs signal that the evidence being presented is obtained from a source that is neither present nor accountable. They also authorize a speaker to report evidence without committing to a stance on its veracity, avoiding responsibility for sharing unconfirmed information (Rozumko 2019). Hearsay is typically understood to be the weakest form of evidence, often rendering it inadmissible in legal contexts. Yet, in the context of #ufotwitter, evidence explicitly marked as weak through the use of the hearsay adverb "allegedly" receives an astonishing *tenfold* increase in downstream engagement. We named this paradoxical pattern the *hearsay effect* but to make sense of it required a return to qualitative methods of textual exegesis (Figure 5.3).

Finding 4: evidential sociability

Our first thought was that perhaps more influential, prominent, or prolific tweeters might be heavier users of hearsay adverbs, but we could find no

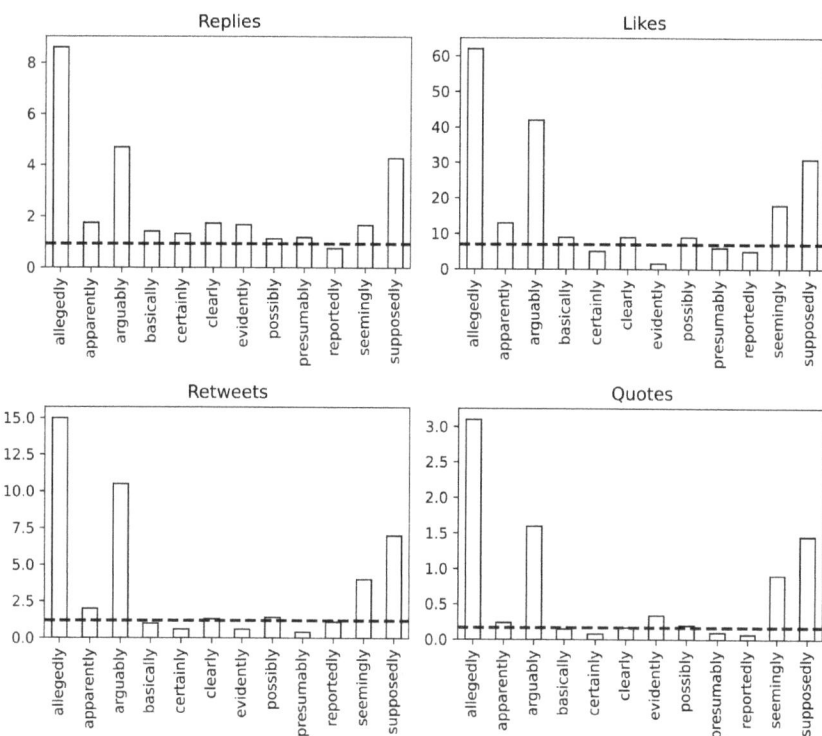

Figure 5.3 Measures of downstream engagement for tweets with different epistemic adverbs. Dashed lines represent corpus averages.

significant correlation between status within the community and adverb use. So, to understand why the hearsay adverb "allegedly" correlates so strongly with dramatic increases in downstream engagement, we turned to the interpretation of specific threads, sampled as cases. Consider the following Twitter thread, dating from June 7, 2021, a few weeks before the release of the Pentagon report. The original poster, a newspaper journalist who covers UFO news, shares what appears to be a military video featuring one such phenomenon. He writes:

> $Allegedly_1$ new, "leaked" #UFO footage $allegedly_2$ from someone inside the DHS which $allegedly_3$ shows a UFO "chasing" an A-10 Warthog near Douglas, AZ. $Allegedly_4$ filmed from a "Mobile Scope Truck." Thoughts or more info on this #ufotwitter?

Like other tweets in this category, this one received significantly more engagement than most tweets in the #ufotwitter corpus: 95 retweets (corpus average ≈ 1.5); 26 quotes (corpus average ≈ 0.25); 445 likes (corpus average ≈ 8); and 80 replies (corpus average ≈ 1).

This author uses "allegedly" four times in one tweet. Because epistemic adverbs are syntactically mobile, adverb placement is deliberate and thus reveals something about what aspect of evidentiality the speaker is choosing to modify, whether consciously or not. The four tokens of "allegedly" distance the speaker from responsibility for, respectively: (1) the veracity of the video as *representation*; (2) the identity of the *animator* who circulated the video; (3) the interpretation of what the *representation* shows; and (4) the identity of the *author* who created the original recording. There is a complex, multidimensional depiction of the overall unreliability of the evidentiary situation indexed by the selection and placement of these hearsay adverbs. To better understand how the representation of evidence as hearsay might correlate with increased engagement, we qualitatively analyzed the 80 replies to this tweet. This analysis suggests at least five possible explanations for the hearsay effect.

The first possible explanation is *newsworthiness*: perhaps hedging evidence as hearsay signals that a tweet is newsworthy, since hearsay adverbs are so often associated with journalism, and the author, in this case, is indeed a journalist. Thus, one respondent characterizes circulating hearsay evidence as an epistemically irresponsible way of sharing news:

> It's extremely irresponsible if these are not vetted correctly. If only a single vid is actually a bird or something prosaic [it] will be debunked & undermines all the work professional journos [have] been doing.

Confirming that adverbial modulation indeed enters into reader awareness, another user counters that the inclusion of the hearsay adverb is, in fact, a sign of epistemic responsibility:

> Hold up … [the Original Poster] is also a professional journalist who has done some outstanding work in the field of ufology. Plus he used the word "allegedly" 4 times making it obvious that he's not confirming the video's authenticity. He's simply asking UFOtwitter 2 take a look.

This exchange clearly underscores a connection between hearsay adverbs and the announcement of newsworthy information, even if the two respondents seem to differ on standards of journalistic responsibility.

A second possible explanation of the hearsay effect is that hedging evidence as unreliable or unconfirmed invites additional scrutiny and promotes *skepticism*. Perhaps it invites people to engage in practices of scientific literacy by disenchanting and debunking candidate evidence. This is a common leitmotif in many of the replies, which offer mundane explanations for the unidentified phenomena: drones, secret government vehicles, optical artifacts of the recording process, etc. Some of these replies are coolly dismissive, suggesting epistemic self-assurance. "Some kind of drone. Not seeing any extraordinary performance," writes one.

A third possibility is that hedging evidence as hearsay produces exactly the opposite effect, promoting enchantment rather than disenchantment. Some respondents simply express awe: "Dude this is incredible." Others go further in embellishing paranormal interpretations, suggesting that hearsay may invite speculative engagement. Thus, one reply reads:

> Here's my thought. With all these governments "leaks" they portray them as a threat yet how many of them have shot down a jet or a plane? How many fired one shot. NONE. THEY ARE FRIENDLIES!

This message seems to presume that the unidentified phenomenon in the video is indeed an alien craft, taking the apparent lack of hostility—in spite of superior technology—as a sign of benevolence.

A fourth possible explanation concerns the construction of a frame of play. Within #ufotwitter, hedging evidence as hearsay functions as a signal for play (Bateson 1972: 179): self-conscious about their traffic in questionable evidence, ufologists seize upon "allegedly" as an opportunity to engage in mildly self-deprecating humor. In a reply to his own tweet, the original poster jokes, "I only used the word 'allegedly' 4 times. I probably should've added a 5th or a 6th for good measure." A number of replies contain outrageous, humorous conjectures, clearly parodying the knowing tone of debunkers: "That's a flying rubber ducky," writes one. "Flying Tesla," jokes another.

A fifth possibility is perhaps the most intriguing, though the hardest to substantiate: marking evidence as hearsay embeds a straightforward referential statement about the world into a more information-rich depiction of a social situation involving multiple parties with differential access to knowledge. Insofar as hearsay adverbs are indexical of secondhandedness, might they invite questions about the intentions, motivations, abilities, and relationships among other parties implied by the circulation of evidence? As one respondent writes:

> You're right. Post "Alien Autopsy" every video is deemed fake until proven otherwise. I don't disagree with this stance either.
> Would be interesting if a genuine HD, up close [UFO] photo was leaked without chain of custody.

In other words, this respondent reflects that hearsay—which separates evidence from a clear provenance—inevitably demands *forensic* social analysis, no matter how compelling the evidence might be.

How could one adverb correlate with the activation of such diametric responses: expressing curiosity about newsworthy information; exercising scientific rationality; indulging in paranormal belief; engaging in unbridled play; and performing social forensics? We believe that "allegedly" can do so much because "hearsay adverbs point to some polemic issue and ... leave it up to the addressee to form a judgment. Hearsay adverbs might therefore be considered both disassertive and addressee-oriented" (Celle 2009, 282). We conjecture that this quality of addressee-orientation may be central to the hearsay effect—and, as we can see from the original tweet, it is signaled not only by the hearsay adverbs but by a direct invitation to participants in #ufotwitter to assess the evidence for themselves. In short, hearsay adverbs announce an opportunity for addressees to get involved in a conversation.

Recall that this #ufotwitter is a community of practice that is: engaged in a shared empirical pursuit; highly decentralized; highly egalitarian; skeptical of evidence; but eager for new evidence to adjudicate. We ultimately suggest that messages marked as hearsay are uniquely generative of engagement in such a context because of the way they allow participants to enact culturally specific norms of evidentiality and thereby occasion culturally specific forms of *evidential sociability*, the pursuit of social interaction for the primary purpose of evaluating evidence. This in turn allows for the continual construction and proliferation of possible worlds where multiple interpretations of the evidence could exist simultaneously (Hanks 2016), perpetuating #ufotwitter as a community.

Theoretical discovery: the Strength of Weak Evidence

Mark Granovetter (1973) famously makes the counterintuitive argument that "weak" social ties to distant acquaintances can prove surprisingly "strong" in terms of a social network's capacity to circulate information or mobilize resources. We propose a loose parallelism with Granovetter's argument: under certain sociocultural conditions, "weak" evidence—and, indeed, we are talking here about evidence that participants themselves mark as weak—proves surprisingly "strong" in terms of its capacity for circulation.

On some level, this flies in the face of Enlightenment understandings of a liberal, democratic public sphere: in a perfectly rational information ecology, strong evidence should theoretically always out-compete the weak. In that sense, it might seem that we are suggesting that ufologists, who are often linked with conspiracy theorists, engage in a flourishing trade in gossip, rumor, and innuendo. This is emphatically not our contention. Among the factors contributing to their elevated engagement with information marked as hearsay, ufologists lavish particularly rigorous scrutiny on tweets in this category, subjecting their claims to protracted analysis in perfectly rational Enlightenment fashion.

In discursive spaces like in #ufotwitter, hearsay evidence might generate engagement not in spite of, but because of its obvious epistemic unreliability. When evidential markers are mobilized to deflect accountability from the speaker and invite recipients to construct their own point of view, seemingly subtle inflections of epistemic modulation can correlate with dramatic changes in the volume of engagement online. Parsing the interactional dynamics within #ufotwitter more closely reveals that such an increase in participation is not necessarily siloed within one particular "camp" or "tribe" in the discursive community. Rather, it is by allowing different perspectives to activate simultaneously, thereby creating a kind of polyphonic dialogism, that ostentatiously weak evidence boosts participation.

Conclusion

This analysis of the strength of weak evidence within an arena of contested knowledge production offers new ways of conceptualizing how information and misinformation alike are animated in the context of an increasingly fragmented and cacophonous online public sphere. Social media analysts typically differentiate between legitimate information as *true* content and mis- or disinformation as *false* content (Murphy 2023). Our analysis of the hearsay effect suggests that the objective truth or falsity of content may be beside the point when it comes to understanding how communities form through the circulation of evidence: What may matter more are the opportunities that content affords for the enactment of mutually valued forms of sociability.

In a poignant twist, this pattern reflects our own research. Like the ufologists we were studying, we were driven by a conviction that there might be a signal in our noisy data. The process of attuning ourselves to detect it was also a social process of cultivating a small but robust community of practice, in which researchers at different career stages—a professor, a grad student, and an undergrad—could co-construct the craft of mixed-methods digital ethnography. We could not have discovered the strength of weak evidence without Graham's background in linguistic anthropology, Jisoo's skills with machine learning, and Maya's aptitude for formal linguistic analysis. Responding to each other's insights challenged us to reimagine tools from our respective fields and to develop a shared idiom unique to our collaborative effort.

By narrating our research process, we hope to have illustrated three somewhat unconventional lessons relevant to the practice of digital ethnography more broadly. First, deliberate theoretical sampling can help identify strategic foci within the immensity of digital discourse. Second, mixed-methods research allows digital ethnographers to computationally leverage quantitative metadata already baked into the language of social media. Third, team-based collaboration can make mixed-methods research particularly dynamic and rewarding, as collaborators learn from both the data and each other. Although these lessons apply to digital ethnography writ large, we feel they may be particularly germane for analyses focusing on the principal building block of digital culture: language.

Acknowledgments

This research was generously supported by a Fang Fund grant for interdisciplinary computing research from MIT's School of Humanities, Arts, and Social Sciences. Several people were instrumental in supporting this project: Crystal Lee, Arvind Satyanarayan, Bambi Schieffelin, and David Valentine. We thank them, along with audiences who responded to presentations in the Language and Technology Lab, Anthropology Program, Technology and Public Policy Program, and Summer Research Program, all at MIT; the Anthropology Departments at Yale, Harvard, and Cambridge Universities; and the "Disciplinary Relatives and Relativities" panel at the 2022 meeting of the American Anthropological Association in Seattle.

References

Agrama, Hussein Ali. 2021. "Secularity, Synchronicity, and Uncanny Science: Considerations and Challenges." *Zygon®* 56(2): 395–415.
Bateson, Gregory. 1972. *Steps to an Ecology of Mind*. New York: Ballentine.
Blondel, Vincent D., Jean-Loup Guillaume, Renaud Lambiotte, and Etienne Lefebvre. 2008. "Fast Unfolding of Communities in Large Networks." *Journal of Statistical Mechanics: Theory and Experiment* 10: P10008.
Bonilla, Yarimar, and Jonathan Rosa. 2015. "#Ferguson: Digital Protest, Hashtag Ethnography, and the Racial Politics of Social Media in the United States." *American Ethnologist* 42(1): 4–17.
Celle, Agnès. 2009. "Hearsay Adverbs and Modality." In *Modality in English: Theory and Description*, edited by Raphael Salkie, Pierre Busuttil, and Johan van der Auwera, 269–93. Berlin: Mouton de Gruyter.
Conrad, Susan, and Douglas Biber. 2000. "Adverbial Marking of Stance in Speech and Writing." In *Evaluation in Text: Authorial Stance and the Construction of Discourse*, edited by Susan Hunston and Geoffrey Thompson, 56–73. Oxford: Oxford University Press.
Dietrich, Alex. 2021. "'Just Disappeared': Veteran Combat Pilot Describes UFO Sighting." Interview by Anderson Cooper. CNN, May 19. Video, 5:38. https://www.cnn.com/videos/politics/2021/05/19/alex-dietrich-ufo-sighting-ac360-intv-vpx.cnn, accessed December 8, 2024.

Du Bois, John W. 2007. "The Stance Triangle." In *Stancetaking in Discourse: Subjectivity, Evaluation, Interaction*, edited by Robert Englebretson, 139–82. Amsterdam: Benjamins.

Eghigian, Greg. 2017. "Making UFOs Make Sense: Ufology, Science, and the History of Their Mutual Mistrust." *Public Understanding of Science* 26(5): 612–26.

Engaging the Phenomenon. 2020. "Welcome to UFO Twitter." *YouTube*. https://www.youtube.com/watch?v=3AFhDxyahko, accessed December 8, 2024.

Espírito Santo, Diana, and Alejandra Vergara. 2020. "The Possible and the Impossible: Reflections on Evidence in Chilean Ufology." *Antípoda* 41: 125–46.

Goffman, Erving. 1981. *Forms of Talk*. Philadelphia: University of Pennsylvania Press.

Goffman, Erving. 1989. "On Fieldwork." *Journal of Contemporary Ethnography* 18(2): 123–32.

Granovetter, Mark S. 1973. "The Strength of Weak Ties." *American Journal of Sociology* 78(6): 1360–80.

Guest, Greg. 2015. "Sampling and Selecting Participants in Field Research." In *Handbook of Methods in Cultural Anthropology*, edited by H. Russell Bernard and Clarence C. Gvarlee, 215–49. New York: Rowman & Littlefield.

Günel, Gökçe, and Chika Watanabe. 2024. "Patchwork Ethnography." *American Ethnologist* 51(1): 131–39.

Hanks, Michele. 2016. "Between Electricity and Spirit: Paranormal Investigation and the Creation of Doubt in England." *American Anthropologist* 118(4): 811–23.

Hong, Jisoo. 2022. *A Thesis, Allegedly*. Master's thesis, Massachusetts Institute of Technology. DSpace Digital Repository. https://hdl.handle.net/1721.1/144608.

Jamieson, Mike. 2020. "The #ufotwitter Loka." *Cosmic Pluralism Studies*. https://cosmic-pluralism-studies.academy/the-ufotwitter-loka, accessed July 31, 2021.

Johnson, Amy, and Graham M. Jones. 2021. "Language, the Internet, and Digital Communication." In *The International Encyclopedia of Linguistic Anthropology*, edited by J. M. Stanlaw. Malden, MA: Wiley-Blackwell.

Jones, Graham M., and Bambi B. Schieffelin. 2016. "The Ethnography of Inscriptive Speech." In *eFieldnotes: Makings of Anthropology in a Digital World*, edited by Roger Sanjek and Susan W. Tratner, 210–28. Philadelphia: University of Pennsylvania Press.

Kiesling, Scott F., Umashanthi Pavalanathan, Jim Fitzpatrick, Xiaochuang Han, and Jacob Eisenstein. 2018. "Interactional Stancetaking in Online Forums." *Computational Linguistics* 44(4): 683–718.

Kuipers, Joel. 2013. "Evidence and Authority in Ethnographic and Linguistic Perspective." *Annual Review of Anthropology* 42: 399–413.

Lee, Crystal, Tanya Yang, Gabrielle D. Inchoco, Graham M. Jones, and Arvind Satyanarayan. 2022. "Viral Visualizations: How Coronavirus Skeptics Use Orthodox Data Practices to Promote Unorthodox Science Online." In *Proceedings of the 2021 CHI Conference on Human Factors in Computing Systems, Yokohama Japan*, 1–18.

Lewis-Kraus, Gideon. 2021. "The U.F.O. Papers." *The New Yorker*, May 10.

Lepselter, Susan. 2016. *The Resonance of Unseen Things: Poetics, Power, Captivity, and UFOs in the American Uncanny*. Ann Arbor: University of Michigan Press.

Murphy, Keith M. 2023. "Fake News and the Web of Plausibility." *Social Media + Society* 9(2). https://journals.sagepub.com/doi/full/10.1177/20563051231170606.

Pasulka, Diana Walsh. 2019. *American Cosmic: UFOs, Religions, Technology*. Oxford: Oxford University Press.

Radin, Paul. (1966 [1933]). *The Method and Theory of Ethnology: An Essay in Criticism*. New York: Basic Books.

Rozumko, Agata. 2019. "Between Acknowledgement and Countering: Interpersonal Functions of English Reportative Adverbs." *Journal of Pragmatics* 140: 1–11.

San Roque, Lila. 2019. "Evidentiality." *Annual Review of Anthropology* 48: 353–70.

Small, Mario Luis. 2011. "How to Conduct a Mixed Methods Study: Recent Trends in a Rapidly Growing Literature." *Annual Review of Sociology* 37(1): 57–86.

Small, Mario Luis, and Jessica McCrory Calarco. 2022. *Qualitative Literacy: A Guide to Evaluating Ethnographic and Interview Research*. Berkeley: University of California Press.

Timmermans, Stefan, and Iddo Tavory. 2012. "Theory Construction in Qualitative Research: From Grounded Theory to Abductive Analysis." *Sociological Theory* 30(3): 167–86.

Wierzbicka, Anna. 2006. *English: Meaning and Culture*. Oxford: Oxford University Press.

Chapter 5.1

Concept
Meme

İdil Galip

The word "meme" was coined by British evolutionary biologist Richard Dawkins in his 1976 book "The Selfish Gene." He came up with this neologism to understand how culture comes about and how it is transmitted between people through an evolutionary framework. He claimed that we could think of memes as "units of culture" that replicate themselves, creating their own "high-fidelity" copies as they are shared from person to person. This was an evolutionary analogy he used to explain how some bits of culture remain and some are lost to time. According to Dawkins, units of culture, or memes, with high survival value would stick around and be reproduced in human communities, while those with low survival value would die out. Some examples of memes he provided were tunes, ideas, catch-phrases, styles, and techniques of making or constructing things such as pots and arches (Dawkins 1989). Dawkins, who is now more well known for "militant atheism" (Dawkins 2008), also argued that the most successful meme of all is the "God meme" due to its strong psychological appeal for humans (Dawkins 1989).

This evolutionary theory of cultural transmission and production came to be known as "memetics" in the following years and faced a great deal of scrutiny from the wider scientific community for its reductionist and determinist tendencies. Particularly within the humanities and social sciences, evolutionary or biological explanations of culture are unpopular as they focus on mechanistic accounts of cultural transmission rather than, for instance, how culture is created by individuals, communities, structures, rituals, practices, etc. Following such critiques from the humanities and social sciences, as well as Dawkins's peers in the natural sciences, memetics as a theory and a field of thought was deemed to be pseudoscientific by most scholars and developed a contentious reputation in academia.

These discussions about the shortcomings of memetics were at their height during the 1980s and 1990s. However, this debate, along with memetics itself, declined in visibility and somewhat disappeared from academic consciousness after this period of activity. That is, until Limor

Shifman, a communications scholar interested in digital culture and internet humor, rehabilitated the concept of the "meme" by dislodging it from the tumultuous heritage of memetics and recontextualizing it for the purposes of internet research (Shifman 2013, 2014). In the early 2010s, Shifman recognized that internet users were describing jokes, stories, images, and videos which are reproduced and circulated online as "internet memes." She also identified that there was a gap between the practices and knowledge of internet users and that of academics studying internet culture. As a result of this discrepancy, Shifman found that it was important to explore the intellectual history of memes and memetics and investigate how it could be connected to the use and practice of internet memes. This period, also marked by a rise in political use of memes, was followed by a flurry of academic research about memes as media (see: Miltner 2014; Phillips and Milner 2017; Nagle 2017; DeCook 2018; Tuters and Hagen 2020; Peeters et al. 2021; Zulli and Zulli 2022).

Meme research is not defined by a set of methodological principles and is open to methodological experimentation, with many contemporary scholars mixing methods to capture different facets of memes and meme cultures. However, we could confidently argue that textual analysis often forms a large part of any study that engages with memes. This presupposes that the researcher sees memes as "media texts" that can be analyzed just like a written work. Textual analysis of memes involves a decoding process, where the researcher analyzes the visual and linguistic elements found in the meme or memes. Characters or personas, aesthetic styles, colors, captions, and grammar used in memes can communicate layers of meaning. Therefore, researchers need to have a degree of *meme literacy*—the ability to understand the meaning, context, and nuances of the meme as a whole. Note that memes are *multimodal* (Phillips and Milner 2017), which means they are texts that convey meaning through many modes, not only visually but also gesturally, socially, aurally, and so on. Meme literacy is then by default multimodal as well.

A particularly useful way of exploring the *social layer of memes* is through digital ethnography, or by observing how meme-makers and communities create, disseminate, and engage with memes. Since a large part of meme research is done by media and communications scholars, digital ethnography is a less common method in the field. However, an advantage of digital ethnography is that it allows scholars to go beyond textual analysis of memes and understand the social, ritual, and communal practices that foreground memes as artifacts in greater detail. Digital ethnography can help researchers find *the people behind the memes*, so to speak.

Tactics such as lurking, scrolling, and screenshotting are part of the toolkit of a digital ethnographer but must be used with discretion due to the ethical complexities of collecting digital data. One way of approaching this issue can be through the application of "ethical consent" through interviews. Researchers can contact interlocutors for interviews and ask for their express permission to collect their memes or material from their social media pages. This can also help with issues that may arise when publishing images in academic texts, for instance. This takes more time and effort for a researcher but also results in complex and nuanced "small data" that can bring context to a meme community or a genre of memes. Digital ethnography, when combined with a platform studies framework, is also useful when investigating how platforms and their respective platform cultures shape and are shaped by memes and meme communities.

Digital ethnography for memes takes the onus from the memes as referent-objects and shifts it to the practices of creativity, belonging, sociality, and antagonism that emerge around memes. It helps bring to light the social and ritualistic connections that underscore meme-making and sharing practices and can show us who makes memes and why and how they do it. Despite the lack of agency prescribed to *people* in memetics and Dawkins's theorization of memes and culture, culture is a deeply social endeavor. As a result, meme research has to interact with methods that address not only visuality but also sociality as well; therefore, digital ethnography is a viable method to gather information about the social formation of memes and meme cultures.

References

Dawkins, Richard. 1989. *The Selfish Gene*. New ed. Oxford; New York: Oxford University Press.

Dawkins, Richard. 2008. "Richard Dawkins: Militant Atheism." *Richard Dawkins Foundation for Reason & Science* (blog). https://richarddawkins.net/2008/04/richard-dawkins-militant-atheism/.

DeCook, Julia R. 2018. "Memes and Symbolic Violence: #proudboys and the Use of Memes for Propaganda and the Construction of Collective Identity." *Learning, Media and Technology* 43 (4): 485–504. https://doi.org/10.1080/17439884.2018.1544149.

Milner, Ryan M. 2017. *The World Made Meme: Public Conversations and Participatory Media*. Cambridge: The MIT Press.

Miltner, Kate M. 2014. "'There's No Place for Lulz on LOLCats': The Role of Genre, Gender, and Group Identity in the Interpretation and Enjoyment of an Internet Meme." *First Monday*, August. https://doi.org/10.5210/fm.v19i8.5391.

Nagle, Angela. 2017. *Kill All Normies: The Online Culture Wars from Tumblr and 4chan to the Alt-Right and Trump*. Winchester; Washington, DC: Zero Books.

Peeters, Stijn, Marc Tuters, Tom Willaert, and Daniël De Zeeuw. 2021. "On the Vernacular Language Games of an Antagonistic Online Subculture." *Frontiers in Big Data* 4(August): 718368. https://doi.org/10.3389/fdata.2021.718368.

Phillips, Whitney, and Ryan M. Milner. 2017. *The Ambivalent Internet: Mischief, Oddity, and Antagonism Online*. Cambridge; Malden, MA: Polity.

Shifman, Limor. 2013. *Memes in Digital Culture*. Cambridge, MA: The MIT Press.
Shifman, Limor. 2014. "The Cultural Logic of Photo-Based Meme Genres." *Journal of Visual Culture* 13 (3): 340–58. https://doi.org/10.1177/1470412914546577.
Tuters, Marc, and Sal Hagen. 2020. "(((They))) Rule: Memetic Antagonism and Nebulous Othering on 4chan." *New Media & Society* 22 (12): 2218–37. https://doi.org/10.1177/1461444819888746.
Zulli, Diana, and David James Zulli. 2022. "Extending the Internet Meme: Conceptualizing Technological Mimesis and Imitation Publics on the TikTok Platform." *New Media & Society* 24 (8): 1872–90. https://doi.org/10.1177/1461444820983603.

Chapter 5.2

Case study

Evaluating emergent Kazakh anti-proverbs using corpus linguistics

Erik Aasland and Gulnara Omarbekova

What exactly is an anti-proverb, and where does one encounter it? One could say that it is a traditional saying with a twist. The change can be as subtle as swapping out a word or as drastic as flipping the meaning of the traditional proverb on its head. We come in contact with anti-proverbs anywhere discourse is used and creativity is valued. This can range from "dad jokes" to advertising and political speeches.

Let's consider an anti-proverb that is formed by swapping out a word. You may be familiar with the proverb "An apple a day keeps the doctor away?" This adage emphasizes the importance of eating healthful foods—an apple—leading to avoiding illness, or "keeping the doctor away." Here is one variation:

> "An onion a day keeps the doctor away" is used as the title of an essay on the health benefits of onions.[1] The meaning has stayed the same, but the specific food has been swapped out.

Here is an example of the anti-proverb contradicting the traditional proverb (O'Toole 2013):

> There is an old motto that runs, "If at first you don't succeed, try, try again." This is nonsense. It ought to read—'If at first you don't succeed, quit, quit at once.
>
> (Leacock 1918, 245)

Leacock provides the traditional proverb followed by his proposed anti-proverb. Since that publication, this anti-proverb has been widely distributed in an abbreviated form: "If at first you don't succeed, quit."

In terms of traditional sayings, there are both proverbs and aphorisms. For proverbs, we don't know the author, but for aphorisms we do. Both forms of traditional sayings are contextually specified with their meaning established through historical, intertextual, personal, and discourse connections as well as the setting-specific application (Finnegan 1981, 15, 27, 34; Kirshenblatt-Gimblett 1981, 112, 118–19). At the same time, we can say that proverb variations such as anti-proverbs are a more frequent occurrence in our globalized world of the internet and social media (Tóthné Litovkina et al. 2021, 20); there are also key local aspects to the process. Anti-proverbs emerge through the playful action of one author to fit the "language use, mentality, and context" of that age (Tóthné Litovkina et al. 2021, 21, 232).

There are three reasons why our focus should be on Kazakh. First, anti-proverbs are a new development for Kazakh, thus the reference to them as "emergent" in the title. The first collection of anti-proverbs in Kazakh was put together by Gulnara Omarbekova (2023). Advertising introduced many of these changes. Second, for Kazakhs, proverbs are the traditional resource for defining problems, making moral judgments, and suggesting remedies (Tabıldıyev 2001). What changes led to the emergence of the current Kazakh anti-proverbs? Third, many of the metaphors and images present in Kazakh proverbs are archaic, having their origin in Kazakh's nomadic past. As the scholar Qayratulı (2015) pointed out, the "nomadic ideal" no longer matches up with what most Kazakhs do in contemporary society.

During both the Russian Empire and the Soviet era, there was an emphasis placed on ethnographic research to catalog and categorize other cultures. Traditions of the past were represented that would not interfere with future priorities, whether of the Empire or Soviet State (Adams 1999). Kazakh writers and other members of the intelligentsia explored the nomadic past as a way to consider current issues (Kudaibergenova 2013). Individuals and institutions also presented aspects of their nomadic past as central to their self-understanding. For example, schools would include a purported section from the seventeenth-century speech by Kazibek Bi on Kazakhs being sheep-herding people as part of the values they wanted to pass on to the youth (Aasland 2023, 26–27). In this way, reflections on nomadic heritage went from being a point of contrast with other cultures to highlighting values within Kazakh culture to which they could aspire.

What is the difference between the use of a traditional saying and an anti-proverb? A Kazakh mother might share an aphorism with her daughter, introducing it with the phrase "The Kazakhs say," followed by:

"Ел болам десең, бесігіңді түзе!" [Yel bolamyn deseŋ, besigiŋdy tüze] (If you want to live in a strong country, take care of raising your children!)

The message: It is necessary to pay special attention to the upbringing of the next generation, since they are the future of the people. This has consistently been a concern of Kazakh oral tradition. The mother has her statement backed up by the weighty authority of tradition, as shown in Figure 5.2.1.

Let's consider how a Kazakh anti-proverb develops. Here is an example:

Ел боламын десең, масканды түзе. [Yel bolamyn deseŋ, maskaŋdy tüze] (If you want to live in a strong country, wear the mask.)

In context, this means wearing a mask in the event of COVID-19 protects the health of the country. If you want to be a healthy country, put on a mask. It sounds like a traditional Kazakh saying, but its authority will be based, to a large extent, on the degree to which it gains currency and corresponding vernacular authority (Howard 2022).

Vernacular authority for anti-proverbs develops as the anti-proverb gains distribution, or as it is commonly referenced, goes viral. Here, the process is similar to how a specific meme might catch on with a wider audience. Memes and anti-proverbs are different, with the meme being more focused on the picture and the anti-proverb more on word play and pun. Still, in terms of vernacular authority, both can be spread by social media, and anti-proverbs' use of metaphor is pictorial (Kövecses 2021). This is shown in Figure 5.2.2.

You will notice the arrows on the left hand side of the figure. These indicate intertextual links. The meme does not appear out of thin air but needs to connect present societal frames and understanding.

Figure 5.2.1 The weighty authority of tradition.

Figure 5.2.2 The effect of vernacular authority.

How does this work in the case of anti-proverbs? Lord John Russel in 1823 defined a proverb as "One man's wit and all men's wisdom" (Mackintosh 1853, 190); however, this definition masks how proverbiality develops. What we see with proverbs is the wit of one that becomes the wisdom of many. This is an especially vital process in the case of anti-proverbs for which familiar plots are played out in a new way, using the general meaning of the expression.

How are anti-proverbs perceived and received so that they have the potential to go viral? There is generally a traditional saying on which the anti-proverb is based. Do those encountering the anti-proverb connect it with a traditional saying, or do they recognize anti-proverbs as being proverb-like? Just like proverbs, anti-proverbs have proverbial markers, such as rhymes, key themes, and logical structures that allow the reader/hearer to see that the sentence being considered is proverb-like (Arora 1994).

What is corpus linguistics?

A corpus consists of a large set of texts that can be analyzed using computers. Corpus linguistics allows us to analyze the language in specific collections of texts to describe language use and change. Corpus (one set) or corpora (multiple sets) can range in the number of entries from a few hundred to millions. With the aid of software, corpora can be used to understand societal stereotypes (Baker et al. 2008), explore language use over time (Steyer 2015), or to delve into the dynamics of different types of discourse in one society (Aasland 2023).

Among the largest sets of corpora are monitor corpora, which are used to explore changes to languages over time. These are referred to as diachronic corpora (Collins 2019, 19). One example of such corpora is the British National Corpus.[2] Editors for dictionaries utilize corpora to locate and evaluate the frequency of new words and phrases. They evaluate both novelty and currency in considering new terms for the dictionary.

There are also topical corpora focused on a specific time period. Consider the corpora collection relating to COVID[3] or the Corpus of American Soap Operas.[4] These are referred to as synchronic corpora. You can access all of these by going to English-Corpora.org. There are also corpora set up by scholars such as folklorists. These include a parallel Ukrainian-English folktale corpus (Burda-Lassen 2022) or an English-Italian parallel corpus of proverbs intended for use in analyzing metaphors in proverbs in the two languages (Özbal et al. 2016).

The use of corpus linguistic tools allows us to explore the co-text of a word (Collins 2019, 9), that is, the linguistic surroundings of a word. We understand what a word means by the co-text. For example, the word "club" can mean a variety of things:

1 He enjoyed going with friends to the *club* to hear new musical groups.
2 She grabbed a stick and used it like a *club*, swatting away the bats flying toward her.
3 They formed their own stamp collectors *club*, sharing finds and projects online.

In corpus linguistic work, the standard practice is to consider the five words before and the five words after the selected key word. Let's look at sentence #1:

going with friends to the -*club*- to hear new musical groups

The participial phrase "going to the" before club makes it clear that what is being referred to is a location rather than a tool for hitting. We understand a word based on the words and phrases around it.

Working with a Kazakh proverb corpus

In the current case study, we set up two corpora using the anti-proverb research completed by Omarbekova (2023). This included one hundred Kazakh anti-proverbs as one corpus and a second corpus of the corresponding traditional Kazakh proverbs on which the anti-proverbs are based. The corresponding traditional proverbs operate as a reference set to the corpus of anti-proverbs. Anti-proverbs in the corpus were located by a Google search.

Here is a most fascinating side-by-side comparison of traditional proverb and anti-proverb:

Ашу—дұшпан, ақыл—дос, ақылыңа ақыл қос. [Aşw—duşpan, aqıl—dos, aqılıŋa aqıl qos.] (Anger is enemy, intelligence is friend, add wisdom to your mind.)

Anti-proverb: Ашу—тапанша, Ақыл—доллар. [Aşw—tapanşa, Aqıl—dollar.] (Anger is a pistol; wisdom is a dollar.)

There are three times when Ақыл (wisdom) is used as part of the traditional proverb or the anti-proverb. However, a new anti-proverb is created with a new borrowed lexis: "dollar," which is a picture of the modern economy of Kazakhstan in the mirror of the language. Kazakh has relatively few proverbs about money, trade, and entrepreneurship. They were not part of the nomadic ideal.

There is a connection in the traditional proverb between money and friendship:

Жүз теңгең болғанша, жүз досың болсын! [Jüz teŋgeŋ bolğanşa, jüz dosıŋ bolsın!] (Rather than one hundred Tenge, have one hundred friends!)

What has happened here? We can use software to compare the co-text for the sayings in question. The traditional proverb connected wisdom with friendship; the anti-proverb has swapped out "friendship" for the semantically related collocate of money represented here by the dollar. However, this also shifts the equation. The traditional proverb valued friendship more highly than money. Now the tables have turned, and the dollar may be as desirable as wisdom. This could be another example of the shift away from the nomadic ideal, but further research would be required.

Future research could involve work in four areas:

1 Expand the Kazakh anti-proverb corpus.
2 Build a corpus of Kazakh proverbs and anti-proverbs for computational linguistic analysis to identify patterns in word use, structure, and theme.
3 Research whether individuals who recognize and understand the given anti-proverb are doing so based on knowing the related traditional proverb and/or based on the proverbial markers in the anti-proverb.
4 Study the rise of anti-proverbs in digital platforms like social media, blogs, and forums. How is the internet shaping the evolution of Kazakh anti-proverbs?

Conclusion

According to Howard and Blank, tradition is what we enact in relationship with others, gaining authority from the past and pressing into a hopeful future together (2013, 10). Why would the enactment of tradition be accompanied by a sense of hope? We would suggest that it is connected with what Michael Herzfeld describes as "cultural fixity" (2016, 27–28). Research into this area would contribute to understanding the evolving nature of Kazakh identity, humor, and communication in the twenty-first century.

Notes

1 https://www.holland-onions.org/gb/media/newsletter/19/46.
2 https://www.english-corpora.org/bnc/.
3 https://www.english-corpora.org/corona/.
4 https://www.english-corpora.org/soap/.

Bibliography

Aasland, Erik. 2023. "Contrasting Two Kazakh Proverbial Calls to Action: Using Discourse Ecology to Understand Proverb Meaning-making." In *Contemporary Kazakh Proverb Research: Digital, Cognitive, Literary, and Ecological Approaches*, edited by Gulnara Omarbekova and Erik Aasland, 19–32. New York: Peter Lang.

Adams, Laura L. 1999. "Invention, Institutionalization and Renewal in Uzbekistan's National Culture." *European Journal of Cultural Studies* 2 (3): 355–73.

Arora, Shirley L. 1994. "The Perception of Proverbiality." In *Wise Words: Essays on the Proverb*, edited by Wolfgang Mieder, 3–30. New York and London: Garland Publishing.

Baker, Paul, Costas Gabrielatos, Majid KhosraviNik, Michał Krzyżanowski, Tony McEnery, and Ruth Wodak. 2008. "A Useful Methodological Synergy? Combining Critical Discourse Analysis and Corpus Linguistics to Examine Discourses of Refugees and Asylum Seekers in the UK Press." *Discourse & Society* 19 (3): 273–306.

Burda-Lassen, Olena. 2022. "Ukrainian-to-English Folktale Corpus: Parallel Corpus Creation and Augmentation for Machine Translation in Low-Resource Languages." In *Proceedings of the 15th Biennial Conference of the Association for Machine Translation in the Americas (Workshop 2: Corpus Generation and Corpus Augmentation for Machine Translation)*, Orlando FL, 28–31.

Collins, Luke. 2019. *Corpus Linguistics for Online Communication: A Guide for Research*. London: Routledge/Taylor and Francis Group.

Finnegan, Ruth. 1981. "Proverbs in Africa." In *The Wisdom of Many: Essays on the Proverb*, edited by Wolfgang Mieder and Alan Dundes, 10–42. Madison: University of Wisconsin Press.

Herzfeld, Michael. 2016. *Cultural Intimacy: Social Poetics and the Real Life of States, Societies, and Institutions*. Third edition. Abingdon, Oxon: Routledge.

Howard, Robert Glenn, and Trevor J. Blank. 2013. "Introduction: Living Traditions in a Modern World." In *Tradition in the Twenty-First Century: Locating the Role of the Past in the Present*, edited by Trevor J. Blank and Robert Glenn Howard, 1–21. Logan: Utah State University Press.

Howard, Robert Glenn. 2022. "Manufacturing Populism: Digitally Amplified Vernacular Authority." *Media and Communication* 10(4): 236–47. https://doi.org/10.17645/mac.v10i4.5857.

Kirshenblatt-Gimblett, Barbara. 1981. "Toward a Theory of Proverb Meaning." In *The Wisdom of Many: Essays on the Proverb*, edited by Wolfgang Mieder and Alan Dundes, 11–121. Madison: University of Wisconsin Press.

Kövecses, Zoltán. 2021. "Standard and Extended Conceptual Metaphor Theory." In *The Routledge Handbook of Cognitive Linguistics*, edited by Wen Xu and John R. Taylor, 191–203. London: Routledge.

Kudaibergenova, Diana T. 2013. "Imagining Community in Soviet Kazakhstan: An Historical Analysis of Narrative on Nationalism in Kazakh-Soviet Literature." *Nationalities Papers* 41 (5): 839–54. https://doi.org/10.1080/00905992.2013.775115.

Leacock, Stephen. 1918. *Frenzied Fiction*. New York and London: John Lane Co. https://www.gutenberg.org/ebooks/28919.

Mackintosh, James. 1853. *Memoirs of the Life of the Right Honourable Sir James Mackintosh*. Edited by R. J. Mackintosh. Boston, MA: Little, Brown, and Co.

Nazpary, Joma. 2002. *Post-Soviet Chaos: Violence and Dispossession in Kazakhstan*. London: Pluto Press.

Omarbekova, Gulnara. 2023. "The Anti-Proverbs of the Kazakh Language." In *Contemporary Kazakh Proverb Research: Digital, Cognitive, Literary, and Ecological Approaches*, edited by Gulnara Omarbekova and Erik Aasland, 171–233. New York: Peter Lang.

O'Toole, G. 2013. "If at First You Don't Succeed, Try, Try Again. Then Quit. There's No Use Being a Damn Fool About It." *Quotesearch*. August 12. https://quoteinvestigator.com/2013/08/11/try-again/.

Özbal, Gözde, Carlo Strapparava, and Serra Sinem Tekiroğlu. 2016. "PROMETHEUS: A Corpus of Proverbs Annotated with Metaphors." In *Proceedings of the Tenth International Conference on Language Resources and Evaluation (LREC'16)*, 3787–93. Portorož, Slovenia: European Language Resources Association (ELRA).

Qayratulı, Beken. 2015. *Qazibek Bidiŋ Sözi Nemese Qazaq Qanday Halıq Edi [Kazibek Bi's Words or What Kind of People Are the Kazakhs]*. https://vk.com/wall-26449296_19846.

Steyer, Kathrin. 2015. "Proverbs from a Corpus Linguistic Point of View." In *Introduction to Paremiology: A Comprehensive Guide to Proverb Studies*, edited by Hrisztalina Hrisztova-Gotthardt and Melita Aleksa Varga, 206–228. Berlin: De Gruyter.

Tabıldıyev, Ädibay. 2001. *Qazaq Etnopedagogıykacı [Kazakh Ethnopedagogy]*. Almaty: Sanat.

Tóthné Litovkina, Anna, Hrisztalina Hrisztova-Gotthardt, Péter Barta, Katalin Vargha, and Wolfgang Mieder. 2023. *Anti-Proverbs in Five Languages: Structural Features and Verbal Humor Devices*. Basingstoke: Palgrave Macmillan.

Chapter 6

Data analysis
Thick Big Data

Anna M. Górska, Dariusz Jemielniak, and Nina Kotula

Introduction

In the ever-evolving landscape of social sciences, the study of digital environments has transitioned from a novel subject to a foundational research aspect, as Bainbridge (1999) predicted, foreseeing the internet becoming the primary environment for sociological research, while social scientists must engage with real societal dilemmas within these digital spaces (Bonenfant and Meurs 2018; Hynes 2018) in various ways. The dialogue between quantitative and qualitative analyses highlights a crucial paradox: as the volume of quantitative data increases, so does the necessity for qualitative interpretation. While offering unprecedented access to information, Big Data often needs a more contextual framework necessary for meaningful analysis. The integration of qualitative research helps to fill this gap, providing the critical context and narrative depth required to make sense of vast datasets.

This chapter presents the concept of *Thick Big Data*, combining highly quantified datasets with deeply qualitative insights, developed by Jemielniak (2020). This approach is essential for unraveling the rich mix of online social dynamics, behaviors, and cultural expressions often overlooked by traditional research paradigms. It leverages the strengths of both quantitative and qualitative methods while minimizing their individual drawbacks. Thick Big Data in social research emphasizes a nuanced interpretation of large datasets by enriching Big Data analysis with deep, qualitative insights. This approach moves beyond mere data accumulation to focus on meaningful interpretation, offering a comprehensive understanding that quantitative data alone cannot achieve. Incorporating qualitative data ensures that research remains grounded, relevant, and contextually informed. This mixed-methods approach aligns with calls to integrate quantitative breadth and qualitative depth for comprehensive and rigorous inquiries (Jemielniak 2020; Jick 1979).

The chapter begins by highlighting the importance of studying digital environments within contemporary social sciences. It traces the migration

DOI: 10.4324/9781032672663-23

of various activities into online spaces, necessitating new methodological frameworks. We introduce Thick Big Data as a paradigm that synthesizes large-scale quantitative analysis with qualitative contextualization to reveal nuanced insights into online behaviors and cultural dynamics.

Further, the chapter outlines the philosophical assumptions underpinning Thick Big Data and presents a model for converging diverse data collection tools and analytical techniques. It critically examines the dichotomy between statistical and contextual approaches, advocating for a pragmatic, iterative methodology that harnesses their respective strengths. The next sections detail the significance of differentiating between declarative and behavioral data in online research. The chapter presents various quantitative techniques, including questionnaires, computational social science, Big Data analytics, social network analysis (SNA), and data scraping. It also explores major qualitative approaches like digital ethnography, case studies, and narrative analysis. The chapter ends with a presentation of a real case study of #MGTOW and #feminism Twitter (now X) communities, demonstrating a practical use of the Thick Big Data method.

Theoretical background

The discourse around mixed-method approaches in the social sciences has long highlighted an unnecessary (and artificial) division between quantitative and qualitative methodologies, each with its exploratory and explanatory strengths (Stebbins 2001, Czarniawska-Joerges 1992). Increasingly, scholars advocate for an integrative, pragmatic methodology that harnesses the advantages of both statistical analysis and contextual interpretation. This convergence proves useful for unraveling the intricate realities of digital domains. Specifically, synthesizing Big Data's extensive breadth with ethnography's in-depth *thickness* offers comprehensive insights into individual behaviors and collective cultural dynamics facilitated by the internet (Jemielniak 2020).

Especially, as the digital age's information and communication technologies have vastly expanded data access, there is a need for new analytical frameworks and paradigms that address this new data. The Thick Big Data approach signifies a paradigm shift that leverages the analytical prowess of Big Data while embedding it within qualitative thickness. This mixed methodology aligns with calls for pragmatism in internet research (Sudweeks and Simoff 1999). Qualitative context weaves meaning into the statistical analyses, echoing perspectives that raw data require interpretive framing (Halavais 2015).

Thick Big Data's interpretivist orientation seeks to comprehend digital communities by elucidating members' social realities and meanings. This perspective, rooted in seminal works, facilitates insights into the structures and processes constituting communities, whether physical or virtual (Geertz 1973, Denzin 1997).

Declarative and behavioral data

The distinction between declarative and behavioral data in social sciences, especially when studying online communities, is essential. *Declarative data* comes from direct participant responses like survey answers or interviews and relies on self-reporting, making it subjective and prone to inaccuracies due to memory or the desire to present oneself favorably (Scharkow 2016, Jürgens et al. 2020). For example, surveys can reflect aspirations more than actual behavior due to societal pressures or reluctance to share the truth. This difficulty is amplified in online studies, where self-reported data often deviates from objective tracking data, as seen in racial preferences in matchmaking (Robnett and Feliciano 2011).

Behavioral data captures actions, free from self-reporting biases, providing a more objective reflection of online engagement and preferences. Tracking real activities bypasses inaccuracies inherent in self-reporting and offers a factual account of user interactions. This data is valuable in online research due to the abundance of digital footprints. In the age of digital transformation that affects all aspects of our lives, tracking users' online activity allows for unique research opportunities (e.g., Vlassenroot et al. 2015). Behavioral data, collected through various technological methods, offers an actual account of user interactions, eliminating biases from self-reported data; however, it should be noted that these still may include the researcher's bias introduced by the data collection and analysis data itself (Seely-Gant and Frehill 2015).

Below, we outline methodologies, including both quantitative and qualitative, used to collect data in the study of online communities. While a comprehensive analysis of each method is beyond the scope of this chapter, the chapter aims to highlight key approaches proven effective in understanding online interactions and behaviors.

Quantitative data

The quantitative dimension has naturally been an important approach to studying online communities. Online social analysis and Big Data have had a profound effect on the entire discipline of social sciences. The vast amounts of data available from billions of internet users provide an unprecedented opportunity to observe subtle social behaviors and changes in communication patterns. For example, by analyzing public tweets, researchers can track shifts in mood across populations or understand reactions to global events in real time.

This part of the chapter aims to showcase various approaches, methods, and tools for quantitative studies in the online world, highlighting the most commonly used methods in the social sciences. This chapter also addresses the challenges associated with quantitative research, including ethical concerns, data access issues, and the risk of misinterpreting data correlations.

Questionnaires

Questionnaires and surveys have long been essential tools for gathering declarative data in social science research. Traditionally, these methods were carried out using offline formats, such as paper-and-pen or telephone questionnaires. However, there has recently been a significant shift toward online platforms. Online questionnaires have become the standard due to their logistical advantages, allowing for instantaneous data compilation, basic analysis, and data presentation (Fricker 2017; Van Selm and Jankowski 2006), and also many offer open access, such as Google Forms and Microsoft Forms.

Despite their convenience, online surveys are not without limitations. They often face challenges related to skewed samples, difficulty in controlling demographics, low response rates, and reliance on self-reported data (Scharkow 2016, Jürgens et al. 2020). "Opt-in" polls, where participants voluntarily sign up, can lead to overrepresentation of certain demographics or those particularly interested in the topic, skewing the results (Bethlehem 2010). Moreover, researchers need to be mindful of potential biases when creating surveys, as these can manifest unconsciously in the wording of questions, making them manipulative or emotionally charged. Questions that require participants to quantify behaviors with high precision may not yield reliable data due to the recall challenge. To address these limitations, scholars are increasingly turning to behavioral data analysis.

Big Data

Big Data in online communities refers to the large-scale collection, analysis, and interpretation of behaviors in digital settings, providing insights into human actions and sentiments. This approach allows for a real-time understanding of societal moods, habits, and reactions without direct engagement with participants, highlighting the potential of digital footprints to reveal previously unseen behavioral patterns. Additionally, Big Data permits the analysis of online behaviors, sentiment in user-generated content like movie reviews, and cross-community comparisons, contributing to a deeper understanding of diverse demographics and shared human experiences (Thet et al. 2010).

A key source of Big Data is the growing range of information accessible from various online sources, including social media, blogs, and human health data from wearable devices such as Fitbit or Garmin. This expansion of data sources allows the analysis of new aspects of social behavior, facilitated by the development of computational social sciences. However, much Big Data is controlled by corporations, limiting academic access and leading to data restrictions. This creates a hierarchy of "research elites" who have privileged access to data. In contrast, databases like those provided by Wikimedia Projects offer free, legal access to diverse information formats, democratizing data access and its analysis. Platforms like datacommons.org aim to make Big Data more accessible for scholars.

Free-of-charge tools like Google Correlate, which previously analyzed trends based on Google search queries, offered potential for Big Data analysis. Despite Google Correlate being discontinued, there are other remaining tools providing similar functionalities; however, these operate on a for-profit basis. Nevertheless, caution is needed with correlational data, as demonstrated by Tyler Vigen's humorous yet cautionary "Spurious Correlations," which illustrates how seemingly unrelated variables can show strong correlations. Vigen provides an AI-generated explanation for absurd correlations, highlighting the danger of concluding without considering underlying factors and potential confounders.[1]

Social network analysis

One of the essential methods in studying online communities' analysis is SNA (Khan and MacEachen 2022), which offers a framework for investigating the structures and patterns of connections within and between online groups (Scott 1988). SNA focuses on the networks between entities, which can be individuals, groups, organizations, or even concepts, rather than classifying subjects based on individual attributes. This approach allows researchers to map out and analyze the complex networks of interactions, identifying key nodes or actors, subnetworks, cliques, and the roles individuals play within these networks. Such analyses are particularly effective in online environments where data on connections, such as friendships, collaborations, or communications are readily accessible and can be mined to reveal the social fabric of virtual communities.

SNA also allows exploration of social phenomena where individuals act as bridges between disparate groups or communities, facilitating the sharing of knowledge and information across the network (Tushman and Scanlan 1981). Open-access tools such as SocNetV and SocioViz are useful to collect and visualize peaks in the conversations, flow of information, and the most relevant users.

However, SNA is not without its limitations. A critical challenge lies in interpreting the context and implications of network interactions. For instance, understanding the significance of a "like" on a social media post requires more than just recognizing a connection—it demands insight into the intent and meaning behind the action. Is it an expression of agreement, support, or something else entirely? Without delving into the contextual and qualitative aspects of network interactions, SNA risks oversimplifying social relations' complex, nuanced nature.

Data scraping

When studying online communities, data scraping is a useful method for gathering data that is not readily accessible through standard interfaces such as APIs or HTML (Dogucu and Çetinkaya-Rundel 2021; Jemielniak 2020). Scraping thus allows researchers to automatically collect vast amounts of data from various online sources. This can range from collecting prices of items on e-commerce sites like Amazon to analyzing social media content. The necessity for scraping arises from the need to handle large volumes of data that would be too time-consuming to collect manually. Data scraping allows the analysis of digital traces left by various online interactions, providing a rich dataset for various analyses, including sentiment analysis, market trends, and social network dynamics. For practical applications, tools like Web Scraper, a Chrome plugin, and OctoParse offer user-friendly interfaces for scraping data without the need for advanced programming skills. These tools can automate the extraction of information from various sources, including social media platforms and websites, into manageable formats such as CSV files for further analysis.

It should be emphasized that, when data scraping, we can access a vast amount of data, also on the individuals' interactions. Thus, it is important to approach scraping with consideration for ethical guidelines and the terms of service of the websites being scraped. The practice should be conducted responsibly to avoid placing undue strain on web services and respecting privacy and copyright norms.

Qualitative methods

It is beyond the scope of this chapter to present all the qualitative tools used in the social sciences, although we aim to present the most useful ones used in the Thick Big Data approach. Qualitative studies add the "thickness" of description to the study of Big Data, whereas researchers can look beyond the statistical analyses to contextualize results better.

Qualitative research is characterized by its diversity, encompassing methodologies like hermeneutics, case studies, grounded theory, ethnography, and narrative research. Each approach offers unique insights but differs in its application and the type of data it generates. For instance, grounded theory aims to develop theories directly from data, while ethnography provides a "thick description" (Geertz 1973) of social phenomena, focusing on detailed observations rather than theory generation. Despite their differences, these methodologies share a common goal: to uncover the underlying dynamics of social interactions within online communities.

Digital ethnography

Ethnography, at its core, embodies a mindset that emphasizes an anthropological approach, fostering deep engagement and reflection. Its goal is to weave stories that interpret social realities, drawing readers into the world of the subjects through comprehensive fieldwork. This storytelling is not about creating an objective depiction of reality, but rather offering an interpretation based on the ethnographer's insights into societal dynamics, power structures, and cultural nuances. Ethnography begins with curiosity and questions rather than hypotheses, emphasizing the ethnographer's openness and reflexivity throughout the research process.

Digital ethnography extends the ethnographer's field to online avatars and digital personas, requiring consideration of the complexities behind online identities, including the presence of bots and the multiplicity of user representations. Digital ethnography's tools and methods are crucial for deep engagement with the field. From participatory observation to narrative analysis, these tools facilitate a comprehensive understanding of the culture under study. The digital ethnographer navigates a landscape where interactions can be asynchronous and multi-sited, challenging traditional notions of fieldwork and requiring a nuanced understanding of online communication dynamics.

Case study

The case study method is a principal method in qualitative research, particularly in examining organizational transformations or specific community events. Unlike ethnography, which delves into understanding a community's cultural context and local logic over extended periods, case studies zero in on analyzing distinct occurrences or shifts. This focused approach may sometimes be perceived as simpler, not necessitating prolonged cultural immersion. However, this perception can be misleading, as it might undervalue the depth of qualitative interpretation or overlook the clarity brought by quantitative analysis.

Case studies embrace a comprehensive understanding of specific social situations, anchored in the local context, to dissect the origins, progression, and outcomes of events or transformations that highlight critical aspects of the research interest. Furthermore, they permit a blend of methodologies, including interviews, SNA, and observation, tailored toward explaining a particular event or transformation. This adaptability emphasizes the method's goal: to explicate a unique or illustrative occurrence.

In the realm of online data, case studies can illuminate the dynamics within digital communities, where every interaction is archived. This allows for historical analysis, providing insights into community-shaping events and the evolution of community regulations. Such studies underscore the importance of being deeply acquainted with the community's culture to identify and analyze events of significance effectively.

Narrative analysis

Classical narrative analysis, traditionally applied in research to dissect texts and spoken narratives, has evolved with the advent of the narrative turn, emphasizing the role of storytelling in shaping our understanding of the world. This approach is deeply rooted in literary research and focuses on the narrative itself rather than the author's intentions or the circumstances of creation. In narrative analysis, the emphasis is on the plot and the structure of stories, exploring how narratives construct the world and negotiate meanings within a social context.

The digital era has significantly impacted narrative studies, especially with the prevalence of written and archived interactions in online communities. These persistent conversations, whether synchronous or archived, offer a rich field for narrative analysis. Online discussions often serve as a form of public discourse, making them accessible for analysis as public narratives. This allows researchers to examine how arguments are formed and identify recurring motifs and conversation patterns within digital communities.

Online narratives also reveal the phenomenon of echo chambers, where opinions are reinforced within like-minded groups, and the effect of digital propaganda in shaping public perceptions and normalizing radical views (Mahmoudi et al. 2024, Flaxman et al. 2016). Furthermore, anonymity and para-anonymity online facilitate extreme arguments and trolling, contributing to the radicalization of online discourse. These elements underscore the complexity of online narratives. Narrative analysis in this context requires an understanding of the digital medium's unique characteristics as its audience, character, performance aspect, and cultural codes.

Thick Big Data

As emphasized in the above discussion, when studying the online environment, both quantitative and qualitative approaches have their benefits and

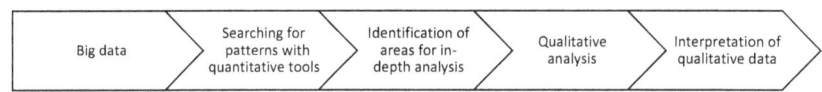

Figure 6.1 Process of the Thick Big Data approach.

limitations. Through merging those two approaches, we can gain a more nuanced understanding of the studied phenomena. This mixed-methods strategy aligns well with studying the internet due to the vast, structured data accessible online that requires nuanced analysis beyond mere numbers. The integration of qualitative and quantitative methods in social sciences is a pragmatic and strategic response to the data-rich environment of the digital age.

Below, we present a possible sequence of research stages from a quantitative to a qualitative approach. Naturally, depending on the aim of the project, research questions, or the type of available data, one needs to choose appropriate research tools and methods of data collection. Moreover, depending on the aim of the study, the opposite sequence may also be possible, progressing from the qualitative analysis, generating theories, formulating hypotheses, and further testing them with the use of a quantitative approach (Figure 6.1).

Feminism vs. MGTOW case study

In this part, we explore the practical application of the Thick Big Data methodology through a case study derived from an article examining online communities using hashtags *#MGTOW*, an acronym for Men Going Their Own Way, and *#feminism* on Twitter (Górska et al. 2023). This research illustrates a comprehensive approach to understanding complex social phenomena by combining quantitative and qualitative analyses along with the Thick Big Data approach. The aim was to investigate the discourse and engagement within these communities, highlighting the differences in sentiment, language use, and media references.

The context of the study

The aim of the article was to better understand the objectives and dynamics of #MGTOW community tweets and place #MGTOW in the context of gender and power struggles. The research specifically targeted MGTOW, an online sphere where men identify as involuntarily celibate, or "incels" (Jones et al. 2020), considering it one of the largest and most rapidly expanding groups in the manosphere. Members of the manosphere blame women and feminist movements for the perceived loss of masculinity.

MGTOWs mainly consist of straight, white, middle-class men from North America and Europe (Lin 2017). The focus on MGTOW stemmed from its claim of non-association with violence against women, distinguishing it from other meninist groups. MGTOW men opt out of romantic relationships with women, seeking self-empowerment instead and rejecting what they perceive as a gynocentric world order. Lin (2017) emphasizes that "unlike other anti-feminist groups, MGTOW espouse the abandonment of women and Western society, which they believe has been corrupted by feminism." (2017, 78) The existing system, they argue, is beyond reform; hence, MGTOWs are "going their own way".

Step 1: quantitative data collection and analysis

The first step in the study was *data scraping*—gathering data through the GetOldTweets3 Python script. The analysis was restricted to tweets available online at the time of collection, which was from April 2018 to January 2020. This was considered an advantage, as it allowed the study of tweets conforming to Twitter's community standards. Such an approach aligns with the current research ethics practices recommended by the Association of Internet Researchers (AoIR). The method facilitated a comparative analysis of large datasets of tweets with the #MGTOW and #feminism hashtags. A total of 167,582 tweets were collected; of these, 139,302 tweets from 52,619 unique usernames used #feminism, while 28,280 tweets from 4,481 unique usernames used #MGTOW. Each user was anonymized, and minor adjustments were made to the tweets to preserve their original meaning, adhering to AoIR guidelines. Extremely misogynistic, offensive, and violent tweets were avoided to prevent the promotion of misogyny and violence. This was based on our subjective evaluation and discussions within the research team. For the initial quantitative analysis, we used Excel spreadsheets and SPSS.

Step 2: engagement analysis

As part of the study, data about *engagement such as retweets, favorites, and likes* was collected using the GetOldTweets3 Python script. Based on the research, a comparative analysis was conducted to gauge user engagement through replies, retweets, and favorited tweets. Statistically significant differences were observed. In the #MGTOW group, 51% of all collected tweets received replies, compared to only 14% of #feminist tweets ($p < 0.001$). This may suggest that, although #MGTOW is a smaller group, there is more active participation in the online conversation. A similar pattern was observed with retweets and favorited tweets: 42% of all #MGTOW tweets received replies, compared to only 25% of #feminist tweets. For favorited tweets, the disparity was even more pronounced: 92% of #MGTOW tweets were favorited, while less than half of #feminist tweets were. Despite the #MGTOW community being smaller than the #feminism community, the data suggests that it is more actively engaged in online discussions and more tight-knit in comparison.

Step 3: sentiment analysis

In this study, *understanding the "tone" of the messages* by measuring the sentiment of the collected tweets was essential. Sentiment analysis was conducted using TextBlob, a Python library that evaluates each tweet's semantic orientation and word intensity (Micu et al. 2017). The analysis captured the emotions and tone of the tweets, which were then described using a numerical scale from –1 to 1, and categorized as very positive, positive, neutral, negative, or very negative.

Below is an example of positive sentiment in #feminist:

You thought 2018 was the Year of the Woman? Wait until you see the BEST #feminist moments of 2019. It will make you smile, laugh and feel PROUD of all the women owning their voice, rewriting history and embracing their power. Bring on 2020.

Here is an example of negative sentiment in #MGTOW:

I'm sure everyone can see what's wrong with this, wrong and how toxic living with a weemin is, on top of that they hold you back and you can't achieve your goals because they want to monopolize your time Go #mgtow gents, don't take this abuse.

The quantitative analysis of the hashtags showed notable differences, which were especially pronounced for extreme sentiments: #feminism was more likely to use very positive sentiment (Clark-Parsons 2021, Jackson et al. 2020), while #MGTOW used very negative sentiment, indicating a focus on criticism and attack (Jones et al. 2020).

Step 4: subjectivity analysis

The *subjectivity analysis* distinguished tweets expressing personal opinions, emotions, and judgments from those providing general information. Subjectivity in phrasing didn't necessarily imply the accuracy of the information; disinformation often used neutral, objective language to appear more credible (Jemielniak and Krempovych 2021). A notable difference in phrasing was found between #feminist and #MGTOW tweets ($p < 0.001$), with feminists tending to express more subjective views. They often shared personal opinions and experiences, whereas MGTOWs tended to adopt a more authoritative tone, using language that sounded factual or scientific to support their views.

This finding suggests that the feminist movement may be less objective than MGTOW. However, the qualitative analysis showed that this "objectivity" in MGTOW tweets often involved making strong, know-it-all, and arrogant statements, whereas feminist tweets were more likely to share individual experiences.

#feminist tweets were more likely to refer to one's own experiences and use subjective phrases:

> *I have attended many panels on #Feminism. This one is undoubtedly the most insightful, conclusive and progressive. These women on stage @yoginisd @Shubhrastha @psitsgayatri Som Dutta and moderated by Pallavi Joshi. So positive. So insightful. And so spiritual.*

#MGTOW tweets, in contrast, were more likely to present definitive statements as facts:

> *Marriage can be seen as a type of modern day slavery for men, except you can buy your freedom by paying half your life savings and your house. #Marriage is #slavery go #mgtow instead.*

This example showcases that quantitative, numerical analysis on its own may lead to wrong conclusions. The MGTOW statements that present definite statements as facts similarly assume "that the way the world appears to oneself is the way it appears to everyone" (Anderson 1995). And this could be found only through "diving" into the data and contextualizing it.

Step 5: collective vs. individualistic and internal vs. external focus

To understand the groups, collective vs. individualistic and internal vs. external focus were analyzed:

- Internal, individual approach—tweets using "me" language ("me," "mine," "myself," and "my").
- An internal, collective approach—tweets using "we" language ("we," "us," "our," "ourself," and "ourselves").
- An external, individual approach—tweets using "you" language ("you," "your," "yourself," and "yourselves").
- An external, collective approach—tweets using "they" language ("they," "them," "their," "themself," and "themselves").

Interestingly, while "me" and "you" were used with similar frequency, #feminism tweets used "we," internally focused language more often (12% vs. 7% of #MGTOW tweets).

An example follows: A #Feminist #PrideMonth PSA:

Remember that our #feminism must be inclusive not only to ciswomen, but to transwomen as well.

#MGTOW tweets used "they" language much more often (18% vs. 9% of #feminism tweets):

Make no mistake, they'll find a way to rationalize screwing your life #mgtow

The discussion above demonstrates how the quantitative Big Data approach may lack depth and substance on its own. In the study, specific tweet examples were showcased to provide context to the data. However, it was only the subsequent analysis that delved into the depth of the data and allowed a deeper understanding of the differences between the two, seemingly opposing movements.

Step 6: qualitative analysis

A *qualitative content analysis of the 1,000 most popular tweets from both communities* was conducted. The popularity of the tweets was understood as the sum of replies, retweets, and favorites, and we chose the top 500 tweets from each dataset based on these criteria.

Visualizing the most common words in #MGTOW and #feminism tweets through a word cloud provided a general understanding of what these two groups discussed. Surprisingly, both groups primarily focused on feminism and women, despite MGTOW's name suggesting a distancing from women. However, their perspectives were opposite. #feminism users emphasized women's rights and stories, while the MGTOW community utilized social media to criticize feminists and women in general. Contrary to the official narrative that MGTOW supports men's autonomy, this word cloud analysis demonstrated that the MGTOW group is largely directed toward women and displays hostility not only toward women themselves but also toward the feminist movement, women's emancipation, and women asserting their rights (Figure 6.2).

Each of the 1,000 tweets was manually coded and analyzed. The coding scheme was based on an inductive approach, drawing on the observations and analysis of tweets (see, e.g., Saldaña 2021). All tweets for the qualitative analysis were manually coded, according to our coding scheme, following the three levels of codes. First, each tweet was coded using open

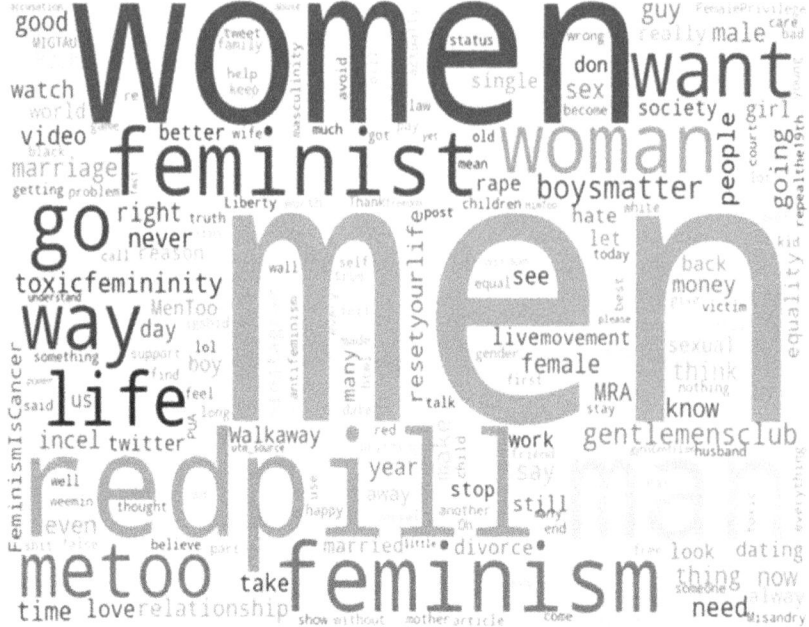

Figure 6.2 Word cloud of the most common words used in #MGTOW tweets.

coding, which was specific and allowed for a high degree of freedom. Then, the codes were clustered into broader categories and themes. This additional qualitative analysis enabled closer examination and comparison of both datasets' words, actions, and experiences.

In the chapter, pseudonyms were used, and minor changes were made to tweets to maintain their original meaning without being easily traceable to the author. This practice is recommended by the AoIR to ensure ethical research (Lin 2017). Extremely misogynistic, offensive, and violent tweets were not quoted verbatim to avoid providing a platform for misogyny and violence.

A total of 40 codes were developed in the initial coding phase, which included examples such as "harassing married women," "supporting MGTOW movement," and "promoting male violence against women." These codes were then grouped into broader categories like "negativity towards women" and "supporting men," with a limit of 10 categories. A narrative was presented, reflecting the character and essence of the tweets, and divided into three parts: the general nature of the MGTOW movement compared to feminism, the focus on defending the patriarchal system, and the relationship between MGTOWs and other men.

Summary of the case study

Although the quantitative analysis allowed acknowledging how the MGTOW movement differs from feminism, showcasing the type of language (internal vs. external, subjective vs. objective), the tone of the messages (sentiment), as well as the sources used to legitimize their views, it still did not show what MGTOW is. However, the qualitative analysis revealed more than just hostility toward women in the #MGTOW movement. The tweets are aimed at preserving a patriarchal system of dominance and entitlement. Thus, only the combination of both approaches, as depicted in the Thick Big Data method, allowed seeing the true nature of the meninist movement MGTOW.

Summary of the chapter

The chapter provided a comprehensive overview of the Thick Big Data approach for studying online communities and social dynamics. This mixed-methods framework combines quantitative Big Data analysis with qualitative "thick" data to gain deeper, contextualized insights. As we highlight, while Big Data offers unprecedented access to information, the sheer volumes of data necessitate qualitative interpretation and "thickness" to make sense of the findings (Jemielniak 2020). The concept of Thick Big Data represents an emerging paradigm for internet research that harnesses the analytical power of large-scale datasets along with ethnographic depth and thick description (Geertz 1973). This interpretivist approach aligns with calls for mixing quantitative breadth with qualitative context to ensure research rigor and relevance (Jick 1979, Stebbins 2001). The chapter outlined the philosophical underpinnings of Thick Big Data and presents a model for integrating diverse data collection tools and analytical techniques.

We argue for a pragmatic and iterative approach that leverages the strengths of both quantitative and qualitative methods. We advocate moving beyond the artificial dichotomy between statistical analyses and contextual interpretation to adopt a holistic perspective. Our proposed framework of Thick Big Data enables us to capture the complex realities of online communities, from individual behaviors to the collective production and consumption of culture facilitated by the internet. By combining exploratory inductive inquiry with hypothesis-testing deductive approaches, we can develop more insightful analyses of the rich mix of social dynamics and cultural expressions in the digital sphere. This convergence of methodologies provides a comprehensive understanding that neither quantitative nor qualitative approaches can achieve independently. Through integrating diverse data sources and analytical techniques, we seek to gain novel insights into the structures, processes, and contexts that shape the digital world.

To demonstrate the application of the Thick Big Data approach, we presented an illustrative case study analyzing and comparing Twitter communities using the hashtags #MGTOW and #feminism. This analysis showcases the synthesis of large-scale quantitative analysis of tweets with manual qualitative coding of a sample to elucidate key differences between the groups. While computational techniques efficiently processed extensive datasets, the subsequent qualitative phase was crucial for a nuanced interpretation, revealing novel insights into the nature of the MGTOW community that statistics alone could not provide. This practical example highlights the importance of qualitative contextualization to enhance the meaning and validity of quantitative findings. Our proposed framework offers a model for conducting rigorous, ethical, and comprehensive analyses of digital trace data to further the understanding of online social dynamics and culture. By combining Big Data breadth with thick data depth, we can drive innovative social research that embraces both the science and the art of studying the virtual world.

Note

1 www.tylervigen.com/spurious-correlations.

References

Anderson, Elizabeth. 1995. "Feminist Epistemology: An Interpretation and a Defense." *Hypatia* 10: 50–84.

Bainbridge, William S. 1999. "Cyberspace: Sociology's Natural Domain." *Contemporary Sociology* 28: 664–67.

Bethlehem, Jelke. 2010. "Selection Bias in Web Surveys." *International Statistical Review* 78: 161–88.

Bonenfant, Marianne, and Marie-Josée Meurs. 2018. "Collaboration Between Social Sciences and Computer Science: Toward a Cross-Disciplinary Methodology for Studying Big Social Data from Online Communities." In *Second International Handbook of Internet Research*, edited by Jeremy Hunsinger, Lisbeth Klastrup, and Matthew M. Allen, 1–17. Dordrecht: Springer Netherlands.

Clark-Parsons, Rosemary. 2021. "'I SEE YOU, I BELIEVE YOU, I STAND WITH YOU': #MeToo and the Performance of Networked Feminist Visibility." *Feminist Media Studies* 21: 362–80.

Czarniawska-Joerges, Barbara. 1992. *Exploring Complex Organizations: A Cultural Perspective*. Thousand Oaks, CA: Sage Publications.

Denzin, Norman. 1997. *Interpretive Ethnography: Ethnographic Practices for the 21st Century*. Thousand Oaks, CA: Sage Publications.

Dogucu, Mine, and Mine Çetinkaya-Rundel. 2021. "Web Scraping in the Statistics and Data Science Curriculum: Challenges and Opportunities." *Journal of Statistics and Data Science Education* 29: S112–22.

Flaxman, Seth, Sharad Goel, and Justin M. Rao. 2016. "Filter Bubbles, Echo Chambers, and Online News Consumption." *Public Opinion Quarterly* 80: 298–320.

Fricker, Ronald D. 2017. *The SAGE Handbook of Online Research Methods*. London: Sage Publications Ltd.
Geertz, Clifford. 1973. *The Interpretation of Cultures*. New York: Basic Books.
Górska, Anna M., Katarzyna Kulicka, and Dariusz Jemielniak. 2023. "Men Not Going Their Own Way: A Thick Big Data Analysis of #MGTOW and #Feminism Tweets." *Feminist Media Studies* 23: 3774–92.
Halavais, Alexander. 2015. "Bigger Sociological Imaginations: Framing Big Social Data Theory and Methods." *Information, Communication & Society* 18: 583–94.
Hynes, Michael. 2018. "Shining a Brighter Light into the Digital 'Black Box': A Call for Stronger Sociological (Re)Engagement with Digital Technology Design, Development and Adoption Debates." *Irish Journal of Sociology* 26: 94–126.
Jackson, Sarah J., Moya Bailey, and Brooke Foucault Welles. 2020. *#HashtagActivism: Networks of Race and Gender Justice*. Cambridge: The MIT Press.
Jemielniak, Dariusz. 2020. *Thick Big Data: Doing Digital Social Sciences*. Oxford: Oxford University Press.
Jemielniak, Dariusz, and Yuriy Krempovych. 2021. "An Analysis of AstraZeneca COVID-19 Vaccine Misinformation and Fear-Mongering on Twitter." *Public Health* 200: 4–6.
Jick, Todd D. 1979. "Mixing Qualitative and Quantitative Methods: Triangulation in Action." *Administrative Science Quarterly* 24: 602–11.
Jones, Callum, Verity Trott, and Scott Wright. 2020. "Sluts and Soyboys: MGTOW and the Production of Misogynistic Online Harassment." *New Media & Society* 22: 1903–21.
Jürgens, Pascal, Benedict Stark, and Max Magin. 2020. "Two Half-Truths Make a Whole? On Bias in Self-Reports and Tracking Data." *Social Science Computer Review* 38: 600–15.
Khan, Tanya H., and Ellen MacEachen. 2022. "An Alternative Method of Interviewing: Critical Reflections on Videoconference Interviews for Qualitative Data Collection." *International Journal of Qualitative Methods* 21: 16094069221090063.
Lin, Kaibin. 2017. "Integrating Ethical Guidelines and Situated Ethics for Researching Social-Media-Based Interactions: Lessons from a Virtual Ethnographic Case Study with Chinese Youth." *Journal of Information Ethics* 25: 114–31.
Mahmoudi, Amir, Dariusz Jemielniak, and Łukasz Ciechanowski. 2024. "Echo Chambers in Online Social Networks: A Systematic Literature Review." *IEEE Access* 12: 9594–620.
Micu, Adrian, Anca Elena Micu, Mihai Geru, and Robert C. Lixandroiu. 2017. "Analyzing User Sentiment in Social Media: Implications for Online Marketing Strategy." *Psychology & Marketing* 34: 1094–100.
Robnett, Belinda, and Cynthia Feliciano. 2011. "Patterns of Racial-Ethnic Exclusion by Internet Daters." *Social Forces* 89: 807–28.
Saldaña, Johnny. 2021. *The Coding Manual for Qualitative Researchers*. London: Sage Publications Ltd.
Scharkow, Michael. 2016. "The Accuracy of Self-Reported Internet Use—A Validation Study Using Client Log Data." *Communication Methods and Measures* 10: 13–27.
Scott, John. 1988. "Social Network Analysis." *Sociology* 22: 109–27.

Seely-Gant, K., and Lisa M. Freehill. 2015. "Exploring Bias and Error in Big Data Research." *Journal of the Washington Academy of Sciences* 101, no. 3: 29–37.

Stebbins, Robert A. 2001. *Exploratory Research in the Social Sciences*. Thousand Oaks, CA: Sage Publications.

Sudweeks, Fay, and Simeon J. Simoff. 1999. *Doing Internet Research: Critical Issues and Methods for Examining the Net*. Thousand Oaks, CA: Sage Publications.

Thet, Tun Thura, Jin-Cheon Na, and Christopher S. G. Khoo. 2010. "Aspect-Based Sentiment Analysis of Movie Reviews on Discussion Boards." *Journal of Information Science* 36: 823–48.

Tushman, Michael L., and Thomas J. Scanlan. 1981. "Boundary Spanning Individuals: Their Role in Information Transfer and Their Antecedents." *The Academy of Management Journal* 24: 289–305.

Van Selm, Martine, and Nicholas W. Jankowski. 2006. "Conducting Online Surveys." *Quality and Quantity* 40: 435–56.

Vlassenroot, Sven, Dimitri Gillis, Ruben Bellens, and Sarah Gautama. 2015. "The Use of Smartphone Applications in the Collection of Travel Behaviour Data." *International Journal of Intelligent Transportation Systems Research* 13: 17–27.

Chapter 6.1

Concept

Data

Tone Walford and Hannah Knox

What is data?

In this short conversation, Tone Walford and Hannah Knox discuss how they came to study data in their research, and how they have learned to approach it as an object of ethnographic attention.

Hannah: How did data first appear in your research?
Tone: I suppose it started during my master's degree at the Museu Nacional in Brazil. I conducted an ethnography of a scientific project in the Brazilian Amazon, but I wasn't really interested in data at the time. When I was there, however, I noticed most of the people I was speaking to were obsessed with data. And then, in 2012, just as I was finishing up my PhD, suddenly Big Data became this exciting topic that everyone, in the UK at least, was talking about—and so it snowballed from there, though that had not been my intention at all to begin with! In fact, when I think about it, what could tie all my research together is an interest in ethnographies of knowledge. I was very influenced by anthropologists in the 1990s and 2000s who were looking on the one hand at the emergence of audit culture and, on the contrary, were excavating anthropology itself as a knowledge-practice. Marrying that with an STS-inflected sensibility to materiality, it seemed obvious for me to empirically explore the material forms that knowledge takes in the context of climate science in the Amazon.
Hannah: That's so interesting, because for me, what prompted me to look at data was also an interest in audit and knowledge. This happened around 2000 when I was researching a European funded economic development organization in Manchester, UK, which was responsible for a project to develop a new digital media sector in the city. As a public sector organization everything they

DOI: 10.4324/9781032672663-24

were doing seemed to be framed in data terms. They had to evidence their impact by metrics like "jobs created," and defined themselves as an information-sharing network. So I got really interested in the role of their incessant metricization and the way it underpinned their use of public funds.

Reflecting back, like you, it was more the conversations about the anthropology of knowledge, audit, management, and governance that took me into thinking about data.

Tone: Because of this, I often wonder, what we are even talking about when we talk about data. Is it just the newest iteration of a long history of the way information has been mobilized around power? Or is there something coalescing over the last decade which is qualitatively different and needs new forms of inquiry?

Hannah: For me it comes back to the question of how we conceptualize data in our own work. To what extent is it equivalent to numbers or techniques of governance, power, and knowledge—things that people have been writing about for a long time - or is there something more that characterizes a focus on (big) data?

Tone: One of the things Rachel Douglas-Jones, Nick Seaver, and I tried to do in a recent essay (2021) was to think through this question of newness by going back to the hubbub around New Reproductive Technologies in the 80s and 90s in the UK, which anthropologists recognized as unsettling the categories of "nature" and "culture." We drew on Sarah Franklin's amazing ethnography (2013) of IVF clinics. Franklin noticed that couples using the clinic were stuck in this extremely awkward, unsettling position, trying to do the most "natural" thing in the world, at least from a cisheteronormative standpoint, and yet they had to do it in the most unnatural or artificial way possible. Franklin was developing Strathern's ideas about what it means to be "after nature" (Strathern 1992)—that is, both in a time ostensibly governed by technology (post-nature) and nevertheless in endless pursuit of "naturalness." And this helped us think about how technological configurations around data can work to create continuity and a rupture, simultaneously. For example, it helped us think how novel practices of datafication, profiling, biometrics, data mining—are certainly continuous with past practices of state, colonial or other forms of power and control, but also that ethnography is useful to explore how something is also making people feel newly uncomfortable about them, like they don't recognize them, or that something is different.

That said, I do have what I find to be a useful way of thinking about data, which continues this comparison with reproduction. I have come to think of data as a form of potential—as something which is valuable exactly because it is *not yet*; like a seed or gamete, the point is what it will become. This was drawn directly from conversations I had with scientific researchers and data managers about how data must be worked on to become "knowledge." But even being *not yet* known, there was clearly value being placed in scientific data in this *not-yet* state. Later, I saw a resonance between this and the "Big Data moment," where we were told that there is this reservoir of untapped value in personal data that companies originally collected "accidentally." Though no one can say exactly what the value necessarily is yet, there is no question that it is valuable. So, potential seemed to be useful as a way to think about data as a specific social form or artifact.

Hannah: I'm more familiar with discussions about the value of data being framed as a relationship between data and capitalism, rather than science. Do you see a difference when you approach data from the viewpoint of scientists rather than, say, a tech corporation?

Tone: Since I started working on this, the worlds of environmental data have changed quite radically, and there is a lot of great work coming out of political ecology now on the commodification of environmental data (Goldstein and Nost 2022). But originally, I was interested in forms of valuing aside from those arising from commodification and alienation; in fact, I was exploring how scientists explicitly differentiated what they did from the commercial, through different notions of property. I was struck by the labor of producing data as means for social reproduction, that is as a means for people to grow—I was looking at the work of the people who painstakingly processed the scientific data being collected from the forest, but never published on it themselves, and the intimate relations they had with the data, data which they then passed on so other people could work with it and publish it. So I started to think about data as a form of reproduction, because of the relations presumed to be latent within it (back to potential again!). But, of course, this isn't to deny its imbrication also in capitalism: what this sort of relational form allows for is for commodity relations to also be in there—genomic data and biocapital are the most well-known examples, maybe of that in the terms I am talking about.

Hannah: Thinking about how I would define data, I don't think I came to data with a strong feeling of wanting to define what data is, either. It appeared and disappeared in my research, and that was fine. I dealt with it when it was there, and I didn't when it wasn't. So, for example, after my work in Manchester, I did a project on road construction in Peru. Part of that project involved working with engineers, who were engaging with soils and construction materials through numbers and measurements and data. But then there were equally other people engaging with the soil and the landscape in completely different ways—through ritual, animism, memory, or physical work on the land. So I was always interested in keeping data in its place as one material practice that would sit alongside others. In this work I didn't need to come up with a conceptual understanding of what data was in a kind of universal or abstract sense.

This changed when I started to be involved in UK policy discussions about data. From 2016 to 2017, I sat on a working group for a project run by the Royal Society and the British Academy on data governance, and I found that the conversation there was revolving around all the kinds of questions you have been talking about, including the question of what data is. So we were looking at things like the use of data for accumulation and profit and asking—is that OK? And how would we adjudicate if that were OK? We were thinking about who should have access to data and who shouldn't have access, so data opened up all these fascinating questions. But I also found I was often really unclear what people were talking about when they were talking about data! And I think maybe others felt the same. So I really started to think, then, what do I mean when I say data—what am I thinking of when talking about this thing?

Funnily enough given your earlier thoughts about IVF clinics, one way people tackled this question in these discussions was by comparing data with new reproductive technologies (NRTs)! There was a sense that the challenges policy makers were facing about how to govern data had similarities with challenges they had faced in the 1990s regarding how to govern NRTs.

Intrigued by this comparison and wondering how to participate anthropologically, I went back to Marilyn Strathern's work in *Property, Substance and Effect* (1999). This helped me see data as something whose challenge lies in the way it troubles existing notions of ownership. It made me realize that many conversations about data are trying to grapple with the fact that it is both a thing (an inscription) and a relationship between things (an object in the world, the actor making the inscription, the user of that inscription). This makes questions over who owns data very difficult. In the working group, there were lots of discussions about whether people should be able to charge micro amounts of money for other people to use their data. But this opened up the question regarding in what sense it is even their *own* data in the first place. This also reminded me of a little book by Tom Boellstorff and Bill Maurer in which there is a really nice moment where they talk about data as being kind of between in between (2015).

Tone: Where Maurer also draws on Strathern's work to explore how data can be kin!

Hannah: We keep coming back round to this!

Tone: Yes, these relationships between knowledge and kinship keep resurfacing! And like you say, the way property enters is intriguing, weaving in and out of the two in terms of the appropriate relations to have with both people and data. In science, for example, there are all these Open Data policies and regulations which privilege sharing over owning. But at the same time, for some of the Latin American scientists I worked with, their experience of data collection can be experienced as a continuation of colonial practices of resource extraction and biopiracy. But others I spoke to, often from the US, would argue that data is just a raw material, it's not anything yet that can be "extracted" as such. So the point at which you can assert ownership is contested, and seemingly common-sense regulations around Open Data smuggle in all sorts of assumptions and violence.

References

Boellstorff, Tom, and Bill Maurer. 2015. *Data: Now Bigger and Better!* Chicago, IL: Prickly Paradigm Press.

Franklin, Sarah. 2013. *Biological Relatives: IVF, Stem Cells and the Future of Kinship*. Durham, NC: Duke University Press.

Goldstein, Jesse, and Eric Nost. 2022. *The Nature of Data: Infrastructures, Environments, Politics*. Lincoln: University of Nebraska Press.

Strathern, Marilyn. 1992. *After Nature: English Kinship in the Late Twentieth Century*. Cambridge: Cambridge University Press.

Strathern, Marilyn. 1999. *Property, Substance, and Effect: Anthropological Essays on Persons and Things*. London: Athlone Press.

Walford, Antonia, Douglas R. Jones, and Nick Seaver. 2021. "Introduction: Towards an Anthropology of Data." *Journal of the Royal Anthropological Institute* 27(Supplement 1): S1.

Chapter 6.2

Case study

Over-the-shoulder observation of Facebook Group admins

Anna D. Gibson

In 2020, nearly a quarter of all humanity used Facebook Groups (Simo 2020). The popular social media platform's group feature allows people to connect and share content related to common interests, from local happenings to diaspora to shared experiences of chronic disease and more. By and large, these groups are run by unpaid volunteers in the roles of admins and moderators. The Facebook Group architecture gives them a lot of power to make choices about who gets to join, what the rules are, what posts are allowed, and who else can share power (Malinen 2021; Matias 2019; Schneider 2022).

For my dissertation research, I was interested in how these kinds of volunteers make decisions, especially what kind of justification they use. The public hears a lot from big social media companies about how they consider and justify their policies. But what about decision makers who aren't professionals; do they use the language of justice? Or the language of social harmony?

Between the years 2020 and 2022, I interviewed over 40 different admins[1] from a variety of Groups, ranging in size from 250 to several million people and ranging in topic from housing to writing to fangirling and meme-sharing. I also wanted to get richer data by observing this moderation in action, so I asked participants if I could join their Groups. Many said yes, and for much of the COVID-19 lockdown, I spent every day checking in on my Facebook Groups. My goal was to carry out digital ethnography, letting me talk to these admins but also letting me be "co-present" with them in their spaces.

It soon became apparent that it was difficult to watch moderation in action. To gain familiarity with how these Groups worked, I became an admin of a Facebook Group with around 10,000 members. Multiple times a day I used my personal Facebook account to decline and approve posts, remove content, and discipline Group participants. But none of these actions would be visible or salient to a general Group member unless they were the ones being disciplined or carefully watching and counting comments.

As I checked in on my Groups daily, I felt like a wildlife photographer waiting weeks at the same tree to catch footage of secretive animals interacting in plain sight. Posts and comments from group members were common, but seeing moderation in action was incredibly rare. During our interview, Autumn, an admin of a shopping Group, told me that her moderation team resorted to deleting comments or disabling comments on posts when there was conflict. Once I managed to catch this process live, as I refreshed the page, the comments disappeared, and finally the comments were locked. This sighting was lucky, though, and I didn't witness another one.

Frustratingly, even getting sight of that action didn't help me understand what exactly was happening; I couldn't tell if it was Autumn herself deleting the comments or one of her teammates. Even though I was *in* the Facebook Group, in the "room where it happens," I wasn't in the right vantage spot to actually see what was happening.

Interactions online are highly mediated by digital technologies in ways that are invisible; the affordances of social media platforms do not necessarily represent their mediation. For example, what if a person using Facebook is uncertain about a comment they are posting online? They may alter their comment repeatedly using an "edit" feature, which marks the post as having been edited. Such an affordance allows an ethnographer to explore this indecisiveness through an inversion of this particular "digital trace" (Geiger and Ribes 2011) of a small icon indicating the author has edited the text. On other sites, ethnographers may be able to uncover previous versions of the comment with automated immediate capture of all posted comments, or even Internet Archive's historical screens through the Wayback Machine.

What these digital traces cannot capture, however, are the moments around the creation of the comment. What did the author write out, and then delete, before she hit the button to publish? What words did she linger over? What about the long posts, carefully written out, that are eventually second-guessed and deleted before ever being shown on any other person's screen? Or the posts that are published but quickly deleted without a trace? In interviews, first-person narratives generally focus on the actions that people feel are consequential. Outside observers, however, may focus on different details, including friction with infrastructure or hesitation and indecision. Such moments are of utmost importance to ethnographers but will necessarily be elided when ethnographers rely solely on digitally mediated representations of online interaction.

In the same department where I was a student, a few of my friends were working in the Screenomics Lab. Many media psychology studies seek to understand the effect of "screen time" on well-being, but results have been mixed; the Screenomics approach argues that this is because the activities in which people engage on screens, rather than the time spent with screens, are ultimately more impactful on mental health (Reeves et al. 2021). It is difficult to gain data about how people spend their time online because people use lots of different sites and apps simultaneously, and switch activities many times a minute (Yeykelis et al. 2014). People are also very bad at recalling the specifics of how they use their devices and with what frequency, so the only way to understand the experience of a digitized world is to directly track or log real-time usage of digital screens (Reeves et al. 2021, 153–54).

It occurred to me that this powerful idea of simply watching someone's screen could help me get at the otherwise hidden background of moderation work. Furthermore, it suddenly seemed possible in a way that couldn't have happened a year earlier. The COVID-19 lockdowns of 2020 in the United States led to widespread adoption of Zoom software. Zoom allows people to easily conduct meetings online, and when in-person gatherings were restricted, many people who had never worked remotely found themselves conducting their professional and social lives through this software. Affordances of the software, such as filters and screen-sharing, became a part of daily practice for many people. Such familiarity with the software meant that participants felt technically and emotionally comfortable sharing their desktop screens with me. Zoom meant I could actually go behind the scenes and watch "over my participants' shoulders" as they went about their moderation work, even if not physically co-present.

The ethical considerations of such observation are tricky. Admins could give their consent for such observations, but the members of their Groups could not. Additionally, admins' privileged perspectives of Facebook Groups meant that I would be able to see much more of the goings-on in a Group than most regular members. On the one hand, there was probably little expectation of privacy, as many tens of thousands of members make up these Groups, and admins do not tend to have personal relationships with most members. However, I was keenly aware of the vulnerable position I was placing the admins in by viewing their personal screens, and I did not have deep relationships with these participants. Therefore, I decided not to record screenshots, video, or sound during these sessions to preserve the confidentiality of members of the Groups who did not give consent to participate in the study. Instead, I took notes during the session using my laptop screen, and, then after the session was complete, I wrote down as much as I could remember about what I had witnessed, using my notes to guide and reflect on the session.

The first thing I noticed when conducting these observations was that many participants moderated only through their smartphones. I had assumed that people used their laptops, like I did, but that was not the case. One participant even told me he couldn't even remember how to log on to his web account. This added a layer of complexity to the Zoom observation sessions, but I was able to solve it with a QuickTime workaround. It was a good reminder of how many people access digital platforms primarily through their phones and how others often experience the same platforms that researchers use in substantially different ways.

In total, I was only able to conduct five of these over-the-shoulder observation sessions, each of which only lasted an hour or two, but I gathered rich data that I would not have otherwise been able to find. For example, in my interviews with admins, they often described making decisions about submitted content quickly and confidently. When I began my over-the-shoulder session with Mikael, who is an admin of a meme Group, he started working his way through the "post approvals" queue. Initially, he made decisions silently, with swift evaluations. After I asked him to narrate his decision process, he started making specific references to rules as he chose to decline posts; rather than declining a post and trying to find a rule that matched, he clearly had the rules memorized and top-of-mind as he read the submitted posts. Furthermore, I noticed that, as he moved through the queue, he did not rule on every piece of content. He hesitated, deliberated, and sometimes decided that he could not make a decision, skipping over that content, either another admin to deal with or for "later." This revealed an important element of ambivalence in making decisions, especially for posts that fell into gray areas or that other admins might have different judgments about.

Another important finding had to do with racial and ethnic stereotyping. During my interviews, many admins discussed new member approvals at length. Moderators must make judgment calls about including or excluding people from the Group based on relatively few signals. While some described the potentially problematic stereotyping that results from this process, few wanted to discuss it at length. Over-the-shoulder observations allowed me access to the moments when admins encountered these problematic situations and needed to navigate them.

Here are fieldnotes from my session with Larry, who admins a US-based sports Group, following him as he went through the new member approval queue:

> Larry also points out someone he deleted because he was pretty sure it was a scammer. This person's name is [redacted] and Larry could tell this person was from the "Middle East." As he says it out loud, that he was banning someone because they were foreign, he clearly feels somewhat embarrassed. "Saying it out loud sounds really bad" he tells me, even though it's a tactic that he uses every day and works somewhat by instinct because he's "been doing it long enough that we can tell."

He clicks on another profile that he banned: [Middle-eastern name], who is from Bangladesh. Again, Larry says somewhat ashamedly, that with someone from Bangladesh, they don't even check his profile because he's clearly not a local sports team fan. I ask him about the kind of threat this person poses, and Larry tells me that these are the guys who sell photoshopped t-shirts that his Group members will buy and then never receive. So, a scammer.

Larry tells me again that one of the Group's most active members is from Jordan, with the implication that [his practices] are justified and not racist.

The fact that I was watching Larry make decisions with actual stakes for his Group meant that his actions were quite meaningful, even if he felt uncomfortable discussing them. The animus of racial and ethnic bias hung over the queue in a meaningful way with him and other participants, not as easily dispelled as it was in an interview.

Screens are important for ethnographers not just as portals into a digital world but as a key material site of the experience of digital sociality. I found over-the-shoulder observation important for creating co-presence with participants in field sites, revealing not just truth-in-action but a more concrete and thorough context of my participants' material and practical considerations for their daily moderation practices.

Note

1 While there is a subtle distinction between Facebook's roles of admin and moderator, in this piece, I use the term "admin" to encompass both.

References

Geiger, R. Stuart, and David Ribes. 2011. "Trace Ethnography: Following Coordination through Documentary Practices." In *2011 44th Hawaii International Conference on System Sciences*, 1–10. Kauai, HI: IEEE. https://doi.org/10.1109/HICSS.2011.455.

Malinen, Sanna. 2021. "Boundary Control as Gatekeeping in Facebook Groups." *Media and Communication* 9(4): 9. https://doi.org/10.17645/mac.v9i4.4238.

Matias, J. Nathan. 2019. "The Civic Labor of Volunteer Moderators Online." *Social Media + Society* 5 (2): 205630511983677. https://doi.org/10.1177/2056305119836778.

Reeves, Byron, Nilam Ram, Thomas N. Robinson, James J. Cummings, C. Lee Giles, Jennifer Pan, Agnese Chiatti, Mj Cho, Katie Roehrick, Xiao Yang, Anupriya Gagneja, Miriam Brinberg, Daniel Muise, Yingdan Lu, Mufan Luo, Andrew Fitzgerald, and Leo Yeykelis. 2021. "Screenomics: A Framework to Capture and Analyze Personal Life Experiences and the Ways That Technology

Shapes Them." *Human–Computer Interaction* 36 (2): 150–201. https://doi.org/10.1080/07370024.2019.1578652.

Schneider, Nathan. 2022. "Admins, Mods, and Benevolent Dictators for Life: The Implicit Feudalism of Online Communities." *New Media & Society* 24 (9): 1965–85. https://doi.org/10.1177/1461444820986553.

Simo, Fidji. 2020. "Supporting Online Communities When They're Needed Most." *Meta Newsroom* (blog). October 1. https://about.fb.com/news/2020/10/supporting-online-communities/.

Yeykelis, Leo, James J. Cummings, and Byron Reeves. 2014. "Multitasking on a Single Device: Arousal and the Frequency, Anticipation, and Prediction of Switching Between Media Content on a Computer: Multitasking and Arousal." *Journal of Communication* 64 (1): 167–92. https://doi.org/10.1111/jcom.12070.

Chapter 7

Spatial analysis
Practicing geospatial ethnography
Greyson Harris

Introduction

Communities exist within physical geographies and landscapes. The positioning and interaction of people and things hold a material power which shapes lived experience. If a picture is worth 1,000 words, then a map illuminates millions of relationships. The ethnographer who engages with these geographic connections is better equipped to more fully describe the full complexity of their subjects.

Geospatial technology provides a powerful suite of tools for painting a rich picture of the world and its peoples through places, qualities, and spatial relationships. Drawing on Clifford Geertz's (1973) notion of culture as publicly visible webs of meaning, geography becomes the spatial medium through which these webs are expressed. While Geertz explained thick description in terms of the written word, technologies like audio, photography, and video have long expanded the ethnographer's toolkit beyond writing (1973). Mapping is another such method—technology-driven and spatial—that deepens the potential for thick description.

Geographic information systems (GIS) is the term for today's technology used to manage, analyze, and visualize location-based data.[1] Traditionally, GIS consists of:

- **Hardware:** Physical infrastructure like computers and servers;
- **Software:** Code and algorithms powering GIS applications;
- **Data:** Information linked to geographic coordinates;
- **Methods:** Techniques for collecting, managing, and visualizing data;
- **People:** The professionals and practitioners who use GIS.

GIS is a computational framework for analyzing spatial relationships, with maps being just one possible output. GIS stands apart from other data-driven tools by featuring geography as an organizing principle to locate people, things, and their circumstances at a spot on the Earth.

DOI: 10.4324/9781032672663-26

Rather than assuming the shape of a paragraph of text or the stacked rows in a spreadsheet, GIS offers an iconic representation of reality modeled on the physical geometry of the planet. While maps are as much a fiction as the written word, they uniquely mimic geographic space and convey spatial meaning.

To grasp what GIS and modern mapping can do, think of a lens, a prism, and an X-ray. As a lens, GIS brings diverse location data into focus. As a prism, it breaks complex datasets into analyzable parts. Like an X-ray, it reveals hidden patterns by layering information. Researchers shift between lensing, prismatic, and X-ray modes of GIS to visualize where people and places are situated and uncover unseen social, economic, and environmental relationships.

This article lays the groundwork for applying GIS to ethnographic and sociocultural research. It begins by situating GIS within social theory, explores the diversity and ethics of mapping, and concludes with a practical case study from emergency management to illustrate how geospatial methodologies can inform and support human-centered inquiry.

Locating GIS in context

GIS, geospatial technologies, and maps have come to permeate modern life. Whether using a smartphone app for directions or checking the weather radar online, people routinely engage with digital representations of geographic space. This widespread adoption is no accident. It reflects deeper shifts in governance and computing.

GIS and mapping align with Michel Foucault's (1989) concept of governmentality. Governmental rationality is the ensemble of strategies and techniques by which modern societies manage populations (1989). As power transitioned from sovereign rulers to decentralized systems embedded in social institutions like health and education, governance began relying on tools that could measure and calculate populations. Geospatial methods fit seamlessly into this logic: they quantify territory, make people legible to the state, and support the management of space and population (Elden 2007; Scott 1998).

Yet governmentality alone does not fully explain the rise of GIS. The cyborgic nature of humanity and the installation of dispersed computing technologies within the landscape itself are critical pieces of the equation. Donna Haraway's (1985) notion of the cyborg—a fusion of organism and machine—offers a complementary perspective. Humanity has long blended the organic and the technological, but this tendency has intensified with the proliferation of digital devices. Mapping technologies, embedded in everyday tools like smartphones, illustrate this cyborg condition. They mediate our relationships with space, data, and each other.

The effect is amplified by ubiquitous computing and the rise of networked cities. As Crang and Graham (2007) describe, today's urban spaces are equipped with technologies that observe, record, and anticipate human behavior. Tasks once carried out manually are now performed by algorithms, increasingly autonomous and interactive (Kitchin 2011). GIS, location tracking, and digital maps serve as central mechanisms in this smart, cyborgic landscape—linking people, devices, data, and place into a dynamic spatial system.

The variety and limitations of maps

Wayfinding and mapping are ancient human practices. From cave paintings to printed atlases to interactive web maps, our mapping tools have evolved with technology. Yet mapping takes many unexpected forms, each with its own limitations and ethical implications.

A striking historical example is the Tabula Peutingeriana, or Peutinger Map—a medieval copy of a Roman-era road map rediscovered in the 1500s.[2] Spanning roughly one foot by 22 feet of vellum, it depicts the Roman Empire's road network and Mediterranean Sea as a long, compressed strip, distorting physical geography to emphasize connectivity (Talbert 2010). Like a modern subway map, it sacrifices spatial accuracy for utilitarian use.

Mapping, however, need not involve a physical artifact. In Aboriginal Australian traditions, songlines[3]—also known as dreaming tracks—are oral maps encoded in song. These verses, shared across clans, mnemonically preserve cultural knowledge and guide navigation across vast landscapes, pointing out features like water sources and sacred sites (Chatwin 1987). Some believe songlines once provided enough guidance to traverse the entire Australian continent (First Australians 2008).

Maps are not neutral. Throughout history, they have been used as instruments of power and control. During the "scramble for Africa," European colonial powers imposed arbitrary borders across the continent, ignoring local languages, cultures, and histories (Bassett 1994). These lines—drawn for political convenience—exercised cartographic violence on African peoples and continue to shape conflict and governance today (Herbst 2000; Englebert, Tarango, and Carter 2002).

Similarly, under the Soviet Union, publicly available maps were deliberately distorted to obscure accurate distances and directions (Harley 1988). High-precision maps existed but were reserved for military use (Davies and Kent 2017). This strategic disinformation limited both foreign intelligence and the domestic population's ability to navigate reliably (Davies and Kent 2017). In contrast, other national mapping efforts, such as the Geological Survey in the United States or the Ordnance Survey in the United Kingdom, provide nation-wide maps considered to be of high quality and reliability available freely to the public.

Maps are not exact replicas of the world. The map is not the territory—nor should it be. They are models, abstractions, and narratives—they are fictions. As with any representation, they can illuminate or mislead. Ethical cartography acknowledges this: it embraces the inevitable distortions of scale and projection not to deceive, but to communicate something true about the world—whether it's how to reach Constantinople, where to find water, or how to locate your community on a shared public map.

Mapping essentials

In geographic research, ethical cartography requires more than technical skill—it demands awareness of how maps distort reality. A responsible mapmaker acknowledges these distortions and considers how they may affect the map's message. Building a complete map—by layering data, applying symbology, and designing a final layout—means working with, not hiding, the inherent imperfections of maps.

Projection

Map projection is the mathematical process of transforming geographic coordinates from a curved surface (the Earth) to a flat map.[4] A common metaphor likens this process to peeling an orange—tears, stretches, and compressions are inevitable. During projection, areas, shapes, distances, and directions are distorted in different ways:

- **Areal distortions:** Land or water areas may appear larger or smaller than they are in the real world. *Solution*: Equal-area projection.
- **Shape distortions:** Geographic forms like coastlines or borders may be warped. *Solution*: Conformal projection.
- **Distance distortions:** Measured distances may be inaccurate. *Solution*: Equidistant projection.
- **Directional distortions:** Compass directions between locations may be altered. *Solution*: Azimuthal projection.

No projection preserves all properties. Ethical map design involves selecting a projection suited to the map's purpose. Navigation maps require accurate distance and direction; land comparison maps need area-preserving projections. Public mapping authorities often provide regional guidance on appropriate projections.

Scale

Scale determines how much a map is zoomed in or zoomed out and influences what details are visible. A zoomed-out map offers a broad overview but may miss local nuance. A zoomed-in map captures fine detail but can obscure broader trends. Neither is inherently right or wrong—the correct scale fits the research question and what the map aims to show.

Extent

Extent refers to the visible area shown on a map, whether printed or digital. Like scale, extent shapes what is included or excluded. A tight extent might omit important surrounding context (and the people who live there); a wide extent may overwhelm the reader with information. Setting the right extent involves balancing focus and context based on the subject of study and the viewer's needs.

Enumeration

Enumeration units—also called areal units or features—are the shapes on a map that represent data, such as points, lines, or polygons. These are typically stored in one of two GIS data formats: vector or raster.

Vector data includes discrete features like address points, roads, rivers, and boundaries. GIS software like QGIS and ArcGIS reads this data as x, y coordinate points (nodes) connected by lines (arcs). Raster data, such as satellite imagery or elevation models, is stored as a grid of pixels. Each pixel contains a value, making rasters well suited for representing continuous phenomena (Figure 7.1).[5]

While vector data is ideal for mapping discrete features, raster data excels at visualizing gradual variation like land cover or temperature. All enumeration units are modifiable and often arbitrary (Openshaw 1983). In other words, their boundaries may not reflect meaningful social or environmental divisions. Moreover, how they are projected, colored, scaled, and framed introduces a variety of biases. The goal, then, is to choose

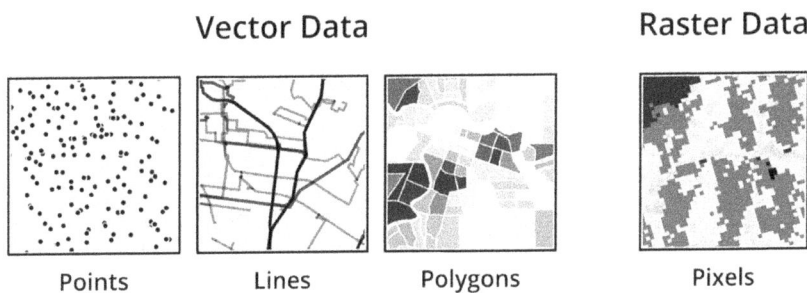

Figure 7.1 Vector data consists of point, line, and polygon features, while raster data consists of a grid of cells, each storing a value.

enumeration units that best match the subject of research while offering just-enough visual and analytical resolution.

Cartography

Once projection, scale, extent, and enumeration are set, attention turns to symbology—the visual language of maps. Cartography is the overall science and the art of making maps. Symbology is like the palette and brushes cartographers use to paint a compelling picture, transforming data into meaningful visual information. Choices of color, shape, and layout are key to communicating meaning effectively.

To avoid overwhelming the viewer, novice mapmakers should start from three principles:

1 **Be descriptive:** Choose symbols that visually represent the map's subject.
2 **Be thematic:** Use consistent color schemes and design motifs across layers.
3 **Be simple:** Clarity trumps complexity; more nuanced maps come with practice.

There are a dozen or more configurable visual variables of symbology (Roth 2017). Most GIS software allows users to manipulate the following elements:

- **Shape:** The look of a symbol such as circles, squares, icons, or custom graphics;
- **Size:** The size of the symbol as it appears on the page, depicting magnitude;
- **Color (hue):** The palette used for fill and borders, depicting categories or gradients;
- **Orientation:** The angular position of the symbol for directional meaning;
- **Height:** The 3D elevation or extrusion up or down to show volume or intensity;
- **Transparency:** The ability of overlapping layers to reveal information;
- **Blending:** The mode by which layers visually interact (e.g., Multiply, Overlay).

Symbology is decorative. It also forms a semiotic system, producing meaning driven by data (Bertin 1983). A single symbol can encode multiple variables. For example, a circle placed at a neighborhood center might scale with the number of households and change color based on median income. This allows a map to simultaneously show condition (wealth), prevalence (households), and spatial distribution (Figure 7.2).

Types of Maps and Symbology

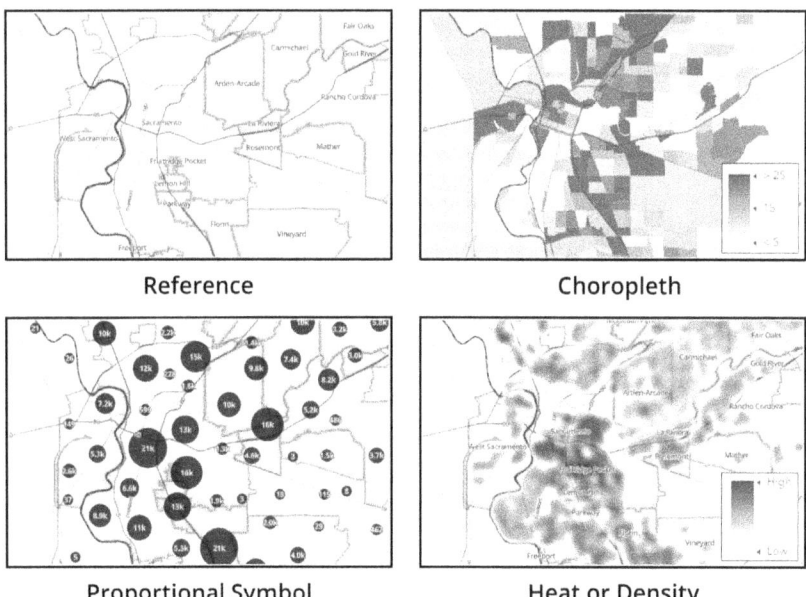

Figure 7.2 From upper left to lower right: The same area of Sacramento, CA, showing examples of a reference map, a filled choropleth map of poverty rate, a proportional symbol map of count of households, and the same household data depicted as a heat or density surface.

Whether creating a reference map, a choropleth map, a proportional symbol map, or a heat map, the final product is the result of many layered decisions. Effective cartography synthesizes projection, scale, extent, enumeration, and design into a cohesive and thick visual narrative.

Geographic communication in a disaster

Natural disasters disrupt every facet of life—from housing and clean water to food security, energy, communication, and healthcare. As such, emergency management offers a powerful example of how GIS can support human-centered research and real-time decision-making.

Yet even the most advanced geospatial analysis is ineffective if its insights are not clearly communicated to the right audience. Nowhere is this truer than in the fast-paced environment of disaster response. While collecting and analyzing quality data is essential, so too is translating those findings into formats that decision makers can quickly interpret and act upon. Effective GIS communication—as with any visual communication—depends on two core considerations:

- **Audience:** Who is the intended recipient? Is the output for the general public or for a specialized group with technical expertise? Does the audience prefer static or interactive formats? Online access or offline briefings?
- **Message:** What is the main insight the audience should take away? What decision will this information inform? Is the message simple and direct, or does it require layered interpretation?

Natural disasters are inherently spatial—they unfold across landscapes and affect communities unevenly. GIS is uniquely equipped to address key questions of where and when a hazard will strike, who is at risk, and how much damage may occur. By integrating geographic and demographic data—such as household size, income, age, disability, or poverty status—GIS reveals not just the areas impacted but the vulnerabilities that shape how people experience disaster.

This section explores how GIS supported emergency response efforts during the 2023 atmospheric river storms in California. In that event, geospatial modeling played a central role in helping emergency managers rapidly identify risks, target resources, and communicate a clear picture of unfolding conditions. The case highlights the value of combining multiple datasets into a single, thick visualization that supports swift and informed decisions.

California's atmospheric river storms

Between late December 2022 and January 2023, a series of nine warm, moisture-laden storms—known as atmospheric rivers—swept across California and the US West Coast (NESDIS 2023). These storms brought an average of 11 inches of rainfall to the state, amounting to an estimated 32 trillion gallons of water (NESDIS 2023). Flood levels in some regions reached heights not seen in a century, resulting in multiple fatalities and widespread property damage (NESDIS 2023).

Although atmospheric rivers are a regular and beneficial source of winter precipitation in the western US, the magnitude and frequency of these storms exceeded the capacity of local infrastructure. Federal disaster declarations soon followed. Particularly hard-hit were the agricultural communities of Watsonville and areas along the Pajaro River in Santa Cruz and Monterey Counties—regions characterized by high social vulnerability and limited resources.

In an emergency such as this, state and local agencies lead the initial response, coordinating efforts on the ground. When additional support is needed, the state may request assistance from the Federal Emergency Management Agency (FEMA). FEMA can provide staffing and subject matter expertise, procure essential goods for disaster survivors, and supply critical data—including geospatial products—to inform decision-making. If the financial impact of the disaster exceeds specific thresholds, FEMA may recommend that the President issue a major disaster declaration, unlocking further federal funding.[6]

Disaster response is inherently collaborative. Federal, state, and local emergency managers typically operate from a central coordination center, where they conduct regular briefings to identify resource needs, share situational updates, and coordinate logistics. In this setting, GIS plays a vital role—supporting real-time analysis, data integration, and effective communication. Throughout the disaster lifecycle, GIS enables stakeholders to maintain a shared operating picture, ensuring that decisions are informed, timely, and spatially grounded.

Throughout the 2023 disaster response, GIS served to communicate flood impacts, estimate population exposure, and visualize community vulnerabilities. This analysis helped emergency managers prioritize needs, allocate limited resources efficiently, and maintain a shared understanding of the situation as it evolved.

Thick visualization

For data and information to be effective, it must all come together in one place. Data visualizations are powerful vehicles to help centralize information and drive home the meaning of key messages in a nuanced way. By featuring the geographic relationships between people, places, and hazards, maps are well suited to synthesize multiple streams of data and analysis into a complete and thickly described picture.

The way GIS compiles and shares information in emergency management may take the form of a web map or dashboard shared as a link, a story map, or a PowerPoint briefing slide show presented orally or simply an email containing tabular summary statistics and two or three key takeaways. The audience and message should determine the format and delivery. Subject matter experts (SMEs) may benefit from a more complex map or dashboard, giving them the freedom to explore and filter data on their own. Executive-level leaders—frequently with less time to dedicate to any one subject—may be better served by a brief, high-level summary with key points clearly stated in a short slide deck or concise email. When there is doubt, ask the intended recipient how and in what format they prefer to receive information.

Composite hazard map

During disaster response, emergency managers—whether SMEs or executives—must maintain a shared understanding of unfolding events, often referred to as a common operating picture. In the 2023 California atmospheric river storms, this need was met through a composite hazard map: a centralized GIS product that aggregated diverse datasets into a single, flexible visualization configurable to various audiences.

By layering up to a dozen spatial datasets, the composite hazard map provided a holistic view of the evolving hazard. While abundant data layers can overwhelm, careful cartographic design—using color theory and visual variables—ensures readability and visual harmony by displaying layers tactically. More art than science, the successful application of tactical visualization results in layers which render in such a way as to fit into the visual context, building upon and complementing interacting layers. Though each layer of data is distinct, a well-designed map allows them to blend seamlessly, producing an integrated picture greater than the sum of its parts.

Each disaster is unique, requiring different inputs. Figure 7.3 illustrates a sample composite hazard map, including:

1 Proportional point symbols showing population size and social vulnerability at the county level;
2 River gage points indicating flood status in key areas of concern;
3 Clusters of stream lines to denote particularly hazardous areas of flash flooding;
4 Precipitation shading to show the overall geographic extent of the storm event;
5 Hatched polygons identifying zones of the most severe rainfall;
6 Vignetting or geographic masking to focus user attention on the most relevant areas.

The composite hazard map is intentionally rich and layered. It requires brief orientation but offers intuitive understanding with repeated use. For example, dark-filled symbols identify socially vulnerable communities, while larger circles represent a greater population. Hatched rainfall zones combined with areas downstream of flooded rivers and streams signal heightened risk. Though the map shows a wide geographic extent at a zoomed-out scale, such an overview can guide deeper inquiry. It prompts users to zoom in, isolate areas of concern, and generate more targeted analyses.

In the 2023 response, one web map served as the master composite hazard map, integrating real-time meteorological and demographic data. Driven by live and near-real-time feeds, the map captured the ebb and flow of the event as conditions unfolded from hour to hour and day to day.

Anatomy of a Composite Hazard Map

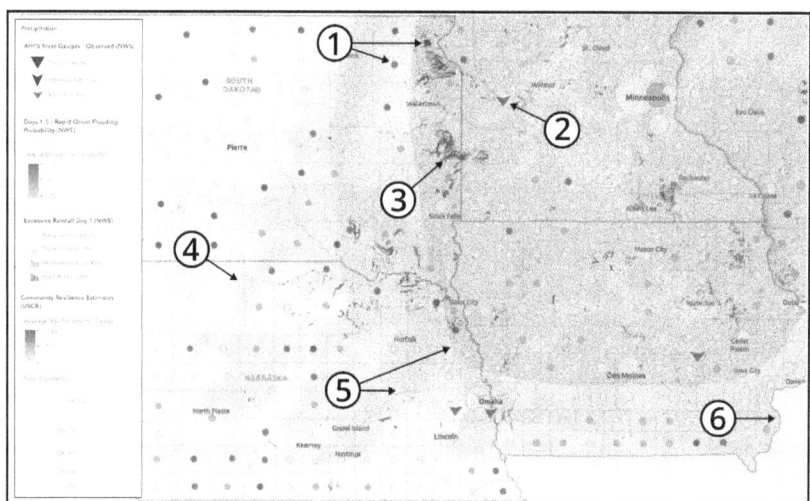

Figure 7.3 This hypothetical example of a composite hazard map combines critical data layers such as (1) vulnerability, (2, 3) riverine flooding, (4, 5) precipitation, and (6) administrative boundaries to form a thick visualization.

Users could adjust scale and extent to focus on communities of interest, revealing localized impacts as conditions changed hour by hour.

This centralized GIS product powered multiple outputs—dashboards, briefings, and analytical reports—ensuring consistency across formats. Because all visualizations were drawn from the same source web map, each tool conveyed aligned information tailored to its audience. Thanks to the flexibility of web mapping platforms, the composite hazard map also supported time-sensitive analysis, evolving in step with the lifecycle of the disaster.

Temporalities of data and analysis

Disasters follow a lifecycle, often described by emergency managers in three phases: before, during, and after an event. Each temporal phase requires different data and analytical approaches. For GIS practitioners, this means aligning geospatial activities with the specific temporal needs of each stage.

Hazard exposure analysis

In the lead-up to the 2023 atmospheric river storms, GIS was used to process forecast data and predictive models from authoritative sources like the National Weather Service. Key inputs included river gage readings, high water and flash flooding streams, excessive rainfall forecasts, and flood inundation models (FIMs). These datasets—points (river gages), lines (streams), and polygons (rainfall and FIMs)—formed the basis of exposure analysis. The hazard and population exposure workflow included:

1 **Attribute selection** to filter river gages, stream segments, and rainfall zones with the most severe forecasts;
2 **Spatial selection** to identify overlaps between these layers and define areas of concern where all three datasets co-occur;
3 **Clipping** populated areas to isolate communities located within the areas of concern, reducing the noise of California's 1,500 communities to a couple of dozen of the most worrisome;
4 **Joining** demographic attributes (e.g., household size, income, age) to enrich at-risk community profiles;
5 **Summarize within** to calculate and rank risk levels, producing a list of the most vulnerable communities and their demographic profile for prioritization.[7]

The output was a daily updated briefing slide deck. Starting with a zoomed-out overview, the presentation drilled down to detailed community-level maps and tables. A typical hazard exposure map used proportional point symbols to represent the number of impacted households and color fills to indicate demographic characteristics such as vulnerability (see Figure 7.4).

Exposure Analysis   Damage Assessment

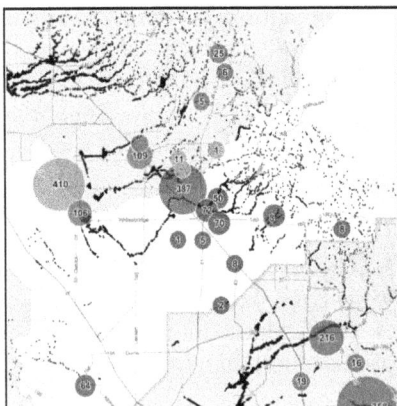
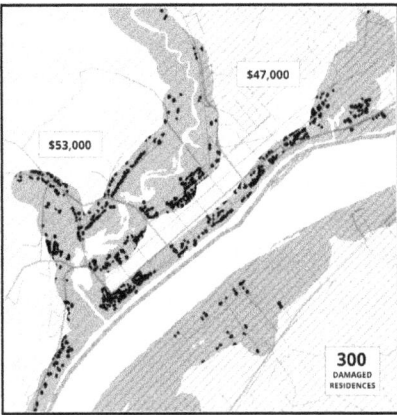

Figure 7.4 Left: Hypothetical example of a flood inundation model (FIM) with forecasted counts of homes exposed to inundation; Right: Hypothetical example of observed flooding along a river with the point locations of actually flooded homes and median household income for context.

This GIS analysis helped emergency managers make informed decisions in a state of nearly 40 million people. It turned disparate data into a clear, structured description of projected severity, location, and timing—allowing responders to focus attention where it was needed most.

Damage assessment modeling

Once a disaster has manifested, the focus shifts from forecasting to documenting observed impacts in real time. Rapid damage assessment is critical to fulfilling requirements under the Stafford Act, which governs requests for federal disaster declarations. Quantifying damage quickly helps justify the need for federal assistance.

While field teams can assess damage onsite, large-scale events often require faster, remote methods. During the 2023 California storms, geospatial operations leveraged Synthetic Aperture Radar (SAR) imagery collected using specialized satellites to detect floodwater through cloud cover and generate high-resolution models of damaged residential homes. The geospatial damage assessment modeling process included:

1 **Image classification** to isolate floodwater visible in SAR imagery;
2 **Conversion** of classified flood water raster outputs into vector polygons;
3 **Overlay** of flood polygons with building footprint data to identify inundated homes, overlaid with demographic data for social context;
4 **Zonal statistics** to calculate the average flood depth and produce a modeled count of damaged households and their demographic conditions.[8]

The outputs included summary tables of damage estimates and maps showing both broad disaster impacts and localized views of the hardest-hit areas. These maps, at finer scales, revealed detailed information down to individual residential structures and contextualized the impacts using indicators like median household income (see Figure 7.4).

For a disaster that spanned the entire state, geospatial damage assessment provided a rapid, scalable way to quantify impacts—saving time and supporting swift federal response. It gave emergency managers a reliable, data-driven snapshot of damage severity across hundreds of communities, supporting a speedier disaster declaration process than what otherwise might have been possible.

Conclusion

Geospatial technologies, geographic information systems (GIS), and maps offer ethnographers a powerful means of achieving what Clifford Geertz (1973) called thick description. These tools iconically represent geographic space, enabling researchers to observe, analyze, and convey the complex interplay between people, culture, and place. Mapping takes many forms, from modern web-based visualizations to historical examples like the subway-like Peutinger Map and the oral tradition of Aboriginal Australian songlines. Yet all maps involve distortions—of projection, scale, or extent—that can lead to both unintentional and strategic misrepresentations.

Researchers can navigate these limitations by applying core GIS concepts: projection, scale, extent, enumeration, and thoughtful cartographic design. The 2023 California atmospheric river storms provide a compelling case study of GIS principles in action. Through exposure analysis and damage modeling distilled into thick visualizations such as composite hazard maps, GIS synthesized environmental and demographic data to support emergency management. Across each temporal phase of the 2023 disaster, GIS emerged as a dynamic tool to integrate diverse data sources, reveal critical spatial relationships, and inform decisions aimed at supporting communities most in need.

Technology statement

GIS as a field is not proprietary to any one software or company. There are, however, common products of which readers should be aware. For general-purpose geospatial applications, QGIS is a desktop-based Free and Open Source Software (FOSS) developed by volunteers. Anyone can download the software for free from the QGIS website (https://qgis.org/en/site/). A parallel for-profit system commonly licensed by public sector agencies and many private and nonprofit enterprises is Esri's ArcGIS product suite and the ArcGIS Pro desktop software (https://www.esri.com/en-us/about/about-esri/overview). One benefit of ArcGIS is its accompanying cloud-based environment, ArcGIS Online, for hosting data and maps suitable for developing online web applications. Many colleges and universities are already ArcGIS customers, and current students may be able to acquire a license by reaching out to their Geography Department or IT Services. Additionally, a limited, free tier of access is available to ArcGIS Online for non-commercial use (https://doc.arcgis.com/en/arcgis-online/get-started/create-account.htm). Meanwhile, a host of libraries and methods for processing and automating geographic data are available within the Python language ecosystem (https://pythongis.org/).

In addition to desktop software, modern GIS is increasingly capable of supporting web development, cloud computing, and automation as both FOSS and proprietary systems (https://forrest.nyc/what-is-modern-gis/). The choice of software should be driven based upon the needs of the project. There are many products available, both desktop and web-based (https://gisgeography.com/gis-software/).

Notes

1 See the Technology Statement for suggestions for getting started with GIS software.
2 See a digital facsimile of the Peutinger Map at https://commons.wikimedia.org/wiki/File:Tabula_Peutingeriana_-_Miller.jpg.
3 Watch excerpts from the documentary series First Australians (2008) discussing songlines from the National Film and Sound Archive of Australia: https://dl.nfsa.gov.au/module/1539/.
4 See "What are projections?" https://www.e-education.psu.edu/geog160/node/1918. See also the "Album of Map Projections" https://projections.mgis.psu.edu/.
5 Discrete data occurs at specific places and has well-defined boundaries. Continuous data lacks clearly defined boundaries and typically varies along a range. See https://www.geographyrealm.com/what-is-continuous-versus-discrete-data-in-gis/.
6 See "How a Disaster Gets Declared" https://www.fema.gov/disaster/how-declared.
7 See the following for examples and explanations of the tools:

   Attribute Selection https://pro.arcgis.com/en/pro-app/latest/help/mapping/navigation/select-features-using-attributes.htm.
   Spatial Selection https://pro.arcgis.com/en/pro-app/latest/help/mapping/navigation/select-features-by-location.htm.
   Clip https://gisgeography.com/clip-tool-gis/.
   Spatial Join https://gisgeography.com/spatial-join/.
   Join and Relate https://gisgeography.com/relate-vs-join-attribute-tables-arcgis/.
   Summarize Within https://pro.arcgis.com/en/pro-app/latest/tool-reference/analysis/summarize-within.htm.

8 See the following for further examples and explanations:

   Image Classification https://gisgeography.com/image-classification-techniques-remote-sensing/.
   Raster to Polygon (Conversion) https://pro.arcgis.com/en/pro-app/latest/tool-reference/conversion/raster-to-polygon.htm.
   Overlay https://gisgeography.com/mapping-overlays/.
   Zonal Statistics https://gisgeography.com/zonal-statistics/.

Bibliography

Bassett, Thomas J. "Cartography and Empire Building in Nineteenth-Century West Africa." *Geographical Review* 84, no. 3 (1994): 316–35. https://doi.org/10.2307/215456.
Bertin, Jacques. *Semiology of Graphics: Diagrams, Networks, Maps*. Translated by Georg Jensch, Dieter Schade, and Wolfgang Scharfe. University of Wisconsin Press, 1983.
Chatwin, Bruce. *The Songlines*. Franklin Press, 1987.
Crang, Mike, and Stephen Graham. "Sentient Cities: Ambient intelligence and the politics of urban space." *Information, Communication and Society* 10, no. 6 (2007): 789–817. https://doi.org/10.1080/13691180701750991.
Davies, John, and Alexander J. Kent. *The Red Atlas: How the Soviet Union Secretly Mapped the World*. University of Chicago Press, 2017.
Elden, Stuart. "Governmentality, Calculation, Territory." *Environment and Planning D: Society and Space* 3, no. 25 (2007): 562–580. https://doi.org/10.1068/d428t.

Englebert, Pierre, Stacy Tarango, and Matthew Carter. "Dismemberment and Suffocation: A Contribution to the Debate on African Boundaries." *Comparative Political Studies* 35, no. 10 (2002): 1093–118. https://doi.org/10.1080/17531055.2010.487338.

First Australians. Blackfella Films, 2008, documentary series. https://www.sbs.com.au/ondemand/tv-series/first-australians.

Foucault, Michel. "Governmentality." In *The Foucault Effect: Studies in Governmentality*, edited by Graham Burchell, Colin Gordon, and Peter Miller, 87–104. The University of Chicago Press,1989.

Geertz, Clifford. "Thick Description: Toward an Interpretive Theory of Culture." In *The Interpretation of Cultures: Selected Essays,* 3–30. Basic Books,1973.

Haraway, Donna. "A Cyborg Manifesto: Science, Technology, and Socialist-Feminism in the Late Twentieth Century." In *Simians, Cyborgs and Women: The Reinvention of Nature,* 149–181. Routledge, 1991.

Harley, J. B. "Maps, Knowledge, and Power." In *The Iconography of Landscape*, edited by Denis Cosgrove and Stephen Daniels, 277–312. Cambridge University Press, 1988.

Herbst, Jeffrey. *States and Power in Africa: Comparative Lessons in Authority and Control*. Princeton University Press, 2000.

Kitchin, Rob. "The Programmable City." *Environment and Planning B: Planning and Design* 38, no. 6 (2011): 945–951. https://doi.org/10.1068/b3806com.

National Environmental Satellite, Data, and Information Service (NESDIS). "Atmospheric Rivers Hit West Coast." National Oceanic and Atmospheric Administration (NOAA), January 25, 2023. https://www.nesdis.noaa.gov/news/atmospheric-rivers-hit-west-coast.

Openshaw, Stan. *The Modifiable Areal Unit Problem*. Geo Books, 1983.

Roth, Robert E. "Visual Variables." In *The International Encyclopedia of Geography*, edited by D. Richardson, N. Castree, M. F. Goodchild, A. Kobayashki, W. Liu, and R. A. Marston, 1–12. Wiley, 2017.

Scott, James C. *Seeing Like a State: How Certain Schemes to Improve the Human Condition Have Failed*. Yale University Press, 1998.

Talbert, Richard J. A. *Rome's World: The Peutinger Map Reconsidered*. Cambridge University Press, 2010.

Chapter 7.1

Concept

Space

Mark Nunes

My writings on the concept of space date back to another time—to "the cyberspace decade." That space is *gone*. More accurately, what "we" had conceived of as a networked social space in the 1990s had become, by the mid-2000s, *something else*. And that something else became, in turn, *yet another something else*. What I offer in this short chapter is a set of *reflections* on the concept of space—and what happens to space when it is lived in its absence.

My entry into the field of internet research came by way of the concept of space, as I found myself in the early 1990s starting to explore the sense of place produced online as individuals engaged with each other, mediated as much through metaphor as through the materiality of software and networks and devices, in a wide range of social, professional, and personal interactions. It was sometime in early 1993 when I first began to engage with others online through telnet, logging into what we referred to at the time as a "text-based virtual reality" called PMC-MOO, a "multi-user dimension" hosted by the online scholarly journal *Postmodern Culture*, that used object-oriented programming to allow its users to chat but also to build "rooms," and "passages," and program "objects" that could be passed and shared between and among users.

It was in that context that I began to ask: What space is cyberspace (Nunes 1997)? And: How do we map the virtual topographies that our actions and interactions write onto these digital networks (Nunes 1999)? My scholarship was informed both by the work of Henri Lefebvre (1994), who emphasized that space was *produced*, brought about through the interrelation of material, conceptual, and experiential processes, as well as by Max Jammer's (1993) *Concepts of Space*, which provided me with an historical and philosophical frame of reference for understanding the growing dominance in Newtonian physics of a concept of space as abstract, empty, and absolute, as well as competing concepts of space as dynamic, interactive, and relational—concepts that are no less "scientific" in their relevance to and application in physics. The *problem* of cyberspace, I argued, framed a more general spatial problematic: by what means do subjects and objects not only "occupy" space in material form but also participate in conceptual processes that both reflect and produce those forms, and how do these lived practices map spatial relations in everyday life?

By the time I had written *Cyberspaces of Everyday Life*, (2006) the project had already taken on a retrospective orientation, looking back at cyberspace rather than mapping its ongoing material, conceptual, and lived expressions. To speak of cyberspace in 2006 was already a nostalgic act, laying claim to a mapping of human-computer interactions that was rapidly approaching the past tense.

If I am guilty of nostalgic musings, I would characterize that nostalgia as more "reflective" than "restorative" (Boym 2001). Unlike restorative nostalgia, with its agenda of returning to a lost (and better) era, reflective nostalgia keeps the past in the past: it "lingers on ruins, the patina of time and history, in the dreams of another place and another time" (Boym 2001, 41). Reflective nostalgia serves a purpose that has nothing to do with making anything "great again"; rather, it offers a structure of feeling (to borrow Raymond Williams's term), mapping a relation between our individual experience of a past and a collective experience of what once was, drawing out, through its absent or ruined presence, "the common landmarks of everyday life [that] constitute shared social frameworks of individual recollections" (Boym 2001, 53).

Nostalgia maps a personal, affective encounter with one's memory of a past, for certain, but it also marks a collective rupture, a site and a scene that may indeed already mark something akin to Lefebvre's (1996) "ephemeral cities" (155): topographies that bring into relief the material, conceptual, and experiential forces caught up in the co-production of conflicting and interpenetrating social spaces. If I linger nostalgically over the digital ruins of the cyberspace decade, I do so to offer up a mapping of the lost spaces and places of networked everyday life that are not so easily rendered by way of GIS.

So perhaps I am homesick for PMC-MOO, and the set of lived, online practices from around 1993 to 1997—a period prior to a framing of the internet as a space for a participatory culture, packaged and branded as Web 2.0 (Jenkins 2006; O'Reilly 2005). But that nostalgic reflection on the cyberspace ruins of everyday, online life in the early 1990s likewise calls attention to the ruptures in social space that were already well underway by 1993: in material form, as the internet took its "neoliberal turn" (Starr 2019) from federally-supported infrastructure and university-dominated R&D efforts to venture capital investment and Silicon Valley entrepreneurialism; in conceptual frames of mind, as "browser" came to describe not only the dominant user interface for the web but also our own role within an expanding online marketplace (of ideas and goods); and in lived experience as well, as the world online and the world offline began to overlay one another in an increasingly seamless fashion.

In this mapping of individual and collective experience of ruptures in social space, nostalgia is, of course, a variable tool. For those who came online in the early 2000s, perhaps they may find themselves confronted with other mappings of digital spaces in conflict, gazing nostalgically, perhaps, at the ruins of the lived spaces of Web 2.0, in that period before the materiality of smartphones and 3G, a concept of the world as "clickable" (Wise 2015), and a set of everyday practices that would make ubiquitous computing increasingly mundane and increasingly banal.

And, of course, by the time William Gibson (2011) was declaring that "cyberspace is everywhere now, having everted and colonized the world," we can already sense other mappings of spaces in conflict on the point of rupture—a *topos* for a nostalgia-to-come—between the-web-as-everywhere of the late 2000s and the growing platformization of the web in the 2010s.

And what spaces in conflict might I find myself mapping now, as I write this short (nostalgic, meandering, self-indulgent) piece? How might the AI-ization of the internet mark yet another rupture in material, conceptual, and lived processes that produce the conflicting social spaces of our collective, contemporary networked lives?

And what maps will we make years from now, as we reflect nostalgically upon this current moment: the soon-to-be ruins of the spaces in which we once lived our digital everyday lives?

References

Boym, Svetlana. 2001. *The Future of Nostalgia*. New York: Basic Books.
Gibson, William. 2011. Interview by D. Wallace-Wells. "William Gibson: The Art of Fiction No. 211." *The Paris Review* 197. https://www.theparisreview.org/interviews/6089/william-gibson-the-art-of-fiction-no-211-william-gibson.
Jammer, Max. 1993. *Concepts of Space: The History of Theories of Space in Physics*. New York: Dover.
Jenkins, Henry. 2006. *Convergence Culture*. New York: New York University Press.
Lefebvre, Henri. 1994. *The Production of Space*. Translated by Donald Nicholson-Smith. Malden, MA: Blackwell.
Lefebvre, Henri. 1996. *Writings on Cities*. Translated and edited by Eleonore Kofman and Elizabeth Lebas. London: Blackwell.
Nunes, Mark. 1997. "What Space Is Cyberspace?" In *Virtual Politics: Community and Identity in Cyberspace,* edited by David Holmes, 163–78. London: Sage.
Nunes, Mark. 1999. "Virtual Topographies: Smooth and Striated Cyberspace." In *Cyberspace Textuality,* edited by Marie-Laure Ryan, 61–77. Bloomington: Indiana University Press.
Nunes, Mark. 2006. *Cyberspaces of Everyday Life*. Minneapolis: University of Minnesota Press.

O'Reilly, Tim. 2005. "What Is Web 2.0: Design Patterns and Business Models for the Next Generation of Software." *Oreilly.com*, September 30. https://www.oreilly.com/pub/a/web2/archive/what-is-web-20.html.

Starr, Paul. 2019. "How Neoliberal Policy Shaped the Internet—And What to Do about It Now." *American Prospect,* October 2. https://prospect.org/power/how-neoliberal-policy-shaped-internet-surveillance-monopoly/.

Wise, J. Macgregor. 2015. "A Hole in the Hand: Assemblages of Attention and Mobile Screens." In *Theories of the Mobile Internet*, edited by Jan Hadlaw, Andrew Herman, and Thom Swiss, 212–231. New York: Routledge.

Chapter 7.2

Case study: implementing GIS in Malmiñañ, Cameroon

From challenges to collaborative solutions

Veronica Bayiha ñwa Quillien, Jean-Baptiste Quillien, and Eugene Bayiha ba Makonn

Initial intentions

The 2022–2023 fieldwork project titled "Implementing GIS to advance rural agro-food systems in Malmiñañ (Cameroon)" was initiated with the primary objective of addressing the pressing issue of food insecurity within the region. The role of agriculture in sustaining livelihoods is pivotal, particularly in rural areas where approximately 70% of the population in Cameroon relies on farming as a way of life (Molua 2008). This project aims to delve into the environmental and ecological challenges affecting agricultural productivity. This mini-chapter offers insights into the methodological strategies employed to overcome challenges encountered during the implementation of geographic information systems (GIS) technology in Malmiñañ, Cameroon. It explores the challenges faced by the research team, the innovative solutions devised in response, and the reflexive considerations regarding the cultural and political stakes inherent in technological interventions.

The initial intentions of the project encompassed several key components. First, there was a focus on coordinating spatial base data using GIS to facilitate a comprehensive understanding of land use and crop dynamics. By leveraging GIS technology, the project sought to gather essential spatial data on approximately 20 hectares of land encompassing various crops such as palm trees, cacao, plantains, macabos, sweet potatoes, and peanuts at the Centre Agroecology Jean Makonn Bayiha (CAE/JMB). This data collection effort hoped to provide a foundational understanding of the existing agricultural landscape and its associated challenges.

Furthermore, the project aimed to engage rural farmers with data by employing innovative methodologies to communicate and disseminate information about the land and crops. This approach would not only empower farmers with valuable insights but also foster a collaborative

DOI: 10.4324/9781032672663-28

environment conducive to addressing food security concerns collectively. Additionally, the project emphasized the documentation of traditional farming practices and stories of the land through interviews, utilizing culturally specific tools rooted in the knowledge and practices of the Bàsàa people of Cameroon.

The statement of need underscored the urgency of collaborating with rural agro-ecological centers to advance natural resources and agro-food systems, thereby enhancing human security and potential. With projections indicating a significant increase in temperatures and the exacerbation of climate change impacts on agriculture in Cameroon, there is a critical need to bolster resilience and adaptive capacity within the agricultural sector. The project aimed to address this need by recording the agricultural history of the land, implementing new technologies, and enhancing monitoring capabilities to respond effectively to production variations and potential food crises.

To achieve its objectives, the project outlined various activities, including the utilization of GIS to coordinate spatial base data collection, accessing satellite imagery for monitoring purposes, and mapping soil data and plot perimeters during field visits. Moreover, the project emphasized the importance of community engagement through the creation of GIS survey forms for farm school learners to track plant growth and maintenance, thereby fostering a participatory approach to data collection and analysis.

Overall, the 2022–2023 fieldwork project sought to combine scientific inquiry with community participation to address the multifaceted challenges confronting food security in Cameroon. By integrating traditional knowledge with modern technologies, the project intended to not only mitigate the immediate threats to agricultural productivity but also foster sustainable practices that would benefit future generations; documenting ancestral agricultural knowledge while incorporating modern technologies to improve people's quality of life.

Problem

In preparing for the fieldwork in Malmiñañ, our team encountered significant challenges related to the implementation of GIS, particularly in the context of the community's unique linguistic and anthropological characteristics. Malmiñañ's community primarily speaks Bàsàa, which posed a formidable language barrier as we sought to introduce GIS concepts and methodologies. Our team is composed of two elders—native speakers of Bàsàa, fluent in English and French. Alongside them are other members who are learners of Bàsàa and proficient in English as well as French. Our intergenerational team recognized the necessity of adapting its approach to effectively convey the intricacies of GIS to the community. In the solution section of this mini-chapter, we delve into our "future" course of action.

Following our team's participation in four GIS workshops, where we gained essential geospatial skills, including an introduction to ArcGIS and field data collection techniques, we convened with the elders to strategize our implementation approach. Emphasizing the importance of oral tradition and community involvement, we deliberated on how best to contextualize GIS concepts within the framework of Bàsàa culture. However, despite our efforts to bridge the gap between Western GIS terminology and Bàsàa understanding, we encountered three primary challenges: anthropological, linguistic, and geopolitical.

Anthropologically, the community's reliance on oral tradition presented a significant hurdle. In a culture where information is predominantly transmitted orally rather than through written form, the concept of utilizing digital mapping tools and data visualization techniques posed a novel and complex challenge. Moreover, the absence of written documentation in Bàsàa meant that conveying technical concepts associated with GIS implementation became inherently challenging in existing words or concepts (e.g., digital mapping).

Linguistically, our efforts to articulate the importance of GIS and land mapping encountered limitations due to gaps in the Bàsàa vocabulary. Certain essential terms and concepts integral to understanding GIS, such as spatial analysis or web mapping, lacked direct equivalents in Bàsàa. This linguistic barrier hindered our ability to effectively communicate the relevance and significance of GIS to the community members, thereby impeding our implementation efforts.

On the world scene, prophetically, a couple of months after receiving the Institute on the Environment mini-grant research award, the Ukraine-Russia war started and led to a global wheat crisis. This world crisis had some notable repercussions in Cameroon. The shortage in wheat supply and the consequent rise in its price threatened the daily nutrition of many in Cameroon. Wheat is the basis of a popular breakfast diet to make bread or beignets. The abrupt rupture in this diet led to the reclamation and re-introduction of culturally significant flour made from, for example, sweet potato, plantain, or cassava. Creative thinking is the child of reasoning and constraints.

Solutions

The Russia-Ukraine war presented an unexpected but invaluable opportunity for experiential learning within the Malmiñañ community. As our team engaged with local farmers at the CAE/JMB, we listened attentively to their experiences and concerns regarding food insecurity. During these interactions, the women shared their innovative solution to the shortage of wheat: bakwèdè or sweet potatoes. Inspired by their resilience and resourcefulness, the eldership at CAE/JMB generously donated three acres of land to support this initiative. Rather than immediately introducing GIS technology, we recognized the importance of first acknowledging and amplifying the community's indigenous knowledge and practices.

In response to the community's needs and preferences, we adopted a participatory approach that prioritized the use of accessible tools such as mobile phones and action cameras to document the current land use practices. By capturing images and videos of the land's transformation and agricultural activities, we worked to create a visual narrative that reflected the community's connection to their environment. These moving images served as dynamic representations of the community's efforts in land cultivation, from cleaning and tilling the soil to planting crops.

The utilization of mobile technology allowed us to collect valuable spatial data, including coordinates, which were essential for mapping and monitoring purposes. Collaborating with the University of Minnesota Duluth Computing Research office (U-Spatial[1]), we explored advanced imagery resources such as Planet Imagery and Esri subscription-based imagery. This collaborative effort enabled us to create a high-resolution imagery map that not only documented the current state of the land but also served as a vital reference point for future agricultural planning and management.

The culmination of our efforts was the creation of a documentary film titled "We, The Women of the Forest: Protecting Bàsàa Knowledge of Sweet Potato Vines in Malmiñañ" by Likinè (2023).[2] This film showcased the resilience and wisdom of the Malmiñañ women, highlighting their innovative approach to addressing food insecurity through the cultivation of sweet potatoes. By sharing their story with the world, we hope to celebrate and preserve the community's indigenous knowledge while inspiring others to embrace sustainable agricultural practices.

Most notably, the creation of this documentary film was made possible through the active involvement of individuals across all age groups in the field. Babies, children, youth, mothers, and grandmothers assumed various roles, from acting to operating cameras and teaching. This intergenerational, participatory approach and collaborative effort enabled us to effectively introduce technological tools (such as cameras and mobile phones) to the Malmiñañ community. The incorporation of these new techniques and tools involved games and hands-on components, which, combined with our cultural connection (represented by elders in our team), facilitated discussions with the people of Malmiñañ around the importance of preserving agricultural knowledge transmission and utilizing new technologies for this purpose.

Words of wisdom

In conclusion, the challenges encountered during the implementation of GIS in Malmiñañ prompted us to adopt a flexible and community-centric approach that prioritized local knowledge and resources. By embracing the use of mobile technology and collaborative partnerships, we were able to capture the essence of the community's agricultural practices and contribute to the sustainable development of agro-food systems in the region. Moving forward, we remain committed to empowering communities like Malmiñañ to harness their collective wisdom and innovate solutions to pressing challenges such as food insecurity.

Transitioning from the initial intentions of the project to the encountered challenges and subsequent solutions, the narrative of the 2022–2023 fieldwork project unfolds with a journey marked by determination, adaptation, and community collaboration. As the project set out to address food insecurity in Malmiñañ through the implementation of GIS technology, it encountered formidable obstacles shaped by the linguistic, anthropological, and geopolitical landscape of the community. Despite these challenges, the research team's commitment to overcoming barriers and embracing innovative methodologies led to a transformative approach rooted in community empowerment and knowledge exchange. In navigating the complexities of GIS implementation within a culturally rich and diverse context, the project exemplifies the intersection of scientific inquiry, community engagement, and technological innovation.

This mini-chapter offers a comprehensive exploration of the methodological strategies employed to navigate these challenges, showcasing the resilience and resourcefulness of the research team and the Malmiñañ community alike. Through reflective analysis and practical insights, the narrative unfolds to reveal not only the intricacies of GIS implementation but also the profound impact of cross-cultural collaborative partnerships in fostering sustainable solutions to pressing agricultural and environmental challenges.

Acknowledgment

We gratefully acknowledge the funding support from the University of Minnesota's Institute on the Environment small grant, which made this work possible.

Notes

1 https://rc.umn.edu/uspatial.
2 https://vimeo.com/1061447319.

References

Likinè, S. 2023. *We, The Women of the Forest: Protecting Bàsàa Knowledge of Sweet Potato Vines in Malmiñañ*. https://youtu.be/pyCkd1_Wpjg?si=V5CjEw6EqOR7WlTn.

Molua, E. L. 2008. "Turning up the Heat on African Agriculture: The Impact of Climate Change on Cameroon's Agriculture." *African Journal of Agricultural and Resource Economics* 2 (311-2016-5519): 45–64.

Chapter 8

Artificial intelligence

The anthropology life cycle of + by + for AI

Matt Artz

Introduction

Since the debut of OpenAI's ChatGPT in November 2022, much has been said about the transformative potential of artificial intelligence (AI). However, the story of AI is much older and broader than the current excitement around large language models (LLMs). In fact, it is a field with a 70-year history that includes many subfields, each with its challenges and opportunities. It is also a field that anthropology has flirted with since its inception. Accordingly, this chapter is not about the hype surrounding LLMs but instead a meditation on the opportunities for digital anthropology to study, work with, and contribute to the development of all subfields of AI.

Given business leaders' profound interest in AI at this time, our engagement with AI is increasingly relevant. A 2023 Accenture survey found that 91% of global executives view it as a critical area of innovation shaping their long-term strategy, and 96% expressed that they were either "very" or "extremely" inspired by novel capabilities offered by foundation AI models. In response, academia is revamping curricula to incorporate AI and rethinking how faculty approach and conduct research in the age of AI.

These implications stretch far and wide, impacting the social sciences, including anthropology (Artz 2023b). Despite anthropologists having studied AI (Seaver 2022; Bell et al. 2021) for decades, and having explored AI as a tool to conduct anthropological research (Munk, Olesen, and Jacomy 2022; Cunningham 1997), relatively limited attention has been given to how anthropology can actively contribute to and shape AI algorithms (Artz 2024b; Forsythe 1993).

Consequently, while all of these previous efforts are valuable, it is of the utmost importance that digital anthropologists get more involved in the development of AI as soon as possible to ensure we contribute to creating human-centered AI during this critical window of technological development. As is, the AI market has already witnessed a meteoric rise in recent years, with the global market for all AI technologies estimated to reach USD$1,847.58 billion by 2030 (Next Move Strategy Consulting 2023).

Staggering as these projections may be, the best anecdote showcasing AI's success and why we ought to get involved now can be found in the case of the most popular AI product to date. Indeed, the meteoric rise of OpenAI's ChatGPT (GPT 3.5) has become a defining moment in AI's mainstream adoption. It became the fastest-growing consumer application in history, attracting 100 million monthly active users within its first two months (Hu 2023).

Given these developments and the pace at which AI systems are being deployed at scale, it is imperative that we, as digital anthropologists, actively engage with AI and contribute to shaping its trajectory. To this end, in this chapter, I put forward the AI Anthropology Lifecycle (AAL), which I use to research and develop AI systems. It is a process that combines three different relationships between anthropology and AI: Anthropology *of* AI, anthropology *by* AI, and anthropology *for* AI. These are combined in a cycle of research and development.

Anthropology *of* AI involves the study of AI as a cultural artifact and the work practices that shape and are shaped by AI. Anthropology *by* AI leverages AI tools and techniques to enhance anthropological and other social science research, expanding the scope and scale of data collection and analysis. Anthropology *for* AI involves applying anthropological insights to developing AI models and products. To illustrate how these three relationships come together in the AAL, I will draw on insights from a company I co-founded, which I will refer to as ArtTech. ArtTech demonstrates how anthropology can be applied to the development of an AI system and how AI can be used to enable and conduct anthropological research, highlighting the transformative potential of AI for the discipline.

By examining these relationships and presenting a concrete example of the AAL in practice, this chapter aims to contribute to the ongoing dialogue about digital anthropology's role in shaping the future of AI and the reciprocal influence of AI on digital anthropology. Further, by reinforcing the importance of critically examining AI and leveraging it to enhance our research methods, it ultimately serves as a call to action for digital anthropologists to become active participants in developing and deploying AI guided by our human-centered principles and grounded in a deep understanding of cultural context.

Digital anthropology and AI

In this section, I will explore the foundations and evolution of digital anthropology and AI, setting the stage for understanding their intersection with the AAL. By examining these two fields' history, methods, and fundamental concepts, we can better grasp the opportunities and challenges that arise when combining the anthropological study of AI, anthropological research enhanced by AI, and the application of anthropological insights to AI development into the AAL process.

Digital anthropology

Digital anthropology explores the complex interplay between humans and information technologies. It investigates how individuals and communities engage with and through digital technologies and how these technologies shape and are shaped by cultural, social, economic, and political factors. As digital technologies have continued to evolve and permeate every aspect of human life, digital anthropology has emerged as a critical lens through which to understand and navigate our lived experience, which increasingly transcends the physical and digital. Further, it has become vitally important for its contributions to the design of digital products (Artz 2024b) and for its potential to carry out machinic anthropology (Pedersen 2023).

Accordingly, the scope of digital anthropology is vast and ever-expanding, as reflected in Daniel Miller's (2018) multifaceted conceptualization of the field. This includes the study of social media and mobile technologies, diverse digital worlds and cultures, disability in the digital age, political engagement and digital activism, museum digitization, and the impact of digital technologies on various domains of human experience such as gaming, personal communication, and development (Geismar and Knox 2021; Horst and Miller 2012).

In addition to its thematic diversity, digital anthropology has significantly contributed to developing new research methods and approaches. These include earlier foundational methods, such as digital ethnography (Pink et al. 2015) as well as computational and techno-anthropology (Munk, Olesen, and Jacomy 2022). Despite the fact that AI was initially overlooked as a field site within digital anthropology, and the foundational methods did not inherently require AI, the discipline has increasingly embraced it as a field of study and augmented its approaches with AI capabilities in recent years. Indeed, this integration of AI and computational methods has become so central that Munk et al. (2023) identify it as one of three critical missions for the future of digital anthropology. Likewise, let us now turn our attention to AI.

Artificial intelligence

AI has been described as "a system's ability to interpret external data correctly, to learn from such data, and to use those learnings to achieve specific goals and tasks through flexible adaptation" (Haenlein and Kaplan 2019). As a field, it originated in the 1950s with early research focused on general problem-solving abilities, seeking to mimic human cognition. Notable early successes included Newell & Simon's Logic Theorist program, which could prove mathematical theorems, and Arthur Samuel's Checkers program, which learned to play at a robust amateur level through self-play. However, the limitations of early AI soon became apparent, given that most programs relied on task-specific rules that needed to be defined by experts in cooperation with software engineers. Likewise, progress slowed after the initial excitement (Crevier 1993).

However, since the early 1980s, the field has steadily advanced with the development of expert systems in the 1980s (Feigenbaum 1981), machine learning (ML) algorithms in the 1980s and 1990s (Fradkov 2020), and deep learning neural networks more recently (LeCun et al. 2015). These advances have led to headline-grabbing, if not somewhat novel, milestones, such as the defeat of the 2016 AlphaGo world champion, Lee Sedol, demonstrating AI's strategic thinking abilities. AI systems have also mastered Poker, surpassing top professionals in 2017, and demonstrated natural conversational phone calls with Google's Duplex AI booking an appointment in 2018. Nevertheless, the progress has not been limited to what some might call novelties. In 2020, DeepMind, a subsidiary of Alphabet, also Google's parent company, unveiled AlphaFold, a revolutionary protein structure predictor, proving AI can solve some of the most complex problems. Also in 2020, OpenAI released GPT-3, an LLM capable of generating human-like text. Over the next two years, GPT-3 found its way into products, many of which were widely adopted by marketers and other business professionals who were following the developments (Barnard and Artz 2024).

Then, in November 2022, OpenAI released GPT-3.5, more commonly known as ChatGPT, significantly altering the perception and adoption of AI. Within two months, it had become the fastest-growing consumer application in history, causing competitors to flood the market with similar products to catch up quickly. Foundational LLMs, such as Google's Bard and Anthropic's Claude, were released, as well as fine-tuned LLMs for specific use cases, such as Bloomberg's financial model and BloombergGPT. Seemingly overnight, the business landscape was transformed.

This transformation is likely to affect all areas of our lived experience, with profound impacts on business and the future of work, from designing innovative business models to identifying new markets and scaling products and services. Beyond these broad transformations, AI is also poised to enhance efficiency, productivity, and decision-making capabilities, presenting entrepreneurs with new opportunities for growth and success (Artz and Ren 2025). However, the widespread adoption of AI in society also harbors the potential for creative destruction, transformation, and massive disruption (Dwivedi et al. 2021), leading 62% of American workers to believe that AI in the workplace will significantly affect them (Pew Research 2023). While it almost certainly will impact a large swath of workers worldwide, changes to the future of work are also not the only considerations. Ethical concerns, including biases in AI models (Sartori and Theodorou 2022), data privacy concerns (Peltz and Street 2020), labor displacement (Gruetzemacher et al. 2020), income distribution disparities (Korinek and Stiglitz 2017), and health inequities (Berdahl et al. 2023), all represent challenges that must be carefully navigated.

Recognizing these multifaceted concerns and the interconnectedness of AI in society, it is essential to approach it from an inherently anthropological systems thinking perspective and acknowledge the widespread impact across various sectors of society, including anthropology. By doing so, we can work to address, or at least mitigate, these concerns, ensuring that AI is implemented responsibly and culturally sensitively. However, to accomplish this, we first must understand the anthropology *of*, *by*, and *for* AI, exploring their potential applications and implications for digital anthropology.

Anthropology of, by, and for AI

Anthropologists have been discussing and involved with the design of information communication technologies for many decades, dating back to at least the 1960s. A notable early demonstration of this is Dell Hymes' 1965 book *The Use of Computers*, which included a quote in the epigraph from Claude Levi-Strauss, who advocated for the idea of computational structuralism, among other critical anthropological concepts. In the book, Levi-Strauss is quoted as saying: "The fundamental requirement of anthropology is that it begin with a personal relation and end with a personal experience, but in between, there is room for plenty of computers" (Hymes 1965).

Yet, despite this early interest in computing, AI remained a relatively unexplored area for most anthropologists. Prominent examples of anthropological research related to AI include Lucy Suchman's (1987) seminal book *Plans and Situated Actions: The Problem of Human-Machine Communication*. In this work, she provided a provocative critique of the assumptions underlying machine intelligence research at the time and called for incorporating insights from the social sciences to better account for the situated nature of human behavior. Building on Suchman's call for a more grounded approach, other anthropologists began to engage with AI systems and technologies. Diana Forsythe (1993), for instance, applied her anthropological lens to expert systems. In her paper on research with computer scientists engaged in knowledge engineering and the development of AI expert systems, she highlighted the role of tacit knowledge and informal practices in shaping these systems. Forsythe illuminated how the engineers' positivist view of knowledge as formal, stable, and transferable rules contrasted with anthropological understandings of knowledge as socially constructed, leading her to critique aspects of AI, notably the "engineers' epistemological stance."

A few years later, in 1996, Alexander Chablo spoke more favorably of expert systems and AI's potential benefits for anthropology in his article "What Can Artificial Intelligence Do for Anthropology?" published in *Current Anthropology*. In the piece, Chablo characterizes AI as offering several advantages, including knowledge elicitation techniques, tools for analyzing field notes and cross-cultural comparisons, and new logics to understand human reasoning (Chablo 1996, 555). Then, in 1997, Sally Jo Cunningham's paper on "Machine Learning Applications in Anthropology: Automated Discovery over Kinship Structures" discussed the use of ML for automated analysis of kinship relationships. She used an inductive logic programming (ILP) system, FOIL, to generalize rules about kinship ties from examples collected during ethnographic fieldwork. Her work demonstrated how AI could aid anthropologists in the difficult task of deriving the implicit rules governing complex social relationships and structures from specific observed instances and stands as an essential early milestone in efforts to bring AI techniques to bear on anthropological research questions (Cunningham 1997).

Yet, despite these examples, the volume of AI literature didn't pick up in earnest until the early 2010s. Since then, it has gained significantly more attention from anthropologists and anthropology-adjacent social scientists, with leading figures such as Genevieve Bell, danah boyd, and Kate Crawford publishing prolifically, especially in the past few years (Bell 2021; Elish and boyd 2017; Crawford 2021). This growing body of work can broadly be categorized into the three aforementioned relationships: anthropology *of* AI, anthropology *by* AI, and anthropology *for* AI, albeit with some overlap.

Anthropology of AI

The anthropology *of* AI involves the study of AI as a cultural artifact, investigating its social, cultural, ethical, and organizational implications. Historically, this work has often involved critically examining AI using traditional ethnographic methods, offering in-depth analysis and critique of AI's effects on society. However, it has also entailed studying how work practices involved in AI development shape these technologies and how AI, in turn, transforms those very practices. By employing anthropological approaches to understand AI's application in real-world contexts and its impacts on the lived experience, the anthropology *of* AI offers crucial insights into the social dimensions of these technologies.

Within this space, anthropologists and cognate disciplines have critically examined AI's development, deployment, and impact from many perspectives. Building on the work of early innovators such as Suchman and Forsythe, the past decade has seen a rise in interest in Big Data and data science, both antecedents to the current era of AI. (Douglas-Jones et al. 2021; Madsen, Blok, and Pedersen 2018; Boellstorff and Maurer 2015; Blok and Pedersen 2014).

Anthropology *of* AI has also engaged with the epistemological and ontological implications of AI systems, approaching them not simply as technical artifacts but as heterogeneous sociotechnical systems that are enacted through varied cultural practices and meanings (Seaver 2017). Critiques have also been waged about using computational approaches to study AI, arguing that purely quantitative or positivist approaches to studying AI and its social impact fail to capture the nuances, complexities, and cultural meanings embedded in AI systems and their use. Researchers emphasize the need for interpretive, ethnographic descriptions of AI that attend to its cultural, historical, and political dimensions through committed fieldwork, trusting relationships with participants, and careful attention to subtle or ambiguous data (van Voorst and Ahlin 2024).

This ethnographic approach has enabled scholars to explore how AI shapes various aspects of social life and cultural production. For example, researchers have studied how AI transforms knowledge production and meaning-making practices, such as translating music styles into statistical patterns (Seaver 2022). They have also explored how AI systems embed political classifications and societal biases through image recognition and labeling practices (Crawford and Paglen 2021) and how they can act as a social gatekeeper, creating power imbalances in digital markets, such as art marketplaces (Artz 2022). A critical area of focus has been the examination of power dynamics, biases, and inequalities in AI models and their impacts on society. Scholars draw attention to the colonial legacies, racial implications, gender, and the broad potential for discrimination in data collection and algorithmic decision-making (Batista Lima 2023; Govia 2020).

Anthropology by AI

Anthropology *by* AI leverages AI tools and techniques to enhance traditional anthropological research, expanding the scope and scale of data collection and analysis. By incorporating AI, anthropologists can analyze larger and more diverse datasets, especially when making use of emergent multimodal capabilities. These datasets certainly include digital data sources but increasingly include digitized data collected as part of traditional ethnographic research. Collectively, these approaches support our ability to triangulate findings from multiple data sources and modalities, strengthening our research's validity and robustness.

While early examples of applying AI to anthropological endeavors included Cunningham's (1997) use of ILP algorithms for automated discovery of kinship structures, more recent approaches use modern AI approaches. Examples include the increasing use of unsupervised ML techniques and natural language processing (NLP) to assist with n-gram analysis, sentiment analysis, topic modeling, named entity recognition (NRE), and word embeddings for analyzing large textual corpora (Pedersen 2023).

Such methods have been used to study cultural meanings and associations and identify themes in ethnographic data (Nelson et al. 2021; Kozlowski et al. 2019). Further, these methods have been employed in use cases such as gaining insights into the semantics and context of drug experiences (Krieg et al. 2017), mapping controversies (Coromina et al. 2023), exploring complexity (Hoy et al. 2023), and charting future directions in business anthropology (Artz 2023c). Other related methods used by anthropologists include social network analysis (Gluesing et al. 2014), knowledge graphs (Artz 2023a), and computer vision for analyzing visual data (Munk 2022).

Paff (2022) has also put forward the idea of "anthropology by data science," which involves using data science tools and methods, particularly ML, to conduct anthropological work. He argues that ML algorithms, like ethnography, are abductive approaches that refine and reformulate conceptualizations based on new data. While I agree that this work is grounded in many data science principles, I argue that anthropology by AI is more fitting because natural language interfaces are making sophisticated data science capabilities accessible without requiring specialized technical expertise, enabling anthropologists to leverage advanced computational methods directly in their research.

Anthropology for AI

Anthropology *for* AI applies anthropological insights to designing and developing AI systems, ensuring they align with human values, needs, and aspirations. Compared to the anthropology *of* and *by* AI, there is a notable scarcity of published literature explicitly focused on this area. While many scholars cited in this chapter have undoubtedly contributed to model and product development, the published works often emphasize the research applications rather than the practical aspects of developing and commercializing AI products informed by anthropological knowledge.

Despite anthropologists having produced rich academic scholarship examining AI's societal and cultural implications, published accounts of anthropological engagement in applied AI development remain more limited, likely due to intellectual property considerations and competitive dynamics in corporate settings. To contribute to this emerging area of applied practice, I have been documenting my AI work practice and system development experiences (2022, 2024a, 2024b) with ArtTech. This work, which resulted in a pending patent for a gamified participatory recommender system (Artz and Speicher 2023), demonstrates one approach to applying anthropological insights in AI design and development. In the following sections, I will describe my approach to the AAL and how it influenced ArtTech.

The AAL

The AAL is a process that combines the three interrelated areas of anthropology *of*, *by*, and *for* AI into a holistic approach to understanding and shaping AI from a digital anthropology perspective. It spans the entire research and development process, incorporating critical analysis, methodological innovation, and human-centered design. The AAL represents a departure from the siloed nature of much existing work in this field, where anthropologists often focus on only one or two of these areas. Instead, by synthesizing anthropology *of*, *by*, and *for* AI into an iterative process, the AAL ensures that anthropological insights and methods are incorporated at every stage, from the initial study of AI as a cultural artifact to the use of AI tools in anthropological research and the application of anthropological knowledge in AI design and development (Figure 8.1).

It begins with studying AI as a cultural artifact and associated work practices through the lens of the anthropology *of* AI. This critical examination of AI's development, deployment, and impact provides insights into the social, cultural, and ethical implications of AI. Within this phase,

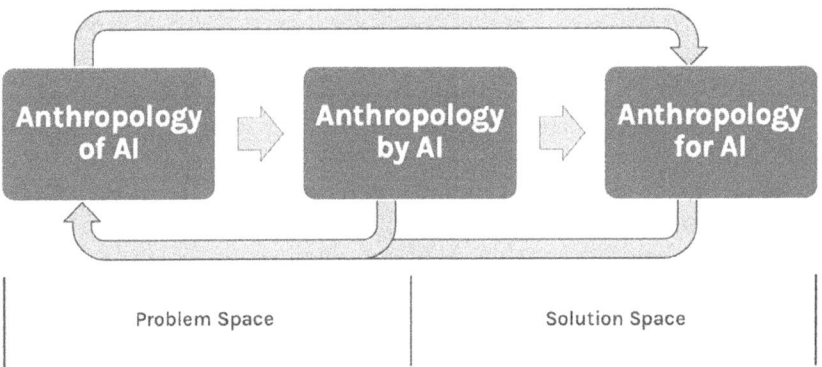

Figure 8.1 The AI Anthropology Lifecycle (AAL).

secondary research is conducted to understand AI's state of the art. Sources may include academic literature, industry white papers, market reports, intellectual property, government reports, and policies. Further and critically, primary research is conducted to gather firsthand accounts and observations from practitioners, stakeholders, and communities impacted by AI, revealing nuanced perspectives and lived experiences that may not be captured in existing literature or public discourse, especially regarding the product being developed.

The insights from this first stage then inform the next stage of the lifecycle, where AI tools and techniques are leveraged to enhance our research capabilities. This involves collecting other multimodal datasets, such as social media and forum content, podcast and video transcripts, product reviews, product analytics, and other digital traces that collectively can contribute to a big data approach to understanding the problem space. Further and critically, all of the data from the anthropology *of* AI stage is also analyzed using the computational methods discussed in this chapter to uncover insights that may not be readily apparent through traditional qualitative analysis alone. By applying techniques like NLP, ML, and network analysis, anthropologists can extract nuanced meaning, identify emergent themes, and detect hidden relationships within the complete dataset collected, ultimately triangulating findings from multiple sources to build a comprehensive understanding.

The insights gained from the first two stages then feed into the final stage of the lifecycle, anthropology *for* AI. In this stage, anthropologists apply their unique understanding of human culture, behavior, and values to designing and developing AI systems. By bringing an anthropological perspective to the AI development process, anthropologists can help ensure that AI technologies are created in a way that aligns with human needs, values, and aspirations. Further, as new data becomes available during the development process through user testing, it is fed back into early research activities and simultaneously influences product development. Similarly, as state-of-the-art changes and new AI technologies are developed and deployed, they become the subject of renewed anthropological study and critique, starting the cycle anew with the latest technological developments.

Likewise, the AAL represents a holistic approach to understanding and shaping AI by combining the critical lens of anthropology *of* AI, the enhanced research capabilities of anthropology *by* AI, and a human-centered design orientation to anthropology *for* AI. Through this approach, digital anthropologists can contribute to the responsible development and deployment of AI systems, which I will endeavor to demonstrate next through the ArtTech example.

ArtTech

As an anthropologist working in the tech sector, I co-founded ArtTech, an AI-enabled platform for the art market, which aimed to address issues of equity, access, and inclusion in the art world. We came to this mission based on exploratory research, which found that individuals with greater economic, social, and cultural capital found it significantly easier to carve out a niche and succeed in the art market. Conversely, those who lacked such capital found it much harder to penetrate the art market, let alone thrive in it. Troubling as that was, the inequalities were not just present in the traditional art market; they were also mirrored and even exacerbated by online markets, given the reliance on machine learning recommender systems. These systems, designed to suggest artwork and users based on preferences, inadvertently result in "rich-get-richer" dynamics, a phenomenon also known as the "Matthew effect" (Ge et al. 2021).

This concept, initially coined by sociologist Robert K. Merton, refers to the social process where those who already have an advantage tend to accrue more advantage over time, while those who are disadvantaged become increasingly so (Merton 1998). In the context of online platforms, such as art markets, the Matthew effect manifests as a bias where popular artists, gallerists, and artworks get recommended more often, benefiting from increased visibility and sales. At the same time, the lesser-known remain in obscurity, struggling to break through. This bias creates a feedback loop that homogenizes recommendations and stunts the chances of discovery, creating an environment that works against those without significant pre-existing capital.

These insights informed our research approach and methodology design. Our aim was to investigate how digital platforms could potentially address existing inequities in the art market, with a particular focus on improving visibility and opportunities for lesser-known artists and gallerists. We sought to explore methods that could potentially make it more equal for all art market participants, regardless of their access to existing forms of capital.

The project started by conducting ethnographic research that involved secondary and primary research. In the secondary research phase, I studied art market reports from UBS, Deloitte, and other industry sources to understand the market size, trends, and external environment. Next, I interviewed 30 participants, including artists, gallerists, curators, critics, educators, and consultants. A subset of those interviews included observations with individuals using other art platforms like Artsy and Saatchi Art. As part of this phase, I also conducted a digital ethnography of Reddit and carried out a competitor analysis, which included other AI-based platforms.

Part of the research involved the study of other similar platforms and, most importantly, academic literature and intellectual property on recommender systems and gamification, both of which rely on machine learning. Notably, I found that the traditional methods of collaborative and content-based filtering, as well as more modern deep learning approaches, all have weaknesses that can lead to numerous forms of algorithmic bias, such as popularity bias, over-specialization, and homogenization, resulting in unfair treatment and a lack of exposure for specific items or users in platforms.

With the data collected through the anthropology *of* AI, I then employed anthropology *by* AI techniques. This involved web scraping to collect more data and using ML and NLP-based methods to analyze all of the data computationally. In this stage, I blended conventional qualitative analysis approaches such as thematic analysis and affinization with AI-based methods like NRE, topic modeling, and sentiment analysis.

NRE was used to quickly identify the individuals, organizations, and places mentioned in interviews, industry reports, and online discussions. It is helpful to gain an initial understanding of the actors and even the language of a new market. This information can assist in developing fluency in the space and map out the relationships and networks among these entities, revealing patterns of influence, collaboration, and competition.

Latent Dirichlet allocation (LDA), a generative probabilistic topic modeling technique, was used to represent documents as a mixture of topics, with each topic characterized by a word distribution. By leveraging LDA, I uncovered the main themes discussed in the interviews, online forums, and market reports, providing a high-level overview of the art market's key concepts, issues, and opportunities. This technique can be helpful in anthropological research to uncover latent themes in large text corpora that would be very challenging to analyze manually.

Sentiment analysis using TextBlob was also conducted to gauge the overall sentiment expressed in the various datasets. By analyzing the sentiment of product reviews, forum discussions, and interviews, I could assess the general attitudes and opinions toward various aspects of the art market, such as the perceived fairness and accessibility of existing platforms.

Collectively, the insights gained from the manual and computational analyses were compared and contrasted to identify areas of convergence and divergence, strengthen the validity of the findings, and uncover potential blind spots or biases. By triangulating the results from the different techniques, I developed a more comprehensive and nuanced understanding, revealing that the art market suffered from problems related to relationships, knowledge, and access, which were not adequately addressed by existing digitalization efforts.

Informed by the findings from the anthropology *of* and *by* AI, I transitioned to anthropology *for* AI, where I applied the insights to design the product and machine learning recommender system. The key innovation in this phase was the development of a novel machine learning system that leverages the concept of "behavioral capital" to promote equity and inclusivity within the platform. Drawing from the insights about the importance of relationships, knowledge sharing, and access uncovered in the earlier phases, we designed a model that rewards users for their productive contributions to the community and filed a US Patent Application for a Gamified Participatory Recommender System (Artz and Speicher 2023).

The system assigns scores to user actions that generate value, such as uploading artwork, providing thoughtful feedback, engaging in discussions, attending events, and supporting other users. These scores are then used to boost the visibility of the user's content in others' recommendation feeds. Significantly, the system also factors in the influence level of the users who engage with the content, creating a virtuous cycle that amplifies the reach of high-quality contributions.

The recommender system leverages a hybrid approach that combines collaborative filtering and content-based filtering. The collaborative filtering component leverages user interaction data to identify similar users and artworks, while the content-based filtering analyzes the metadata to recommend items with similar characteristics. The behavioral capital scores are incorporated into the recommender model as weights that modulate the importance of specific user actions and interactions. This ensures that the system prioritizes the content and connections that are most valuable to the community rather than just optimizing for popularity or similarity. The result is a recommendation system that connects users with relevant and high-quality content and actively promotes community-building within the art market. By leveraging anthropological insights, we aimed to create a more inclusive and sustainable platform for artists, collectors, and enthusiasts alike.

Throughout the product development process, I worked through the AAL, engaging in successive loops of research, design, and development. This approach allowed me to refine the system and the overall product continuously based on ongoing insights from conventional and digital data sources. At each stage, I gathered feedback and data through various methods and analyzed the data using qualitative and computational methods to compare and contrast the findings. The insights gained from this ongoing process enabled us to create a product that resonated with our target audience, resulting in recognition at the 2022 South by Southwest Pitch Competition and partnerships with 25 museums and eight art fairs internationally.

Considerations and next steps

It is essential to recognize that the AAL is not a linear process but rather an iterative one. This continuous loop allows for the constant refinement and improvement of AI informed by anthropological insights and grounded in a deep understanding of human beliefs and behavior that contribute to AI as a cultural contrast worth our intervention. Moreover, the AAL should be seen as a flexible process that can be adapted to different AI projects' specific needs and contexts. The relative emphasis placed on each stage of the lifecycle may vary depending on the nature of the project. However, the core principles of critical analysis, enhanced research capabilities, and human-centered design should remain central to the process.

Additionally, as digital anthropologists increasingly engage with AI, it is crucial to develop a set of best practices and ethical guidelines to navigate the complex landscape of AI development. This should involve collaborating with other disciplines, such as computer science, design, and ethics, to ensure a holistic and responsible approach to AI. It should also include developing new models and frameworks that help us make sense of our engagement with AI. I've attempted to put some structure to the way I approach my AI work, but others are needed.

Finally, anthropologists need to actively get involved in AI development and policy. We cannot just study and critique it. We need to be engaged at every touch point, from the research and development process outlined in this chapter to the development of public policy, if we are to help reduce the potential negative harms of AI.

Conclusion

The AAL represents a holistic approach to understanding and shaping AI from a digital anthropology perspective. Leveraging the three interrelated areas of anthropology *of*, *by*, and *for* AI, the AAL ensures that anthropological insights and methods are incorporated at every stage of the research and development process.

The anthropology *of* AI involves the critical study of AI as a cultural artifact and the work practices that shape and are shaped by AI. This area of inquiry builds on the lineage of digital anthropology, offering crucial insights into the human dimensions of AI by examining it in real-world contexts and its impacts on lived experiences. Anthropology *by* AI leverages AI tools and techniques to enhance conventional anthropological research, expanding the scope and scale of data collection and analysis and strengthening the validity and robustness of the research. Anthropology *for* AI applies anthropological insights to developing AI systems, ensuring they align with human values, needs, and aspirations by building on the critical understanding gained through the study *of* AI as a cultural artifact and the expanded research capabilities enabled *by* AI.

The ArtTech case study presented demonstrates the real-world potential of the AAL in guiding the development of socially responsible AI products. By leveraging the unique combination of critical analysis, enhanced research capabilities, and human-centered design principles, anthropologists can contribute to creating AI solutions that address industry-specific challenges while promoting social equity and inclusion.

The future of digital anthropology will be intricately linked with AI. I hope you will join me there.

Bibliography

Artz, Matt. 2022. "Design Anthropology, Algorithmic Bias, Behavioral Capital, and the Creator Economy." *Practicing Anthropology* 44 (1): 33–36. https://doi.org/10.17730/0888-4552.44.2.33.

Artz, Matt. 2023a. "From Machine Learning to Machine Knowing." *UNESCO Digital Library*. https://unesdoc.unesco.org/ark:/48223/pf0000384902.

Artz, Matt. 2023b. "Ten Predictions for AI and the Future of Anthropology." *Anthropology News* 64 (2): 15–17. https://doi.org/10.1111/AN.1605.

Artz, Matt. 2023c. "The Digital Turn in Business Anthropology." *Journal of Business Anthropology* 12 (1): 78–91. https://doi.org/10.22439/jba.v12i1.6919.

Artz, Matt. 2024a. "Design Anthropology by Co-Becoming: Reimagining Participation in the Pursuit of New Possibilities." In *The Routledge Companion to Practicing Anthropology and Design*, edited by Jenessa Spears and Christine Miller. New York: Routledge. https://doi.org/10.4324/9781003340188-31.

Artz, Matt. 2024b. "Reimagining Recommender Systems: Towards a More Equitable Model for Creators." In *EmTech Anthropology: Careers at the Frontier*, edited by Matt Artz and Lora Koycheva. New York: Routledge. https://doi.org/10.4324/9781003458555-3.

Artz, Matt, and Yaya Ren. 2025. "Beyond the GenAI Gold Rush: Mapping Entrepreneurial Tensions in the Age of Generative Artificial Intelligence." *Annals of Anthropological Practice*.

Artz, Matthew R., and Geoffrey C. Speicher. 2023. "Gamified Participatory Recommender System." United States Patent US20230046646A1. https://patents.google.com/patent/US20230046646A1/.

Barnard, Jason, and Matt Artz. 2024. "Search Marketing in the Age of AI: Understanding the Marketing Implications of Search, Assistive and Answer Engines." *Journal of Digital & Social Media Marketing* 11 (3): 244–60. https://ideas.repec.org/a/aza/jdsmm0/y2023v11i3p244-260.html.

Batista Lima, Mayane. 2023. "Computer Vision: Anthropology of Algorithmic Bias in Facial Analysis Tool." In *Numerical Simulation - Advanced Techniques for Science and Engineering*, edited by Ali Soofastaei, 27–36. London: IntechOpen. https://dx.doi.org/10.5772/intechopen.110330.

Bell, Genevieve. 2021. "Talking to AI: An Anthropological Encounter with Artificial Intelligence." In *The SAGE Handbook of Cultural Anthropology*, edited by

Lene Pedersen and Lisa Cliggett, vol. 1, 442–59. New York: SAGE Publications Ltd. https://doi.org/10.4135/9781529756449.n25.

Bell, Genevieve, Ellen Broad, Brenda Martin, Ellen O'Brien, Juliette Parsons, and Alexandra Zafiroglu. 2021. "Gender and Artificial Intelligence." In *The International Encyclopedia of Anthropology*, edited by Hilary Callan, 1–11. John Wiley & Sons. https://doi.org/10.1002/9781118924396.wbiea2458.

Berdahl, Carl Thomas, Lawrence Baker, Sean Mann, Osonde Osoba, and Federico Girosi. 2023. "Strategies to Improve the Impact of Artificial Intelligence on Health Equity: Scoping Review." *JMIR AI* 2: e42936. https://doi.org/10.2196/42936.

Blok, Anders, and Morten Axel Pedersen. 2014. "Complementary Social Science? Quali-Quantitative Experiments in a Big Data World." *Big Data & Society* 1 (2): 1–6. https://doi.org/10.1177/2053951714543908.

Boellstorff, Tom, and Bill Maurer. 2015. *Data: Now Bigger and Better!* Chicago, IL: Prickly Paradigm Press.

Breiger, Ronald L., Robin Wagner-Pacifici, and John W. Mohr. 2018. "Capturing Distinctions While Mining Text Data: Toward Low-Tech Formalization for Text Analysis." *Poetics* 68: 104–19. https://doi.org/10.1016/j.poetic.2018.02.005.

Chablo, Anthony. 1996. "What Can Artificial Intelligence Do for Anthropology?" *Current Anthropology* 37 (3): 553–55. https://doi.org/10.1086/204518.

Coromina, Òscar, Alexei Tsinovoi, and Anders Kristian Munk. 2023. "Digital Marketing as Digital Methods: Repurposing Google Ads for Controversy Mapping." *Big Data & Society* 10 (2): 1–15. https://doi.org/10.1177/20539517231216955.

Crawford, Kate. 2021. *The Atlas of AI: Power, Politics, and the Planetary Costs of Artificial Intelligence*. New Haven, CT: Yale University Press.

Crawford, Kate, and Trevor Paglen. 2021. "Excavating AI: The Politics of Images in Machine Learning Training Sets." *AI & Society* 36: 1105–16. https://doi.org/10.1007/s00146-021-01162-8.

Crevier, Daniel. 1993. *AI: The Tumultuous History of the Search for Artificial Intelligence*. New York: Basic Books.

Cunningham, Sally Jo. 1997. "Machine Learning Applications in Anthropology: Automated Discovery over Kinship Structures." *Computers and the Humanities* 30: 401–06. https://doi.org/10.1007/BF00057936.

Douglas-Jones, Rachel, Antonia Walford, and Nick Seaver, eds. 2021. *Towards an Anthropology of Data*. Hoboken, NJ: Wiley-Blackwell.

Dwivedi, Yogesh K., Laurie Hughes, Elvira Ismagilova, Gert Aarts, Crispin Coombs, Tom Crick, Yanqing Duan, et al. 2021. "Artificial Intelligence (AI): Multidisciplinary Perspectives on Emerging Challenges, Opportunities, and Agenda for Research, Practice and Policy." *International Journal of Information Management* 57: 101994. https://doi.org/10.1016/j.ijinfomgt.2019.08.002.

Elish, Madeleine Clare, and danah boyd. 2017. "Situating Methods in the Magic of Big Data and AI." *Communication Monographs* 85 (1): 57–80. https://doi.org/10.1080/03637751.2017.1375130.

Feigenbaum, Edward A. 1981. "Expert Systems in the 1980s." In *State of the Art Report on Machine Intelligence*, edited by edited by Bond, A., 23. Maidenhead: Pergamon-Infotech.

Forsythe, Diana E. 1993. "Engineering Knowledge: The Construction of Knowledge in Artificial Intelligence." *Social Studies of Science* 23 (3): 445–77. https://doi.org/10.1177/0306312793023003002.

Fradkov, Alexander L. 2020. "Early History of Machine Learning." *IFAC-PapersOnLine* 53 (2): 1385–90. https://doi.org/10.1016/j.ifacol.2020.12.1888.

Geismar, Haidy, and Hannah Knox, eds. 2021. *Digital Anthropology*. 2nd ed. London: Routledge. https://doi.org/10.4324/9781003087885.

Ge, Yingqiang, Shuchang Liu, Ruoyuan Gao, Yikun Xian, Yunqi Li, Xiangyu Zhao, Changhua Pei, Fei Sun, Junfeng Ge, Wenwu Ou, and Yongfeng Zhang. 2021. "Towards Long-Term Fairness in Recommendation." In *Proceedings of the 14th ACM International Conference on Web Search and Data Mining*, 445–53. https://doi.org/10.1145/3437963.3441824.

Gluesing, Julia C., Kenneth R. Riopelle, and James A. Danowski. 2014. "Mixing Ethnography and Information Technology Data Mining to Visualize Innovation Networks in Global Networked Organizations." In *Mixed Methods Social Networks Research*, edited by Silvia Domínguez and Betina Hollstein, 203–34. Cambridge: Cambridge University Press. https://doi.org/10.1017/CBO9781139227193.011.

Govia, Leah. 2020. "Coproduction, Ethics and Artificial Intelligence: A Perspective from Cultural Anthropology." *Journal of Digital Social Research* 2 (3): 42–46. https://doi.org/10.33621/jdsr.v2i3.53.

Gruetzemacher, Ross, David Paradice, and Lee Kang Bok. 2020. "Forecasting Extreme Labor Displacement: A Survey of AI Practitioners." *Technological Forecasting and Social Change* 161: 120323. https://doi.org/10.1016/j.techfore.2020.120323.

Haenlein, Michael, and Andreas Kaplan. 2019. "A Brief History of Artificial Intelligence: On the Past, Present, and Future of Artificial Intelligence." *California Management Review* 61 (4): 5–14. https://doi.org/10.1177/0008125619864925.

Horst, Heather A., and Daniel Miller. 2012. *Digital Anthropology*. 1st ed. London: Routledge. https://doi.org/10.4324/9781003085201.

Hoy, Tom, Iman Munire Bilal, and Zoe Liou. 2023. "Grounded Models: The Future of Sensemaking in a World of Generative AI." *Ethnographic Praxis in Industry Conference Proceedings* 2023: 159–82. https://doi.org/10.1111/epic.12158.

Hu, Krystal. 2023. "ChatGPT Sets Record for Fastest-Growing User Base - Analyst Note." *Reuters*. https://www.reuters.com/technology/chatgpt-sets-record-fastest-growing-user-base-analyst-note-2023-02-01/.

Hymes, Dell. 1965. *The Use of Computers in Anthropology*. The Hague: Mouton. https://stacks.stanford.edu/file/druid:hd684mh5338/hd684mh5338.pdf.

Jemielniak, Dariusz. 2020. *Thick Big Data: Doing Digital Social Sciences*. 1st ed. Oxford: Oxford University Press. https://doi.org/10.1093/oso/9780198839705.001.0001.

Korinek, Anton, and Joseph E. Stiglitz. 2017. *Artificial Intelligence and Its Implications for Income Distribution and Unemployment*. Cambridge, MA: National Bureau of Economic Research.

Kozlowski, Austin C., Matt Taddy, and James A. Evans. 2019. "The Geometry of Culture: Analyzing the Meanings of Class through Word Embeddings." *American Sociological Review* 84 (5): 905–49. https://doi.org/10.1177/0003122419877135.

Krieg, Lisa Jenny, Moritz Berning, and Anita Hardon. 2017. "Anthropology with Algorithms? An Exploration of Online Drug Knowledge Using Digital Methods." *Medicine Anthropology Theory* 4 (3): 21–52. https://doi.org/10.17157/mat.4.3.458.

LeCun, Yann, Yoshua Bengio, and Geoffrey Hinton. 2015. "Deep Learning." *Nature* 521: 436–44. https://doi.org/10.1038/nature14539.

Luitse, Dieuwertje, and Wiebke Denkena. 2021. "The Great Transformer: Examining the Role of Large Language Models in the Political Economy of AI." *Big Data & Society* 8 (2): 1–14. https://doi.org/10.1177/20539517211047734.

Madsen, Mette My, Anders Blok, and Morten Axel Pedersen. 2018. "Transversal Collaboration: An Ethnography in/of Computational Social Science." In *Ethnography for a Data-Saturated World*, edited by Hannah Knox and Dawn Nafus, 183–211. Manchester: Manchester University Press. https://doi.org/10.7765/9781526127600.00017.

Merton, Robert K. 1998. "The Matthew Effect in Science, II: Cumulative Advantage and the Symbolism of Intellectual Property." *Isis* 7 (4): 606–23. https://doi.org/10.1086/354848.

Miller, Daniel. 2018. "Digital Anthropology." *Open Encyclopedia of Anthropology*. https://www.anthroencyclopedia.com/entry/digital-anthropology.

Munk, Anders Kristian. 2022. "How to Use Computer Vision to Study Large Corpora of Images." In *SAGE Research Methods: Doing Research Online*. SAGE Publications, Ltd. https://doi.org/10.4135/9781529611465.

Munk, Anders Kristian, Asger Gehrt Olesen, and Mathieu Jacomy. 2022. "The Thick Machine: Anthropological AI between Explanation and Explication." *Big Data & Society* 9 (1): 1–14. https://doi.org/10.1177/20539517211069891.

Munk, Anders Kristian, Mette Simonsen Abildgaard, Astrid Oberborbeck Andersen, Torben Elgaard Jensen, Mathieu Jacomy, and Anders Koed Madsen. 2023. "Three Missions for Digital Anthropology." *UNESCO Digital Library*. https://unesdoc.unesco.org/ark:/48223/pf0000384922.

Nelson, Laura K., Derek Burk, Marcel Knudsen, and Leslie McCall. 2021. "The Future of Coding: A Comparison of Hand-Coding and Three Types of Computer-Assisted Text Analysis Methods." *Sociological Methods & Research* 50 (1): 202–37. https://doi.org/10.1177/0049124118769114.

Next Move Strategy Consulting. 2023. "Artificial Intelligence Market." *Next Move Strategy Consulting*. https://www.nextmsc.com/report/artificial-intelligence-market.

Paff, Stephen. 2022. "Anthropology by Data Science." *Annals of Anthropological Practice* 46 (1): 7–18. https://doi.org/10.1111/napa.12169.

Pedersen, Morten Axel. 2023. "Towards a Machinic Anthropology." *Big Data & Society* 10 (1): 1–9. https://doi.org/10.1177/20539517231153803.

Peltz, James, and Anita C. Street. 2020. "Artificial Intelligence and Ethical Dilemmas Involving Privacy." In *Artificial Intelligence and Global Security*, edited by Yvonne R. Masakowski, 95–120. Bingley: Emerald Publishing Limited. https://doi.org/10.1108/978-1-78973-811-720201006.

Pew Research. 2023. "AI in Hiring and Evaluating Workers: What Americans Think." *Pew Research Center*. https://www.pewresearch.org/internet/2023/04/20/ai-in-hiring-and-evaluating-workers-what-americans-think/.

Pink, Sarah, Heather Horst, John Postill, Larissa Hjorth, Tania Lewis, and Jo Tacchi. 2015. *Digital Ethnography: Principles and Practice*. Thousand Oaks, CA: SAGE Publications Ltd.

Sartori, Laura, and Andreas Theodorou. 2022. "A Sociotechnical Perspective for the Future of AI: Narratives, Inequalities, and Human Control." *Ethics and Information Technology* 24 (4): 1–12. https://doi.org/10.1007/s10676-022-09624-3.

Seaver, Nick. 2017. "Algorithms as Culture: Some Tactics for the Ethnography of Algorithmic Systems." *Big Data & Society* 4 (2): 1–12. https://doi.org/10.1177/2053951717738104.

Seaver, Nick. 2022. *Computing Taste: Algorithms and the Makers of Music Recommendation*. Chicago, IL: The University of Chicago Press.

Sekara, Vedran, Arkadiusz Stopczynski, and Sune Lehmann. 2016. "Fundamental Structures of Dynamic Social Networks." *Proceedings of the National Academy of Sciences* 113 (36): 9977–82. https://doi.org/10.1073/pnas.1602803113.

Suchman, Lucy A. 1987. *Plans and Situated Actions: The Problem of Human-Machine Communication*. Cambridge: Cambridge University Press.

van Voorst, Roanne, and Tanja Ahlin. 2024. "Key Points for an Ethnography of AI: An Approach towards Crucial Data." *Humanities and Social Sciences Communications* 11: 337. https://doi.org/10.1057/s41599-024-02854-4.

Chapter 8.1

Concept

Algorithm

Heiner Heiland

Algorithms are key technologies of contemporary societies and have a profound impact on people's daily lives. As "encoded procedures for transforming input data into a desired output, based on specific calculations" (Gillespie 2014, 168), they are not a new phenomenon. At their core, they are simple "if A, then B" instructions, so that every traffic light, every assembly manual, and every cooking recipe is an algorithm, and every computer is based on them.

However, algorithms are not just computational procedures. Kowalski (1979) states that "Algorithm = Logic + Control." Logic refers to the underlying data on which a decision is made. And control describes the actual decision-making process. In the first place, this puts the focus on the data being used and not only on the control and outcomes of algorithmically controlled processes. Data is never "raw" (Gitelman 2013); it is always processed and contains a subjective component and as such also influences algorithmic decisions. And, second, artificial intelligence can be identified as an evolvement of algorithmic systems. AI is also based on algorithms, but these are not fixed and can adapt themselves and their decisions independently based on the data. Analyses of algorithms must therefore also take into account their data basis and at the same time allow for a critical perspective on AI.

With increasing digitalization and computing capacity, the use and power of algorithms have grown significantly, influencing what people consume, how they live, and where and how they spend their everyday lives. In doing so, algorithms reproduce social inequalities (Eubanks 2018) and power structures (O'Neil 2017). They exert their influence by defining "grammars of action" (Agre 1994). Their decisions frame how individuals should or must act. Depending on the context—be it the selection of a film on a streaming service or a work instruction under algorithmic management—these grammars force or compel the decisions to be followed. And since, as Lawrence Lessig (1999) points out, "code is law," it is often impossible to deviate from them, just as an online form will not allow you to proceed until you have filled in all the required fields.

A key characteristic of algorithms is their opacity, in contrast to the documented and transparent nature of bureaucratic processes, for example. Algorithms are "black boxes" of which only the outcomes are visible, and their mechanisms are kept "behind veils of trade secrecy" (Pasquale 2015, 2), so that their opacity is legally protected. This obfuscated nature of algorithms undermines the identification of biases in their decision-making and thus also undermines their accountability.

The black box nature of algorithms is a significant factor contributing to their mythical status. They are often regarded with a high level of effectiveness, efficiency, and objectivity. This perception, though, can be considered a form of "agency laundering," whereby the individuals, structures, and interests behind and within the algorithms become obscured. Thus, the critical analysis of algorithmic systems is of paramount importance. However, this endeavor is accompanied by significant "conceptual, epistemological, and methodological challenges when it comes to actually studying and knowing them" (Bucher 2016, 82).

A variety of approaches are available for the analysis of algorithms, which can be selected depending on the respective research question (Kitchin 2017). First and most obviously, there are attempts to open the black box and analyze the source code, i.e., the DNA of an algorithm that controls its processes. If there is no access to this code, an attempt can be made to reverse engineer the algorithm. But both approaches require appropriate expertise. Second, source code can be very difficult to comprehend, meaning that even experts do not necessarily understand the decisions made by the algorithm, which is exacerbated in the case of machine learning algorithms that adapt their decision-making structure (Kroll et al. 2017). Alternatively, the ethnographic study of programming teams during the production of algorithms can yield valuable insights into the social processes and assumptions that underpin algorithms. This approach offers only limited insight into the specific effects of algorithms.

The aforementioned approaches share a common perspective on algorithms as computational processes, positing that they are technologies with unfiltered effects on the world. However, the congruence between the programming of an algorithm and its effects is not always guaranteed, as numerous other factors can intervene, ranging from technical issues such as bugs to human agency. While most algorithms can make decisions and induce specific actions in individuals, the ultimate responsibility for implementing these decisions rests with the individuals themselves. They must translate the decisions into social reality. In other words, neither an automatic product recommendation nor an algorithmic work instruction has consequences if they are not followed.

Such a socio-material perspective posits that technology is not merely an objective process, but rather a social process that only materializes in practice (Orlikowski 2007). This perspective engenders a shift in the understanding of algorithms and the manner in which they can be analyzed. Accordingly, there is a "social construction of algorithms" (Heiland 2023) in the context of which individuals not only actualize but also exert influence over their effects through their interactions with algorithms.

This highlights the significance of algorithm awareness among individuals (Eslami et al. 2016) and the influence of their assumptions on actions and attempts to influence algorithms. Studies of YouTube vloggers (Bishop 2019) and platform workers (Heiland 2023; Möhlmannn et al. 2023) provide empirical evidence of this phenomenon. This can also result in the controlling effects of algorithms being based not on their decisions, but on their opacity. In the course of so-called black box power (Heiland 2022), the opacity of algorithms forces individuals to make assumptions about how they function and to act accordingly. The Thomas theorem (Thomas and Thomas 1928) posits that if individuals perceive a situation as real, it is indeed real in its consequences. This suggests that such assumptions, despite their objective inaccuracy, can nevertheless influence behavior.

Algorithms are a particularly salient and potent technological artifact, the analysis of which engenders novel challenges. A socio-material understanding facilitates the employment of ethnographic methods for the analysis of algorithmic mechanisms. The analysis of algorithms within the social practices in and with which they achieve their effects enables a realistic perspective on these technologies.

References

Agre, Philip E. 1994. "Surveillance and Capture: Two Models of Privacy." *The Information Society* 10, no. 2: 101–27. https://doi.org/10.1080/01972243.1994.9960162.

Bishop, Sophie. 2019. "Managing Visibility on YouTube through Algorithmic Gossip." *New Media & Society* 21, no. 11–12: 2589–2606. https://doi.org/10.1177/1461444819854731.

Bucher, Taina. 2016. "Neither Black nor Box: Ways of Knowing Algorithms." In *Innovative Methods in Media and Communication Research*, edited by S. Kubitschko and A. Kaun, 81–98. Cham: Springer International Publishing.

Eslami, Motahhare, Karrie Karahalios, Christian Sandvig, Kelsey Vaccaro, Aimee Rickman, Kevin Hamilton, and Ali Kirlik. 2016. "First I 'Like' It, Then I Hide It." In *Proceedings of the 2016 CHI Conference on Human Factors in Computing Systems*, edited by Jofish Kaye, Allison Druin, Cliff Lampe, Dan Morris, and Juan Pablo Hourcade, 2371–82. New York: ACM.

Eubanks, Virginia. 2018. *Automating Inequality: How High-Tech Tools Profile, Police, and Punish the Poor.* New York: St. Martin's Press.

Gillespie, Tarleton. 2014. "The Relevance of Algorithms." In *Media Technologies*, edited by Tarleton Gillespie, Pablo J. Boczkowski, and Kirsten A. Foot, 167–94. Cambridge: The MIT Press.

Gitelman, Lisa, ed. 2013. *"Raw Data" is an Oxymoron.* Cambridge: MIT Press.

Heiland, Heiner. 2023. "The Social Construction of Algorithms: A Reassessment of Algorithmic Management in Food Delivery Gig Work." *New Technology, Work & Employment.* https://doi.org/10.1111/ntwe.12282.

Heiland, Heiner. 2022. "Black Box Power: Zones of Uncertainty in Algorithmic Management." In *Digital Platforms and Algorithmic Subjectivities*, edited by Emiliana Armano, Marco Briziarelli, and Emanuela Risi, 75–86. Westminster: Westminster University Press.

Kitchin, Rob. 2017. "Thinking Critically About and Researching Algorithms." *Information, Communication & Society* 20, no. 1: 14–29. https://doi.org/10.1080/1369118X.2016.1154087.

Kowalski, Robert. 1979. "Algorithm = Logic + Control." *Communications of the ACM* 22, no. 7: 424–36. https://doi.org/10.1145/359131.359136.

Kroll, Joshua A., Joanna Huey, Solon Barocas, Edward W. Felten, Joel R. Reidenberg, David G. Robinson, and Harlan Yu. 2017. "Accountable Algorithms." *University of Pennsylvania Law Review* 165: 633–705.

Lessig, Lawrence. 1999. *Code and Other Laws of Cyberspace.* New York: Basic Books.

Möhlmann, Mareike, Carolina Alves de Lima Salge, and Marco Marabelli. 2023. "Algorithm Sensemaking: How Platform Workers Make Sense of Algorithmic Management." *Journal of the Association for Information Systems* 24, no. 1: 35–64. https://doi.org/10.17705/1jais.00774.

O'Neil, Cathy. 2017. *Weapons of Math Destruction: How Big Data Increases Inequality and Threatens Democracy.* New York: Broadway Books.

Orlikowski, Wanda J. 2007. "Sociomaterial Practices: Exploring Technology at Work." *Organization Studies* 28, no. 9: 1435–48. https://doi.org/10.1177/0170840607081138.

Pasquale, Frank. 2015. *The Black Box Society: The Secret Algorithms That Control Money and Information.* Cambridge, MA: Harvard University Press.

Thomas, William I., and Dorothy S. Thomas. 1928. *The Child in America: Behavior Problems and Programs.* New York: Alfred Knopf.

Chapter 8.2

Case study
Using AI for deradicalization

Andrea Russo

Radicalization, which refers to the adoption of extreme ideologies that promote violence for political or ideological reasons (Serafim 2005), is thriving in digital spaces. Platforms like Telegram have become key places where inappropriate or illegal content becomes normalized, partly due to the ease of sharing information and the anonymity these platforms provide, fostering a sense of "safety in numbers" (Semenzin and Bainotti 2020). While there is a lot of research on how radicalization occurs online, much less attention has been given to deradicalization, the process by which individuals reject the extreme beliefs they once held. This chapter addresses that gap by presenting an action-research study that explores how AI can facilitate deradicalization in digital environments.

Radicalization is a gradual and complex process through which individuals or groups come to adopt a radical ideology that justifies violence for achieving specific political or ideological aims (Serafim 2005). This process can occur on different levels: at the individual level, it often involves identity struggles, social integration failures, and feelings of alienation; at the social level, it takes place within a "radical milieu"; and at the governmental or political level, it may result from state policies or shifts in public opinion (European Commission 2024). The journey to radicalization is highly personal, with no single path and manifesting in various ways (Kkienerm 2024), driven by a mix of triggers and motivating factors (European Commission 2024).

Despite the alarming nature of this issue, empirical research—mostly conducted through digital means—has significantly downplayed its scope. Numerous computational analyses of extensive video datasets have shown that users are generally more exposed to mainstream news rather than extreme content (Hosseinmardi et al. 2021; Munger and Phillips 2022). When it comes to the role of bots in spreading disinformation, scholars argue that empirical studies need to go beyond merely counting bots in social media datasets to understand the full impact (Krizhevsky, Sutskever, and Hinton 2012). Qualitative methods are essential for

DOI: 10.4324/9781032672663-31

exploring how people respond to bots and the misinformation they spread (Caliandro et al. 2024).

Deradicalization is the process through which individuals reject previously held extremist ideologies. In developing strategies for deradicalization, it is essential to consider group dynamics and the inter-group contexts that form the basis of radicalization (Caliandro 2018). Radical groups often foster a strong in-group identity, which they see as superior, while viewing the out-group as inferior and hostile, blaming them for the grievances of the in-group. This, in turn, justifies the use of violence for societal or political change (Doosje et al. 2016). Interestingly, an individual's resilience may not only protect them from radicalization but can also make them resistant to deradicalization efforts once they have joined a radical group. However, there's scant literature on initiating deradicalization with online radical groups, especially leveraging digital and computational methods. My research aims to fill this gap.[1]

Methodology

The first phase is obviously to observe and test whether the group is radicalized. After some time, elements of the group showed extreme behavior, evidencing a desire to even make violent and dangerous gestures. After ascertaining that the group was radicalized and violent, I began with data collection.

I started to gather data from the Italian chat group "Put down the covid-mask" on Telegram using the Telethon tool.[2] A baseline was set from November 10, 2022, predating vaccine and Ukraine-Russia conflict concerns. Before this date, topics were varied, driven by Italian elections and anticipation for updates on vaccinations. Subsequent data collection confirmed increased group interactions from early October, averaging a weekly rise of around 20% compared to prior weeks, totaling about 1,000 posts per week. This data also helps assess bot influence on group dynamics.

Analyzing acquired data reveals daily initial conditions for temporal analysis.[3] I performed a Sentiment analysis process via Italian VADER to enhance nuanced understanding compared to translation-based approaches of the original tool.[4] For the AI system, I opted for the GPT-3.5 Davinci model with the API service connected with Telegram API, with the goal to improve conversational agents in bot-human interactions, providing more natural and engaging conversations that better meet user needs (Bender et al. 2021; Brown et al. 2020). This linguistic aspect is significant since GPT generates responses based on probabilistic information without explicit reference to meaning, resembling a "stochastic parrot" (Bender et al. 2021).

Regarding the strategy of deradicalization, I used the Juan Pujol García fake-agent network intelligence method. Juan Pujol García, known as GARBO, was a Spanish double agent loyal to Great Britain during WWII, conducting fictitious spying for the Germans (Vecchioni 2016). Disliking extremism after the Spanish Civil War, Pujol chose espionage for Britain "for the good of humanity" (Vecchioni 2015). Rejected by the British Embassy, he crafted a false pro-Nazi identity and became a German agent, producing deceptive reports on Britain from diverse sources in Lisbon (Vecchioni 2015). In emulation of GARBO's strategy, I employ controlled fictitious accounts to build a network. I use five accounts with the same strategic principle. To enhance credibility, each account is endowed with a story crafted from information gathered through qualitative sociological analysis and the anthropological "follow the native" principle (Caliandro 2018).

Results

From October 10, 2022, until November 11, 2022, I collected data on the group "Drop the covid-mask!" to assess the initial conditions of the system. It had about 450 people—with an average of about 70 people online—when I started observing interactions in December of 2022. The deradicalization phase of the research spanned from March 23, 2023, to May 7, 2023.[5]

The initial condition

Analyzing data from October 14, 2022, around 1,300 interactions revealed initial system conditions—reference network, prevalent words, topics, ecosystem, and influence network. The reply network (Figure 8.2.1) reveals a central hub identified as the group administrator and reveals group influencers and associated communities.[6] Notably, a majority of comments are succinct, while a few individuals contribute extensive text. This observation offers valuable insights into the group's structural composition and community interactions. Regarding message content, I assessed the group's overall sentiment[7] as: Negative: 0.125332436; Neutral: 0.724032301; Positive: 0.149318977; and Compound: 0.481011844. Despite a notably high negative value, the average sentiment remains usually positive, with a minimal 0.024 difference. The compound value, at 0.48, suggests a generally medium-positive tone, influenced by a prevalent neutral value.

I found that there is a substantial presence of comments endorsing weapons, revolt, and conspiracy theories such as those involving George Soros and Klaus Schwab. Thanks to the data collected, I created the network animation highlighting group interactions of the initial condition.[8]

Case study: using AI for deradicalization   267

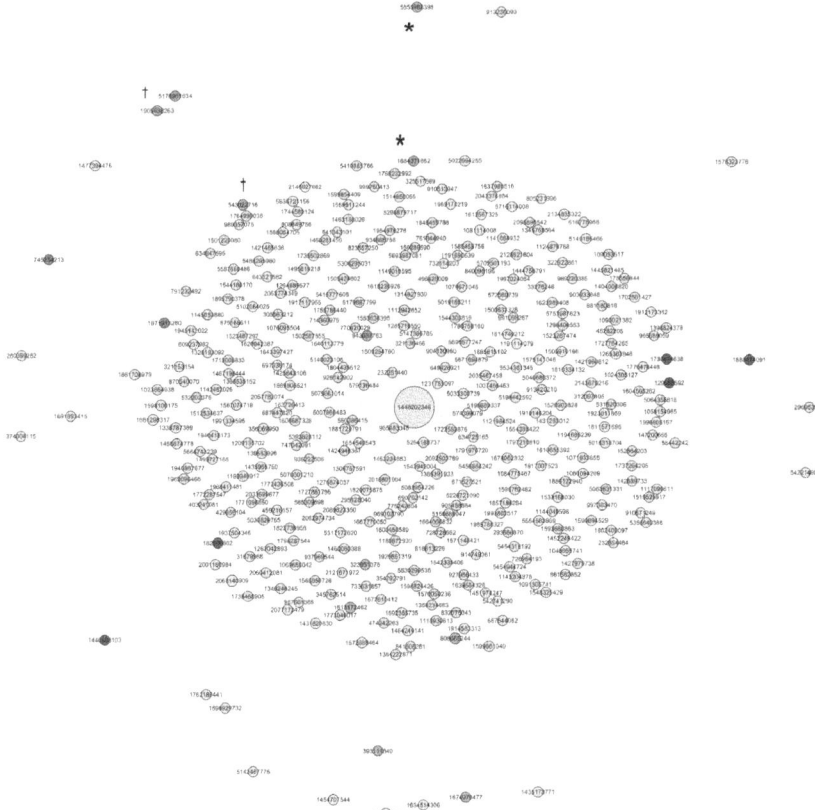

Figure 8.2.1 The full reply network.

Before dynamics

The initial conditions of the system and the observed social dynamics, unfortunately, described a difficult and hostile environment for my goals. I admit I was discouraged by the possible results after the interaction with my bots and ChatGPT, but starting with the channel network after the deradicalization dynamics,[9] there was a change from the initial conditions.

While the administrator remains the main hub of the network, their centrality has decreased significantly. Since the implementation of my accounts and the dynamics they bring, the relative weight of other accounts in the network has shifted considerably. As shown in Figure 8.2.2, the gray nodes representing my accounts (marked with *) indicate that interactions with other accounts cover roughly ~17% of the entire community (represented by light green and light blue nodes in the

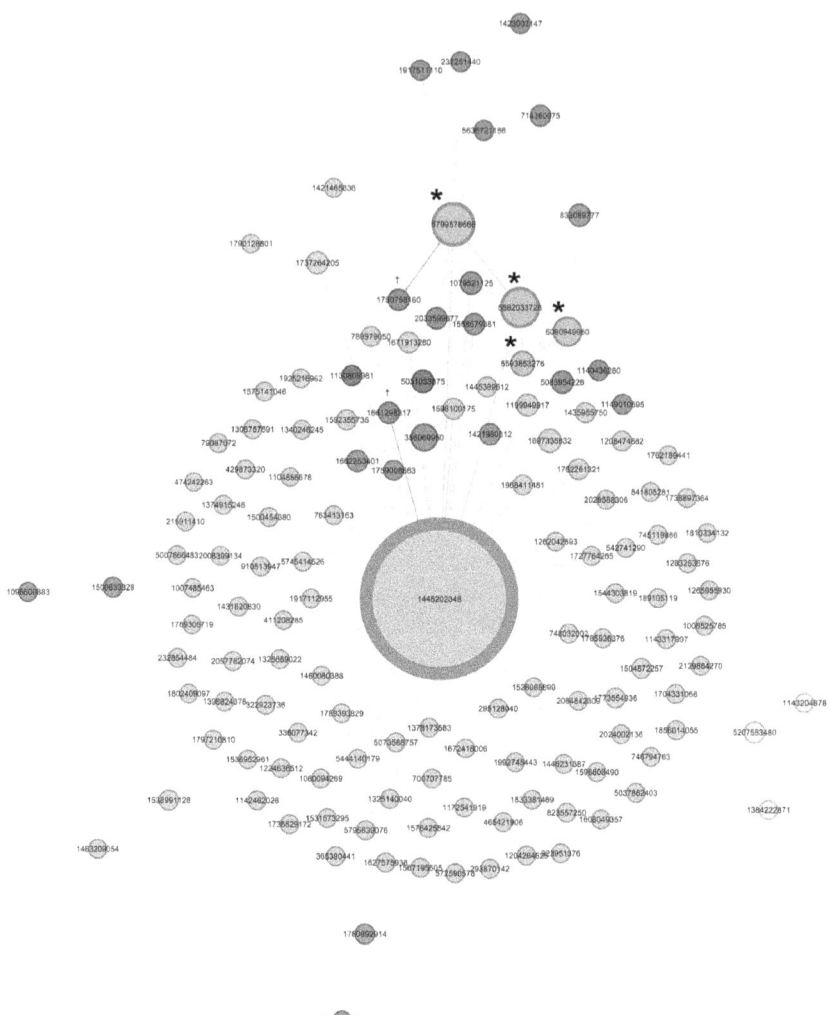

Figure 8.2.2 The reply network with representative interactions marked.

linked online version).[10] Concerning accounts displaying violent behavior, I encountered several, with two particularly prominent ones represented by dark orange nodes (marked with †) still in the same figure. Despite their violent tendencies, frequent interactions occurred, forming a cluster in the graph's top center where open discussions took place. This led to the formation of new, smaller communities (light green, light blue, and dark green nodes) distinct from the violet one directly connected to the administrator—an "anti-echo chamber." Thanks to the data collected, I created the network animation highlighting group interactions after the dynamics of deradicalization.[11]

Another noteworthy result that I found is the variation in weight and importance in the network during the two phases.[12] The administrator initially has the highest number of connections (degree) with 349, which drops to 122 after the dynamics, though it retains a significant influence as seen from its weighted degree of 222. My accounts appear in varying degrees after the dynamics, indicating different levels of activity and influence. Notably, they are positioned as second, third, fourth, and sixth of the most important accounts in the network. The accounts associated with violent behavior have low degrees (few connections) but relatively high weighted degrees, suggesting that, despite having fewer interactions, these connections are particularly strong or important.

With the Sentiment analysis, I wanted to see if significant results could emerge in people's discussions and interactions. The average text sentiments present as: Negative: 0.078551515; Neutral: 0.938115152; Positive: 0.104549495; and Compound: 0.067783434.[13] The post-dynamic sentiment outcomes illustrate variations from the initial sentiment: Negative: –0.046780921; Neutral: 0.214082851; Positive: –0.044769482; and Compound: –0.41322841.[14] The findings indicate a decline in negative sentiment, an uptick in neutral sentiment, and a corresponding reduction in positive sentiment. Additionally, the compound sentiment appeared more negative post-dynamic, attributable to increased neutral sentiment fostering balanced and less radical discussions within the group.

[Stay Human]

Notes

1 Tables and Figures results mentioned in this chapter can be found at https://github.com/AndreaRussoAgid/Devin-Proctor-Book---AI-device-for-deradicalization-process and https://zenodo.org/records/10987637 (Russo 2024).
2 https://docs.telethon.dev/en/stable/.
3 Table 1 in the Link Results: https://github.com/AndreaRussoAgid/Devin-Proctor-Book---AI-device-for-deradicalization-process/blob/main/Table%201.png.
4 https://github.com/AndreaRussoAgid/VADER-Italian-Sentiment.
5 Table 2 in the Link Results: https://github.com/AndreaRussoAgid/Devin-Proctor-Book---AI-device-for-deradicalization-process/blob/main/Table%202.png.
6 ACC_Reply_ALL in the Link Results: https://github.com/AndreaRussoAgid/Devin-Proctor-Book---AI-device-for-deradicalization-process/blob/main/ACC_Reply_ALL.png.
7 Table 3 in the Link Results: https://github.com/AndreaRussoAgid/Devin-Proctor-Book---AI-device-for-deradicalization-process/blob/main/Table%203.png.

8 Animation as GIF Before_dynamics_animation: https://github.com/Andrea RussoAgid/Devin-Proctor-Book---AI-device-for-deradicalization-process/blob/main/Before_dynamics_animation.gif.
9 Channel_network in the Link Results: https://github.com/AndreaRussoAgid/Devin-Proctor-Book---AI-device-for-deradicalization-process/blob/main/Channel_network.png.
10 Channel_network_Grigio_cattivi in Link Results: https://github.com/Andrea RussoAgid/Devin-Proctor-Book---AI-device-for-deradicalization-process/blob/main/Channel_network_Grigio_cattivi.png.
11 Animation as GIF After_dynamics_animation: https://github.com/Andrea RussoAgid/Devin-Proctor-Book---AI-device-for-deradicalization-process/blob/main/After_dynamic_animation.gif.
12 Table 4 in Link Results: https://github.com/AndreaRussoAgid/Devin-Proctor-Book---AI-device-for-deradicalization-process/blob/main/Table%204.png.
13 Table 5 in Link Results: https://github.com/AndreaRussoAgid/Devin-Proctor-Book---AI-device-for-deradicalization-process/blob/main/Table%205.png.
14 Table 6 in Link Results https://github.com/AndreaRussoAgid/Devin-Proctor-Book---AI-device-for-deradicalization-process/blob/main/Table%206.png.

Bibliography

Bender, Emily M., Timnit Gebru, Angelina McMillan-Major, and Shmargaret Shmitchell. 2021. "On the Dangers of Stochastic Parrots: Can Language Models Be Too Big?" In *Proceedings of the 2021 ACM Conference on Fairness, Accountability, and Transparency*, 610–23. Canada. https://doi.org/10.1145/3442188.3445922.

Brown, Tom, Benjamin Mann, Nick Ryder, Melanie Subbiah, Jared D. Kaplan, Prafulla Dhariwal et al. 2020. "Language Models Are Few-Shot Learners." *Advances in Neural Information Processing Systems* 33: 1877–1901.

Caliandro, Alessandro. 2018. "Digital Methods for Ethnography: Analytical Concepts for Ethnographers Exploring Social Media Environments." *Journal of Contemporary Ethnography* 47 (5): 551–78. https://doi.org/10.1177/0891241617702960.

Caliandro, Alessandro, Alessandro Gandini, Lucia Bainotti, and Guido Anselmi. 2024. "The Platformisation of Consumer Culture: A Digital Methods Guide." Alessandro Caliandro, Alessandro Gandini, Lucia Bainotti, and Guido Anselmi, In *The Platformisation of Consumer Culture*, edited by Alessandro Caliandro, Alessandro Gandini, Lucia Bainotti, and Guido Anselmi. Amsterdam: Amsterdam University Press.

Doosje, Bertjan, Fathali M. Moghaddam, Arie W. Kruglanski, Arjan De Wolf, Liesbeth Mann, and Allard R. Feddes. 2016. "Terrorism, Radicalization and De-Radicalization." *Current Opinion in Psychology* 11: 79–84. https://doi.org/10.1016/j.copsyc.2016.06.008.

Extremists, Violent. 2024. *Prevention of Radicalisation – European Commission*. https://home-affairs.ec.europa.eu/policies/internal-security/counter-terrorism-and-radicalisation/prevention-radicalisation_en.

European Commission. 2024. *Prevention of Radicalisation – European Commission*. https://home-affairs.ec.europa.eu/policies/internal-security/counter-terrorism-and-radicalisation/prevention-radicalisation_en.

Hosseinmardi, Homa, Amir Ghasemian, Aaron Clauset, Markus Mobius, David M. Rothschild, and Duncan J. Watts. 2021. "Examining the Consumption of Radical Content on YouTube." *Proceedings of the National Academy of Sciences* 118 (32): e2101967118. https://doi.org/10.1073/pnas.2101967118.

Kkienerm. 2024. "Counter-Terrorism Module 2 Key Issues: Radicalization & Violent Extremism." https://www.unodc.org/e4j/zh/terrorism/module-2/key-issues/radicalization-violent-extremism.html.

Krizhevsky, Alex, Ilya Sutskever, and Geoffrey E. Hinton. 2012. "ImageNet Classification with Deep Convolutional Neural Networks." In *Advances in Neural Information Processing Systems* 25: 1097–1105. https://proceedings.neurips.cc/paper_files/paper/2012/hash/c399862d3b9d6b76c8436e924a68c45b-Abstract.html.

Munger, Kevin, and Joseph Phillips. 2022. "Right-Wing YouTube: A Supply and Demand Perspective." *The International Journal of Press/Politics* 27 (1): 186–219. https://doi.org/10.1177/19401612211052922.

Russo, Andrea. 2024. *Telegram Italian NoVax*. https://zenodo.org/records/10987637.

Semenzin, Silvia, and Lucia Bainotti. 2020. "The Use of Telegram for Non-Consensual Dissemination of Intimate Images: Gendered Affordances and the Construction of Masculinities." *Social Media + Society* 6 (4): 2056305120984453. https://doi.org/10.1177/2056305120984453.

Serafim, Ana. 2005. "Terrorism—A Cultural Phenomenon?" *Connections* 4 (1): 61–74. https://www.jstor.org/stable/26323155.

Vecchioni, Domenico. 2016. "Garbo, La Spia Che Rese Possibile Lo Sbarco in Normandia." *Sistema di Informazione per la Sicurezza della Repubblica*. https://www.sicurezzanazionale.gov.it/sisr.nsf/storie-di-spie/garbo-la-spia-che-rese-possibile-lo-sbarco-in-normandia.html.

Chapter 9

Multimodal anthropology

Publics and encounters

Isaac Marrero-Guillamón and Ethiraj Gabriel Dattatreyan

The argument for multimodality

In the last decade or so, multimodality has become something of a buzzword in anthropology. For many, multimodality has offered an exciting re-orientation toward ethnographic research and dissemination that is open to experimenting with more-than-textual media and different modes of encounter. Under the banner of multimodal anthropology, we may find exhibitions, workshops, graphic novels, games, digital interfaces, multimedia websites, theater plays, music videos, and collaborative films. As one can, for instance, observe in *American Anthropologist*'s pioneering "Multimodal anthropologies" section, the range and heterogeneity of projects under its banner is remarkable.[1]

Many of those who have adopted the moniker have argued that the point of multimodality, however, is not to simply signal this plurality but rather to contribute to the discipline's transformation. Collins, Durington, and Gill define it as "not only an anthropology that works across multiple media but one that also engages in public anthropology and collaborative anthropology through a field of differentially linked media platforms" (2017, 142). For these authors, multimodality is a way to conceptualize the potential of new relations between researchers, students, participants, and publics configured around novel media ecologies. They invite practitioners to embrace these mediated worlds and experiment with ways of opening up anthropological research to new publics and collaborations.

In our own work, we have argued that "multimodality offers a line of flight for an anthropology yet to come: multisensorial rather than text based, performative rather than representational, and inventive rather than descriptive" (Dattatreyan and Marrero-Guillamón 2019, 220). These three conceptual pairings point at key areas of transformation for the discipline—certainly not new, as we will discuss below, but still relevant. First, multisensoriality centers the need to go beyond the logocentrism that has characterized anthropology; it points to the multiple ways in which we make sense of the world beyond language, for instance, through embodied experience. Here, multimodality is an invitation to imagine and devise forms of anthropology that enable us to learn from and with others through an expanded sensorium: by making, crafting, drawing, stitching, cooking, etc. As many authors have claimed before us (e.g., Ingold 2013; Pink 2009; Vidali 2016), these practices have the potential to tune the discipline into more-than-textual knowledges, as well as reconfiguring its field methods through new embodied devices such as do-it-together workshops (Pérez-Bustos and Bello-Tocancipá 2024), apprenticeships (Grasseni 2004), and stagings (Giordano and Pierotti 2020).

Second, we invoke performativity as a way out of the hegemony of representation in ethnographic and anthropological work. Instead of anchoring our practice to the craft of description and analysis, we have defended the relevance of a performative approach. Fieldwork, as well as ethnography, need not be limited to "capturing" what is already in existence; it can also take the shape of performative encounters in which new ideas, entities, and even realities are co-created. Jennifer L. Biddle and Tess Lea, for instance, have theorized the ways in which indigenous artists and scholars working with digital media have used artifice "to make the real *more* real, when the real is itself what is at risk, at stake: namely, indigenous history, language, presence, silenced, denied, ignored" (2018, 6). This orientation toward "performative realism"—which they dubbed *hyperrealism*—may offer new possibilities and horizons for multimodal ethnography. It allows us to reimagine fieldwork as an activity geared toward co-creation; interventionist and open to reshuffling the very relations it depends on.

Third, we have posited invention as a productive companion concept to multimodality. We understand it as "a creative, immanent mode of engagement with the subjects and objects with whom we work, through which unforeseeable knowledges, events, and encounters may be produced" (Dattatreyan and Marrero-Guillamón 2019, 221). In other words, doing inventive research means participating in the inventiveness of social life: rather than simply attempting to "capture" reality through established descriptive techniques, an inventive approach to multimodal ethnographic research "aspire[s] instead to contribute to enacting new entities, new relations, new worlds" (Dattatreyan and Marrero-Guillamón 2019, 221). Crucially, we do not intend this commitment to creative approaches to signify a (re)turn to more centered forms of authorship—far from it. As we have argued elsewhere "a politics of invention in ethnographic practice refers in the first instance to the ability and willingness to attune ourselves to the inventiveness that surrounds us, and to work with it in ways that are contextually appropriate" (Marrero-Guillamón and Dattatreyan 2023, 216). Caterina Sartori's collaboration with housing activists in the form of the exhibition *Fight 4 Aylesbury*[2] is a great example of the kind of "distributed creativity" we are advocating for. Rather than curating an exhibition based on her long-term fieldwork on the demolition of this housing estate in London, she partook in the co-creation of a collaborative platform—the exhibition was in fact a device for collectively building an archive of life and displacement in the estate.

Our theoretical work on multimodality has thus attempted to shift the debate from an interest in the possibilities of using different media to a focus on the modes of encounter and address we generate as researchers, and how they may reconfigure the practice of ethnography. One of the key components in this regard is a renewed sense of the role and purpose of collaboration in ethnographic research. For us, the challenge here is to go beyond instrumental uses of collaboration: "the question is less one of devising and implementing collaborative methodologies *in order to achieve certain disciplinary goals* than creating anthropological *encounters in which the very question of what matters, and to whom, can be asked*" (Dattatreyan and Marrero-Guillamón 2019, 223, emphasis added). Henceforth, the collaborative dimension we envision as part of multimodal ethnography links back to the inventive and performative ethos explained above: it speaks of a commitment to learning with and from others, in embodied ways, through relevant and creative devices.

Ancestors and allies

The kind of multimodality we have advocated for may indeed be seen as part of a longer history and a wider constellation of transformative practices in anthropology and ethnography. We have found inspiration, for instance, in Jean Rouch's "ethnofictions," films in which participants created fictional selves and staged their lives. Rather than scripted fictions, though, the results are improvisational and collaborative films such as *Moi un Noir* (1958) and *Jaguar* (1967), which explore the desires, aspirations, and frustrations of young migrants in (post)colonial West Africa in an open-ended way. Ultimately, film was, for Rouch, a platform that enabled a different kind of research to take place: more playful and inventive than traditional methods, more open in its form and feel (see Henley 2009).

Rouch's ethnofictional work has continued to offer inspiration, less as an actual method to be implemented and more as an orientation toward creative collaboration. For example, we can look toward Nick Mai's *Travel* (2016), produced in collaboration with migrant sex workers in France. The film is constructed around a fictional character written and acted by several participants: a collective subject of enunciation devised over the course of creative writing workshops (see Mai 2021).

Taking the spirit of Rouch's shared anthropology (*anthropologie partagée*), Mai's work offers opportunities for the women involved to develop a sense of their own stories in relation to the co-constructed character they have created.

More recently, Dattatreyan's *Desiring Bollywood* (2020) remixed the notion of ethnofiction in the context of a research project examining the relationship between India and Nigeria vis-à-vis popular Hindi film. In this project Dattatreyan gathered a troupe of amateur actors to "restage" recounted scenes from the life of Ola Jason, an aspiring Nigerian actor who made his home in India for over a decade. Together, they explored how the improvisation of ethnographic stories opens new sites to approach historical and contemporary relationships between Africa and India (Dattatreyan, 2020).

Given the centrality of collaboration to our understanding of multimodality, it is worth, however briefly, opening up the concept for further scrutiny. As Kiven Strohm has argued (2012), the ethics and politics of collaboration in anthropology are often linked to the will to decolonize the discipline. Collaborative ethnography is seen as a response to colonial legacies and a way to interrupt their reproduction. But as Strohm has forcibly argued, collaboration per se may not subvert power relations; indeed, it may reinforce them inasmuch as it *presupposes* an inequality (of knowledge, of status) that must then be alleviated. Inspired by the work of Jacques Rancière, Strohm has argued instead for a practice that presupposes and tests "the principle of equality," that is, that reconstructs the ethnographic encounter as a "polemical space wherein the egalitarian logic of those with whom anthropology works confronts the anthropological episteme" (2012, 119). Put differently, the point of collaboration for Strohm is not to "give voice" but to listen to those we work with as "already equal." Related and equally important are the ways, as Elena Guzmán and Emily Hong (2022) argue, that multimodal approaches offer a way to engage in the sensorial and affective worlds we share, even for just a time. Here, equal footing emerges out of a shared exploration of the entanglements that bring us together while keeping us apart.

Miyarrka Media offers a powerful example in this regard. Miyarrka is a collective of Yolngu artists from Gapuwiyak in northern Australia who work alongside university-based anthropologists. Over the years, Miyarrka has generated a body of work that develops what they call a "*yuta* anthropology." As they explain it: "if 'old' anthropology understands its task to be revealing one world to another, the challenge of *yuta* anthropology is to bring different worlds into relationship" (Miyyarka Media, 2019, 11). Miyarrka creatively and skillfully utilizes digital media technologies to convey Yolnu ways of seeing, being, and understanding the world in relation to—but not subject to—anthropology's epistemic project. A new and exciting aesthetically attuned project emerges from their experimentation—one that is founded on a commitment to research that is inventive and grounded in Yolnu epistemologies.

The remainder of this chapter extends the discussion above by engaging with two areas of specific interest for multimodal ethnography: the first explores how different modes of encounter and relation may be enacted through particular multimodal strategies; the second centers the relations (and tensions) between media forms and publics. These two areas, of course, are linked, in part through the kinds of digital networks and infrastructure that enable encounter and circulation. They are also linked, as we have mentioned previously, to a way of imagining anthropological research as collaborative and for audiences beyond an expert community of practice.

Toward a politics of ethnographic encounters

One of our overriding concerns when thinking about multimodality has been to avoid offering ready-made methodological recipes and insist, instead, that we think of research strategies as locally relevant and situated. In this sense, focusing on the modes and politics of encounter—as opposed to methods per se—is crucial. A similar argument has been put forward by Adolfo Estalella and Tomás Sánchez-Criado (2023) in their inventory of creative research practices in anthropology. They conceptualize these in terms of "field devices" as opposed to "methods"—a distinction that seeks to highlight an orientation to research based on provisional, situated *arrangements* rather than standardized methodologies. Relatedly, one of the potentials of multimodality in an ethnographic context is, in our opinion, its capacity to pluralize the modes of relation we generate and that underpin the possibility of ethnographic research. The question is how to produce modes of encounter and relation between ethnographers and collaborators capable of generating pertinent, respectful, and inventive research.

The work of the Ecuadorian research center Kaleidos[3] is a case in point. This interdisciplinary center for ethnography has, since 2018, experimented with a range of multimodal and collaborative approaches to engaged research. Here, we will focus on EthnoData, an online platform for the study of data concerned with violent deaths in Ecuador. The project started as a critical investigation into official statistics but evolved into a collaborative inquiry into such data as well as a collaborative platform to make them public (see Núñez and Suárez 2023). The platform offers different data visualization tools that can be used and tweaked by users and also contains other modes of address such as short narratives, documentaries and podcasts. Apart from opening up the very notion of data to public scrutiny and debate, the platform is interesting as an online space for collaboration, negotiation, and tension. EthnoData created a "digital ecology" that allowed encounters between state officials, activists, and families of victims: "a collective instrument that allowed us to share and produce knowledge, make data, and present interpretations to build more just, diverse, democratic, inclusive, and equitable societies" (Núñez and Suárez 2023, 35).

Inspired by projects such as the Platform for Experimental, Collaborative Ethnography,[4] Kaleidos set out to create a digital meeting ground where different collectives concerned by the question of violent deaths and missing persons could meet, discuss, and intervene multimodally. Interactive data interfaces, maps, audiovisual productions, or paintings were some of the results of the dialogues and collaborations made possible by the platform and the data it hosted—an online space capable of facilitating connections between the victims' families, official statistics, artists, activists, etc. As Núñez and Suárez put it:

> EthnoData is a space for the production of responsive scholarship understood as ethnographic interventions in the face of crisis, disaster, and massacre. EthnoData works with civil society organizations and government agencies but does not work for them. The basis of the platform is the interaction between data, images, words, and sounds interwoven in a critique of violence and death.
>
> (2023, 41)

In a very different context—the study of "digital folklore" in Barcelona—artist/anthropologist Ezequiel Soriano has experimented with ethnographic devices that can speak to, and partake in, the ways and dynamics of the field. In *Hyperpublication 100/24*, a project exploring "digital vernacular creativity," for instance, he invited a group of programmers, gamers, visual artists, meme-makers, amateur filmmakers, and art students to participate in two performative workshops modeled after a hackathon: the challenge, respectively, to write 100 books and make 100 films in 24 hours (Soriano 2023a). For Soriano, the absurdity of the challenge is part of its appeal, for the workshops are designed to emulate the playfulness and unseriousness characteristic of the kind of digital creativity he was interested in studying. He describes the workshops as having created a welcoming space for experimentation, play, joy, boredom, or improvisation—all of which are drivers of vernacular forms of creativity. These are spaces of "collaboration without teamwork" (i.e., of shared aims and co-presence, but without coordination) in which digital folk practices such as copy-pasting, shitposting, AI-generated content, or meme-making proliferated. In the end, 82 books[5] and 73 films[6] were completed and made publicly available online during the workshops.

Soriano's broader argument is that these "minor" forms of creativity and digital folklore couldn't be studied discursively, for instance, through interviews. Indeed, his collaborators repeatedly rejected analyzing them or even taking them seriously. Participant observation would have been extremely complicated, considering this is a completely decentralized phenomenon. This online underground scene, therefore, was best approached by adopting and embracing its vernacular, "lowkey" ways and ethos (Soriano 2023b). The hackathon-style workshops were one way to create the possibility of an appropriate ethnographic encounter.

The very significant differences between EthnoData and *Hyperpublication 100/24* are also relevant to the argument we are putting forward. Both represent situated, specific strategies that respond to their aims, the topics they work with, and the groups and people that participated. Their methods are not directly exportable; we provide these examples not as models to be copied, but as case studies to think with. Multimodal ethnography may well have to be reinvented each time if it wants to be relevant.

Playing with form: publishing intermedial explorations, creating public(s)

A key question that emerges when thinking about multimodal approaches to anthropology is whether and how the heterogeneous experiments with encounter and shared learning that fall under its banner will find form and circulate. In academic anthropology, the journal article and the monograph have long taken precedence as legitimate and legitimating forms that garner prestige and access into the discipline's communities of practice. While there is a long and rich tradition of film and photography in the discipline under the banner of visual anthropology, historically these works didn't circulate in the same networks as written works, nor were they given the same pride of place. In many cases, twentieth-century filmic and photographic materials didn't circulate at all. Rather, they became archival "salvage" materials for anthropologists of the future to engage with as visual data and evidence. If anything, images produced during fieldwork were utilized as illustrations rather than sites of collaborative inquiry and theoretical potential.

In the last decade or so, as web-based publications have become the norm in journalism and other domains and access to digital technologies has increased globally, there has been a growing interest within the discipline to experiment with online publication and open access (Corsín Jiménez et al. 2015). The turn to web-based publishing opens new possibilities for images, video, and sound clips to be combined with text in ways that were previously unattainable. This opportunity to publish differently coincides with and amplifies the interest in multimodal dispositions toward ethnographic fieldwork.

These shifts toward what has been described as "intermediality" in anthropology (see Deger et al. 2024) take on different dimensions than in journalism or other popular forms of modal experimentation. While in journalism intermediality might offer a kind of layered approach to storytelling that is more illustrative, in anthropology, as Steven Feld (2024) argues, the composition of different media forms offers an opportunity to create a different epistemological horizon for the discipline. Through composition, one can explore (with others) how perception and the senses come together in ways that give us insight into relationships between mediated subjects and processes of mediation. Multimodality extends, as such, to include not only the ways we might approach fieldwork differently but how we might compose our experiences for audiences to immerse and encounter worlds in-between text, images, and sound—as well as to reflect on composition as a generative practice. In this light, web-based, multimodal works offer the exciting promise of sharing work beyond an academic audience, even if they are still, particularly within academic journals, limited in terms of what kind of content a platform can host or even in how images and videos are labeled. Historically, journal articles have been behind paywalls, and academic monographs have been relegated to small batch publications for expert audiences. Web-based, open-access publishing opens up an entirely new range of possibilities for engaging broader *public(s)* to encounter and engage with anthropological work.

Public is a conceptual term that draws attention to the multiple, different, and overlapping audiences that have the potential to come together in and through media. It anticipates media as a site for deliberative dialogue and affectively charged exchange (see Kelty, in this volume). For anthropologists publishing in spaces that are no longer behind a paywall, a web-based, multimodal piece has the potential to be seen, read, and heard by several intersecting publics, including a scholarly anthropological audience, publics linked to participants involved in a project, and other as yet unanticipated groups. This potential to serve multiple publics creates an interesting and perhaps exciting tension. On the one hand, the composition of intermedial works offers different epistemological grounds to engage and understand the worlds we inhabit, theoretically informing our understandings of experience, encounter, and mediation. On the other hand, intermedial works offer the promise of a more public anthropology. This move toward public(s) suggests a more digestible and accessible form might need to be produced to attract and engage broader publics. While we are not saying these two propositions are mutually exclusive, the unconscious pull toward creating more transparent, easily accessible anthropological works can push against a more academically committed yet potentially opaque and "experimental" intermedial project. This tension, we assert, should be met directly and thoughtfully as an opportunity to think through what relevant knowledge might be and for whom.

Opportunities and challenges

We conclude with a few thoughts on how multimodality indexes particular challenges in an anthropology to come—one that remains committed to theoretical innovation that challenges and complicates quantitative and increasingly AI-driven social science research. Anthropology, grounded in long-term, slow, and relational approaches, has always offered a different take on the "social" than more statistically oriented research. Given the increasing focus and intensity on "Big Data" approaches to studying social phenomena, multimodal anthropology, as it signals anthropology's twenty-first-century potential for collaborative research and public engagement, offers a viable alternative to an increasingly distant epistemological project that traffics in aggregate data and analysis. However, there are practical and disciplinary obstacles that make realizing the full potential of a multimodal anthropological project difficult.

First, there is the issue of publication for career advancement. For tenure and promotion, anthropologists, like all academicians, need to publish in recognized peer-reviewed journals and presses. In US-based R1 institutions, there is an additional pressure to publish in top-tier peer-reviewed journals and university-based publishing houses. Textual production remains the standard for career advancement. For anthropologists who are part of the tenured or tenure-track professoriate, it continues to be the case that the more public, accessible, and extra-textual research that they publish outside of paywalls is not recognized or valued by their institutions or the discipline at large. For multimodal work to thrive, established journals (and presses) that promote the discipline need to facilitate the creation of infrastructures that are able to host more-than-textual forms.

This is already underway, albeit in fits and starts. As we mentioned, *American Anthropologist*, the flagship journal of the American Anthropological Association, inaugurated a section in 2019 called Multimodal Anthropologies, which enables more-than-textual works to be published. Similarly, *Cultural Anthropology* has enabled more-than-textual publication on its website. Recently, *The Australian Journal of Anthropology (TAJA)* published a special double issue that promotes extra-textual scholarship. Several university presses have also developed ways to support born-digital book projects to facilitate improvisation and experimentation in form.

Yet, (Gabriel) speaking as a co-editor for the multimodal section of *American Anthropologist*, there have been issues around how to create a way to make these extra-textual publications (that are web-based and not downloadable), legitimate peer-reviewed works. To date, large publishers have not been willing to invest in the necessary infrastructure to host non-textual forms. By leaving the labor of creation and maintenance of web interfaces to authors, several issues emerge. First, there is a danger that non-textual work becomes ephemeral. If authors—rather than publishers—are responsible for the creation and maintenance of web interfaces, there is a real risk that these works will only be maintained for a period of time, due to costs and other factors. There is also an issue of searchability. Non-textual forms often don't benefit from the well-developed digital identification strategies that are utilized for textual publications such as articles and books. These issues need to be addressed and resolved by publishers for there to be a robust multimodal future.

Finally, and, as importantly, there is the question of evaluation and how to peer-review work that doesn't fall into simple logocentric textual conventions of argument, evidence, and analysis. If peer review is to extend to and legitimize more-than-textual outputs, it requires that those in the discipline are able to critically assess non-standard, multimodal research. The Stadtlabor Lab at Humboldt University[7] has taken on this challenge, investigating and exploring how we can educate our peers in the discipline to read and evaluate extra-textual work. At *American Anthropologist* multimodal section editors have experimented with a "crit review" process where blind peer review is put aside in favor of a collegial set of discussions that bring together author-makers who wish to publish new works with those working in the media/medium that is up for discussion. More of these sorts of initiatives need to be taken up if multimodal ethnography is to thrive and the discipline of anthropology is to continue to stay relevant.

All of these movements toward legitimating and codifying extra-textual scholarship signal a shift toward a different way to produce knowledge within the discipline of anthropology, a shift that is heavily influenced by the potential of multimodal research. While there are risks and challenges in forging this path forward, we feel that they are worth taking on, given the state of the world we inhabit and precarious futures that stretch in front of us. As Tsing et al. (2024) correctly argue, "we need new kinds of knowledges and new processes of becoming knowledgeable together" in this time of climate catastrophe, rising fascism, and collapsing systems. Multimodal approaches offer a way forward, a means to think differently about how to produce knowledge and who we are producing knowledge for.

Notes

1 https://www.americananthropologist.org/online-content/category/Multimodal+Anthropologies.
2 The exhibition took place between April and May 2023 and had an associated Instagram account (https://www.instagram.com/fight4aylesbury/). Luisa De la Concha Montes' review (2023) offers valuable contextual information.
3 https://www.kaleidos.ec/.

4 https://worldpece.org/.
5 https://www.artefactosnativos.com/100.24.html.
6 https://www.artefactosnativos.com/100-pelis-24-horas.html.
7 https://www2.hu-berlin.de/stadtlabor/.

References

Biddle, Jennifer L., and Tess Lea. 2018. "Hyperrealism and Other Indigenous Forms of 'Faking It with the Truth.'" *Visual Anthropology Review* 34 (1): 5–14. https://doi.org/10.1111/var.12148.

Collins, Samuel Gerald, Matthew Durington, and Harjant Gill. 2017. "Multimodality: An Invitation." *American Anthropologist* 119 (1): 142–46. https://doi.org/10.1111/aman.12826.

Corsín Jiménez, Alberto, Dominic Boyer, John Hartigan Jr., and Marisol de la Cadena. 2015. "Open Access: A Collective Ecology for AAA Publishing in the Digital Age." *Cultural Anthropology*. https://culanth.org/fieldsights/open-access-a-collective-ecology-for-aaa-publishing-in-the-digital-age. Retrieved on June 6, 2024.

Deger, Jennifer, Victoria Baskin Coffey, Caleb Kingston, Sebastian J. Lowe, and Lisa Stefanoff. 2024. "Epistemic Attunements: Experiments in Intermedial Anthropology." *The Australian Journal of Anthropology* 35 (1–2): 3–19. https://doi.org/10.1111/taja.12492.

Dattatreyan, Ethiraj Gabriel. 2020. "Desiring Bollywood: Re-Staging Racism, Exploring Difference." *American Anthropologist* 122 (4): 961–72. https://doi.org/10.1111/aman.13463.

Dattatreyan, Ethiraj Gabriel, and Isaac Marrero-Guillamón. 2019. "Introduction: Multimodal Anthropology and the Politics of Invention." *American Anthropologist* 121 (1): 220–28. https://doi.org/10.1111/aman.13183.

De la Concha Montes, Luisa. 2023. "Fighting for the Aylesbury Estate." *Shado Magazine* (blog), July 18. https://shado-mag.com/see/fighting-for-the-aylesbury-estate/.

Estalella, Adolfo, and Tomas Sanchez-Criado. 2023. "Introduction: The Ethnographic Invention." In *An Ethnographic Inventory: Field Devices for Anthropological Inquiry*, edited by Tomás Sánchez-Criado and Adolfo Estalella, 1–14. London & New York: Routledge.

Feld, Steven. 2024. "Hearing Heat: An Anthropocene Acoustemology." *The Australian Journal of Anthropology* 35 (1–2): 143–44. https://doi.org/10.1111/taja.12493.

Giordano, Cristiana, and Greg Pierotti. 2020. "Getting Caught: A Collaboration On- and Offstage between Theatre and Anthropology." *TDR/The Drama Review* 64 (1): 88–106. https://doi.org/10.1162/dram_a_00897.

Guzman, Elena H., and Emily Hong. 2022. "Feminist Sensory Ethnography." *Visual Anthropology Review* 38 (2): 184–210. https://doi.org/10.1111/var.12273.

Grasseni, Cristina. 2004. "Skilled Vision: An Apprenticeship in Breeding Aesthetics." *Social Anthropology* 12 (1): 41–55. https://doi.org/10.1111/j.1469-8676.2004.tb00089.x.

Henley, Paul. 2009. *The Adventure of the Real: Jean Rouch and the Craft of Ethnographic Cinema*. Chicago, IL: University of Chicago Press.

Ingold, Tim. 2013. *Making: Anthropology, Archaeology, Art and Architecture.* London & New York: Routledge.

Mai, Nick. 2021. "Films Collaboratifs, Ethnofiction et Vérité Socio-Anthropologique à l'Ère de l'Humanitarisme Sexuel." *Images du Travail, Travail des Images*, no. 10 (February). https://doi.org/10.4000/itti.1511.

Marrero-Guillamón, Isaac, and E. Gabriel Dattatreyan. 2023. "Interlude III: The Politics of Invention." In *An Ethnographic Inventory: Field Devices for Anthropological Inquiry*, edited by Tomás Sánchez-Criado and Adolfo Estalella, 213–21. London & New York: Routledge.

Miyarrka Media. 2019. *Phone & Spear: A Yuta Anthropology.* London: Goldsmiths Press.

Núñez, Jorge, and Maka Suárez. 2023. "How to Produce Responsive Ethnography of Data." In *An Ethnographic Inventory: Field Devices for Anthropological Inquiry*, edited by Tomás Sánchez-Criado and Adolfo Estalella, 33–42. London & New York: Routledge.

Pérez-Bustos, Tania, and Andrea Bello-Tocancipá. 2024. "Thinking Methodologies with Textiles, Thinking Textiles as Methodologies in the Context of Transitional Justice." *Qualitative Research* 24 (5): 1121–41. https://doi.org/10.1177/14687941231216639.

Pink, Sarah. 2009. *Doing Sensory Ethnography.* Los Angeles & London: Sage.

Soriano, Ezequiel. 2023a. "Hiperpublicación 100/24: Dos Workshops Performáticos Para La Investigación En La Creatividad Vernácula de Internet." *Artnodes*, no. 32 (July): 1–9. https://doi.org/10.7238/artnodes.v0i32.411264.

Soriano, Ezequiel. 2023b. "How to Do It Lowkey in a Meme Ethnography." *Xcol* (blog). https://xcol.org/invention/how-to-do-it-lowkey-in-a-meme-ethnography/.

Strohm, Kiven. 2012. "When Anthropology Meets Contemporary Art: Notes for a Politics of Collaboration." *Collaborative Anthropologies* 5 (1): 98–124. https://doi.org/10.1353/cla.2012.0004.

Tsing, Anna Lowenhaupt, Jennifer Deger, Alder Keleman Saxena, and Feifei Zhou. 2024. *Field Guide to the Patchy Anthropocene: The New Nature.* Stanford, CA: Stanford University Press.

Vidali, Debra Spitulnik. 2016. "Multisensorial Anthropology: A Retrofit Cracking Open of the Field." *American Anthropologist* 118 (2): 395–400. https://doi.org/10.1111/aman.12595.

Chapter 9.1
Concept
Public

Christopher M. Kelty

What is a public?

The "public" is one of the few concepts in this book which is explicitly a political concept. It is both descriptive and normative: it refers to something out there, somewhere, called a (or the) public, but it also implies a theory of what a public *should be like* to promote democracy or justice. Publics are central to Western institutions of liberal representative democracy but are not restricted to them; there are Islamic publics and Confucian publics, and publics also change over the decades and centuries, as technologies and societies change.

Publics have three elements: they concern the *common good*, they are opposed to *private* power, and they are *discursive*. The "common good" derives from the *res publica* of Roman Law, which literally means "the public things"—the things that concern everyone, the origin of the term *republic*. *Res publica* includes material things, such as the water supply, a public plaza, or printed money, as well as immaterial things like laws or the procedures used in courts. *Res publica* ensures that no person or set of persons controls any one thing that concerns everyone. The public good is central to political theory, but also fiendishly difficult to protect.

When opposed to *private*, public refers to notions of property and ownership, and the autonomy and rights of individuals. A public thing cannot be owned by any individual, whereas a private thing is something that cannot be taken away by either a public or a private entity. Privacy is a form of control over one's individual person or property which cannot be forced into the public without consent. Privacy law is today a central locus of debate about what happens online, and how individuals, states, and corporations relate to things like data, images, or ideas.

To say that the public is *discursive* is to say that it is a matter of communication, language, imagery, or writing. A public is the medium through which a collective of people deliberates about the common good, and it represents the will of that collective. Elections are the most visible form of deliberation. But humans also argue, explain, cajole, lie, and manipulate. It is through this deliberative activity that individuals might come to understand what their interests are, even the kind of persons they are. Such deliberation is not restricted to speech: images, sounds, films, theater, games, and other media shape understanding and emotion in political debate.

By this third criterion, a public consists of all the places where words, images, sounds, and ideas circulate. Two people in a bar can argue about an issue, such as whether some chemical used to make beer should be regulated. One of them might post on social media. That post might spark another discussion in another bar or at a private dinner table. The other might change their mind and write an op-ed for a newspaper which many more people will read. Those readers, in turn, might form an interest group to lobby a local city council or congressional representative. Collectively, a shared "imaginary" emerges through this process. In this example, it is the *issue* which defines the public first—and only then do people come to it. The ideal form of a public is therefore an emergent space of discussion among a "community of the affected" independent of other organized forms of power like the state, church, or corporations.

The ideal public rarely exists; many scholars have pointed out that not everyone gets to participate equally: gender, class, sexuality, and disability are all used to exclude forms of speech from the public. When it does work, however, a public matters because it helps shape what people think about the common good: what issues are important, what they think about them, and what they think we should do about them. Ideally then, people should be able to *access* the public, people should be able to *participate* in it, and people should be able to *freely decide* based on it. Where these norms fail, the public fails to exist, and the common good becomes an object of private manipulation by a few.

The nature of public has changed over time. It can refer to a coffee house or salon in eighteenth-century France, or to the broadsheets and pamphlets of the American Revolution, or to nineteenth-century Indian newspapers. In the twentieth century, mass media such as radio, film, and television dominated individuals in new ways and led to "counterculture" critiques of mass society. Habermas' famous *Structural Transformation of the Public Sphere* (1989) is both a theory and an account of changes to newspapers, the rise of a mass media, and the social transformation of the distinction between public and private spheres. According to Habermas, changes to the *structure* of the public changed the *power* of the public: it limited the role that some people could play in government and vastly expanded something called "opinion," which could be measured and tallied and paved the way for the form of democracy we have today—focused intensively on polling, elections, and campaigns for votes.

In the late 1990s, people started to ask: Is the *internet* part of the public? Well before social media emerged, debates raged about "net neutrality," "digital divides," and equality of access. Scholars and politicians compared it to newspapers, television, public space, private homes, highways, and colonialism. Proponents of "free and open source software" demanded unrestricted access to ideas—whether written in words, images, or software code. These "punk rock" attitudes of opening up the airwaves, networks, and tools to everyone were grounded in democratic ideals, for better or for worse.

The smartphone and social media created several "structural transformations:" the creation of valuable "Big Data," debates about privacy and surveillance, and the increasing power of large platform companies. Edward Snowden's 2012 revelations about corporate and government spying changed the debate about the role of data and networks in democracy. Algorithmic processing of this data, and the creation of a monetized system of attention-channeling, raised fundamental questions about the existence of the public. Can it be a public if the ideas are computationally generated with the goal of controlling or extracting revenue from everyone? Platforms are not publics—in fact, many increasingly take on features of states themselves. Meta, for example, has a "supreme court" designed to adjudicate some of the questions brought to it by its users. The ideal public stands outside such processes, and it is a mistake to confuse the two.

Publics always find a way to emerge, though. Hackers are political and technical tinkerers, adept at locating vulnerabilities in sociotechnical systems. Some, like the original collective Anonymous, supported classical liberal norms of democratic freedom and resistance to state and corporate power. Others, such as the trolls and alt-right hackers associated with QAnon, or the troll armies of India or Turkey, have done so to support authoritarianism. Both are publics by definition, but raise the question of whether the current configuration of the public sphere supports the ideals of democracy or threatens them. Our current definition of publics requires that they are spaces where individuals and collectives can contest the power of large organizations or of states. If those organizations control the public, what then? Where will the people go? What could the public become?

References & Further Reading

Bruns, Axel. 2023. "From 'the' Public Sphere to a Network of Publics: Towards an Empirically Founded Model of Contemporary Public Communication Spaces." *Communication Theory* 33 (2–3): 70–81. https://doi.org/10.1093/ct/qtad007.

Coleman, Gabriella. 2014. *Hacker, Hoaxer, Whistleblower, Spy: The Many Faces of Anonymous*. 1st ed. London: Verso.

Dewey, John. 1954. *Public & Its Problems*. 1st ed. Athens, OH: Swallow Press.
Fraser, N. 1990. Rethinking the Public Sphere: A Contribution to the Critique of Actually Existing Democracy. *Social Text* 25/26: 56–80. https://doi.org/10.2307/466240
Habermas, Jürgen. 1989. *The Structural Transformation of the Public Sphere: An Inquiry into a Category of Bourgeois Society*. Translated by Thomas Burger with the assistance of Frederick Lawrence. Cambridge: Polity.
Hirschkind, Charles. 2006. *The Ethical Soundscape: Cassette Sermons and Islamic Counterpublics*. New York: Columbia University Press.
Kelty, Christopher M. 2008. *Two Bits: The Cultural Significance of Free Software*. Durham, NC: Duke University Press.
Mahmood, Saba. 2011. *Politics of Piety: The Islamic Revival and the Feminist Subject*. Princeton, NJ: Princeton University Press.
Marres, Noortje. 2012. *Material Participation: Technology, the Environment and Everyday Publics*. London: Palgrave Macmillan.
Taylor, Charles. 2004. *Modern Social Imaginaries*. Durham, NC: Duke University Press.
Warner, Michael. 2002. "Publics and Counterpublics." *Public Culture* 14 (1): 49–90.

Chapter 9.2

Case study

SAPIENS magazine as anthropology for the public

Emily Sekine

Many anthropologists hesitate to call themselves writers. They produce writing; they're almost always drafting a journal article, revising a book, or composing a conference paper (sometimes on the plane, on the way to said conference). They often care deeply about this written work, worrying over an em-dash or the precision of a given phrase. But, in spite of how much they author, present, and publish, more often than not, writing in an academic mode remains a means to an end: scholars write to fulfill their professional obligation to share their research insights and theoretical interventions, typically within peer-reviewed publications, with other scholars.

So, one of the toughest but most satisfying parts of my job as an editor at the online magazine SAPIENS is encouraging my fellow anthropologists to claim the identity of writer—especially those who are writing for a non-academic audience for the first time. I don't explicitly tell them that's what I'm doing, of course. But my role, as someone who develops stories for a public-facing digital outlet, is to gently but determinedly shepherd people accustomed to scholarly writing conventions into the craft of narrative storytelling.

Welcome to the world of characters and setting, I tell them. Remember colors and textures and scents? Yes, write those down. Oh, and the sound of laughter and the moments of tension, too. And can you say a few words about what the soup you ate in the market tasted like, and what the air felt like in the room when the interviewee made that snide remark about their neighbor?

Not all these sensory details will make it into the final version of a published story. But I ask authors to start there, in the stuff of daily life, because grounding the story in a vivid scene where something *happens* is where the stakes come in.

Anthropologists know as well as anyone that broader structures and histories—capitalism, colonialism, patriarchy, white supremacy, ableism, and so on—show up both in the formal spaces of institutions and in the banality of our everyday and intimate encounters. Behind every anthropological theory or concept are real people and places, with layered longings and anxieties and memories and aches and resentments. But if a reader can't picture these people and places or feel some investment in their material lives and in their survival, they're less likely to keep reading to learn about how, say, the privatization of water systems could destroy longstanding communal farming practices in X region, or how a new education policy impacts families in Y place.

If I'm successful, the writer in the anthropologist eventually emerges, along with a sense of why their work matters to the broader world. But the process requires patience, collaboration, and, perhaps most importantly, a willingness to meet potential readers where they're at. And that means understanding the realities—the good, the bad, and the ugly—of writing for a popular audience in today's saturated, fast-paced digital media environment.

A brief history of SAPIENS anthropology magazine

SAPIENS launched in 2016 as a publication with the Wenner-Gren Foundation (SAPIENS 2016). In the early planning stages, it had been envisioned as an open-access news portal where anthropologists from around the world and across the disciplinary subfields could write and post short, digestible pieces about "everything human." Institutional gatekeeping had made anthropological knowledge unapproachable to most people outside the field—hidden behind costly paywalls, siloed in conferences and classrooms, and communicated through alienating jargon. Publishing pieces online, and making the content free and accessible, would allow for much wider dissemination of scholarly research and ideas into the public sphere than typical academic publishing processes.

However, it quickly became apparent that translating scholarly work for non-academic, global audiences came with its own challenges. With Chip Colwell as the founding editor-in-chief and Amanda Mascarelli as the founding managing editor, science journalists, editors, and other experts were brought in to establish procedures to make SAPIENS into a successful magazine. The staff set up systems for soliciting, assessing, and tracking story pitches; commissioning and developing essays and other content; selecting and navigating ethical issues with images; managing a consistent production schedule; and promoting content digitally to audiences. They also established guidelines for copy editing and fact-checking content (in lieu of the peer-review process typical of academic journals).

By the time I joined the editorial team in 2020, SAPIENS had reached millions of readers with stories about humanity's past, present, and future. Editorial and production processes had become more established (though still in flux to some degree). Over the years I've been with the magazine, we've continued to experiment with the form and content we offer. In addition to written essays, we've published book excerpts, poetry, videos, comics, photo essays, and even ethnographic fiction. SAPIENS also offers a podcast, writing workshops and trainings, a Public Scholars Training Fellowship program, a poet-in-residence program, teaching curricula, translations, and online webinars and events ("SAPIENS Podcast" 2025; "SAPIENS Public Writing Training" 2024; "Teaching" 2023). As social media trends have changed, we've adapted some of our content, from creating poetry reels on Instagram to hosting audience polls on X. Our weekly newsletter, which reaches tens of thousands of subscribers, features roundups of new and archival stories, weekly trivia questions, and other informative content related to the magazine and the field of anthropology.

Navigating the digital media landscape

Working in digital media ensures our team at SAPIENS remains agile and responsive to change. But working in this space has also taught me an important lesson: you can't assume an online reader will stick around to hear what you have to say. The numbers confirm this; according to data SAPIENS gathered in 2023, the average time a reader stays on a given page is one to two minutes. I found this statistic disheartening at first but then thought about how I read today: Even in a moment when I'm taking deep pleasure in a piece of writing, I can easily be pulled out of my reverie by the buzz of a calendar notification or text message.

We urge our authors to take seriously these technologically mediated constraints on readers' attention spans. Imagine a person on the other side of the world encountering your story while scrolling on their smartphones during a morning train commute, waiting in line at the doctor, or—yes, sitting on the toilet. We can't expect readers to be drawn in; it's the task of writers and editors to make audiences want to engage.

With those constraints in mind, each SAPIENS piece goes through a rigorous editing process. Our development editors collaborate with authors, often over the course of months, to craft stories that communicate nuanced ideas clearly and compellingly—in around 2,000 words or less. We hone strong openings (or "ledes"), knowing the first few sentences might determine whether a reader keeps scrolling or clicks away. We pace out our main points to build suspense and intrigue. We refrain from jargon (or make sure it's clearly defined), reduce "to be" verbs and passive language, and slice apart dense sentences and paragraphs. And because images rule in the digital landscape, our art editor collaborates with authors to select striking, high-quality images that aid in storytelling. These images usually lean photojournalistic, but sometimes a story demands a more conceptual or instructive approach, such as an illustration, map, or infographic.

Our editorial team asks authors to write in the first-person and share at least a little bit about themselves with the audience. For some scholars, especially those trained in more reflexive approaches to writing, stepping into this narrative voice seems to come easily. We regularly get pitches for stories with an auto-ethnographic bent, or that otherwise blend ethnography, history, and memoir. I find those stories especially meaningful to work on because the authors are opening up about how their research connects with the more intimate parts of their lives. For other academics, however, writing in first-person still feels uncomfortably vulnerable or indulgent. To help authors over that hurdle, I often ask about what made them want to learn about the people and places and events they're writing about in the first place. That's another way of trying to understand the stakes of a story; returning to the beginning usually tells me about *why* an author cares deeply about the central conflict or question at the heart of a story—and thus why I (and potential readers) might care too.

First-person point of view not only makes the writing more concise and easier to understand but also builds trust with readers by showing the author as an active agent in the construction of the story they're telling. In 2024, the online publication Allegra Lab and the journal *Anthropology and Humanism* published a set of guidelines to review creative work within anthropology (Allegra Lab 2024). In an accompanying article, the collaborative writing team behind the guidelines reflects on the transformative power of work that blends the academic and the personal (Borpujari et al. 2024). "When we produce creative work, we reveal parts of ourselves—our uncertainties, our questions, our dreams—that may not fit neatly within academic frameworks," they write. "This act of exposure is both risky and courageous, requiring us to confront and perhaps change our assumptions about knowledge, expertise, and authority."

The stakes of public writing

Publishing on a free, accessible platform like SAPIENS can indeed be an impactful way for scholars to reach audiences beyond the ivory tower—from policymakers to high school students to members of the community where a researcher works. But digital media also carries risks, especially in an era of intensifying censorship and online abuse. For marginalized voices, these risks may be amplified. For instance, during what came to be known as the Woman, Life, Freedom protests in Iran—a Kurdish-led feminist movement that erupted in 2022 after the death of Mahsa Amini under police custody—I was in touch with a political anthropologist who worked in Iran. She went so far as to submit an excellent draft about the movement, only to withdraw it because of online harassment that threatened her safety.

We make every effort to support authors in making choices that protect themselves and their sources, such as following ethnographic conventions of using pseudonyms in many cases to protect interviewees. Once a piece is published on our site, however, we can't control who views it or how they will interpret (or misinterpret) its claims. For example, Agustín Fuentes, a professor of anthropology at Princeton University, published a piece for SAPIENS in 2022 called "Biological Science Rejects the Sex Binary, and That's Good for Humanity" (Fuentes 2022). In the piece, Fuentes relies on extensive scientific evidence to challenge the myth that human biology can be divided into strict categories of male and female. He writes, "'man/woman' and 'masculine/feminine' are neither biological terms nor rooted exclusively in biology." In the first week, over 100,000 people read the piece—or at least viewed the headline. Some responded positively, while others attacked it with misogynistic, sexist, and transphobic comments.

For the author and for our team at SAPIENS, these reactions only underscore the importance of our work as public scholars. When I stepped into the role of Sociocultural & Linguistic Anthropology Editor at SAPIENS, I had struggled to complete my PhD, knowing I didn't want an academic job. It was the first year of the COVID-19 pandemic—and a time of heightened demands for racial justice ignited by months of Black Lives Matter protests. That period crystallized for me how vital anthropological analyses could be in helping people make sense of the complexities unfolding in their daily lives—from the high rates of vaccine hesitancy in the US, to police violence in Kenya, to the rise in anti-Asian violence and scapegoating during the pandemic (Sobo 2021; Kimari 2021; Sekine 2021). I also relished the chance to work on pieces that could spark people's curiosity and wonder during times of uncertainty and upheaval, such as drawing on multispecies ethnography to dig into why so many people started collecting houseplants during lockdown (Lasco 2020).

During that period, our staff at SAPIENS started to hold difficult but necessary conversations about our values and priorities as a magazine—conversations that are still urgent and unresolved. We revised our mission and vision statements to be more explicit about our efforts to "build a more just and sustainable world" through amplifying anthropological insights. Our website now lists the following commitments:

- Share a broad range of human stories with integrity and clarity
- Bring marginalized voices to the center of conversations
- Treat our community of authors, readers, and story subjects with empathy and respect
- Bridge academic and public spaces

- Help anthropologists become engaging storytellers
- Demonstrate the value of anthropology in the wider world
- Confront what anthropology was, challenge what it is, and dream what it could be

I'm especially fond of the final item in the list. It reminds me that our work is not finished—and that we still have time to push against harmful narratives and transform unjust systems. One way to start is by telling different stories about the worlds we want to bring into being.

Postscript: This piece was drafted and submitted in October 2024, shortly after the SAPIENS editorial staff unionized with The Chicago News Guild. In early 2025, the University of Chicago Press informed SAPIENS they would no longer serve as the magazine's publishing partner. In July 2025, the Wenner-Gren Foundation announced they would cease publishing SAPIENS by the end of the year. All staff members, except for the editorial director, were laid off in December 2025. The magazine's archival content remains online and freely accessible as of the publication of this piece.

References

Allegra Lab. 2024. "Reviewing Creative Anthropology: Guidelines." https://allegralaboratory.net/guidelines-reviewing-creative-pieces-for-anthropology-journals/.

Borpujari, Priyanka, Ian M. Cook, Çiçek İlengiz, Fiona Murphy, Julia Öffen, Johann Sander Puustusmaa, Eva van Roekel, Richard Thornton, and Susan Wardell. 2024. "Empathy and Dialogue: Embracing the Art of Creative Review." *Anthropology and Humanism* 49 (2): 83–87. https://doi.org/10.1111/anhu.12536.

Fuentes, Augustín. 2022. "Biological Science Rejects the Sex Binary, and That's Good for Humanity." SAPIENS, May 11. https://www.sapiens.org/biology/biological-science-rejects-the-sex-binary-and-thats-good-for-humanity/.

Kimari, Wangui. 2021. "Kenyan Mothers Take on Police Violence." SAPIENS, August 5. https://www.sapiens.org/culture/police-violence-kenya/.

Lasco, Gideon. 2020. "How COVID-19 Is Changing People's Relationships With Houseplants." SAPIENS, September 17. https://www.sapiens.org/culture/covid-19-houseplants/.

"SAPIENS - Anthropology Magazine." 2016. SAPIENS. https://www.sapiens.org/.

"SAPIENS Podcast." 2025. SAPIENS. https://www.sapiens.org/podcast-seasons/.

"SAPIENS Public Writing Training." 2024. SAPIENS. https://www.sapiens.org/training/introduction/.

Sekine, Emily. 2021. "Anti-Asian Racism's Deep Roots in the United States." SAPIENS, May 6. https://www.sapiens.org/culture/anti-asian-racism-anthropology/.

Sobo, Elisa. 2021. "What Does the American Dream Have to Do With the COVID-19 Vaccine?" SAPIENS, February 25. https://www.sapiens.org/culture/covid-19-vaccine-protestors/.

"Teaching." 2023. SAPIENS. https://www.sapiens.org/teaching/.

Chapter 10

Video games

Interpreting play states and communities, a digital ethnographic framework

Lindsay Grace

Overview

Fundamentally, to understand game ethnography, one must understand the play state. Games, whether analog or digital, are designed to engage the part of the human brain that triggers a play state. From psychology (Brown 2009) and anthropology (Sutton-Smith 2001), researchers understand this is a unique situation in all animals, where the rules of interaction go beyond the pragmatic toward a distinct other. Play is the mental state where experimentation is tolerated without lasting consequences. A dog that plays fights, for example, never bites hard enough to injure, but experiments with the physicality of a real fight. The person who plays, might say, or do things they'd never do in real life, to experiment with how those decisions might play out in the safe space of a play state.

The play state is an alternate state inhabited by two versions of the same subject. The first is the player, who is actively engaged in the state of play. The second is the person who transitioned to the play state and became a player. Since play is a state, the player and the person they were before and after play can be considered distinct. Play behavior isn't always real-life behavior, and real-life behavior isn't play behavior.

With games it's important to interpret both the player and their play. More precisely, to understand the user as separate from the player. The player is the person who is engaged in the play state, while the user is the person before and after they are engaged in the play state. It's useful to recognize that in any play research, there are two versions of the same person: the player and the person they are when not playing. This is similar to how one understands an actor as separated from their role or an athlete in game performance as distinct from the person they might be as a parent or partner.

Understanding this makes the interpretation of game, player, and person (or user) easier and more accurate. It's also an easy way to introduce

DOI: 10.4324/9781032672663-35

the trajectory from which such research begins. Consider that many early, notable works applying digital anthropology focused on the online role-playing game *World of Warcraft* (Nardi and Harris 2006) (Nardi 2010). Role play is at the intersection of both a play state and an interactive narrative. A person role plays to enter the fiction of a narrative, assuming a role to engage in the play state. Researching role player experiences is thus an exercise in researching the game, the roles offered in the game, and the people who play those games. It's also important to note that role play isn't often a solitary experience, so it frames that when understanding players, one must also understand the interaction between players. To do digital ethnography well we can't simply consider the player as a solitary figure, but instead as part of a play community.

Since role play shares vectors with acting and its play, it's important to differentiate the actor from the role, or more specifically the actor from the character role they assume. Just as we do not expect famous actors to carry those behaviors out into the real world, we should not expect the same of our players in games. This duplicity is obvious at first but becomes more nuanced when one thinks more deeply about games, play, and society.

Interest, for example, in playing specific roles may in itself demonstrate something about the user. Prior research notes user identity to player representation in games (Triberti 2017; Van Looy 2015), noting that some players might engage in specific types of play to engage alter egos (Trepte et al. 2009), other genders (Huh and Williams 2010), or to explore spaces they were not engaged in their non-play lives. This most basic interpretation implies that an office worker in the daily safety of a cubicle might crave the adventures of a Lara Croft. It offers that while a teen who is told what to do all day might endeavor to command an army of minions in their play life, it does not mean that their real-life aspirations are the same. Some research in this space demonstrates that game-playing motivations differ significantly from career motivations (Giammarco et al. 2015).

This line of logic is clear when we understand the dimensions of the play state. Fundamentally, play is an opportunity to explore and experiment. The literature that helps humanity understand the psychological and cultural benefits of play points to a pattern of using play as a way to interpret new information and a way to train the brain toward understanding hypotheticals. This is the anthropological (Sutton-Smith 2001) and evolutionary (Smith 1982) benefit of play that has long been held. Play provides a safe space in which to solve problems, a kind of sandbox to experiment without the worry of real-world consequences.

What that also means is that a sloppy interpretation of player and user assumes a linear relationship between the chosen play and the person. It assumes that play is vocational; playing as a soldier, for example, is about aspirations toward soldiering. But such an interpretation fails to recognize that the kinds of problems being solved in a game, the alternative narratives, the differences in the player state, and the user are easily interpreted by their mere subject.

The user motivation and value proposition in play are far more complicated than such linear interpretations might imply. If this weren't true, then why would a player voluntarily choose to place themselves in the middle of the dramatic conflicts, sometimes life or death, that games offer? Conversely, why would users choose to enter entirely mundane worlds, like Job Simulators (Owlchemy Labs 2016) or affection games (Grace 2020)? Why then would players choose work, such as farming simulations and resource management games, when they already have work to do?

The answer is entirely dependent on the user, their community, and the intersection of a variety of factors. There are various vectors that intersect to create communities of players. Players may share motivations or affinities toward specific types of play. They may also simply share an interest in wanting to play with each other. There may be myriad sociocultural factors that encourage or dissuade users from entering specific types of play states.

As a shorthand for these factors, a researcher could begin with the user's—not the player's—demographics, psychographics, and technographics. The demographics cover the simple attributes, like age and occupation. Psychographics identify the psychological state and preferences for the user, such as fear of flying or a history of trauma and anxiety. The third factor is technographics, which cover the technological factors like the users' devices used to play, their access to high-speed internet, and their experience with other technologies. Together, these things help to describe a user.

That user then switches to a new person, a *player*, when they initiate play. Generally, play is recognized as voluntary work (Huizinga 2008), and as such, players must initiate play. This means that the choices a player makes in the freedom of the safe space of play might be very different from the decisions a user might make. This is why it's useful to interpret player and user distinctly and recognize that one transforms into the other.

The result is that analysis of the players is an intersection of the person they are before and after play (aka the user), the person in the play state (aka the player), and as a community member among other players and users. A digital ethnographer in games studies, player, user, and the community of play. This is why it's so important to understand the play state. Not only is it the demarcation between the player and the user, but it's also a way to understand the interplay of community members within a play community. A moment, such as in-game harassment or being banned from a game, often means moving the player out of the play state. It means that the player returns to being a user, even if the community continues to play.

For a digital ethnographer, the result is an opportunity to examine, analyze, and interpret the kinds of play and play communities with which people engage. From historical anthropology, it's clear, for example, that play activities may be linked to community identity and culture. One need only think of the variety of folk games and community rituals to see evidence of this interplay. In some cases, such play propagates beyond the culture, leaving some of the character of the cultural values within the play, even if the cultures that play them may not entirely recognize them. The game of *Snakes and Ladders* (also known as *Chutes and Ladders*) is an ancient Indian game about the relationship of *karma* and *kama* (Bornet and Burger 2012). Toys like Roman dice have origins in cultural value for numerology (Purcell 1995).

Many communities of play have had very linear relationships to their play. Wargaming players, for example, were often former and active military personnel or military history enthusiasts, practicing the strategies of war. Yet notably, the fictional roleplay of globally popular games like *Dungeons and Dragons* is traced back to military wargaming cultures (Laycock 2015). Such play is rooted in a kind of practice and training, but its evolution moves simulation of historical moments into the fictitious world of *Dungeons and Dragons* (Laycock 2015).

Other forms of play, such as the myriad simulations, are often propagated from communities that have an interest in their real-world equivalents (e.g., flight simulators and aspirational pilots, sports simulations and sports fans). What's important to recognize is that quality digital ethnography in games does not jump to assumptions about users, players, or their communities. Part of the work is examining and interpreting those assumptions to understand the more complex intersections of players, users, games, and their community.

It's important to remember that such relationships between user choice in play and the play in which they engage can be very different. While in linear relationships—like aspiring pilots choosing to play flight simulation games—there are clear vocational relationships, but there are others in which the nuances of play are more complicated. The lure of playing *Angry Birds*, for example, doesn't really help explain the user preference and the draw of the play. This is where widely popular play experiences complicate an interpretation of the player's motivations in such environments. It also hints at the value of digital ethnography in games to answer questions about why such play is alluring.

In such cases it is often useful to examine the motivations from multiple perspectives. The lure of a game for communities may be much larger than its mechanics or the virtual propensities the game provides. Some games attract because they signal to peer groups that the player is also part of that community. A small mobile game might be popular among the coolest middle-school students in rural Sweden, or a 25-year-old horror game might be part of the community identity for aficionados of the genre. In this, such game motivations are similar to prior media consumption habits, where music preference may be less about the acoustic qualities of the music than the fact that a community identity is associated with that kind of music.

In other cases, motivation to play may be tied to the complex offerings a game provides. In teaching game design, for example, we often help designers recognize that a widely popular game appeals to a wide variety of play motivations. For some players, the draw of the game is in the competition, for others it's in the sense of creative practice and customization, and for others it's about the richness of the illustrated world. These dynamics and lures can be considered from a play theory anthropological perspective.

For this kind of analysis, it's useful to consider the foundational work of Brian Sutton-Smith (2001). Sutton-Smith tried not only to understand why people play but also to outline the specifics of those motivations. In his seminal work, he described the rhetoric of play. These rhetorics can be framed in two ways. First as the ways in which society recognized the value of such play. This utilitarian perspective is useful in validating why play is an important cultural element. The second is in explaining player motivations. The duality of Brian Sutton-Smith's rhetoric is thus useful for both understanding how communities perceive play and how the individual might be drawn to play. That is, it's a frame for perceiving multiple perspectives in play.

As an example, consider the motivations and value of having a public parade. For Sutton-Smith, the parade is useful in sharing the community's values, the rhetoric of identity, or literally parading what matters to the community's identity as projected or real. For the individual, Sutton-Smith would argue, it also offers the rhetoric of self, as individuals participating have the opportunity to contribute their own play to the larger community's play in the parade. But more interesting, such a parade might also offer the rhetoric of creativity, as players engaged in creative problem-solving, ranging from costume creation to stories they share in parading.

Now then, one can take that same analog interpretation and apply it to the digital space. The value of Nintendo's Wii parade, a parade of Nintendo Wii characters known as Mii's (a portmanteau of "Wii" and "me"), could be interpreted similarly. There's an opportunity to demonstrate the virtual community created within Nintendo's virtual world. Yet there's also the moment of rhetoric of self, when an individual user gets to witness their virtual representation of self, a Mii, walk in the parade.

Understanding the contrast between digital and non-digital games

This is where the intersection of the digital and non-digital anthropology becomes most interesting. A parade itself is by nature a kind of performance space. The costume or character one plays in a parade might be an extension of self, but the fundamental expectation is that the self-representation in a parade is limited to that parade. Whether playing a dragon in a Lunar New Year parade, a prom queen in a homecoming parade, or a marshal at the front of a marching band, the person in the parade maintains that role for the length of the parade.

In the digital space the length and moments of that virtual self vary. Where analog characters are often a temporal extension of self, digital characters are complicated by their existing in a digital space, the scale of the space, and the persistence of that space. In the analog world, there is a moment when the scene ends, the end of the parade is reached, or the costume is put away for use next year. In the digital space, the game may end, but the character may persist. In a digital game, the rules that dictate the played character are not as obvious as those of the physical world. They are mitigated by algorithms, often obscured in an effort to preserve a play state or to protect the intellectual properties of their creators. That then complicates some dynamics of ethnographic research in digital game spaces, while simultaneously simplifying them.

On the simplification end, where society's rules have evolved over hundreds of years, waxing and waning across an immensely complicated interplay of cultural, historical, institutional, religious, and other factors, digital games are dictated by one single guide—the game's code. This is what makes some dimensions of ethnography through games a bit simpler. Before downloadable content, before weekly updates to balance an eSports product, games were created with their rules dictated in immutable code solidified on a CD-ROM, DVD, or downloaded file, and the players were subject to those affixed rules.

That means, in short, that when studying the communities of players in games, there is often a single guiding document of the rules that govern that community. The public availability of that guiding algorithmic decisions, the mechanics, dynamics, and aesthetics that govern that play space are prescribed before play commences. For players, this may also be shaped by a variety of cues they've learned outside the game, such as a sense of what's taboo, what's most important, and who matters. These extrinsic expectations are layered on top of the intrinsic rule sets that games offer and shape both the player and the preceding user. Yet, at least, there is one governing set of rules that binds all players in the community.

This one guiding, common rule set was at least somewhat true before large-scale virtual worlds, with daily updates and moderated communities evolved. Since their advent, the work of digital ethnography has become much more complicated. Contemporary study requires an understanding of the code binding all play, the social contracts of the play community, the prohibitions and proclivities of the play moderating community, and an understanding of the player dynamics. Each one of these dimensions is ripe for research and can be a dimension of focus in a digital ethnography.

This is why digital ethnography is both simplified and increasingly complicated when compared to similar work in other domains. If one wanted to interpret the community of Roblox players, for example, the many dimensions that shape that interpretation are as complex as studying any real-world community. Except that the Roblox community is constantly changing because of the aforementioned dynamics of game production, user-generated content, mediated behaviors, and community management. Add to this milieu considerations in evolving technology and resulting shifts in technographics, the ways that other game experiences shape player psychology, and how the countless forces outside the game affect everything from in-game economies to perceptions of players. The result is an exceptionally complex dynamic of temporal forces and pervasive elements that must be unpacked to accurately understand the research subject.

By analogy, it is as though in classical anthropology, a community, its members, physical environment, and values were shifting daily. The community of game players is at once nomadic, moving between play communities with ease, and pervasive, extending between a variety of play and non-play communities as part of a daily experience. Meanwhile, the scale of those transitions applied across a border where millions of people crossed at will, whimsically, and with little interest in learning the societal rules of the space they've entered.

This illustrates the scale of the complexity of such work, but admittedly, when done well, non-digital anthropological research shares some of these same challenges and can inform effective work. In the first generation work on Black Game Studies (Grace 2021), for instance, I offer a way of interpreting games relating to the global African diaspora through a variety of categorizations. There are for example, games about Blackness, games about being a member of the Black community, games celebrating Black culture, games designed to educate the Black or non-Black communities, games designed to foster community with Black members, games about shared locations within Black culture, games that feature Black people, games that are made by Black game makers, and so on. But these categorizations serve a useful purpose across any cultural, political, religious, or other identity group. That is, one way of thinking about the kinds of ethnographic work is to think about the ways in which the studied game can be considered beyond its outward marketing and perception.

Returning to *Chutes and Ladders*, one recognizes that it was a game about a religious concept, for community members, designed to impart a lesson. Hence, in game studies, there are research foci tied to general groups like indigenous games (LaPensée 2021) and Queer games (Ruberg 2017) but also highly specific case studies like Nordic Live Action Role Play (Stenros and Montola 2010) and Folk Games linked to folk tales (Vesa 2011). It is reasonable to use the following list to help frame the kind of ethnographic work being done, focusing on any given community:

- Games about the culture's internally perceived or externally attributed identity
- Games about the situation of the community
- Games about being a member of the community
- Games that celebrate the good and bad of that community
- Games to educate or serve the community
- Games to foster the community
- Games about shared attributes within the community
- Games that feature the members of the community
- Games that feature the community but are not created by members of it
- Games made by community members

These and more can be applied to a range of communities of players, from players of cooking games to skateboarding simulations. They can also be applied to users, from neurodivergent people to fans of manatee websites. This list reminds the researcher of the many ways in which communities of play can be categorized and analyzed.

The list also stands as a starting point from which any such research could be conducted. The first step in such research is much like other investigations. It begins with a clear lens through which the question will be asked. If a researcher were to begin with an interdisciplinary problem that might involve the mind, culture, or genetics, one would appropriately apply the standards and procedures of a psychological, anthropological, or biological, respectively. In the case of games and interactive narrative, it is similarly useful to frame the line of disciplinary inquiry pursued in the pursuit of knowledge.

From this perspective, digital ethnography in games reads as much more complicated than other endeavors. One could further complicate it by considering that the play space itself is one in which players are encouraged to break rules, to find and push borders, and to even ignore rules in pursuit of more play. By their definition, games are dynamic, offering a changing experience through the interplay of a designed system and its players. Yet too, one could argue so are social systems, governments, and other systems that bind humanity together.

Generative artificial intelligence, with its ability to create even more variable experiences, would seem to multiply the dynamic variables of such research. However, the uniqueness in games is less in its dynamic nature and more in its unique embrace of the play state. The play state is a place to be entered and exited outside of real-world communities but is generative of its own play-focused communities. It is a place that is both outside the ordinary and simultaneously shaped by it. Depending on the game, the play state is at once stage, temple, play field, pulpit, and much more.

A framework for digital ethnography in games

To wrangle this complexity, it's useful to begin with a frame that helps the researcher examine these elements effectively. To do so, they must make two distinctions. First, understanding the difference between the person before play (the user) and the person engaged in play (the player). Second, accepting the threshold between the non-game world and the game world, the voluntary entrance into the play state. That there are at least two people in the ethnography, player and user, and that their threshold is the play state, is essential for a clear framework for this work. From there, the play state and its resulting games can be examined as a confluence of intrinsic rules and their taboos, encoded in part through the game's system as code and algorithm.

Each of these, user and player, play state and non-play state, is shaped by the intrinsic and the extrinsic. The extrinsic forces are the user's anthropological precedence, often shaped by demographics, psychographics, and technographics. The result is a kind of cycle, where users engage in play, they remain in play, or may be pulled from play back to a user who becomes comfortable or uncomfortable with where the play state has taken them.

Figure 10.1 demonstrates this interplay. Doing digital ethnographic work is about recognizing, observing, and interpreting the data that's demonstrated in this dance between the play state. As an example, a person's extrinsic experience with or knowledge about war might shape their in-game response to war, but it's also shaped by the intrinsic rules set about how war is conducted in game. Transgressing intrinsic rules in game may mean "game over" for the player, which is often an algorithmically dictated removal from the play state. If the player fails to meet the criteria to remain in the game, many games simply end and provide the player the opportunity to try again.

Likewise, prior personal extrinsic experience outside of the game may mean the player rejects the experience of the game and disengages with the play state. In between, prior experience with other games may shape how they remain or fail to remain in the play state. Adding to this is their own complex amalgamation of identity, motivation, and more. At the start of

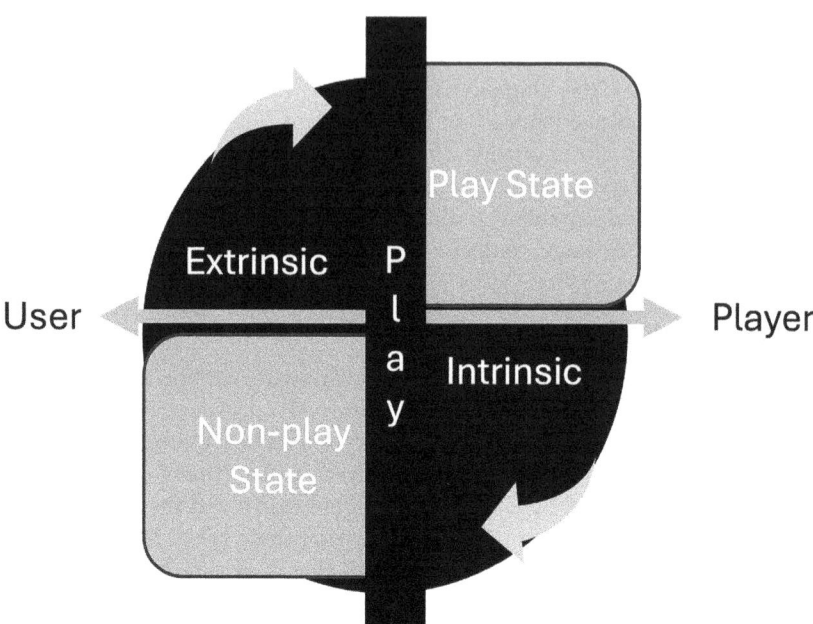

Figure 10.1 The diagram illustrates the heart of playful experiences as games and interactive narrative, demonstrating how the user on the X axis brings extrinsic experiences to the play state. The play state provides intrinsic rules which, when the player leaves the play state, remain in the user for subsequent play and non-play experiences.

the play state, the user becomes the player. Users carry with them some of the outside world but also adopt some of the play state's world. Likewise, when they leave the play state, they are shaped by their in-game experience and carry some portion of that, from the most basic game-specific terminology to the complex emotions that may have been created, back into the non-play world.

This pattern, as diagramed, where the play state forms as a transformation space between the player and the person they are outside of games, is at the heart of my 20-year career in social impact game design. The goal in social impact games is to shape the user-player through gameplay (Grace 2019). It aims to fundamentally change players, as much as play does, by tapping into specific communities' play and leaving an impression on the player that lasts well beyond the play state. To do so, such work employs myriad strategies that overlap with education, psychology, and sociology.

The opportunity in digital ethnography through games

It might feel like such work is extremely complex and perhaps even daunting. Yes, these things might be true, but there's a tremendous opportunity in the domain as well. First, all this activity, each decision, each event, is trapped, logged, and witnessed in microsecond intervals in modern games. Every keystroke, tap of the button, and meaningful and meaningless decision can be recorded if so desired. In such game systems, perception is relatively objectively captured by a system that is not only generating the playful experience but recording it too.

Coupled with this is a community that is eager to share its play. Game players not only broadcast their experiences through streaming communities like Twitch and YouTube Gaming, but they also offer think-aloud sessions for no cost while doing so. Players broadcast their play experiences for any researcher to interpret, sharing their triumphs, their disappointments, and their hopes. Digital ethnographers can begin such research without ever leaving their work chair, in theory.

When users aren't broadcasting, others are contributing to extensive wikis that archive and interpret the game experience publicly. They are sharing bugs, demonstrating exploits, and offering support to each other through public forums as varied as Reddit or online forums. What's incredible about modern massive play experiences is that they are tremendous data producers. Players and users offer diatribes in Discord, theories in chatrooms, and playthroughs on YouTube. All for no cost to the researcher who wants to understand their experience.

This is why the opportunities in digital ethnography for players are such a rich space to investigate. The researcher does not need to fly across the world to collect six months of data; it might just be downloaded within a few clicks. Notably, depending on the games being studied, this includes the decisions of game makers whose own combination of extrinsic and intrinsic values may have contributed to the decisions in making the game. These are often accessible through marketing materials, including development diaries used to show the process of making the game. They are also sometimes made available through postmortems, which reflect on the philosophies, inspiration, and motivation for creating the game. Development diaries are more common in independent, small-scale games, while postmortems are often available in at least one-hour talks at major conferences like the Game Developers' Conference. There's also a community of researchers doing embedded developer studies, for which Casey O'Donnell's work has been influential (2014).

Of course, this only provides one dimension of the complete digital ethnography. Collecting and interpreting data from players is a much easier task than doing so for the user, much like it's easier to examine the performance of an actor than it is to understand their process and retrospectively examine how that performance was created. To this point, traditional research, less mired in large-scale data science, is often more useful. As seminal work in digital ethnography notes, a balance between physical and digital ethnography is essential for productive work that also avoids marginalization and other research problems (Murthy 2008).

Optimistically, some of the fundamentals of user data can be interpreted from those same logs that help games run. Technographics, for example, the data that describes the technology used to play a game, or the speed at which the game was served, are readily available through some basic web tools. Likewise, some large-scale demographics are discernible from web statistics, like the IP address from which they've joined the game. The third, psychographics, is much harder to interpret from public and even private data.

Ethnography

Thus far, there's an evident opportunity in game analysis that supports a kind of anthropological research. This is, of course, sometimes complicated by proprietary systems, content restrictions, and the general lack of transparency by large-scale computer game producers. However, in time, many of these challenges dissipate.

In the relatively recent history of analyzing video games, the treasure troves of *World of Warcraft* data often illustrate such value. Researchers have examined avatar choices (Lee et al. 2011), sometimes by using public data as a means of data mining observations about the community at large scales (Bell et al. 2013). The growth of data mining tools, coupled with the increasing low cost of artificial intelligence solutions, provides fertile ground from which to conduct large-scale analysis of games, players, and their communities. The work conducted on games with especially long user histories, like *World of Warcraft*, provides a new researcher with models for reapplying such work in shorter-lived game franchises. Modern work in this domain benefits from that precedent, offering both lessons learned and models for data collection that extend well beyond self-report and survey instruments.

Similarly, it's important to understand that the production of a modern, large-scale game actually requires some of the same kinds of research a digital ethnographer would be doing. Large-scale games are an enormous financial undertaking, one that requires prudent investment in the community that will ultimately engage in the game. As such, game companies employ psychometricians to help optimize game design and experience.

Working within such organizations offers an opportunity to get access to all such data, but working outside of such organizations presents a challenge of intellectual property.

This is where, methodologically, the reams of player data produced by communities of players become even more useful. The wikis that are produced and maintained by avid players, the Discord servers, the Twitch streams, the transcripts, and comments, etc., all serve as artifacts from which an ethnography can be conducted. But those resources are most commonly maintained for large, commercial experiences from what the industry typically refers to as "AAA games."

This leaves the independent game, or the newly budding breakout hit, or the niche, esoteric 20-year-old game, with a very different set of tools and strategies. In some cases, such games have small communities of dedicated players, streaming speedruns, or demonstrating glitches in 20-year-old code. However, these artifacts are much less richly descriptive than the firehouse of data collected in large commercial games. In such cases, the methods change toward more traditional ethnographic interpretation. The researcher must assemble an understanding from scant datasets, perhaps immersing themselves in the community in an attempt to understand it better.

To this point, it's important to recognize that a digital ethnographer in games must also be cognizant of the ephemeral qualities of language within this domain. While many games have language that is specific to their game worlds, there's also a time-dependent variable to the game-specific language. As an example, researchers 20 years ago had a clear sense of what it meant to "frag" a player in a first-person shooter game. Ten years ago, a "GG" meant a very specific type of quitting in eSports competition. This constant shift in language means that ethnographers must remain vigilant in their work to accurately interpret their case studies. Large-scale tools, like data scraping language through logs, are made distinct in games because the language is so often tied to both the player's game world and the user's community.

Similarly, other challenges that shape the work of archiving games also affect the ethnographic study of them. Some games take a long time to play, and the technology itself atrophies, making old versions of the game experience harder to recreate, and more. For a complete list of these challenges, it's useful to review chapters one and five of Wolf's video game history (Wolf, 2007). However, the act of archiving games has been improved by new technologies that archive original code and make generally publicly playable versions of games on websites like Archive.org.[1] It is reasonable to assume that as the world of digital ethnography develops, so too will systems that aid in these challenges.

Where to begin

With all these observations and reflections on process and concept, studying games may read as far more complex than it is. The process in games begins as most others: the researcher must identify research questions, assess their knowledge and the community's requisite knowledge for participation, and select a perspective from which the work will be conducted. From there, any requisite permissions should be requested as necessary and relationships brokered between community leadership. In commercial game communities, these relationships may be brokered between the companies that own the intellectual property, the moderators managing the communities, or some others.

While digital communities may feel and often do have their own styles of communication and propriety, it's important to acknowledge and follow them. In comparison to other similar research, digital game communities often have explicit terms of service, a luxury that does not often exist for other types of ethnography. While joining a Discord group or posting on a Reddit forum might include accepting some rules of interaction, the subtle transgressions that may invalidate such research are often explicitly spelled out in detail before such researchers enter these spaces. Such clear rule-setting is, of course, simple to misinterpret or to falsely assume members of the community are abiding, but it is a starting place that prior anthropologists in earlier work may not have had.

Once these are determined, the work requires openness, respect, and consistency. As with any scientific method, researchers must avoid the traps of cherry-picking answers they seek and ignoring observations that don't fit their hypothesis. In this context it includes mislabeling the observable start and stop of the play state, which clearly can extend well beyond the time spent in games and their game communities. Cosplayers, for example, might avidly play a game, spend time sewing a costume, meet others at a convention, and participate in an online community. The play states that, for each of those communities, as well as the implicit and explicit rules for interaction and observation in each, would also vary greatly. Hence, effective and valued research in this domain involves understanding the perspective from which the researcher is conducting such work and admitting the practical limits of time and scale. Similarly, digital tools designed to mine and analyze large sets of user data can tempt their users toward asking only the questions that affirm their hypothesis.

Conclusion

The opportunities and value of such work are clear. Play spaces reveal much about society, providing a sense not only of value and taboo but of the wants, desires, needs, aspirations, escapes, and more of the players and users. The propensities of digital ethnography applied to games provide a rich environment for doing such research, albeit with both benefits and drawbacks. The growth of virtual spaces, including potential for a metaverse, only emphasizes the value of such research. In a future involving artificial intelligence-assisted engineering and implementation, the value of individuals who can interpret the play space, players, users, and their community increases. Researchers will be needed to understand what keeps people in a play state, what brings them to it, and what they may want in the future. Digital ethnography in games also has the propensity to help explain the relationships between game worlds and non-game worlds, explaining how each is shaping the other.

As is often the case with new technology, for every problem solved, a new set of problems is created. The result is a fertile environment in which new approaches can be developed that—like much of the technological innovation that has shaped our society—begin in games and can be applied more widely. Using games as a case study for digital ethnography offers an opportunity to experiment with future patterns of research that can be applied more widely.

Note

1 https://archive.org/details/classicpcgames.

References

Bell, Jonathan, Swapneel Sheth, and Gail Kaiser. 2013. "A Large-Scale, Longitudinal Study of User Profiles in World of Warcraft." In *Proceedings of the 22nd International Conference on World Wide Web*, 1175–84. New York, NY: Columbia University.

Bornet, Philippe, and Maya Burger, eds. 2012. *Religions in Play: Games, Rituals, and Virtual Worlds*. Vol. 2. Theologischer Verlag Zürich.

Brown, Stuart L. 2009. *Play: How It Shapes the Brain, Opens the Imagination, and Invigorates the Soul*. Penguin.

Giammarco, Erica A., Travis J. Schneider, Julie J. Carswell, and William S. Knipe. 2015. "Video Game Preferences and Their Relation to Career Interests." *Personality and Individual Differences* 73: 98–104.

Grace, Lindsay D. 2021. *An Overview of Games Made by Black Game Makers*. Black Game Studies.

Grace, Lindsay D. 2020. *Love and Electronic Affection: A Design Primer*. CRC Press.

Grace, Lindsay D. 2019. *Doing Things with Games: Social Impact through Play*. CRC Press.

Huh, Searle, and Dmitri Williams. 2010. "Dude Looks Like a Lady: Gender Swapping in an Online Game." In *Online Worlds: Convergence of the Real and the Virtual*, edited by William Sims Bainbridge, 161–74. Springer.

Huizinga, Johan. 2008. *Homo Ludens*. Amsterdam University Press.

LaPensée, Elizabeth. 2021. "When Rivers Were Trails: Cultural Expression in an Indigenous Video Game." *International Journal of Heritage Studies* 27 (3): 281–95. https://doi.org/10.1080/13527258.2021.1868586.

Laycock, Joseph P. 2015. *Dangerous Games: What the Moral Panic over Role-Playing Games Says about Play, Religion, and Imagined Worlds*. University of California Press.

Lee, Yeng-Ting, Kuan-Ta Chen, Yun-Maw Cheng, and Chin-Laung Lei. 2011. "World of Warcraft Avatar History Dataset." In *Proceedings of the Second Annual ACM Conference on Multimedia Systems*, 123–28. San Jose, CA.

Murthy, Dhiraj. 2008. "Digital Ethnography: An Examination of the Use of New Technologies for Social Research." *Sociology* 42 (5): 837–55.

Nardi, Bonnie, and Justin Harris. 2006. "Strangers and Friends: Collaborative Play in World of Warcraft." In *Proceedings of the 2006 20th Anniversary Conference on Computer Supported Cooperative Work*, 149–58. Banff, AB.

Nardi, Bonnie. 2010. *My Life as a Night Elf Priest: An Anthropological Account of World of Warcraft*. University of Michigan Press.

O'Donnell, Casey. 2014. *Developer's Dilemma: The Secret World of Videogame Creators*. MIT Press.

Owlchemy Labs. 2016. *Job Simulator*. Quest VR. https://www.meta.com/experiences/3235570703151406/.

Purcell, Nicholas. 1995. "Literate Games: Roman Urban Society and the Game of Alea." *Past & Present* 147: 3–37.

Ruberg, Bonnie, and Adrienne Shaw, eds. 2017. *Queer Game Studies*. University of Minnesota Press.

Smith, Peter K. 1982. "Does Play Matter? Functional and Evolutionary Aspects of Animal and Human Play." *Behavioral and Brain Sciences* 5 (1): 139–55.

Stenros, Jaakko, and Markus Montola. 2010. *Nordic Larp*.

Sutton-Smith, Brian. 2001. *The Ambiguity of Play*. Harvard University Press.

Trepte, Sabine, Leonard Reinecke, and Katharina-Maria Behr. 2009. "Creating Virtual Alter Egos or Superheroines? Gamers' Strategies of Avatar Creation in Terms of Gender and Sex." *International Journal of Gaming and Computer-Mediated Simulations (IJGCMS)* 1 (2): 52–76.

Triberti, Stefano, Ilaria Durosini, Filippo Aschieri, Daniela Villani, and Giuseppe Riva. 2017. "Changing Avatars, Changing Selves? The Influence of Social and Contextual Expectations on Digital Rendition of Identity." *Cyberpsychology, Behavior, and Social Networking* 20 (8): 501–7.

Van Looy, Jan. 2015. "Online Games Characters, Avatars, and Identity." In *The International Encyclopedia of Digital Communication and Society*, edited by Robin Mansell and Peng Hwa Ang, 748–58. Wiley-Blackwell.

Vesa, Ileana. 2011. "The Future of Narrative between Folktales and Video Games." *Caietele Echinox* 20: 247–61.

Wolf, Mark JP. 2007. *The video game explosion: a history from PONG to Playstation and beyond*. New York: Bloomsbury.

Chapter 10.1

Concept

Gamer

Florence Chee

This commentary unpacks the conceptual role of "gamer" in the practice of digital ethnography. In working with the concept of "games" as a medium of communication, the "gamer" as ethnographic subject comes rich with sites and sights, boundaries, and liminalities. In the contexts of work, rest, and play, the gamer provides a key access point into myriad technocultural spaces, where we may find fruitful generative insight as we endeavor to interpret and understand people and practices. The gamer as a point of inquiry, especially as an identity that has been fraught with shifting politics and policies, is important to note in the processual aspects of conducting ethnography, digital or otherwise.

In insights emerging from my earliest days of ethnographic fieldwork investigating online game culture in Korea, I addressed some of the cultural, social-structural, and infrastructural explanations for why Koreans had an international reputation for being particularly susceptible to online game addiction (Chee 2006, 2023). In addition to finding a whole host of factors external to any one game, such as the use of PC bangs and other social factors, the promotion and popular play of "old" games such as StarCraft has been key in creating professional online game spectacles, known as eSports, which persist to the present.

In my research of game communities that form the basis for my book, *Digital Game Culture in Korea* (2023), I discuss how the mass media's characterization of Korean youth as a particular population of problematic gamers pointed to a broader journalistic trend that broadly mischaracterized the people (both from afar and yet also proximately). My search for nuanced understandings of the motivations of gamers studies the role of gaming around the world. This set of inquiries lent itself to investigations of culture, social structure, infrastructure, and policy. I attempted to curate the reasons why Korean youth spent their hours at PC bangs and associated spaces of liminality, as they manifested and continue to emerge as signifiers of a broader and deeper culture of play.

DOI: 10.4324/9781032672663-36

Rather than dismiss the participants as "game addicts," I present a few examples of the various motives one might have for spending a lot of time gaming at PC game rooms or otherwise. Those motivations had very little to do with which game was on the screen. However, as far as this fieldwork took me, I would always return to the nucleus of my studies: gamers.

The goal of my work in exploring what it means to be a gamer is ultimately to be of service to those who have been underserved by virtue of their participation in community through games and play. Those who have had special disservice done to them by inaccurate and sensationalist media representations, racial stereotyping, or marginalization through gender and sexuality have been too often lumped into the gamer identity and subsequently scapegoated. To temper the debates surrounding online game addiction by considering how the socio-political and economic imperatives of global society have manifested, particularly in the Korean cultural milieu.

More than binary

Ethnography is a method that is well suited to studying for, and with, the marginalized. Digital ethnography, while purposefully including the nuances of digital spaces and places, presents even more of a case for spotlighting this methodological research practice.

My commentary here focuses on the term "gamer" as an ethnographic subject of study in the process of investigating video games and interactive narratives. The concept of "gamer" is a fraught identity marker in the context of video games and interactive narratives, particularly because, in the ethnographic pursuit of understanding it as an identity, occupies an uncomfortable liminal zone between the categories of "insider" and "outsider."

Not focusing on the game itself, but the human-encompassing identity (gender, race, class, etc.), agency, culture, and many more possible nuances to explore. It is this existence between binaries: in/out groups, fandoms, players, that benefits from ethnographic frameworks. Sometimes we do not know (yet) the *why* and the *how* of someone coming to a practice or identity.

Games as lifelines to the social

The discussion of who gets identified and "counted" as a gamer appears to stem from the proliferation of multiple meanings and connotations associated with the label. Does it indicate a mere fandom, activity, or identity? In my work, I draw attention to ethnography to discern the cultural nuances included in a constellation of meaning-making practices. In particular, the sense-making of a gameworld, including a gamer's own understanding of themselves in relation to others, thereby implicating a system in which the game operates.

Co-design

Understanding the quintessential "gamer" has been intricately tied to game design and development. Through the employment of researchers practicing in social scientific fields, gamers have coordinated with game production personnel to form what has aimed to be more culturally aware in some cases, to further monetize a free-to-play game in others. Ethnography embraces the inductive–that is, the revealing of social phenomena rather than the comparatively prescriptive structure of deductive research. The inductive approach permits a liminal state of unknowing, as well as emergence and dynamism.

Because game spaces ultimately comprise boundaries as well as the in between, ethnography is well suited to walk the analytical line between disciplinary silos, frameworks, and epistemologies. The key here is how ethnography affords the translation of cultural insights into the multitudes represented by a term like "gamer" while also paying attention to context. In so doing, we can include the effect, and affect, of sociotechnical systems and move toward actionable items that demonstrate utility. As we use these insights to talk with and in between, the ethnographic tradition allows for a solid grounding in a theoretical foundation rooted in what we hope is an ethics of care.

For those who wish to make sense of what "gamer" entails for applied/ practitioner settings such as user experience research, the ethnographer must also be included at the concept stage, rather than brought in as an afterthought. Too many times, the afterthought model has prevailed, and a sort of re-entrenchment of marginalization may occur. Except in the cases where ethnographic expertise has been sought out, it may be too late to get "under the hood," so to speak, and instead only be able to speak to ultimately cosmetic changes, if any.

Leveraging ethnography for the purpose of communicating how people understand themselves, how they describe themselves in relation to others, as well as the multitude of standpoints possible are what enables the key insights to manifest. In my experience of collaborating with gamers as an ethnographic subject, my reflections were rich with delight, surprise, and generosity. Put more pointedly, if I had focused on just the game data, or the industry, the workers, players, or any of the matters in isolation from one another, I would not have garnered the insight that ethnography is especially well suited to provide, which is the holistic, open-ended, inclusion of multifaceted social insight and complicated circumstances.

Ultimately, we would do well to remember that the gamer is one who plays, and that the practice of digital ethnography is particularly well suited to the investigation of the cultural nuances in emergent phenomena.

Bibliography

Chee, Florence. 2006. "The Games We Play Online and Offline: Making Wang-Tta in Korea." *Popular Communication* 4 (3): 225–39. https://doi.org/10.1207/s15405710pc0403_6.

Chee, Florence. (2015) "Online Games and Digital Ethnography." In Mansell, R. and Ang, P. (Eds.), *International Encyclopedia of Digital Communication & Society*. Wiley-Blackwell. DOI: 10.1002/9781118290743.wbiedcs086

Chee, Florence. (2023). *Digital Game Culture in Korea: The Social at Play*. Bloomsbury Books.

Chee, Florence M., Larissa Hjorth and Hugh Davies. (2021). "An Ethnographic Co-Design Approach to Promoting Diversity in the Games Industry." *Feminist Media Studies*. DOI: 10.1080/14680777.2021.1905680

Chapter 10.2

Case study

Listening to queer, LGBTQ+, and women Twitch streamers

Jack McLaren and Larisa Kingston Mann

In the months leading up to October 2021, we enthusiastically prepared to undertake a virtual ethnographic project focused on the experiences of women, LGBTQ, queer, nonbinary, transgender, and drag performing streamers on the video game streaming platform Twitch.

Since Jack had been observing these communities for a while as a casual viewer, we knew that these types of streamers often had certain experiences that straight, white, and cisgender men who stream did not have. Jack came to this project as a graduate student who was familiar with Twitch and the video game *Dead by Daylight*, and wanted to experience virtual ethnography in the field, while Larisa came to the project with experience as a professor who studies how communities use cultural practices for liberation and the ways technology and law structure their possibilities, and as a queer participant/organizer/performer of underground musical events, former street medic and union organizer. These experiences led us to be interested in how people were using these online spaces and what affordances the technologies gave them or took away.

This is a methodological reflection on some of our successes, challenges, ethical conundrums, and interesting experiences we encountered while conducting this exciting project. We discuss the strength of our sample in terms of highlighting marginalized voices, negotiating how to participate in Twitch livestreams, some of our ethical decision-making processes, and the surprising interactions between interviewee and interviewer.

We collected data using virtual ethnography between October 2021 and November 2022. We had planned to first observe a pre-selected variety of streamers who all played the horror game *Dead by Daylight* and then interview those streamers. Since Jack was an avid player of this game, he was very familiar with some of the popular streamers of the game, as well as the language and mechanics. This turned out to be a good choice as we were already familiar with the language used to describe the game and the general vibe of the *Dead by Daylight* community.

We were pleased to find interviewees enthusiastic, open, and generally quite candid about their experiences on Twitch and as streamers generally on the margins. This candidness made us wonder the extent to which they considered their voices unheard or under-attended to in the broader conversation about streaming and other participatory media forms. We spoke with streamers with different followings: some with large followings (around 24,500 followers), averaging around a couple of hundred viewers each stream, and other smaller streamers with less than 400 followers. In addition, we had a mix of transgender, nonbinary, drag performing, gender fluid, queer femme, and transmasculine identities, with most of our interviewees describing their race/ethnicity as Black. As Black femme content creators generally must deal with misogynoir, having such a variety of voices with this particular experience was a strength of our research.

While we did not get the interviewees we expected when we set out on this research journey, our interview sample turned out to include an interesting variety of voices and experiences. It was striking that Black folks were so well represented in our interviews, particularly as they are not a large percentage of Twitch streamers. That led us to reflect on the context in which Black community members felt interested and/or safe to share their thoughts with us, and what our role was in contributing to that context.

In our initial contact, we supplied them with Jack's Twitch and Twitter handle, as well as Jack's graduate school profile. This allowed the interviewee to investigate him to decide if they were comfortable interviewing or not. We wondered whether a different race, gender, or identity would have got different responses, and in what ways Jack's choices of self-disclosure, online visibility, or reputation affected people's decisions to meet for an interview. In addition, being vouched for by existing streamers helped interviewees feel more comfortable interviewing with us. We believe a good interviewing reputation, along with giving out information that streamers could look up about our electronic footprint, enabled us to get as many interviews as we did.

At the same time as we were working on this project, we could not avoid the experience of surging transphobic and homophobic rhetoric. Verbal and physical attacks and terrorism targeted meatspace events that center queer, LGBTQ, women, drag performing, and BIPOC communities in the US and beyond. From attacks on queer nightlife spaces to threateningly militarized protests against Drag Queen Story Hours, we knew that many of these streamers were likely experiencing heightened hostility in their daily lives, because we ourselves were experiencing and witnessing them in ours. This made us more careful in how we reached out and mindful of how ambivalent people might feel about publicity. But at the same time, it increased our conviction that understanding sites like Twitch's capacity to support (or endanger) marginalized communities was more important than ever.

Notably, we began our project aware that queer, LGBTQ, women, drag performing, and BIPOC streamers were experiencing massive amounts of bigoted attacks on Twitch. The most dramatic attacks was hate raids, and it was clear that Twitch as a platform was very slow to deal with them. To raid someone's channel means you send your viewers to another streamer's channel to support them. This helps to boost a streamer's active viewership and is a great way for viewers to find new streamers to watch. Since the number of active viewers in a streamer's chat is very important for income purposes and to achieve or maintain certain Twitch levels (partner, etc.), this is a great way to boost fellow streamers. However, this capacity can be used to harm as well as help.

As we conducted our research, some were using this raiding function of Twitch to send a group of users and bots to spam others' chats with hateful messages, commonly in the form of racist, homophobic, and transphobic slurs. At this point, users could create multiple fake or bot accounts and overload the intended targets' chat while spewing hate. An additional impact of this attack was Twitch flagging the victims' accounts for using slurs in their stream and for "paying" for follow bots: both suspendable offenses on Twitch. This was intended, of course, to get the streamer banned while also subjecting them to vehement harassment. As we observed the simultaneous rise in physical-world hate mobs and online ones on Twitch, it clarified for us that marginalized people's cultural expression and social gatherings become targets when socio-political battles are being whipped up.

At the time, streamers had very limited defense against these raids. Both they and their channel moderators would have to try to individually ban the accounts to stop it. If it was a small streamer and the raid was huge, it was predictably difficult for the streamer to try to get an individual handle on the hate raid. We witnessed streamers demanding and pleading with Twitch to help them. In the meantime, some of these streamers banded together to help each other by creating certain applications that streamers could use in the live stream to put the channel in "followers" or "subscribers" only mode, auto-delete the entire chat, or tools that would "catch" the messages first and not post them immediately. One positive outcome that arose from the hate raids was that we witnessed these streamers coming together as a community and developing technological tools for self-defense.

We came into this project as two academics interested in being ethical and empowering our research participants. As such, we often thought about ways we could give back or empower our interviewees. Alongside shaping our research to reflect their voices and address the concerns that appeared to be affecting their lives, we tried to give back in small, direct ways using our own personal funds, including occasionally "subscribing" to a streamer's channel to give them a month's financial support or purchasing merchandise from their online stores. We also made sure we followed each streamer's channel and actively watched when we could. In this way, we thought about the multitude of ways we could support these content creators that did not have to include financial support. We also had to balance our support with anonymity—without directly alerting the streamer that we were doing this, to ensure streamers did not feel persuaded in any way to say yes or no to our interview requests.

Two other ways we dealt with ethics in our research involved announcing our presence as researchers and empowering our participants. We considered "announcing" our presence and intentions as researchers in the streamers' chats but quickly discovered that this would be very impactful and awkward. In short, it would disrupt the space and be quite weird to constantly announce our presence as researchers. Instead, Jack used his real last name and first initial as his Twitch handle. This means that he could be linked to his social media accounts through a quick search of his Twitch handle. While this is risky, we felt it was important not to be "hidden" or anonymous as researchers.

In addition, we considered what it would mean to give participants more control over the research process, especially as we wanted to try to uplift those voices that are often marginalized in the Twitch community. What would it mean to position our participants as part authors by allowing them a say in the written product? Therefore, we committed to our researchers that we would send them anonymized drafts of the manuscript so they could review it. In this way, they would be able to consent to the way we were using their words and add any commentary they had about the way we were conducting our analysis.

A final interesting reflection on our research process we had was something we dubbed "bumping baggage." Bumping baggage happens when participants manage to draw us out and encourage us as interviewers to reveal aspects of ourselves to them as well. For example, Jack found that in interviews he sometimes disclosed more of his own experiences or aspects of his identity that he had not planned to share. This made for a more meaningful interaction when this unexpected exchange occurred. Aside from this unexpected disclosure, it felt like our participants' reactions to our identities were intertwined with their own identity vectors in surprising ways. There are things we can control about our interviews, and there are things about our identity that we cannot control but still come to bear on how our interviewees see us. This intertwining of identities, or bumping baggage, can impact the interview process in beautiful ways. When this bumping baggage occurred in our interviews, there seemed to be a special kind of connection with interviewees who shared parts of our own identity, such as transmasculine experiences or a particular type of queer identity. We found that this often led to a mutual examination of queer or trans experience at these moments between interviewer and interviewee.

At other times, this led to a rich conversation where we empathized with interviewees but had no basis for understanding, such as the power and experience of Black femme identity that some interviewees discussed. While these conversations could be quite challenging, we felt immense gratitude when these unexpected (and very human) interactions occurred during the interview process. For Larisa, as one removed from the interviews but connected at all points to the interpretive and analytic process, the heightened context of violence and political volatility heightened the obligation to clarify the political orientation of this work. It is simply not fair to attempt to build knowledge out of interacting with communities under active attack without working to make that knowledge useful in preventing, protecting, or responding to those attacks. In our conversations with each other, we were increasingly clear that being aware and critical of our own identities provided important analytical and ethical tools. And it makes our data all the more relevant, richer, and more useful.

Chapter 11

Hybrid installations

Making meaning through the body in hybrid ethnography-art

Rob Eagle

Bristol (UK) June 2022—The bassline thumped, and the multi-colored lights twirled above the dancefloor. Clubbers danced, drank, and chatted, their feet at times sticking to the floor and their faces increasingly beading with perspiration. To cool down, they could head outside to the smoking area—or stumble into a quiet backroom where there were chairs, a rack of multi-colored secondhand clothing, and an interactive digital art experience, THROUGH THE WARDROBE.

For three days in June 2022, I, as both an ethnographer and an artist, hosted this installation in a nightclub backroom in the UK city of Bristol. When a visitor encountered the installation, I first instructed them to choose an item of clothing from the rack that they might feel "fabulous" wearing. Then, they donned an augmented reality (AR) headset to learn the story of the item's owner. THROUGH THE WARDROBE featured the stories of four people, all nonbinary and gender-nonconforming, living in Bristol. The installation offered visitors a virtual encounter with someone through listening, watching, and touching fragments from that person's everyday experience of the world. I had developed, iterated, and then exhibited the installation over four years, bringing together ethnographic research and practice-led arts research.

Discussions of the ethnographer-cum-artist or an artist adopting an ethnographic approach are not new in anthropology (Marcus and Meyers 1995; Schneider and Wright 2006; Basu and Macdonald 2007; Cox et al. 2016; Hartblay 2017). Ethnographer-artists might employ creative research methods beyond the orthodox multimodal forms of documentary photography, film, or audio, extending to other tools more associated with fictional representation or art and design practice. Through art-based methods like speculative fiction writing (Anderson et al. 2018), drawing and illustration (Theodossopoulos 2022), animation (Morelli 2021), and more, ethnographers have pushed the sensory and multimodal "turns" in anthropology to spill well beyond disciplinary boundaries. Interdisciplinary groups, such as the Ethnographic Terminalia Collective (Brodine et al. 2011) and the Centre for Imaginative Ethnography (Elliott and Culhane 2017), have expanded how performance, multimodal, and digital art developed through ethnography can be shared and exhibited for both academic and wider audiences (Errington 2012).[1] In his online review of the 2014 Ethnographic Terminalia exhibition, anthropologist Paul Stoller (2015) reflected that one challenge for interdisciplinary ethnographers and artists working today is "to create multi-sensorial spaces" in which stories are "told and retold, understood and comprehended anew through prisms of sound, scent, movement, and touch." Stoller optimistically declares that such an approach is both "the future" and "a much-appreciated tonic" for anthropology.

Art installations resulting from ethnographic research can speak far beyond anthropology and the academy (Degarrod 2013). When arts-based ethnographic research becomes a form of public ethnography, we as ethnographer-artists find ourselves speaking to audiences who find and create new meanings in our work. We are challenged then to consider audiences in an interactive work as potential collaborators in the making process (Pringle 2017) and in actively shaping the work from our original artistic intentions. Art installations as public ethnography come with a set of considerations for user testing and exhibiting in venues beyond the academic institution and sometimes even beyond the walls of a gallery or museum.

This chapter presents theoretical and practical considerations for those bringing together ethnographic research methods and art practices, creating installations with digital interfaces and physical objects, specifically for public, non-academic audiences. I will illustrate key points with *THROUGH THE WARDROBE*, an installation of ethnography-art exhibited almost entirely beyond academic venues. The installation demonstrated how a hybrid physical-digital format can open creative possibilities to present ethnography with meanings that are unfixed, emergent, and contingent upon the unique bodily subjectivities of each visitor. The physical objects and augmented reality in the installation presented stories from nonbinary people who actively questioned and resisted binary notions of gender through their bodies. Visitors, then, were challenged on their own assumptions of gender through wearing a digital device (an AR headset) and physically engaging with furniture, clothing, and multisensory stimuli in the installation.

The process of creating such work requires the ethnographer-artist to embrace hybridity in multiple ways: form (physical-digital), methods (ethnography-arts practice), discipline, and subject matter. Through a physical-digital installation format, we can bring together interactive technology, multimedia, and objects, sharing our research with wider audiences. The stories and experiences in these installations can challenge assumptions and provoke critical thinking about human diversity and societal

Hybrid installations 323

Figure 11.1 Visitor to THROUGH THE WARDROBE in the backroom of the nightclub in Bristol (Photograph taken by the author).

issues—what all good public ethnography does. Art installations with digital media provide a platform for ethnographers to engage the public in a sensory and experiential manner, which fosters dialogue and a deeper understanding of different communities and lived experiences (Figure 11.1).

Ethnography and art?

Working both in ethnography and in art means grappling with the discourses of both simultaneously. While the boundaries and formats of art seem to be ever-expanding, particularly with emerging digital technologies and rapid expansion in the uses of AI, the practice and definition of ethnography are still a source of contention among academics (HAU 2017; Ahmad 2021). The aim of ethnography, according to anthropologist Tim Ingold, "is to render an account—in writing, film, or other graphic media— of life as it is actually lived and experienced by a people, some-where, sometime" (2017, 21). The output of ethnography ought to be a "faithful" representation of someone's life experiences. Ingold disparages the combination of ethnography with art practice, as this generally leads to "bad art and bad ethnography"; the "ethnographer's commitment to descriptive fidelity" is fundamentally incompatible with "art's experimental and interventionist interrogation" (2017, 24). Ingold despairs at what he views as the watering down of ethnography, as the term has become overused and misused by both fellow anthropologists and researchers in other disciplines. The descriptor "ethnographic" has commonly been applied to any form of research, method, or knowledge that involves an encounter with a community.

Consequently, Ingold is keen to "narrow ethnography down" (2014, 284) to its purest form, which is descriptive, factual, explanatory, and insightful (2008, 90, 2014, 285, 393). His surprisingly positivist characterization of ethnography reflecting "life as it is actually lived" seems to conflict with so many examples of ethnography in artistic forms that resist "documentary realism" (Banks and Ruby 2011; Cox and Wright 2012). The practice of ethnography requires the researcher to interpret the participants' lives through a medium or multiple media, but the extent to which the result is a "faithful" depiction varies. Ethnography and art-based practices can form exciting, original outputs, from animation to performance and speculative fiction writing. Are all of these "bad art and bad ethnography?"

Perhaps Ingold also overstates the fixed-ness of ethnographic representation, especially in the combination of ethnography and artistic practice. He views the final outputs of ethnography as offering "insights" and conclusions from fieldwork (Ingold 2014, 393). In treating ethnographic outputs as closed, fixed texts, he neglects the creative potential of both the audiences who interpret and make meaning(s) from the output (especially creative writing, film, and the arts) and the outputs themselves to change and be adapted (Ahmad 2021).

Ingold's provocation provides a useful point of departure to explore the potential of presenting ethnography through an art installation using digital media. How might the ethnography-art installation blend *both* "descriptive fidelity" *and* artistic interpretation? These two qualities and modes of interpretation, as shall be demonstrated in this chapter, are not always mutually exclusive but potentially intertwined. An artistic treatment of ethnography both proposes a creative format to interpret social phenomena and, when employing participatory methods, offers research participants an opportunity to self-reflect and share their experiences with wider audiences (Degarrod 2013). In a physical installation, this constitutes a *mediation* more than a *representation* of ethnographic research (Basu and Macdonald 2007). As visitors navigate ethnography-art installations, they make connections and meaning among what Peter Weibel and Bruno Latour (2007) call the *assemblage* of physical objects and interactive digital elements. That is, meaning is emergent among the constituent visitors, objects, digital technology (including software), subject matter, and more.

For anthropologist and artist-filmmaker Paolo Favero (2017, 284), "ethnographers must start viewing themselves as curators of ethnographic content. Their main task is that of creating a space within which viewers can engender their own searches, interpretations and narratives, to facilitate their path of meaning-making." This is what some immersive media practitioners call "storyliving," rather than storytelling, in which visitors must actively engage with the performative qualities of an immersive work (Maschio 2021). The degree of interactivity in shaping the outcomes of the story allows each visitor to experience the work differently. Depending on the affordances of both the physical elements and digital technologies used, the work itself may also continue to change and adapt to each visitor and location in which it is exhibited.

THROUGH THE WARDROBE provides here an illustration of how descriptive fidelity and artistic interpretation can intertwine in an ethnography-art installation. More than this, we can see how visitors assemble their own experience and meaning through the physical and digital elements, providing open (rather than closed) understandings of a work.

An open mesh of possibilities: AR in THROUGH THE WARDROBE

With the emergence of the latest wave of VR since 2014, a handful of digital ethnographers have turned their attention to immersive virtual worlds. Some ethnographers have taken advantage of the accessibility of cameras that shoot in 360 degrees to be viewed in VR headsets (Shuter and Burroughs 2017; Westmoreland 2020; Schillaci and D'Onofrio 2022). VR places the viewer within an immersive environment, which can be valuable to give the audience a sense of presence in place, the feeling of being transported there at least visually and auditorily. AR, by contrast, whether displayed through a smartphone or a headset, affords a hybrid sense of place and embodiment that is *both* physical *and* digital. In THROUGH THE WARDROBE, for example, the visitor wearing the headset looked down and saw their own physical body in a room, but the 3D animated objects had the illusion of appearing in the room, and the spatial audio gave the illusion of a person's voice speaking from the location of that animation.

The most common uses of AR tend to be visual, such as face and environment filters on social media platforms like Instagram, Snapchat, and TikTok. But the medium can incorporate and be applied to more than visual forms. We can think of AR as a "perceptual phenomenon" (Avram 2016), not as a technology, in which the physical and digital dialogically intermingle. In THROUGH THE WARDROBE, physical actions—including looking, moving, sitting, and lying down—triggered digital reactions in the headset as animations and audio would start, stop, and surround the visitor. Each item of clothing on a hanger had a name tag attached with one of four names: Sammy, Rex, Micah, and Jamie. Once the visitor had put on their chosen item of clothing and the AR headset, they were instructed to look at the name tag, which triggered the 3D animations in the headset. Next, they entered a room-scale installation resembling a bedroom, complete with furniture. In the headset, they saw five orbs around the space that worked as chapters in the story. Upon entering each chapter, 3D animations would appear around the room along with spatialized music and the voice of the person whose story they had chosen.

To progress through each chapter of a story, the visitor needed to move from one item of furniture to the next. The visitor negotiated sensory layers of physical reality—sitting on a chair, trying on jewelry, spraying perfume—simultaneously with a digital, augmented layer of animations and spatial audio. The stories examined how my four main research participants felt getting dressed and going out into a world in which their fashion sense or bodies did not always conform to binary assumptions of gender. From despair to joy, they revealed their everyday strategies for feeling confident in their bodies.

Throughout my fieldwork, my participants described their gender as unstable and emergent. We often spoke of what queerness means for those who are genderqueer. For this, I found it useful to refer to the conceptualization of "queer" from Eve Kosofsky-Sedgwick (1993, 8) as, "the open mesh of possibilities, gaps, overlaps, dissonances and resonances, lapses and excesses of meaning when the constituent elements of anyone's gender, of anyone's sexuality aren't made (or can't be made) to signify monolithically." Genderqueerness, therefore, for my participants meant more than a resistance to binaries (male/female) but a capacious understanding of the infinite possibilities of gender. One could be both male and female simultaneously, neither (agender) or so fluid that any gendered label would be meaningless.

Gender as an "open mesh of possibilities" guided how I approached the use of AR in developing the installation. The medium is constituted of *both* physical objects *and* real-time 3D virtual elements. What results is an experience of a simultaneous physical and virtual space. The visitor, for example, would step through a virtual wardrobe (projected inside the headset) to enter a physical room with physical furniture. The layered medium of the installation matched the content: the participants' stories spoke of negotiating gender as internal, bodily, and socially constructed, while expressing their nonbinary-ness through clothing, accessories, and more.

As I conducted my research among the queer community in Bristol from 2017 to 2019, only a fraction of our discussions focused on gender, the body, and gender presentation. Most conversations with my participants, as in any fieldwork, involved their daily realities of work, dating and relationships, family, hobbies, and the occasional going out to places like the cinema or gigs. In long-term ethnography, we as researchers become entangled in a place and the lives of our participants. And—when employing an artistic practice in our research—our participants may also become involved in our creative process, depending on the format and level of technical complexity. Our participants inhabit the dual roles of being the center of our research (the "subjects" of our ethnography) and producers of this ethnographic knowledge with us. To paraphrase Ingold's characterization of anthropology (2017, 22), we are studying *with* them and not making a study *of* them.

For anthropologist and artist Lydia Nakashima Degarrod (2013), when "arts-based ethnographies" become "public-engaged ethnographies," they open up possibilities for both the participants and audiences. When participants in arts-based ethnographies know that their story will be shared publicly, the process encourages them "to consider the various audiences to whom they can address their stories and images [and] to perform truths" (2013, 407). Artistic methods may help to surface experiences they might not otherwise have an opportunity to express publicly. In fact, there may be a motivation for social justice and activism in sharing their stories with wider audiences. In this process, ethnographic knowledge becomes explicitly relational between the participant (telling the story), the ethnographer-artist (interpreting the story), and the installation visitor (engaging with the story).

In ethnographic-artistic research, our participants can be collaborators or co-creators, from contributing material, such as video, audio, or physical objects, to producing and editing work themselves (Turner 1992). However, while some projects might start out embracing the optimism of co-creation, the complexities of particular digital technologies may prohibit participants from actively producing material themselves (Battaglia 2014). Recording, editing, and—often with advanced digital media formats—complex computer coding are potential barriers to consider in multimodal and participatory arts research methods.

From ideating and developing *THROUGH THE WARDROBE* in 2018 to touring and exhibiting from 2019 to 2022, my participants and I continually negotiated how they might be involved in the creative process. The digital components for the AR headset required professional-level programming in the game engine Unity, a process so technologically specialized that it would not be practical to involve participants. We, instead, discussed options to contribute, including: audio recording their voices, incorporating items of their own clothes within the installation, contributing drawings and photos that we featured in the AR animations, user testing, and helping to install and exhibit the work. Sammy, Rex, Micah, and Jamie became both research participants and creative collaborators. While their contributions could be perceived as a "faithful" account in a documentary tradition, the entire set, resembling a bedroom, was an artificial construct. Many of the animations in the headset used abstract colors and shapes to convey the emotional meaning of their audio. The installation blended the two qualities of "descriptive fidelity" and a collaborative artistic interpretation. Sammy, Rex, Micah, and Jamie were also more than participants, becoming dear friends and artistic collaborators in the process. The installation became a way to share their lived daily realities in an intimate and accessible format while still offering the unapologetically queer voices of four people who defy any attempts to fit into mainstream gendered categorization or labels.

Openness and meaning-making

Returning to the potential openness and artistic interpretation in an ethnography-art installation, what, exactly, makes the format open? Umberto Eco (1989 [1962]) would argue that many works of art of the modern era are inherently "open." Explanations and conclusions may not be obvious or given; the viewer or reader must make connections within the work to form meaning. The pantheon of ethnographic filmmakers, including Robert Flaherty, Jean Rouch, and Timothy Asch, has demonstrated how ethnographic film has never been a closed text (MacDougall 1978, 421). Roland Barthes (1977) takes this line of reasoning a step further in declaring the "death of the author:" after an author completes a work, the meaning now lies in the interpretation of the reader. For Barthes, there is no singular narrative, but multiple, emergent ways of understanding a text. If we apply these strategies of openness to an ethnography-art exhibition, as Weibel and Latour (2007, 107) do, we accept that there is no singular interpretation held by the artist or the curator but a process of assemblage in which meaning is contingent on the emergent relationship among the visitors, the objects, the digital technology, and the artist.

Those meanings, according to film theorist Laura Marks (2000), are not just a cognitive process but are felt in the body of the viewer. According to Marks, the act of viewing the moving image involves physically responding to the story onscreen, what she terms "haptic visuality." The image and sound can resonate with the viewer's own life experiences, including joys and traumas, and their own cultural context. Marks points to the potential of haptic visuality in bridging a gap in intercultural cinema wherein the audience (living in one part of the world) may connect to the humanity of someone onscreen they might otherwise perceive as Other. Building on Marks, Favero (2020, 10) reminds us that how we as viewers engage with digital images is "multisensory, multimodal and relation[al]." The physical context of the viewer can shape the interpretation even of the digital image. While we may often think of digital media as dematerialized, on the contrary, digital technologies have become so pervasive that we can no longer separate the digital from the analog in our visual culture. This, Favero contends, is an era of "post-digital visuality."

Since the 1980s, we have also seen the emergence of *interactive* documentaries (such as web-docs, docu-games, and nonfiction VR experiences) in which the audience can exert some influence on the outcome or pace of the work. The audience makes connections between components through a physical process of choosing a course of action, like clicking a mouse or tapping a screen. We can also think of this process of experiencing an interactive documentary as a form of assemblage (Gaudenzi 2013). The audience might navigate through different materials onscreen, say, text, video, and gameplay. In most interactive documentaries, the audience must actively, physically arrange and create pathways to form their experience of a story.

Physical installations with digital media bring Eco's openness into our era of post-digital visuality. Meaning is made not just by looking but by engaging other senses of the body. It is in those gaps between the digital media content and the physical context and location where the potential for meaning lies. And there are several components for the ethnographer-artist to consider how the audience constructs meanings within an ethnography-art installation, including the digital device, user experience (UX) design, and setting.

Digital devices

Installations with digital media feature interfaces—most commonly screens, projections, and touchscreens, often with speakers, or sometimes just the speakers alone for an audio installation. It is not just the digital device that shapes the physical experience but what sort of actions they demand of the audience. With interactive work involving a digital device, the processes of touching, watching, listening, and more take an experience from haptic viewership to a kinetic, multisensory process of assemblage.

Some ethnography-digital art installations require the visitor to hold or even wear the digital interface. Mobile phones, tablets, headphones, and VR/AR headsets invite the visitor to experience a story through a device connected to their body. The device mediates their experience as they move, as in *THROUGH THE WARDROBE*. The digital interface is more than a display for audio, photos, video, or text content; the device is an object in itself, interactive as visitors move and physically engage with the installation. Wearing the device, especially headphones or a headset, is especially intimate. While such devices contribute to a sense of immersion, surrounded by the digital image and audio, they also shape how the visitor moves among the physical surroundings and objects.

VR/AR headsets and other interactive digital devices allow for communication of ethnography beyond representation. Emerging digital technologies, according to Favero (2017, 285), "force us to go beyond conventional explanatory models, opening up the space for more interactive and participatory strategies of knowledge communication." Especially with ethnography, this allows for the *polysemy* of visual components that can be interpreted in multiple layers of meaning. Digital visual elements (photographs, drawings, film, 3D imagery) are more than representational but contain potentially multiple interpretations and meanings for the viewer.

With AR, the layering of meaning is made literal; a 3D digital image appears to sit atop or to filter the physical environment. That 3D object (or filter) changes how the viewer perceives or interacts with the environment. It is that bringing together of digital objects (interactive animations and spatial audio) with physical objects in THROUGH THE WARDROBE that allows visitors to make their own connections and meanings—often personal and different for each visitor.

User experience design through user testing

For an academic, sharing a research paper as a work-in-progress and inviting feedback helps to sharpen their arguments and ensure that their work is rigorous, scholarly, and in dialogue with the wider discipline. For an ethnographic filmmaker, similarly, screening a rough cut of a film helps to ensure the film communicates what they *hope* it communicates. Ethnographic filmmaker Timothy Asch, for example, screened multiple iterations of his films for test audiences and asked for their feedback to improve the edit (Martinez 1995). As researcher-practitioners sharing our work in unpolished stages, we invite our peers to be an active and vital part of the making process.

Digital art installations often require a similar type of vulnerable testing and evaluation—but in a process that might involve novices as much as knowledgeable peers. User testing is as much about testing the content (asking the user what they understood) as it is about testing the ease of navigating the digital interface. Testing with digital formats requires ensuring the work is at a certain level of technological stability. This means the coding, interface, and physical setup need to be robust enough for multiple visitors, often for several hours in a row in a venue. For most digital artists, user testing is an essential stage of the making process, helping the maker to ensure that the device functions properly but also, more significantly, that the interface facilitates the visitor's ability to make connections and meaning in a work.

Interactive documentary maker Ramona Pringle (2017) writes about her process of testing and iterating for interactive formats. First, there is concept testing to ensure the project is engaging and entertaining and simultaneously thought-provoking and educational. (For the digital artist-ethnographer, the "entertaining" element might be less important, but if we are concerned with sharing our research outputs with public audiences, we still must consider how our work is engaging for non-specialists.) Then, there is pre-production, development, prototype development, production, and testing of multiple iterations. For Pringle (2017, 169), "the user is the creator's silent collaborator—the one who will bring the interactive experience to life once it is released to the public—and testing brings that user into the design process." Pringle notes how makers in the testing phase should focus on how the interface design and the device facilitate (and not hinder) the user's flow in the experience.

The complexity of the digital device might necessitate different approaches to user testing. Most visitors to an exhibition are familiar with touchscreens and mobile phones. The choice of such everyday digital interfaces might require fewer (or no) instructions and less effort on the part of venue staff to demonstrate and guide visitors. At the opposite end of the spectrum, VR and AR headsets require instructions for most audiences. The more complicated an interface, the more clarity is needed for instructions, and often the more user testing is necessary.

For user testing, makers invite test audiences and may hold a feedback session after, live-capture interaction data of the testers, or compare variables with study participants, known as A/B testing. One of the most difficult elements of an interactive digital art installation in a gallery or festival is the complexity of instructions for the visitor. If instructions are unclear or insufficient, the visitor is left confused and lost, feeling self-conscious that they cannot figure out how to navigate the space or operate the device (Scott-Stevenson 2020). Alternatively, instructions can be so overwhelming—text on the wall, instructions from the gallery assistant, instructions within the installation—that the visitor, in a state of information overload, cannot remember how to operate a complicated interface or navigate a complex labyrinth of branching narratives.

In user testing *THROUGH THE WARDROBE*, I set up a mock installation in my office and invited trusted critical colleagues and friends who had varying levels of experience with digital media formats. Testers also included my participants, who were able to experience their own stories and offer suggestions on edits. For A/B testing, I fitted one group of testers with the AR headset and gave them full instructions before going into the installation, plus additional instructions within the headset. I asked for feedback on whether they felt there was too much or too little information to feel confident in navigating the installation and for them to make connections (and therefore find meaning) among the physical objects and AR elements. The other group of testers was given no instructions; the challenge for them was to navigate the headset and the space on their own. When they emerged from the installation, I asked (1) what instructions they wished they had known before they entered and (2) what connections and meanings they made without instructions.

The responses of both groups served a functional purpose in helping me craft the instructions and indicators, like arrows, in the headset. This process is known as UX design. The user testers also demonstrated and reflected on how their respective levels of instruction resulted in making connections among the digital media and physical elements. If instructions (such as "Look here," "Sit here," and "Try this on") are too explicit, the visitor has less opportunity to explore and create their own meanings. Overly controlling instructions risk giving the visitor only a singular experience—thus closing down, rather than opening up, meaning. Conversely, no instruction makes it difficult for the visitor to engage with the work. For the sake of accessibility for wider ages, backgrounds, education, and physical abilities, there are limits to the openness of an open work.

Through user testing and iterative exhibitions, we can ensure (*contra* Barthes) that the author is not "dead"; our role as the maker continues as we learn from our user testers and later the installation visitors when it is publicly exhibited. Often, it is not enough to provide an assemblage and then leave it to our visitors to make meaning. Rather, user testing allows the maker to find a delicate balance in providing *some* instructions, steering visitors on how to make connections among different elements—e.g., clothing and furniture with 3D animations and spatial audio in the headset in THROUGH THE WARDROBE. Without some level of instruction, especially with emerging digital technologies, we risk alienating visitors. They must feel comfortable within the installation and empowered enough to explore and make connections, not intimidated or excluded by the device, and afraid that they will break it.

Setting: emplacement interaction

Once our installations have gone through testing and production, they are ready to be shared with the world, right? Well, there is still one major consideration: just exactly who and where will our audiences be? For ethnographer-artists wanting to share our work with wider audiences, we might look at the potential of exhibiting in galleries, festivals, nightclubs, train stations, city streets, and more. Of course, not every venue or location will facilitate the same type of visitor engagement. Visitors come with their own expectations, subject knowledge (or assumptions), understanding of the content or technologies involved, and physical and skill abilities to interact with digital interfaces. When we examine not just the individual visitor's interaction but the geographical and physical context of an exhibition, we are confronted with a multitude of layers that shape how visitors make connections and meaning in our work.

Much of the literature on the experience of exhibitions examines the embodied processes of meaning-making among physical objects and the framing and interpretation of those objects (e.g., Weibel and Latour 2007; Färber 2007). In his focus on the cultural context of studying the senses, anthropologist David Howes (2005) argues that we ought to consider not just embodiment but what he terms *emplacement*—how the context of place influences the experience of the mind and body. For Howes, the paradigm of embodiment is limited, as it focuses on the relationship between mind and body. This risks neglecting the many factors that shape how we experience the world, namely, our culturally informed sensory regimes. Considering emplacement, rather than embodiment, helps us to situate the stimuli of the mind and body *within* a physical and social context, "the sensuous interrelationship of body-mind-environment" (Howes 2005, 7).

Anthropologist and filmmaker Judith Aston (2017) applies Howes's understanding of emplacement to interactive documentaries, including experiential work. Bringing attention to interaction design together with the emplacement of the person in the experience, Aston coined the term *emplaced interaction*. This emphasizes the physical and social context in which an audience experiences a work with digital elements. The visitor's emplacement (background, location, venue context) shapes how they use their body in interacting with a digital art installation, and that results in the connections they make.

There were different forms of emplaced interactions in *THROUGH THE WARDROBE*, depending on the geographic and cultural context in which it was staged. Before a nightclub backroom in Bristol, the installation had been exhibited in art galleries in the UK, a train station in Amsterdam (as part of International Documentary Festival Amsterdam), and a cultural center in Beijing. For a UK visitor to an art gallery, the themes of transphobia resonated with the recent political and media discourse on trans rights. Some visitors came to the arts venues specifically for the stories of nonbinary experiences precisely because trans rights were so often politicized and "debated" in media representations; trans voices were rarely presented as simple stories of everyday existence and resistance to transphobia. In Amsterdam, the installation sat among an arcade of clothing shops; half of the visitors were passengers who were going through the train station and stumbled upon the installation (Eagle 2020). Much of their attention was on the bold, colorful clothes and the tactile elements of the experience, not the UK's political situation for trans rights. When it was exhibited in Beijing, we collaborated with a local LGBT group that translated the transcripts and then recorded a Mandarin-language version of the stories from Sammy, Rex, Micah, and Jamie. For a Chinese audience, the installation contained a locally specific angle to an otherwise British understanding of genderqueerness and identity.

When we look at the emplaced interaction of visitors in each iteration of THROUGH THE WARDROBE, we see how the installation acquired different meanings. Each geographic location and venue helped to frame how visitors approached the work. The sensory regimes in each place shaped a different sense of emplacement for visitors in each version of the installation, leading to different interpretations and meanings for them. There was also no singular type of visitor: commuters and international travelers in a train station, visitors to an art gallery, or clubbers taking a break from the sweaty main room of a nightclub. The visitor contexts of THROUGH THE WARDROBE demonstrated how the meanings of the work were unstable, mirroring Kosofsky-Sedgwick's (1993, 8) understanding of queer as an open mesh of "possibilities, gaps, overlaps, dissonances and resonances, lapses and excesses of meaning." Interaction with the work was shaped by constituent elements: the physical body of the visitor and their lens in experiencing the work, the venue (gallery, nightclub, train station), and the location.

An ethnography-art installation offers more than a static presentation of research findings. Images and objects acquire new meanings for new audiences. These layers of meaning are what Favero (2017, 285) views as the polysemy of the image. For THROUGH THE WARDROBE, the acquisition of meanings was also physical and literal, as the installation changed ever so slightly from one exhibition to the next. Along the way, clothing acquired smudges, stretches, and even small tears. The secondhand furniture changed completely, as it was not practical to ship around the world and back. THROUGH THE WARDROBE was never static; it acquired new meanings for visitors in each location it toured (Figure 11.2).

Limits to openness

In the ever-growing polysemy of a work over time, does this lead to a dissolution, then, of any core meaning? Again, there are limits to the openness of open work.

When placing so much emphasis on the subjectivity of each visitor, we risk sidelining the voices of our research participants. An ethnography-digital art installation then becomes more about the visitor's opinion of an object or element of the installation, rather than an opportunity for a visitor to listen and learn from the life experiences of another person. Even visual anthropologists can be guilty of seeing their participants through their own lens, incapable of grasping the sensory orders of their research participants (Marks 2000, 230). If we know the world through the body, à la Merleau-Ponty, then surely, we know the world only through our *own* body. While the visitor may be hindered by the limits of their own sensory

Figure 11.2 Visitors to THROUGH THE WARDROBE are given instructions to touch and explore both physical and digital objects to build their own interpretation of the experience (Photograph taken by Li Yinjun, Goethe-Institut China).

regime, the installation presents a potential space to learn—even if only a little—about the emplaced experiences of others.

Of course, experiencing ethnographic media does not always lead to a process of intercultural understanding. As anthropologist Wilton Martinez (1992) found in his studies of student audiences in the 1990s, sometimes ethnographic films work to further entrench the viewer's preconceived views of the ethnographic "Other" onscreen. Martinez examined what he termed the "interpretive gap" between what the ethnographic filmmaker had intended to communicate and how the student audience understood it. In their interpretation of the films, Martinez's California-based students mainly reflected on what they understood as the exoticism of the ethnographic Other onscreen. Rather than "educating" viewers, sometimes ethnographic media compounds an audience's assumptions about the ethnographic Other.

So how, then, ought we to ensure that our ethnography-art installation is open enough to interpretation for public and non-specialist visitors, while not further entrenching notions of exoticism and otherness?

One solution might be to acknowledge that not all ethnographic outputs for public audiences are necessarily for *every*one. THROUGH THE WARDROBE offers snippets of daily experiences of four nonbinary people; the range of visitors was wide and international, but I did not attempt to convince anti-trans visitors suddenly to embrace transgender rights. I accepted that for some people, the content might not appeal, and that is okay. Ethnography-art installations are for those already open to learning from other voices.

Second, when we insist that "all are welcome" to festivals and galleries, how open are these spaces, really? At risk of Euro-American festivals and galleries over-platforming work by white, straight men for audiences also limited to the primarily white and highly educated, we must ask who is absent among our visitors (Verstappen et al. 2021; Gill 2021). To echo past critiques of media and arts festivals, there are multiple barriers to entry for new audiences to attend (Vallejo 2020; Varvantakis 2021). Attendees are those who have access to and knowledge of the festival, requiring a particular level of cultural capital. This eliminates many potential novice attendees who do not have the means to visit these places, do not understand what such festivals are about, or do not feel welcome in such spaces. The particular devices and formats might also mean that wheelchair-users and those with vision or hearing impairments find the work inaccessible for their physical needs. Visitors to festivals and galleries of ethnography-art installations are self-selecting or excluded through several factors. No matter how inclusive festivals and arts venues claim to be, they will be more heavily attended by those with similar levels of economic and cultural capital. Another solution for installation artists might be to leave the gallery and academic festival behind. Even if train stations or nightclubs are not appropriate for all ethnography-art installations, we can make greater efforts to share our work with wider audiences beyond the academy.

Conclusions: an "artistic turn" for digital ethnography?

Contra Ingold, I would argue that arts practice and ethnography (especially *digital* art and ethnography) can intermingle through an installation in exciting ways for the ethnographer-artist, research participant, and visitor. Despite Ingold's attempts to "narrow ethnography down," entwining it with digital arts opens up both practices.

For the hybrid ethnographer-artist, an arts practice is more than an output to create a "faithful" representation of our participants. Rather, like all ethnography, art-making is how we make sense of our position in and experience of our research. Arts practice engages implicit and emplaced forms of knowledge of both the ethnographer and the research participants. The installation is a mediation, not a representation, of our participants, and now visitors are invited to experience that mediation and create their own assemblage. Consequently, stories and meanings are emergent, sometimes ambiguous, as the physical surroundings, digital device, and wider emplacement are imbricated in how an audience constructs meaning. The polysemy of the ethnography-digital art installation acquires different layers of meaning over time and in different contexts. The meaning of a work can even change and deepen for the maker: from the concept design phase to iteration to user testing to touring it over several months or years.

In surveying the rise of tools for digital ethnography, especially the potential for both collaborative research methods and alternative non-text outputs, Sarah Pink in 2011 observed the emergence of a field "still in its infancy" that she called "Digital Visual Anthropology." The next year, reviewing three editions of the pioneering exhibitions of Ethnographic Terminalia, Shelly Errington (2012) proposed "Digital/Intermedia Anthropology" to describe the range of work across digital and installation formats, bringing together art and anthropology. Neither of their terms quite caught on. But Pink and Errington, respectively, were identifying a shift in scholarship and practice, a subfield of a subfield in anthropology that was responding to the growth in digital tools. Since then, both anthropology departments and art schools have produced a new generation of hybrid ethnography-art researcher-practitioners. And we have seen how ethnography (despite Ingold's protests) has become a useful tool for inquiry and practice across arts practice, the humanities, and the social sciences.

Following on from the sensory and multimodal turns in anthropology and the ethnographic turn in art, are we seeing a digital arts turn in ethnography? Or a digital ethnographic turn in the digital arts? Ethnographer-artists find themselves awkwardly struggling to find equitable, non-academic platforms to celebrate their hybrid ethnography-art. In an era of post-digital visuality, these installations of physical objects and digital art assemblages demonstrate the radical potential of ethnography to continue to provoke and facilitate conversations among researchers (including artist-researchers), participants, and non-academic audiences.

Note

1 For more information, see https://ethnographicterminalia.org/ and https://www.imaginativeethnography.ca/.

Bibliography

Ahmad, Irfan. 2021. "Introduction: On the Equivalence between Anthropology and Ethnography." In *Anthropology and Ethnography Are Not Equivalent: Reorienting Anthropology for the Future*, edited by Irfan Ahmad, 1–19. New York: Berghahn Books.

Anderson, Ryan B., Emma Louise Backe, Taylor Nelms, Elizabeth Reddy, and Jeremy Trombley. 2018. "Introduction: Speculative Anthropologies." *Theorizing the Contemporary, Fieldsights*. https://culanth.org/fieldsights/introduction-speculative-anthropologies.

Aston, Judith. 2017. "Interactive Documentary and Live Performance: From Embodied to Emplaced Interaction." In *I-Docs: The Evolving Practices of Interactive Documentary*, edited by Judith Aston, Sandra Gaudenzi, and Mandy Rose, 85–104. New York: Wallflower, Columbia University Press.

Aston, Judith, and Stefano Odorico. 2018. "The Poetics and Politics of Polyphony: Towards a Research Method for Interactive Documentary." *Alphaville: Journal of Film and Screen Media* 15: 63–93.

Avram, Horea. 2016. *The Visual Regime of Augmented Reality Art: Space, Body, Technology, and the Real-Virtual Convergence*. PhD diss., McGill University. https://escholarship.mcgill.ca/downloads/dr26z097w.

Banks, Marcus and Jay Ruby. 2011. "Introduction: Made to Be Seen, Historical Perspectives on the History of Visual Anthropology." In *Made to Be Seen: Perspectives on the History of Visual Anthropology*, edited by Marcus Banks and Jay Ruby, 1–18. Chicago: University of Chicago Press.

Barthes, Roland. 1977. "The Death of the Author." In *Image, Music, Text*, translated by Stephen Heath, 142–48. London: HarperCollins UK.

Battaglia, Giulia. 2014. "Crafting 'Participatory' and 'Collaborative' Film-Projects in India." *Anthrovision* 2 (2). https://journals.openedition.org/anthrovision/1416 (accessed January 19, 2024).

Brodine, Maria, Craig Campbell, Kate Hennessy, Fiona P. McDonald, Trudi Lynn Smith, and Stephanie Takaragawa. 2011. "Ethnographic Terminalia: An Introduction." *Visual Anthropology Review* 27: 49–51.

Cox, Rupert and Christopher Wright. 2012. "Blurred Visions: Reflecting Visual Anthropology." In *The SAGE Handbook of Social Anthropology*, edited by Richard Fardon, Olivia Harris, Trevor H Marchand, Mark Nuttall, Cris Shore, Veronica Strang and Richard A Wilson. 84–100. London: SAGE Publications.

Cox, Rupert, Andrew Irving, and Christopher Wright, eds. 2016. *Beyond Text?: Critical Practices and Sensory Anthropology*. Manchester: Manchester University Press. https://doi.org/10.7765/9781526147233.

Degarrod, Lydia Nakashima. 2013. "Making the Unfamiliar Personal: Arts-Based Ethnographies as Public-Engaged Ethnographies." *Qualitative Research* 13 (4): 402–13. https://doi.org/10.1177/1468794113483302.

Eagle, Rob. 2020. "Multisensory Ethnography through Emplaced Augmented Reality." *Anthrovision* 8 (2): 1–17. https://doi.org/10.4000/anthrovision.6563.

Eco, Umberto. 1989 [1962]. *The Open Work*. Translated by Anna Cancogni. Cambridge, MA: Harvard University Press.

Elliott, Denielle, and Dara Culhane, eds. 2017. *A Different Kind of Ethnography: Imaginative Practices and Creative Methodologies*. Toronto: University of Toronto Press.

Errington, Shelly. 2012. "Exhibition Review Essay Ethnographic Terminalia: 2009–10–11." *American Anthropologist* 114 (3): 538–42.

Färber, Alexa. 2007. "Exposing Expo: Exhibition Entrepreneurship and Experimental Reflexivity in Late Modernity." In *Exhibition Experiments*, edited by Paul Basu and Sharon MacDonald, 219–38. London: Blackwells.

Favero, Paolo. 2017. "Curating and Exhibiting Ethnographic Evidence: Reflections on Teaching and Displaying with the Help of Emerging Technologies." In *The Routledge Companion to Digital Ethnography*, edited by Larissa Hjorth, Heather Horst, Anne Galloway, and Genevieve Bell, 275–87. New York: Routledge.

Favero, Paolo. 2020. "Audio-Visual-Sensory Essays in Post-Digital Times." *Anthrovision* 8 (2): 1–18. https://doi.org/10.4000/anthrovision.7934.

Fluehr-Lobban, Carolyn. 2008. "Collaborative Anthropology as Twenty-First-Century Ethical Anthropology." *Collaborative Anthropologies* 1: 175–82. https://doi.org/10.1353/cla.0.0000.

Gaudenzi, Sandra. 2013. *The Living Documentary: From Representing Reality to Co-Creating Reality in Digital Interactive Documentary*. PhD diss., Goldsmiths, University of London. https://research.gold.ac.uk/id/eprint/7997/.

Gill, Harjant S. 2021. "Decolonizing Visual Anthropology: Locating Transnational Diasporic Queers-of-Color Voices in Ethnographic Cinema." *American Anthropologist* 123 (1): 36–49.

HAU. 2017. *HAU: Journal of Ethnographic Theory*. 7 (1). https://www.journals.uchicago.edu/toc/hau/2017/7/1.

Hartblay, Cassandra. 2017. "This Is Not Thick Description: Conceptual Art Installation as Ethnographic Process." *Ethnography*, ahead of print, August 21. https://doi.org/10.1177/1466138117726191.

Howes, David, ed. 2005. *Empire of the Senses: The Sensual Culture Reader*. Oxford: Berg. https://doi.org/10.4324/9781003230700.

Howes, David. 2019. "Multisensory Anthropology." *Annual Review of Anthropology* 48: 17–28. https://doi.org/10.1146/annurev-anthro-102218-011324.

Ingold, Tim. 2008. "Anthropology Is Not Ethnography." *Proceedings of the British Academy* 154: 69–92.

Ingold, Tim. 2014. "That's Enough about Ethnography!" *HAU: Journal of Ethnographic Theory* 4 (1): 383–95.

Ingold, Tim. 2017. "Anthropology Contra Ethnography." *HAU: Journal of Ethnographic Theory* 7 (1): 21–26. https://doi.org/10.14318/hau7.1.005.

Kosofsky-Sedgwick, Eve. 1993. *Tendencies*. Durham, NC: Duke University Press.

Macdonald, Sharon and Paul Basu, eds. (2007) *Exhibition Experiments*. London: Blackwell.

MacDougall, David. 1978. "Ethnographic Film: Failure and Promise." *Annual Review of Anthropology* 7: 405–25.

Marcus, George, and Fred Myers, eds. 1995. *The Traffic in Culture: Refiguring Art and Anthropology*. Berkeley: University of California Press.

Marks, Laura U. 2000. *The Skin of Film: Intercultural Cinema, Embodiment and the Senses*. Durham, NC: Duke University Press.

Martinez, Wilton. 1992. "Who Constructs Anthropological Knowledge? Toward a Theory of Ethnographic Film Spectatorship." In *Film as Ethnography*, edited by Peter Ian Crawford and David Turton, 131–49. Manchester: Manchester University Press.

Martinez, Wilton. 1995. "The Challenges of a Pioneer: Tim Asch, Otherness, and Film Reception." *Visual Anthropology Review* 11 (1): 53–82.

Maschio, Thomas. 2021. *Digital Cultures, Lived Stories and Virtual Reality*. New York: Routledge.

Morelli, Camilla. 2021. "The Right to Change: Co-Producing Ethnographic Animation with Indigenous Youth in Amazonia." *Visual Anthropology Review* 37 (2): 333–55. https://doi.org/10.1111/var.12246.

Pink, Sarah. 2011. "Digital Visual Anthropology: Potentials and Challenges." In *Made to Be Seen: Perspectives on the History of Visual Anthropology*, edited by Marcus Banks and Jay Ruby, 209–33. Chicago, IL: University of Chicago Press.

Pringle, Ramona. 2017. "Testing and evaluating design prototypes: the case study of Avatar Secrets." In *I-Docs: The Evolving Practices of Interactive Documentary*, edited by Judith Aston, Sandra Gaudenzi, and Mandy Rose, 154–169. New York: Wallflower, Columbia University Press.

Schneider, Arnd, and Christopher Wright, eds. 2006. *Contemporary Art and Anthropology*. Oxford: Berg.

Scott-Stevenson, J. 2020. "Virtual Futures: A Manifesto for Immersive Experiences." In *Handbook of Research on the Global Impacts and Roles of Immersive Media*, edited by J. F. Morie and K. McCallum, 235–52. Hershey, PA: Information Science Reference.

Schillaci, Rosella and Alexandra D'Onofrio. 2022. "Exhibition of a VR Experimental Documentary: Using VR Technology to Work with Children and Mothers in Prison." *Interactive Film & Media Journal* 2 (2). https://doi.org/10.32920/ifmj.v2i2.1583.

Shuter, Jeff, and Benjamin Burroughs. 2017. "The Ethics of Sensory Ethnography: Virtual Reality Fieldwork in Zones of Conflict." In *Internet Research Ethics for the Social Age: New Challenges, Cases, and Contexts*, edited by Michael Zimmer and Katharina Kinder-Kurlanda, 281–85. New York: Peter Lang.

Stoller, Paul. 2015. "The Bureau of Memories: Archives and Ephemera – Review: Ethnographic Terminalia 2014, Hierarchy, Washington, D.C., December 3–7." *Cultural Anthropology Online*, ahead of print, March 20. http://culanth.org/fieldsights/647-the-bureau-of-memories-archives-and-ephemera.

Theodossopoulos, Dimitrios. 2022. "Graphic Ethnography on the Rise." *Theorizing the Contemporary, Fieldsights*, July 28. https://culanth.org/fieldsights/series/graphic-ethnography-on-the-rise.

Turner, Terence. 1992. "Defiant Images: The Kayapo Appropriation of Video." *Anthropology Today* 8 (6): 5–15.

Vallejo, Aida. 2020. "Rethinking the Canon: The Role of Film Festivals in Shaping Film History." *Studies in European Cinema* 17 (2): 155–69. https://doi.org/10.1080/17411548.2020.1765631.

Varvantakis, Christos. 2021. "Ethnographic Film at the Crossroads." *AllegraLab*, July 29. https://allegralaboratory.net/ethnographic-film-at-the-crossroads/.

Verstappen, Sanderien, Christos Varvantakis, Fiona P. McDonald, Alice Apley, Harjant S. Gill, Margot Mecca, Caterina Sartori, and Frode Storaas. 2021. "Rethinking Anthropological Film Exhibition and Distribution (Part II)." *Visual and New Media Review*. https://culanth.org/fieldsights/rethinking-anthropological-film-distribution-part-ii.

Weibel, Peter, and Bruno Latour. 2007. "Experimenting with Representation: Iconoclash and Making Things Public." In *Exhibition Experiments*, edited by Paul Basu and Sharon MacDonald, 219–38. London: Blackwells.

Westmoreland, Mark. 2020. "360° Video". In *The Routledge International Handbook of Ethnographic Film and Video*. Edited by Phillip Vannini. 256–266. London: Routledge.

Chapter 11.1

Concept

Hybridity

Maxi Heitmayer

Over 30 years ago, Mark Weiser conjectured that we would grow accustomed to being constantly surrounded by computing devices:

> Hundreds of computers in a room could seem intimidating at first, just as hundreds of volts coursing through wires in the walls did at one time. But like the wires in the walls, these hundreds of computers will come to be invisible to common awareness. People will simply use them unconsciously to accomplish everyday tasks.
>
> (Weiser 1991, 98)

In a similar vein, Google's Eric Schmidt controversially claimed ten years ago that the internet will disappear: "There will be so many IP addresses, so many devices, sensors, things that you are wearing, things that you are interacting with that you won't even sense it [...]. It will be part of your presence all the time" (Scolaro 2015).

Today, we seem to have already arrived in Weiser's world, and Schmidt's does not seem so distant either (in some places, it has indeed arrived already). More and more technologies we use in our everyday lives are becoming *smart* and connected, beginning with our phones, moving over to fridges, washing machines, household heating and lighting systems, or healthcare tools and applications (e.g., blood-sugar sensors connecting to smartphones, fitness bracelets monitoring our vitals). This profoundly affects how we engage with the space around us (Atzori, Iera, and Morabito 2010; Crabtree and Tolmie 2016; Heitmayer 2021, 2022; Heitmayer and Lahlou 2021). Our lives have further become augmented through various Extended Reality technologies, be it via gaming headsets, smart glasses, smart speakers, heads-up displays in cars, or photo and video filters embedded in social media or communication applications.

These technological developments are often subsumed under the term "metaverse" or "hybrid spaces," which suggest a merging of physical and digital that creates a third space with novel, emergent properties

DOI: 10.4324/9781032672663-39

(Ball 2022; de Souza e Silva 2006, 2023; Wang et al. 2023). Prior to the advent of portable devices and wireless network connections, accessing the internet necessarily entailed a visit to a fixed computer workstation and deliberately dialing into the web. This led to the concept of *cyberspace* as a separate realm from the physical world, and drew a clear distinction between online and offline, virtual and real. Today's digital experiences are more integrated into our physical world, blurring the lines between the two and fundamentally changing how we perceive and interact with technology and the internet in our daily lives.

As a basic observation, technology is becoming more present and more connected, and information on the internet is becoming more visible and more accessible in our daily lives. From an abstract perspective, our lives are becoming *more mediated*. Technology supports our activities, helps us make better and more informed decisions, and sometimes takes care of them for us altogether (e.g., a smart fridge automatically stocking up on consumed items, an AI-assistant taking care of administrative tasks). Some scholars suggest these developments will eventually culminate in the "real-world web," where digital information associated with physical objects becomes immediately accessible to our senses and forms part of our cognitive processes (Halpin 2013; Heersmink & Sutton 2020; Smart 2012; Turner 2022). Recent developments in the fields of Artificial Intelligence and Neuroprosthetics, for example, suggest this, too, may be upon us sooner than we might think.

There is plenty of evidence that our lived reality in the physical world has become inextricably interwoven with the digital world. The notion of *going online* has already almost entirely disappeared from our vocabulary; the dial-up sound of the 56k modem is a faint memory. Spaces that are not augmented by technology and internet connectivity will follow suit. For researchers interested in digital ethnography, this raises several exciting challenges for the future:

First, as the technologies and infrastructure required for people to fully engage with and in hybridity are now becoming widely available, there is an urgent need for in-depth research on the basic experiences that users of these technologies make (e.g., Everri & Heitmayer 2024; Heinrich et al. 2025). Digital ethnographers should therefore pay close attention to the adoption and the subsequent role technologies play in the lives of users. They must provide rich accounts of people's lived experiences and highlight challenges and opportunities for researchers, designers and engineers, and policymakers to build on.

Second, some of today's most pressing questions for digital well-being and workplace productivity such as how we divide our time and attention between physical and digital space, how the two interact, and which one takes precedence at what point in time (e.g., Heitmayer 2025; Mills et al. 2001; Orhan et al. 2021), will take on a completely different nature due to hybridization. Moreover, understanding the impact of the technological augmentation of our bodies and the space around us on our cognitive processes will be crucial. Technologies potentially interfering so deeply with the sensory ways in which we interact with our surroundings, but also our philosophical, social, and epistemological engagement with the world, need to be studied with the utmost care. Digital ethnography will be the first line of inquiry to document the idiosyncrasies and technicalities, the moments of joy and of frustration in the hybrid world of the future that can help us assess the true impact of these technologies.

Finally, the term *digital ethnography* itself may eventually become obsolete in a hybrid world, as it will be impossible to distinguish it from *non-digital* ethnography (or rather, it will be impossible to do ethnography without considering the digital). Digital ethnographers may find themselves sharing best practices and experiences with increasing numbers of researchers from other traditions or disciplines. They must therefore frequently revisit and question the basic assumptions they make about *digital* ethnography as the lifeworld of the people and topics they study shifts toward further digital augmentation. Fostering an engaged and constructive theoretical and methodological dialogue is crucial—the foundations that digital ethnographers of today build may end up carrying a larger part of the scientific edifice in the future than originally anticipated.

References

Atzori, Luigi, Antonio Iera, and Giacomo Morabito. 2010. "The Internet of Things: A Survey." *Computer Networks* 54 (15): 2787–2805. https://doi.org/10.1016/j.comnet.2010.05.010.

Ball, Matthew. 2022. *The Metaverse: And How It Will Revolutionize Everything.* Liveright Publishing Corporation.

Crabtree, Andy, and Peter Tolmie. 2016. "A Day in the Life of Things in the Home." In *Proceedings of the ACM Conference on Computer Supported Cooperative Work, CSCW.* https://doi.org/10.1145/2818048.2819954.

De Souza e Silva, Adriana. 2006. "From Cyber to Hybrid: Mobile Technologies as Interfaces of Hybrid Spaces." *Space and Culture* 9 (3): 261–278. https://doi.org/10.1177/1206331206289022.

De Souza e Silva, Adriana. 2023. "Hybrid Spaces 2.0: Connecting Networked Urbanism, Uneven Mobilities, and Creativity, in a (Post) Pandemic World." *Mobile Media & Communication* 11 (1): 59–65. https://doi.org/10.1177/20501579221132118.

Everri, Marina, and Maxi Heitmayer. 2024. "Cyborg Children: A Systematic Literature Review on the Experience of Children Using Extended Reality." *Children* 11 (8): 1–17. https://doi.org/10.3390/children11080984.

Halpin, Harry. 2013. "Does the Web Extend the Mind?" In *Proceedings of the 5th Annual ACM Web Science Conference, WebSci'13.* https://doi.org/10.1145/2464464.2479972.

Heersmink, Richard, and John Sutton. 2020. "Cognition and the Web: Extended, Transactive, or Scaffolded?" *Erkenntnis* 85 (1): 139–64. https://doi.org/10.1007/s10670-018-0022-8.

Heinrich, Anna J., Maxi Heitmayer, Edward Smith, and Yiming Zhang. 2025. "Experiencing Hybrid Spaces: A Scoping Literature Review of Empirical Studies on Human Experiences in Cyber-Physical Environments." *Computers in Human Behavior* 164: 108502. https://doi.org/10.1016/j.chb.2024.108502.

Heitmayer, Maxi. 2021. "'It's Like Being Gone for a Second': Using Subjective Evidence-Based Ethnography to Understand Locked Smartphone Use Among Young Adults." In *Proceedings of the 23rd International Conference on Mobile Human-Computer Interaction (MobileHCI '21)*, September 27–October 1, 2021, Toulouse & Virtual, France. https://doi.org/10.1145/3447526.3472026.

Heitmayer, Maxi. 2022. "Patterns of Multi-Device Use with the Smartphone: A Video-Ethnographic Study of Young Adults' Multi-Device Use with Smartphones in Naturally Occurring Contexts." *Computers in Human Behavior Reports* 8: 100244. https://doi.org/10.1016/j.chbr.2022.100244.

Heitmayer, Maxi. 2025. "The Second Wave of Attention Economics: Attention as a Universal Symbolic Currency on Social Media and Beyond." *Interacting with Computers* 37 (1): 18–29. https://doi.org/10.1093/iwc/iwae035.

Heitmayer, Maxi, and Saadi Lahlou. 2021. "Why Are Smartphones Disruptive? An Empirical Study of Smartphone Use in Real-Life Contexts." *Computers in Human Behavior* 116: 1–12. https://doi.org/10.1016/j.chb.2020.106637.

Mills, James E., Bo Hu, Sam Beldona, and John Clay. 2001. "Cyberslacking! A Liability Issue for Wired Workplaces." *Cornell Hotel and Restaurant Administration Quarterly* 42 (5): 34–47. https://doi.org/10.1177/0010880401425004.

Orhan, Mehmet A., Stefano Castellano, Imen Khelladi, Luca Marinelli, and Florent Monge. 2021. "Technology Distraction at Work: Impacts on Self-Regulation and Work Engagement." *Journal of Business Research* 126: 341–349. https://doi.org/10.1016/j.jbusres.2020.12.048.

Scolaro, Cristina. 2015. "Why Google's Eric Schmidt Says the 'Internet Will Disappear.'" *CNBC*. https://www.cnbc.com/2015/01/23/why-googles-eric-schmidt-says-the-internet-will-disappear.html.

Smart, Philip. 2012. "The Web-Extended Mind." *Metaphilosophy* 43 (4): 446–63. https://doi.org/10.1111/j.1467-9973.2012.01756.x.

Turner, Charles. 2022. "Augmented Reality, Augmented Epistemology, and the Real-World Web." *Philosophy and Technology* 35 (1): 1–28. https://doi.org/10.1007/s13347-022-00496-5.

Wang, Haibin, Huansheng Ning, Yuqing Lin, Wenbo Wang, Salah Dhelim, Farha Farha, Jianhua Ding, and Mahmoud Daneshmand. 2023. "A Survey on the Metaverse: The State-of-the-Art, Technologies, Applications, and Challenges." *IEEE Internet of Things Journal* 10 (16): 14671–88. https://doi.org/10.1109/JIOT.2023.3278329.

Weiser, Mark. 1991. "The Computer for the 21st Century." *Scientific American* 265: 94–104. https://doi.org/10.1038/scientificamerican0991-94.

Chapter 11.2

Case study
"In America" COVID memorial art installation on the DC National Mall

The Rituals in the Making Collective

This essay examines the long-term digital and in-person ethnographic study of one of the largest and most recognizable COVID-19 memorial efforts in the United States to date, the public art installation, *In America: Remember*. Created by visual artist Suzanne Brennan Firstenberg, the *In America* series seeks to commemorate pandemic loss through combined physical materials and digital spaces of remembrance. Our research team, Rituals in the Making, has collaborated with Firstenberg since November 2020, participating in, supporting, and studying the installation and its archival afterlife. In this case study, we detail the distinctive form of hybrid commemoration and the multimodal ethnographic research that it has elicited. This hybrid memory work is premised on the mirroring effect of the installation's digital and physical features. Finally, through the examples of our team's sustained engagement with the installation and its community of mourners and volunteers, we underscore the ethos of collective research-as-activism that has been so central to this anthropological project.

Begun in May 2020 at the height of pandemic confinement, Rituals in the Making (RIM) posed a fundamental question: How do we mourn when we cannot gather in person? At that time, we were interested in how rituals typically conducted in the physical presence of others were being adapted to virtual spaces through platforms like Zoom and FaceTime. By year two, the project expanded to consider the increasing politicization of COVID death and mourning, including the impact of misinformation about the virus on mourning and remembrance, and the longer-term social effects of extended grief and delayed or suspended rituals. Our work with Firstenberg and the *In America* series has been a through-line of the study, as student and faculty researchers have engaged with it at almost every stage of the art and its post-installation existence.

In America

Originally staged at the DC Armory near RFK Stadium in southeast Washington, DC, in the fall of 2020, the artwork's first iteration, *In America: How Could This Happen* ... comprised over 260,000 white flags—each flag representing a single life lost to the virus. Thousands of people from the DC area and beyond visited, some dedicating flags, writing the names or a few words of tribute in honor of a lost loved one. Shortly after Thanksgiving, the installation came down, but Firstenberg was determined to continue memorializing COVID loss. She teamed up with RIM researchers and other volunteers to create a map—a grid with points plotted for the 1,865 flags bearing an inscription. The impromptu effort became the basis of the installation's original website and planted the seed for the next round of hybrid memorialization.

Ten months later, after almost half a million more deaths, and with a new administration in the White House, Firstenberg brought her artwork to the National Mall. From September 17 to October 3, 2021, a sea of more than 700,000 white flags covered the lawn just north of the Washington Monument. The installation, *In America: Remember*, was the largest public art

Figure 11.2.1 In America: Remember flags in front of the Washington Monument, Washington, DC (Photograph taken by William Atkins/the George Washington University).

Case study: COVID memorial art installation on DC National Mall   347

project to visit the Mall since the AIDS quilt, stretching across 20 acres, 147 sections, and 3.8 miles of walking paths. The National Park Service estimated that approximately 1.2 million people visited the site during those three weeks (Figure 11.2.1).

Millions more visited the *In America: Remember* digital installation. Working with partners at ESRI, a GIS software company, Firstenberg prioritized public participation, both in person and virtually. Mourners could walk up to the physical site and dedicate a flag, or they could submit one online. The website included both types of submission in an interactive map that allowed visitors to search by name and to view the location and a photograph of the flag planted.

Geolocating loss

The interaction between visitors and the digital installation depended on the critical step of geolocation—the crux of the memorial's hybridity and a process the RIM research team spearheaded from its original conception to its implementation on site. ESRI adapted its geolocating app, Survey 123, to enable volunteers to geolocate and photograph the personalized flags; data were then uploaded to the installation's digital map.

For those of us working among that vast field of flags, the task of geolocating was both physically and emotionally demanding. We understood the power and significance of the work: stripped of rituals and forced to grieve alone, for many mourners the installation represented a space of recognition. For some, the flag was a proxy gravesite, and planting it was the funeral they never had. Over and over, we heard visitors express their shock at the sight of the flags. One visitor, overwhelmed by the immensity of it, told us the scene looked like newly fallen snow covering the National Mall, even though it was 75 degrees outside. Another mistook the shimmering white flags for the Potomac River from afar since the sun's reflection made it look like rippling waves of water.

With hundreds of newly dedicated flags being planted each day over the 17-day installation, the sense of urgency was palpable. Occasionally, visitors would seek us out to ask for help in finding "their flag"; in real time, we witnessed the ritual efficacy of the individual site of remembrance, where mourners addressed, touched, and sometimes adorned the flag. They photographed themselves beside it and among the backdrop of the shimmering white field. Some lay flowers, others gathered for a meal or sat in quiet communion. All the while, the team of geolocators, carrying with them a steadily growing sense of responsibility and even reverence, kept on searching for flags to digitize until the final minute of the final day.

Post-installation: archiving against social forgetting

Of the more than 700,000 flags that marked the individual lives lost to the COVID-19 pandemic, some 20,000 bore personal inscriptions memorializing family, friends, coworkers, patients, classmates, and neighbors. Among them, we can trace the preoccupation with loved ones dying in isolation and of troubled grief; many mourners used the small space they were given to eulogize those lost to the disease, writing of the deceased's occupation, achievements, or hobbies. We also see glimpses of a nation divided in its response to the pandemic and COVID-19 death itself. Some wrote messages urging others to get the COVID-19 vaccine or wrote political messages reminding others of the partisan lines that had been drawn during the pandemic.

In their post-installation archival form, the flags resist attempts at "social forgetting" or revisionism. But that wasn't the original intent. When Firstenberg decided to bring the 20,000 dedicated flags back to her studio in Bethesda, MD, she knew only that they needed to be preserved. The complex chain of digital-material activity around that preservation has become a crucial site of RIM's ethnographic engagement with pandemic loss and, equally important, its activism.

Cleaning, storing, ordering

Having been exposed to the elements for those three weeks on the Mall, the flags first required proper care—the painstaking process of removing rust and soil from the metal stems, cleaning the flags' surface, waxing the stems, then ordering and storing them. Volunteers, including members of the RIM team, spent hundreds of hours laboring over the flags for almost two years. In early December 2023, we gathered at the studio for the final push. Restoring the flags became a meaningful gesture in its own right, as volunteers treated each one with the care and respect that one would normally give a sacred object. Elise Shieh, who lost her mother to COVID in early 2020, summed up the effort: "It has been incredibly healing to witness the extreme care and thoughtfulness given to each and every flag throughout this project, something that was not always afforded to our loved ones during the height of the pandemic... It feels like we're putting them to rest."

Transcribing

But the flags had more memory work to do. The next step was the enormous undertaking of transcribing the approximately 11,000 dedications made onsite. Numerous volunteers and researchers worked simultaneously to transcribe the flags on a Microsoft Excel spreadsheet. A transcription begins with an image of a unique flag. The messages range in length, detail, language, and emotion; some mourners choose to document who their loved one was:

> "Her greatest loves were her husband, their enormous family, the color yellow, candy, and the Yankees."
> "[Ella] Lucho duro y fue muy valiente y fuerte. No era su tiempo de irse pero lo volveremos a ver un día. La queremos, nunca dejaremos de extrañarla."

Some choose to write no more than a name; others make sense of their loss to benefit others:

> "[He] fought a warrior like battle against COVID. We will forever carry him in our heart. Please get vaccinated."

Transcribing is repetitive and time-consuming: zooming in on barely decipherable handwriting penned in a rush, or typing "[heart] [heart] [heart] [heart]" to accurately reflect a name's border. No matter the content, the transcriber's work is to maintain the integrity of the flag down to every minute detail. At times this means reproducing grammatical errors, spelling mistakes, or even undecipherable or irregular script.

Despite the mundane intricacy of the data entry task, each flag represents an opportunity for the transcriber, the digital ethnographer-activist, to feel deeply and connect with the loss of a complete stranger. Often, the dedications of the flags are descriptive, featuring inside jokes and hometowns, and signed with the names of immediate and extended family members. The transcriptions urge their beholder to visualize a family, neighborhood, workplace, and, beyond that, how these relations and space were transformed by the loss of a loved one. The unique quality of each flag helps paint a fuller picture of the life lived. The importance of this detailed, at times granular, work lies in the meaningful act of remembering and honoring these lives lost, and of providing evidence of who these people were to those who loved them.

From time to time, something about a dedication makes us, the transcribers, want to learn more. We open a new window and search for the name of the deceased to find the corresponding obituary. In an instant, we are transported into another virtual space of mourning—a memorial page, a newspaper article, a Facebook page. For a moment, we glimpse the wider circle of their mourners, perhaps a face to go with the name.

Coda: Coding

Once the database is complete, the RIM team will embark on a final act of sorting—this time of words rather than materials. Using MAXQDA qualitative database software, we will code and interpret the patterns in the flags' textual inscriptions. The aim is to map out the configurations of language by which the complex geography of national grief is manifest through this artwork.

Conclusion: hybrid futures and the digital/material afterlife of *In America: Remember*

Our team and volunteers for the *In America: Remember* series have dedicated hundreds of hours of physical and emotional labor to caring for the flags. Each flag that has been geolocated, cleaned, archived, and transcribed is the essence of a loved one's memory. Our intention is that both the transcription database and the physical flags will become part of a COVID memory archive at George Washington University. We hope that these flags and their dedications will be accessible to the public and to ensure future generations will be able to learn about and appreciate the lives lost to COVID-19.

In such care work we also recognize a potential for grief support through ethnographic research. In our research, flags are more than just data. They are mementos that grievers have entrusted us with. In our role as geolocators on the National Mall, we shared the visitors' sense of awe and carried the weight of loss and recognition as we canvassed the sections in search of newly planted (not yet geolocated) flags, squinting at the glare of our phones, dropping pins and snapping photos, before pushing on to the next. In our role as transcribers, we practiced a fidelity to mourners' emotions that brought us into a caring relationship with both survivors and the flags they endowed with meaning. It is a tie formed initially through research but one that has moved beyond it. The witnessing we have been invited to partake in also transformed us. We no longer see ourselves as researchers only but also as caretakers and activists.

Index

abduction 103
access and gatekeeping 66–7, 105–6
activism, digital 118–24, 243, 327, 345–50
affect theory 91–6, 105–107
affordance: concept of 87–90; in digital self-tracking 91
AI (artificial intelligence): deradicalization via 264–6; ethics and bias 241–71; gender and AI 256; health equity and AI 256
algorithms 260–2
anonymity 44–5, 52, 78
anti-proverbs 177–83
archives, digital 99–100
audience 23, 48, 62, 127–30, 221–5, 280, 290–2, 322–37
authenticity 50, 78–9

big data 65, 76, 185–200
body and embodiment 92–4
boundary work 98–102

co-presence 2, 44–5, 103
community 13–17, 22–4, 31 97–111
context collapse 23
COVID-19 94–5, 128–9, 157–9, 179–81, 208–10, 265–6, 293, 345–50
critical data studies 185–200
cultural codes 60–3

data ethics 43–57, 65–9, 110, 194, 318
datafication 114–15
deradicalization 264–6
digital divide 27–8, 287

digital infrastructures 114–17
digital resistance 26–31
digital rituals 33–9
digital storytelling 273–94
DIY networks 13–17

echo chambers 192
ethics, research: in digital contexts 43–57; IRB and consent 44–6; paraphrasing and data fabrication 53–4
ethnographic methods 1–6, 43–57, 98–110

Facebook 3, 13–17, 20–4, 26–8, 50, 99–101, 208–12
Feminism 27, 118–23, 193
field delineation 98–102
fieldnotes 106–10

Gab 48–9
gamers and gaming 71–2, 125–37, 146–51, 295–319
gender and technology 6, 26, 91–6
GIS (geographic information systems) 215–28, 235–40
guanxi (social networks in China) 82

habitus 80–1
hashtags 27, 100–2, 120–1, 153–60, 193–200
hybridity 321–37, 341–3, 345–50

identity 29–31, 46–56, 60, 166, 264–6, 296–303, 311–2, 316–9
infrastructure studies 114–17

key informants 105–6

linguistic anthropology 33–4, 153–70, 173–5, 177–83
lurking 4, 45, 50, 103–5, 122, 174

mapping technologies see "GIS"
memes 14, 22, 26, 173–5, 179, 278
metaverse 126–30, 136, 143–4, 309, 341
migration and digital media 71–6
MGTOW (Men Going Their Own Way) 186–200
multimodal anthropology 273–87, 289–94

narrative analysis 192
netnography 8–9, 97
NSFW communities 102, 109

online communities see "community"

participant observation 7, 47, 72–5, 97–105, 132–3, 146
performativity 273–4
platforms 2–5, 21–2, 47–9, 61–2, 78, 97–110, 114–6, 118–121, 125–137, 154–8, 188–90, 208–211, 251–3, 275–8, 336–7
positionality 2, 81–3, 93–110
privacy 43–56, 78, 122–3, 285–7

QAnon 43–57

reflexivity 44, 89, 95, 108–11, 191
representation, connotation and denotation 60–3
resemiotization 60
ritual 33–6, 60, 104, 173–5, 298, 345–50

self-tracking 91–5
shadowbanning 104, 115
social media as field site 97–113
social movements 118–24
surveillance 17, 76–8, 154, 287

TikTok 2, 26, 101, 114, 128, 135
Twitter 2, 51, 119–21, 128, 153–69, 186, 193–4, 316

urban ethnography 71–6
user-generated content 295–319

virtual influencers 125–37
virtuality 13–5, 71–2, 128–9, 143–4, 146–51, 298–300, 326, 347

wearables 91–6
WhatsApp 14, 21, 26–31, 114

YouTube 2, 14–17, 35–9, 114, 127–37, 160, 262, 305

For Product Safety Concerns and Information please contact our EU
representative GPSR@taylorandfrancis.com
Taylor & Francis Verlag GmbH, Kaufingerstraße 24, 80331 München, Germany

www.ingramcontent.com/pod-product-compliance
Ingram Content Group UK Ltd.
Pitfield, Milton Keynes, MK11 3LW, UK
UKHW060636230126
467259UK00022B/1267